Foundations of Nursing Research

Foundations of Nursing Research

Sixth Edition

Rose Marie Nieswiadomy, PhD, RN
Professor Emerita
Texas Woman's University
College of Nursing

Pearson

Boston Columbus Indianapolis New York San Francisco Upper Saddle River
Amsterdam Cape Town Dubai London Madrid Milan Munich Paris Montreal Toronto
Delhi Mexico City Sao Paulo Sydney Hong Kong Seoul Singapore Taipei Tokyo

Editor-in-Chief: Julie Alexander
Acquisitions Editor: Pamela Fuller
Editorial Assistant: Lisa Pierce/Cynthia Gates
Director of Marketing: David Gesell
Senior Marketing Manager: Phoenix Harvey
Marketing Specialist: Michael Sirinides
Senior Managing Editor: Patrick Walsh
Production Editor: Yagnesh Jani
Project Manager: Susan Hannahs
Art Director Interior: Maria Guglielmo-Walsh

Designer Interior: Ilze Lemesis
Senior Art Director Cover: Jayne Conte
Cover Designer: Jodi Notowitz
Full-Service Project Management:
 Kailash Jadli, Aptara®, Inc.
Composition: Aptara®, Inc.
Text Printer/Bindery: R.R. Donnelley/Willard
Cover Printer: Lehigh-Phoenix Color
Text Font: 10/12 Palatino

Credits and acknowledgments borrowed from other sources and reproduced, with permission, in this textbook appear on the appropriate page within the text.

10 9 8 7 6 5 4 3 2 1

ISBN 10:   0-13-275623-4
ISBN 13: 978-0-13-275623-5

To Ben
Thank you for "lighting up my life"
all of these years

Contributor

We extend a sincere thanks to our contributor. His time, effort, and expertise were so willingly given for the development and writing of resources that promote understanding of nursing research in the pursuit of nursing excellence.

Michael L. Nieswiadomy, PhD, BA
Professor of Economics and
Director of the Center for Environmental
Economic Studies and Research
University of North Texas
Denton, Texas

Reviewers

Thank You

Our heartfelt thanks go out to our colleagues from schools of nursing across the country who have given their time generously to help us create this exciting new edition of our book. We have reaped the benefit of your collective experience as nurses and teachers, and have made many improvements due to your efforts. Among those who gave us their encouragement and comments are:

Elizabeth N. Austin, PhD, MA, RN
Assistant Professor
Towson University
Towson, Maryland

Victoria Menzies, PhD, RN, PMHCNS-BC
Assistant Professor
Virginia Commonwealth University
Richmond, Virginia

Deborah Behan, PhD, RN-BC
Clinical Assistant Professor
The University of Texas–Arlington
Arlington, Texas

Donna Mitchell, PhD, RN
Director of School of Nursing
University of Rio Grande
Rio Grande, Ohio

Mary T. Boylston, RN, MSN, EdD
Professor
Eastern University
St. Davids, Pennsylvania

Sue E. Odom, RN, DSN
Professor
Clayton State University
Morrow, Georgia

Joy Longo, DNS, RN-NIC
Assistant Professor
Florida Atlantic University
Boca Raton, Florida

Sandra Millon Underwood, RN, PhD, FAAN
Professor
University of Wisconsin–Milwaukee
Milwaukee, Wisconsin

Deborah Mandel, PhD, MSN, RNC-OB
Assistant Professor
Kutztown University
Kutztown, Pennsylvania

Margaret G. Williams, PhD, RN
Professor
Blessing-Rieman College of Nursing
Quincy, Illinois

Kathy Mayle, RN, BSN, MNEd, MBA
Director, Center for Health Care Diversity
Duquesne University
Pittsburgh, Pennsylvania

Kathleen Z. Wisser, PhD-c, MS, RN
Assistant Professor
Alvernia University
Reading, Pennsylvania

Preface

My main purpose for writing the sixth edition of this book continues to be the promotion of interest in nursing research. I firmly believe that research is essential to evidence-based nursing practice and the growth of the nursing profession. Results of nursing research studies improve patient care and demonstrate that nurses are not only caring, but cost-effective providers of health care.

Research can be interesting and exciting, and I have tried, through the years, to present the material in this textbook in an inspirational manner. Nursing students and practicing nurses tell me that I have accomplished my goal. Many say they have actually read the entire book, which is not the case for most of their textbooks or other books that they read. After reading this introductory research book, you will not be expected to have the skills to conduct research independently or to critique research reports with a great deal of confidence. However, my goals will have been achieved if you:

- recognize the importance of research to evidence-based nursing practice
- are willing to use research findings in your practice
- have gained knowledge about the research process
- possess beginning skills necessary to evaluate research findings
- discuss research study results with your colleagues, family, and friends
- begin to think about conducting your own research study in the future

For those of you just beginning your careers in nursing, the future of the profession depends on you. This book is intended primarily for individuals with little research experience, particularly undergraduate nursing students. However, many students in graduate programs have used this text to supplement their other research textbooks in order to gain a better understanding of nursing research. They have commented that this text explains the research simply and clearly. It is my hope that practicing nurses will also use this book as they evaluate study findings for use in practice and as they begin to conduct their own studies.

FEATURES OF THE BOOK

The informal writing style has been maintained in this sixth edition of the text. Readers have made many positive comments about the writing style. Students have said that they often feel as if they are talking with me, the author. The book continues to be learner-friendly, just like the previous five editions. Please interact with me as you read this text. Get involved! This is the best way to learn about research.

The exercises at the end of the chapters are designed to help you get excited about research. Because most of you will not be conducting research while you are reading this textbook and learning about the research process, exercises in class or with your colleagues will help to simulate what it would be like if you were actually carrying out the steps of a study.

Readers are referred to Web sites throughout the book for additional information and resources. References are cited from more than 60 nursing journals. Excerpts from 85 recent nursing research studies are interspersed throughout this book. These research study excerpts are presented to illustrate various aspects of the research process. Most of these studies were conducted here in the United States. However, a number of these studies were conducted in other countries. I take pride in, once again, introducing nurses and nursing students in this country to research from around the world:

Saturation in Qualitative Studies—Sweden—Chapter 4
Neuman's Systems Model—South Africa—Chapter 7
Directional Research Hypothesis—Taiwan—Chapter 8

Nonequivalent Control Group Design—Hong Kong—Chapter 9
Correlational Study—Korea—Chapter 9
Ethnographic Study—Uganda—Chapter 10
Systematic Random Sample—Australia—Chapter 11
Quota Sample—Jordan—Chapter 11
Delphi Study—United Kingdom—Chapter 13
Barriers to Nursing Research Utilization—Canada—Chapter 17

New terms are highlighted and defined the first time they are discussed. Each chapter in the book concludes with a summary of the content presented in that chapter. At the end of Chapter 2 and the ends of Chapters 5 through 16, a section is devoted to critiquing the specific step of the research process that each of those chapters addresses. Also, a set of critiquing questions is highlighted in a box in each of these chapters. Chapter 19 is a new chapter in this edition. It discusses nursing research and health care economics. This chapter was added because nurses should be aware of the monetary issues involved in health care and demonstrate that they are not only caring but cost-effective providers of health care.

Chapter 20 (which was Chapter 19 in the 5th edition) presents a summary of guidelines for critiquing quantitative study reports. Additionally, this edition presents a summary of guidelines for critiquing qualitative study reports.

Appendix B presents a critiquing exercise, which is a new assignment in this edition. You are asked to obtain a copy of a specific research article and then critique this article, using the questions listed.

Two distinctive features of the book are the Get Involved Activities and the Self-Tests at the end of each chapter. Get Involved Activities challenge you to work with other students or colleagues to evaluate and apply current research. Self-Tests provide readers an opportunity to see how well they have mastered the chapter content. Answers to all of the questions are provided at the back of the book.

Another feature of the text is *Research on the Web*. This feature appears at the end of each chapter and encourages readers to go to My Nursing Kit at www.mynursingkit.com to access the interactive, chapter-specific modules.

For each chapter, resources include:

- Chapter Objectives
- Key Terms
- Chapter Review
- Review Questions
- Research Links
- WebLink Applications
- Critical Thinking Exercises/Challenges

The knowledge that you gain from reading this book will help you to provide evidence-based care for your patients/clients. I also hope that you will gain a greater appreciation of research and can actually picture yourself conducting a research study in the future.

Acknowledgments

When I first decided to write a research textbook in 1985, I never dreamed that one day I would be preparing the sixth edition. The need for this book is evident by its continued use in this country and other countries throughout the world. The text has been translated into several other languages. It looks strange to see your words presented in another language! I always hope the translation is correct.

Instructors usually make the decision about textbooks for their courses. I am so grateful to the instructors who have chosen this textbook. I also want to thank other instructors who have recommended it as a reference source for their students.

I cannot give enough praise to all of the students who have given this textbook great reviews. I continue to receive comments about how learner-friendly the book is and how it is one of the few textbooks that they have read from cover to cover. Of course, it helps that this textbook is much smaller than some of their other textbooks!

Master's and doctoral level nursing students have told me that they use this book to supplement their course research textbooks. They believe this text presents the research process clearly and succinctly. When they review content in this book, they achieve a greater recall and understanding of research concepts.

Heartfelt thanks go to practicing nurses who have had the courage to pick up this research textbook. It demonstrates their awareness of the importance of nursing research, particularly in this day of evidence-based nursing practice.

Once again, Connie Maxwell, librarian at Texas Woman's University, critiqued the chapter on the review of the literature. This chapter is always a challenge because of the continued changes in the ways we access information. With her help, this chapter has been revised and updated.

Many people at Pearson Education deserve my thanks, especially Pam Fuller, Acquisitions Editor, who helped make the decision to publish another edition of this textbook. I am also very grateful to Lisa Pierce, Editorial Assistant, for her e-mails as the book material was being prepared. They were always very timely and encouraging. She was able to find answers to all of my questions. I would also like to thank Susan Hannahs, Project Manager, and Susan Gilbert, Copyeditor, for their positive feedback during critical phases in the book development and production.

Again, my family deserves much credit for my accomplishments. They try not to complain when I am working on book revisions. My daughter, Anne, proofread all of my material. My son, Michael, co-authored the new Chapter 19. Nine grandchildren (ages 6–27) kept our family gatherings lively. They help me to remember what is important in life.

I know that students usually refer to their textbooks by the authors' last names. I have often wondered how they identify this textbook! So, once again, I will try to help with the pronunciation of "Nieswiadomy." The name is of Polish derivation. The i's are silent, and the accent is on the first syllable. The name is pronounced like: *Néss wah dough me*. I might mention that some members of my husband's family pronounce the name differently, particularly those members who speak Polish! I apologize to them, again, for my attempt to simplify the pronunciation of this difficult name.

Rose Marie Nieswiadomy, PhD, RN

Contents

Chapter 1

Development of Nursing Research

OUTLINE

Importance of Nursing Research
Definitions of Nursing Research
Sources of Nursing Knowledge
Scientific Research
Purposes of Nursing Research
Funding for Nursing Research
Goals for Conducting Nursing Research
- Promote Evidence-Based Nursing Practice
- Ensure Credibility of the Nursing Profession
- Provide Accountability for Nursing Practice
- Document the Cost Effectiveness of Nursing Care
Quantitative and Qualitative Research
Outcomes Research
Educational Preparation for Nursing Research
Roles of Nurses in Research
- Principal Investigator
- Member of a Research Team

- Identifier of Researchable Problems
- Evaluator of Research Findings
- User of Research Findings
- Patient/Client Advocate During Studies
- Subject/Participant in Studies
History of Nursing Research
Research Priorities for the Future
National Institute of Nursing Research
The Cochrane Collaboration and The Cochrane
    Nursing Care Field
Summary
Nursing Research on the Web
Get Involved Activities
Self-Test

OBJECTIVES

On completion of this chapter, you will be prepared to:
1. Define nursing research
2. Identify sources of nursing knowledge
3. Describe scientific research
4. Compare two broad purposes for conducting research
5. Discuss four goals for conducting nursing research
6. Compare qualitative and quantitative research
7. Recognize the importance of outcomes research

8. Contrast the various roles of nurses in research
9. Recall some of the historic events in the development of nursing research
10. Determine priority areas for nursing research
11. Explain the significance of the National Institute of Nursing Research
12. Recognize the importance of the Cochrane Nursing Care Field

NEW TERMS DEFINED IN THIS CHAPTER

applied research, pg. 4

basic research, pg. 4

clinical nursing research, pg. 3

empirical data, pg. 3

evidence-based nursing practice, pg. 5

nursing research, pg. 3

outcomes research, pg. 7

qualitative research, pg. 6

quantitative research, pg. 6

replication studies, pg. 13

research utilization, pg. 9

Many people are still unaware that nurses conduct research. A similar statement has been included in each of the previous editions of this book. What kind of response do you think you would receive if you were to ask 10 friends to describe nursing research? Their answers would probably be quite interesting. My guess is that you would hear about some aspect of medical research, such as which drug might be most effective for some specific health problem. As nurses, we have not done a good job of discussing our research or making our research results readily available to the general public.

The primary goal of all professional nurses is "to be the client's advocate and provide optimal care on the basis of evidence obtained through research" (Tingen, Burnett, Murchison, & Zhu, 2009, p. 167). In an editorial in the January 2010 issue of *Nursing Research*, Dougherty asserted, "successful evidence-based practice (EBP) depends on high-quality nursing research" (p. 1). Health care reform in this country has made nursing research more important than ever before. Nurses must show that they make a difference in the lives of the American people.

In other countries, nurses are also emphasizing the importance of nursing research. In an article in the June 2009 issue of *Canadian Nurse*, Helene Sabourin, executive director of the Canadian Nurses Foundation, stated that she talks to corporate executives, government representatives, and philanthropists about the value of nursing research. She wrote that there is a decreasing pool of research funds at a time when innovations in health care have never been more important. Sabourin called for nurses to take the lead in ensuring that nursing research is fully supported.

IMPORTANCE OF NURSING RESEARCH

Right now, you are probably trying to convince yourself that nursing research is important (or you wouldn't be reading this textbook!). You may be trying to meet educational requirements for a baccalaureate degree, or someone has convinced you that you need more knowledge about research.

Sometimes a "hard sell" is necessary on the first day of an undergraduate nursing research class. The folded arms and facial expressions of students indicate that they are not convinced of the importance of learning about research.

Research knowledge will help you become an excellent nurse. As you read this book, you will be challenged to question constantly every intervention you perform or see performed. Questions to ask include these: Am I performing this intervention because someone told me to or maybe even because this is the intervention that has *always* been used? What evidence exists that this is the most effective intervention for the problem? If an intervention is not based on research evidence, there is no way to determine that this intervention is the optimum one. It is hoped that your instructor or your nurse friends, if you are already a nurse, will not have to do a hard sell to convince you that research is of utmost importance to the nursing profession. Your efforts to learn about nursing research will be rewarded in your nursing career in the future.

DEFINITIONS OF NURSING RESEARCH

There is some discrepancy among authors about the definition of nursing research. Polit and Beck (2008) have broadly defined nursing research as "systematic inquiry designed to develop knowledge about issues of importance to the nursing profession, including nursing practice, education, administration, and informatics" (p. 3). Burns and Grove (2009) have more narrowly defined nursing research as "a scientific process that validates and refines existing knowledge and generates new knowledge that directly and indirectly influences the delivery of evidence-based nursing practice" (p. 711). Thus, by their definition, to be called nursing research, study results must directly or indirectly affect clinical nursing practice.

In this book, the term **nursing research** is defined as the systematic, objective process of analyzing phenomena of importance to nursing. Using this definition, nursing research includes all studies concerning nursing practice, nursing education, and nursing administration. Studies concerning nurses themselves are also included in the broad category of nursing research. The term **clinical nursing research** indicates nursing research that involves clients or studies that have the potential to affect the care of clients, such as studies with animals or with so-called normal subjects. To learn about nursing research and how to conduct research, it is important to gain an understanding of what scientific research is all about, and why this method of gaining knowledge is valuable to nurses. The scientific method is only one source of nursing knowledge. It is, however, generally considered to be the most reliable source of knowledge.

SOURCES OF NURSING KNOWLEDGE

Nurses have relied on several sources of knowledge to guide nursing practice. A great storehouse of knowledge for nurses has been tradition. Tradition involves the handing down of knowledge from one generation to another and leads to actions that occur because "we've always done it that way."

Another source of knowledge for nurses has been found in authority. Experts or authorities in a given field often provide knowledge for other people. In the past, nurses looked to physicians for a great deal of their practice knowledge. It has only been fairly recently that nurses have begun to build a unique body of nursing knowledge.

Nurses have also used trial and error as a means of discovering knowledge. If one approach did not work, another one was used. Finally, when a certain approach was found to be effective, the trial-and-error process ceased. Frequently, the reasons behind the failure or success of a certain method were not determined. The goal was "if it works, we'll use it."

SCIENTIFIC RESEARCH

Several features characterize traditional scientific research. The researcher uses systematic, orderly, and objective methods of seeking information. The scientific method is based on **empirical data,** which are data gathered through the sense organs. Information is gained in the form of data or facts that are obtained in an unbiased manner from some aspect of the real world. The researcher tries to exercise as much control as possible over the research situation, to minimize biased results. Various means of exercising such control are discussed throughout this book. The researcher's opinions and personal biases should not influence the findings of a study.

Many similarities exist between scientific research and the problem-solving approach familiar to all nurses. Both processes involve identifying a problem area, establishing a plan, collecting data, and evaluating the data. These two activities, however, have very different purposes. Problem solving attempts to seek a solution to a problem that exists for a person or persons in a given setting. The purpose of scientific research is much broader. It seeks to obtain knowledge that can be generalized to other people and to other settings. For example, the nursing staff might be concerned about the best approach to use in teaching Mrs. Smith, a blind patient, how to operate an insulin pump. This would be an example of an immediate problem that needs a solution. Scientific research, in contrast, would be concerned with the best approach to use in teaching blind people, in general, how to operate insulin pumps. Scientific research is concerned with the ability to generalize research results.

PURPOSES OF NURSING RESEARCH

Research may be classified, according to the general purpose of the study, as basic or applied research. **Basic research** is concerned with generating new knowledge; **applied research** is concerned with using knowledge to solve immediate problems.

Basic research is conducted to develop, test, and refine theories and generate new knowledge (Kerlinger, 1986; Oman, Krugman, & Fink, 2003; Polit & Beck, 2008). Sometimes it is said that basic research seeks "knowledge for knowledge's sake." Whether basic research seeks to generate or develop theories, immediate application of the results usually does not occur. In fact, years may pass before the social usefulness of the results of the research is determined or acknowledged. Basic research often uses laboratory animals as subjects. The following example of a basic research study was conducted with nasogastric tubes. The object was to determine the amount of pressure according to the size of the tubes.

Laboratory Study

Knox and Davie (2009) conducted a laboratory study concerning the pressure of nasogastric tubes according to their size. They attached a manometer to a syringe (with and without a nasogastric tube being attached) and measured negative pressures produced when aspirating and positive pressures produced when injecting fluids. The researchers found that smaller syringes generated lower pressures, which they contended runs counter to current practice that indicates larger syringes are safer and produce lower pressures.

Applied research is directed toward generating knowledge that can be used in the near future. It is often conducted to seek solutions to existing problems (Burns & Grove, 2009; Polit & Beck, 2008). It appears that the majority of nursing studies have been examples of applied research. Many of these studies have focused on nursing interventions for patients and their families.

The distinction between basic and applied research is really not as clear-cut as it may seem. Sometimes the findings of basic research are applied rather quickly in the clinical setting, whereas applied research findings actually lead to basic studies. The distinction between basic and applied research may have more to do with financial support for the project than the purpose of the study. In this sense, basic research may imply that the researcher is provided support to work on a particular project without having to indicate the immediate practical usefulness of the findings.

FUNDING FOR NURSING RESEARCH

The federal government provides the most money for research in this country. Nurses receive the largest amount of government funding through the National Institute for Nursing Research. The 2010 budget for this institute was $145.6 million; the proposed 2011 budget is more than $150 million (http://ninr.nih.gov/AboutNINR/BudgetandLegislation).

Other sources for nursing research include private foundations, corporations, and professional organizations, such as Sigma Theta Tau International, Honor Society of Nursing. This organization, in conjunction with its chapters and grant partners (corporations, associations, and foundations), provides more that $500,000 annually for nursing research through grants, scholarships, and monetary awards (http://www.nursingsociety.org/default.aspx). The American Nurses Foundation (ANF) awarded more than $85,000 in research grants for the 2009 cycle (Blackledge, 2009).

GOALS FOR CONDUCTING NURSING RESEARCH

The importance of nursing research cannot be emphasized enough. Some of the goals for conducting research are to (a) promote evidence-based nursing practice, (b) ensure credibility of the nursing profession, (c) provide accountability for nursing practice, and (d) document the cost effectiveness of nursing care.

Promote Evidence-Based Nursing Practice

The major reason for conducting nursing research is to foster optimum care for clients. In the first three editions of this textbook, this section was titled "Improvements in Nursing Care." However, the title was changed because *evidence-based practice* (EBP) is a more appropriate term today, and one with which you are all familiar. Because of the increasing emphasis on EBP, both this edition and the previous edition include a chapter on evidence-based practice (see Chapter 18).

Evidence-based nursing practice (EBNP) means that nurses make clinical decisions based on the best research evidence, their clinical expertise, and the health care preferences of their patients/clients. Although EBNP may be based on factors other that research findings, such as patient preferences and the expertise of clinicians, the aim of EBNP is to provide the best possible care based on the best available research. To back up the importance of EBNP, Sigma Theta Tau International, Honor Society of Nursing, and Blackwell Publishing initiated a journal in 2004 titled, *Worldviews on Evidence-Based Nursing*. It is a quarterly peer-reviewed journal.

The nursing profession exists to provide a service to society, and this service should be based on accurate knowledge. Research has been determined to be the most reliable means of obtaining knowledge.

Ensure Credibility of the Nursing Profession

In the past, nursing was frequently thought of as a vocation rather than a profession. In fact, the struggle to gain professional status has been long and difficult. One of the criteria for a profession is the existence of a body of knowledge that is distinct from that of other disciplines. Nursing has traditionally borrowed knowledge from the natural and social sciences, and only recently have nurses concentrated on establishing a unique body of knowledge that would allow nursing to be clearly identified as a distinct profession. Through research, nurses can demonstrate what they do that distinguishes them from other groups in the health care field.

Nurses must demonstrate to the general public that nursing makes a difference in the health status of people. In 1999 the nursing profession, for the first time, was included in the Gallup Poll that ranked professionals in regard to honesty and ethical standards. Since then, nurses have ranked highest every year (except for 2001 when firefighters scored higher following the terrorist attack that fall). Nurses must build on this ranking and the admiration of the general public and continue to show what is unique about their services.

Provide Accountability for Nursing Practice

As nurses have become more independent in making decisions about the care of clients, this independence has brought about a greater need for accountability. There is an old saying that every privilege is accompanied by a corresponding duty. The privilege of being independent practitioners brings with it the duty of being accountable to those who receive our care. Although nurses have generally been glad to achieve some degree of independence from the medical profession, in some ways life was easier when physicians were considered to be responsible for all aspects of health care. At that time, if a nurse made an error in providing care, the physician (and sometimes the hospital) was held responsible. The idea of a lawsuit being brought against a nurse was almost unthinkable. The general public has gained more knowledge of health care, and expectations of nurses as providers of care have increased.

To be accountable for their practice, nurses must have a sound rationale for their actions, based on knowledge that is gained through scientific research. Nurses have the responsibility of keeping their knowledge base current, and one of the best sources of current knowledge is the research literature. The ability to critique research articles and determine findings that are appropriate for practice is a skill that is needed by all nurses.

Document the Cost Effectiveness of Nursing Care

Because of nursing's humanistic and altruistic traditions, it has been difficult for nurses to consider the cost effectiveness of nursing care. The goal has been to help people achieve or maintain health, regardless of cost. But the reality of the health care picture has forced nurses to think in monetary terms. Some nurses have acquired additional educational preparation in business and finance to help them better understand the financial aspects of health care. With the increased cost of health care, all disciplines within the health care field have been called on to demonstrate their value in a dollar-and-cents fashion.

Consumers are now more aware of the cost of health care and are asking for explanations of services they receive. These consumers need to be made aware of the importance of nursing care in relation to maintaining the health of well clients and in promoting the recovery and rehabilitation of ill clients.

Nursing services can consume a large percentage of a hospital's budget. With prospective payment systems dictating the amount of reimbursements that hospitals receive, nursing care services are being closely examined. It is not difficult to determine that hospitals could cut costs by curtailing nursing services. If nursing care can be demonstrated to be cost effective, hospitals will look to other sources for saving money. If effective nursing care enables patients to leave hospitals in better condition and in less time than predicted, hospitals will make more profit or, in the case of nonprofit hospitals, lower operating budgets will be needed. To determine that nursing care is effective, research is needed. Unfortunately, only a small percentage of a hospital's budget is allocated for nursing research.

Many studies in the literature demonstrate the cost effectiveness of nursing care. In a classic study, which means it has been cited many times, Brooten et al. (1986) examined early hospital discharge and home follow-up care of very-low-birth-weight infants. They found that follow-up care by a nurse specialist is safe and cost effective. This type of care potentially decreases iatrogenic illness and hospital-acquired infections, enhances parent–infant interaction, and significantly reduces hospital costs for care.

In previous editions of this text, this first chapter presented a few other nursing research cost-saving studies. However, because of the great importance of cost-savings in health care today, a new chapter has been added to this 6th edition. Chapter 19 discusses the economic value of nursing and how nursing research clearly demonstrates the positive effect nurses have on the health care of members of society. The chapter is co-authored by an economist.

QUANTITATIVE AND QUALITATIVE RESEARCH

Nurse researchers conduct both quantitative and qualitative studies. **Quantitative research** is concerned with objectivity, tight controls over the research situation, and the ability to generalize findings. **Qualitative research** is concerned with the subjective meaning of experiences to individuals.

In the past, nurse researchers have primarily conducted quantitative research. Quantitative research has been the traditional scientific approach used by many of the other disciplines. Some people do not consider qualitative research to be scientific. Others view quantitative research as hard science and qualitative research as soft science. Still others view both research approaches as scientific.

The number of nurse researchers who conduct qualitative research has increased. In 1985 Madeleine Leininger wrote that there were approximately 50 qualitative nurse researchers. Although the exact number of nurses conducting qualitative research more than 25 years later is not known, the numbers have increased dramatically.

Consider patients who experience chronic pain. Quantitative research would be concerned with the level of pain that these people were experiencing and how to reduce it, whereas qualitative research would be concerned with what it means to be living with chronic pain. This book focuses more on quantitative research than on qualitative research. However, Chapter 4 presents an overview of qualitative research, and specific qualitative designs are covered in Chapter 10.

OUTCOMES RESEARCH

According to the Agency for Healthcare Research and Quality (AHRQ), outcomes research seeks to understand the end results of health care practices and interventions (www.ahrq.gov/clinic/outfact. htm). End results include quality of life as well as mortality. According to the AHRQ fact sheet on outcomes research, the difference between traditional clinical measurements of outcomes, such as the results of laboratory tests, and the outcomes that matter most to patients, can be very different. An example provided in the fact sheet concerns benign prostate disease. The biomedical measure of urine flow rate, most often used to evaluate the need for treatment, has almost no relationship to a patient's symptoms. Based on this finding, a patient self-administered "symptom index" was developed to evaluate whether treatment is needed and/or desired.

It seems that nursing research has always been interested in outcomes research; we just didn't give it that label. Lake (2006) wrote that although most clinical nursing research studies could be considered outcomes research, the term has come to be associated with "how the organization of nursing impacts nursing (e.g., burnout), system (e.g., retention), and patient (e.g., 30-day mortality) outcomes rather than on the efficacy of an individual nursing intervention" (p. 51).

In this textbook, **outcomes research** is considered the research that focuses on measurable outcomes of interventions with certain patient populations. The increased interest in this type of studies is tied in with the high cost of health care. Health care policymakers, such as managed care organizations, want to know if the care that is being provided is cost effective. Consumers also want to know if the services that they purchase will improve their health.

Outcomes research has been placed in a separate category because the types of designs, methods, and sampling procedures used in these studies may be somewhat different from those used in the traditional quantitative or qualitative studies. For example, rather than exercising tight control over the sample, the goal might be to include a wide range of patients with varying levels of health status and comorbidities to determine the effectiveness of an intervention for this varied group of people.

EDUCATIONAL PREPARATION FOR NURSING RESEARCH

The membership of the American Association of College of Nursing (AACN) approved a research position statement in October 1998, with revisions approved in 1999 and 2006. This statement lists research expectations and outcomes for graduates of baccalaureate programs, master's programs, practice-focused doctoral programs, research-focused doctoral programs, and postdoctoral programs (http://aacn.nche.edu/Publications/positions/NsgRes).

Nurses prepared at the baccalaureate level should be able to understand and apply research findings from nursing and other disciplines in their clinical practice. They should be able to work with others to identify potential research problems and collaborate on research teams.

Masters-prepared nurses should be able to evaluate research findings and develop and implement evidence-based practice guidelines. They should identify practice and systems problems that require research, and collaborate with scientists to initiate research.

Graduates of practice-focused doctoral programs use advanced leadership knowledge and skills to translate research into practice and collaborate with scientists on new health policy research. They focus on the evaluation and use of research, rather than on carrying out research.

Graduates of research-focused doctoral programs are prepared to conduct independent research. They are expected to plan and implement an independent program of research and begin to involve others (students, clinicians, and other researchers) in their research interest area.

Finally, postdoctoral study provides a time for graduates of research-focused doctoral programs to fully develop their research skills. They are able to develop their research program with the help of formal mentoring by senior investigators.

ROLES OF NURSES IN RESEARCH

Overall, nurses can assume many roles in association with research projects. Some of these roles include the following, and are described in the ensuing sections:

1. Principal investigator
2. Member of a research team
3. Identifier of researchable problems
4. Evaluator of research findings
5. User of research findings
6. Patient/client advocate during studies
7. Subject/participant in studies

Principal Investigator

Nurses can and should serve as principal investigators in scientific investigations. To be a principal investigator, special research preparation is necessary. It might be possible for a beginning researcher to conduct a small-scale survey study, but preparation beyond the baccalaureate, or even the master's level, is necessary for independent investigator status in most nursing research studies.

Member of a Research Team

Nurses can serve as members of a research team. They may act as data collectors or administer the experimental intervention of the study. As nurses increasingly participate in research, it is possible that interest and enthusiasm to conduct their own investigations may grow. In 1982 Rittenmeyer wrote that research would become a higher priority as knowledge of the benefits of research increased. She predicted that by 1990 research would be part of the nurse's normal workload. Unfortunately, the 20th century closed without her prediction coming true. Maybe the 21st century will be the magic millennium! However, the first 10 years have not yet seen this change occur.

Nursing research does seem to be gathering momentum because bedside nurses and health care leaders are trying to validate the impact of nursing on patient outcomes and the health care system in general. We can only hope that the trend continues, as evidence-based practice becomes the standard for nursing care.

Identifier of Researchable Problems

All nurses, from associate degree to doctoral-level preparation, have the responsibility of trying to identify areas of needed research. Nurses at the bedside are particularly well situated to identify patient-related researchable problems.

Evaluator of Research Findings

Nurses should be involved in the evaluation of research findings. As research consumers, nurses have the obligation to become familiar with research findings and determine the usefulness of these findings in the practice area. Beginning researchers should critique research articles, first with the help of an experienced researcher and eventually on their own. They may gain knowledge in a structured research course (either in their basic nursing education program or in a continuing education course). The evaluation of research is not an easy task. This book will help you to acquire some of the skills needed to critique research articles and reports.

User of Research Findings

Through the years, nurses have tended to carry out nursing procedures and provide nursing care "the way we've always done it." Change is difficult to bring about, but research findings have no value if they are not put into use. After evaluating research findings, nurses should use relevant findings in their practice. The primary goal of nursing research, as mentioned earlier, is quality nursing care of clients. However, nurses must be judicious in their use of research findings. The results of one small study conducted with a sample of 15 volunteers, for example, would not provide sufficient evidence for a change in nursing practice.

Research utilization and evidence-based nursing practice (EBNP) are related because both processes emphasize research findings. However, **research utilization** focuses on the implementation of findings from specific research studies. The goal of research utilization is to see that the findings of research studies are actually put into action in nursing practice. EBNP is broader and involves searching for the best evidence to use in nursing practice, which includes searching for the best research evidence available.

Patient/Client Advocate During Studies

All nurses have the responsibility to act as advocates when their patients/clients are involved in research. This advocacy involves making sure that the ethical aspects of research are upheld. Nurses should help answer questions and explain a study to potential participants before the study begins. They also might be available during the study to answer questions or provide support to study participants.

Some of the questions that research subjects need to have answered include: Why is the study being conducted? Who is conducting the study? Who is going to be in the study? What kind of tests and treatments are involved? How long will the study last? (Habel, 2005). Nurses should serve as valuable resources for information about clinical trials, both in health care settings and in the community.

Subject/Participant in Studies

Nurses may act as subjects or participants in research. Many nurses (including me) are involved in a long-term survey study, the Nurses' Health Study, being conducted by researchers at Harvard Medical School. The study was designed to examine some of the health risks that pose special threats to women. Nurses were chosen as subjects, according to Frank Speizer, the principal investigator, because the study called for "a sophisticated group of individuals who could report exposure and diseases more accurately than the general population" ("Massive Nurses' Health Study," 1983, p. 998). The study was begun in 1976 and was originally intended to last for 4 years, but additional funding has been received and the study has continued for over 35 years. In 1989 a new cohort of younger nurses was added to the study in what is called Nurses' Health Study II. Hundreds of publications have resulted from the data obtained in these studies. Chapter 11 presents more information on the Nurses' Health Study I and II, under the discussion of samples for longitudinal studies.

HISTORY OF NURSING RESEARCH

Nursing research was slow to develop in the United States, as well as in the rest of the world. Some of this slow growth is related to the development of nursing education. Despite her skill in independent scientific investigation, Florence Nightingale derived the foundation for modern nursing education from the military tradition, which emphasized the concept of authority. The authoritarian system of training deterred the development of inquiring minds (Simmons & Henderson, 1964). Many schools of nursing throughout the world have been influenced by British nursing education and have relied on tradition and authority, as did British schools.

Nursing research was able to develop and expand only as nurses received advanced educational preparation. The growth of nursing research seems to be directly related to the educational levels of nurses. Although the first university-based nursing program in the United States was begun in 1909, the number of such programs increased very slowly. In the early part of the 20th century, nurse leaders were more concerned with increasing the number of nurses and establishing hospital-affiliated nursing schools than with establishing university programs.

Because nurses were not prepared to conduct research, members of other disciplines conducted many of the early nursing studies. Beginning with a 1923 study, whose final report was titled the Goldmark Report, non-nurses became involved in studying nurses and nursing. Sociologists were particularly interested in the "learning, living, and working" experienced by nurses (Abdellah & Levine, 1965, p. 4). Research conducted by sociologists and behavioral scientists added to their respective bodies of knowledge but did not necessarily expand nursing's body of knowledge (Henderson, 1956).

As nurses received advanced educational preparation and became qualified to conduct research, many of the studies they conducted were in nursing education because before 1950 most nurses received their advanced degrees in education. However, even during the early half of the 20th century, the need for clinical nursing research was evident. In an article in the *American Journal of Nursing* in 1927, Marvin proposed many research questions involving procedures. What was the safest, simplest, quickest method of preparing a hypodermic? How long should the hands be scrubbed, by what method, and with what kind and strength of soap? By the 1950s, interest in nursing care studies began to rise. During the 1970s, particularly the last 5 years of that decade, practice-related research expanded rapidly.

Although Florence Nightingale recommended clinical nursing research in the mid-1800s, most nurses did not follow her advice until more than 100 years later. Some of the studies that she recommended, such as those concerning environmental health hazards, are being conducted today. It is only in recent years that Nightingale has come to be appreciated for the truly extraordinary woman that she was. If nurses had begun sooner to follow the example of their first leader, nursing would be much further along in establishing a body of nursing knowledge. However, there is reason for optimism at this time. Both the number and quality of nursing studies have increased dramatically.

The historical development of nursing research has many noteworthy events, including:

- **1850s:** Florence Nightingale studied nursing care during the Crimean War. She called for research that focused on nursing practice. Nightingale admonished nurses to develop the habit of making and recording observations systematically. She used statistics to clearly illustrate her findings.

- **1902:** Lavinia Dock reported a school nurse "experiment" that was begun by Lillian Wald. Nurses gave free care to school children and visited the homes of sick children.

- **1906:** Adelaide Nutting conducted a survey of the educational status of nursing.

- **1909:** The first university-based nursing program was established at the University of Minnesota.

- **1923:** A well-known study of nursing and nursing education was conducted by the Committee for the Study of Nursing Education and funded by the Rockefeller Foundation. Referred to as the Goldmark Report, this study recommended advanced educational preparation for teachers, administrators, and public health nurses, and was instrumental in the establishment of early collegiate nursing schools at Yale, Vanderbilt, and Western Reserve.

- **1924:** The first doctoral program for nurses was established at Teachers College, Columbia University. The EdD degree was offered to nurses preparing to teach at the college level.

- **1927:** Jean Broadhurst and her colleagues researched handwashing procedures. Edith S. Bryan became the first nurse to earn a doctoral degree when she received a PhD in psychology and counseling from Johns Hopkins University.

- **1928:** Ethel Johns and Blanche Pfefferkorn published a study concerning the activities in which nurses were involved. This study was one of the first of many studies that focused on nurses.

- 1932: EliFzabeth Ryan and Virginia B. Miller investigated thermometer-disinfecting techniques.
- 1936: Sigma Theta Tau, National Honor Society for Nursing, began funding nursing research.
- 1948: Esther Lucille Brown, a social anthropologist, published her famous study on nursing education, *Nursing for the Future,* which called for nursing education to take place in university settings. The Brown Report, as the study was called, recommended research in nursing and pointed to the need for nurse educators to be involved in research.

  Doris Schwartz documented the effectiveness of nursing care for inducing sleep in patients and for decreasing their intake of medications.
- 1949: The Division of Nursing Resources was organized within the U.S. Public Health Service.

  Esta H. McNett demonstrated the usefulness of masks in preventing the spread of tuberculosis.
- 1952: The first issue of *Nursing Research* was published.
- 1953: The Institute of Research and Service in Nursing Education was founded at Teachers College, Columbia University. A full-time staff studied nursing and nursing education.
- 1955: The American Nurses Foundation was established with the goal of promoting high-level wellness and the improvement of patient care. This foundation funds nursing research.

  The Nursing Research Grants and Fellowship Programs were established by the U.S. Public Health Service.
- 1957: The first unit directed primarily toward research in nursing practice was established at the Department of Nursing of the Walter Reed Army Institute of Research.

  The Western Council for Higher Education in Nursing (WCHEN) sponsored a nursing research conference at the University of Colorado.
- 1962: The federally supported Nurse Scientist Graduate Training Grants Programs were begun.
- 1963: Lydia Hall published her 5-year study of chronically ill patients who were cared for at the Loeb Center in New York.
- 1970: The National Commission for the Study of Nursing and Nursing Education, established by the American Nurses Association (ANA) and the National League for Nursing (NLN), published the results of a 3-year study on nursing. The report, titled *An Abstract for Action,* was popularly called the Lysaught Report, after Jerome Lysaught, director of the project. The report recommended that research be financed in both nursing practice and nursing education.

  A center for nursing research was established at Wayne State University.
- 1972: The ANA established a Department of Nursing Research.
- 1974: At its national convention, the ANA delineated nursing practice as the area to which nursing research should be directed in the next decade.
- 1976: The Commission on Nursing Research of the ANA recommended that research preparation be included in undergraduate, graduate, and continuing education programs.
- 1977: The Veterans' Administration began employing nurse researchers.
- 1978: The first issue of *Research in Nursing and Health* was published.
- 1979: The first issue of *Western Journal of Nursing Research* was published.
- 1980: The ANA Commission on Nursing Research identified research priorities for the 1980s.
- 1982: Eleven volumes were published of the work of the Conduct and Utilization of Research in Nursing (CURN) project.
- 1983: The first Center for Nursing Research was established. It encompassed the American Nurses Foundation and the American Academy of Nursing.
- 1986: The National Center for Nursing Research (NCNR) was established within the National Institutes of Health.

- **1987**: Dr. Ada Hinshaw, director of the NCNR, called for nursing organizations to identify their research priorities.
- **1988**: The NCNR convened the first Conference on Research Priorities (CORP #1) to establish research priorities through 1994.

   The first issues of *Applied Nursing Research* and *Nursing Science Quarterly* were published.
- **1992**: The first issue of *Clinical Nursing Research* was published.
- **1993**: The National Institute of Nursing Research (NINR) was established within the National Institutes of Health (NIH). This organization replaced the NCNR.

   The second Conference on Research Priorities (CORP #2) was held to establish research priorities for 1995–1999.
- **1994**: The first issue of *Qualitative Nursing Research* was published.
- **1997**: The International Council of Nurses convened a group of experts to establish worldwide nursing research priorities.
- **1999**: The first issue of *Biological Research for Nursing* was published.
- **2001**: The budget for NINR reached almost $90 million.
- **2004**: The first issue of *Worldviews on Evidence-Based Nursing* was published.
- **2005**: The budget for NINR was more than $138 million.
- **2009**: The Cochrane Nursing Care Network (CNCN) was registered as one of the Networks within the Cochrane Collaboration, which produces and disseminates systematic reviews.
- **2010**: The NINR budget was more than $145 million; the 2011 budget was set at more than $150 million.

   The name of the Cochrane Nursing Care Network was changed to the Cochrane Nursing Care Field (CNCF).

RESEARCH PRIORITIES FOR THE FUTURE

Professional nursing organizations and individual nurse leaders are united in identifying the need for research that will help build a scientific knowledge base for nursing practice. In 1980 the ANA Commission on Nursing Research identified priorities for nursing research. These priorities included research concerned with health promotion and preventive health practices for all age groups, health care needs of high-risk groups, life satisfaction of individuals and families, and the development of cost-effective health care systems.

In November 1987 Dr. Ada Sue Hinshaw, director of the National Center for Nursing Research (NCNR), invited nursing organizations to identify their research priorities. Since then, many nursing organizations have conducted surveys of their membership to determine research priorities.

The National Association of Orthopaedic Nurses identified a list of priorities in 1990 (Salmond, 1994). They used a Delphi technique to survey experts in the field. Some of the highest ratings were given to preventing confusion in elderly patients following a hip fracture, determining the most effective safety measures to use with patients with acute confusional state, and differentiating pain responses according to diagnoses, ages, and pain management interventions. In 1997 Sedlak, Ross, Arslanian, and Taggart (1998) replicated the 1990 study. Their respondents expressed the need for more research on pain and patient complications, such as deep vein thrombosis (DVT). Sedlak et al. called for an ongoing and wider dissemination of research results.

In 1999 Pullen, Tuck, and Wallace published a list of priorities in mental health nursing. These priorities were obtained by examining the published literature from 1990 to 1996. Six broad categories were identified: support, holism, mental health nursing practice, quality care outcomes, mental health etiology, and mental health delivery systems. These authors cautioned that as nursing promotes evidence-based practice, there is a need for clear research priorities. They called for mental health nursing experts and organizations to propose a national/international mental health research agenda.

In 2004 the Emergency Nursing Association published the results of a Delphi study on national research priorities for emergency nurses in the United States (Bayley, MacLean, Desy, & McMahon, 2004). Three rounds of mailed surveys were used to gather data. Responses were received from 101 emergency nursing leaders. The study was completed in summer 2001. Interventions for pain management received the highest ranking. Emergency nurses were also concerned with staff shortages and overcrowding of emergency departments and the effects of these two conditions on patients.

A survey was conducted in 2004 among members of the Oncology Nursing Society (ONS) to determine research priorities for 2005 to 2008 (Berger et al., 2005). Responses were received from 431 members. The top 20 research priorities were identified. These included quality of life, participation in decision making about treatment in advanced disease, patient/family education, and pain management. In 2008 the survey was again sent out, by e-mail this time. Participants returned their responses to the survey Web site. Quality of life and pain were the two highest rated topics. Results from this survey were used to develop the 2009–2013 Oncology Nursing Society Research Agenda (Doorenbos et al., 2008).

A three-round electronic Delphi study was conducted to identify and gain consensus benchmarks for effective primary care-based nursing services for adults with depression (McIlrath, Keeney, McKenna, & McLaughlin, 2010). Surveys were completed by 67 multi-professional experts in the United Kingdom. They reached consensus on 73 benchmarks, of which 45 were related to structures, 18 to processes, and 10 to outcomes. The "top-ranked benchmarks focused on the need for alternative service delivery models, an identified level of training and competency for nurses, and the availability of advice and support from secondary care specialists, when necessary." (p. 277).

Priorities for public health nursing were published by the Association of Community Health Nursing Educators (ACHNE) Research Committee in the January 2010 issue of *Public Health Nursing*. They identified the most important priorities as population-focused outcomes, and workforce issues. This research committee called for "multisite studies, clinical trials, community-based participatory research, development and/or analysis of existing large data sets" (p. 94).

Although clinical nursing research is essential for the profession, other types of research are also needed. Tucker-Allen (2003) wrote an editorial in which she bemoaned the fact that nursing education research has not always been respected. She called for nurse educators to conduct research on both clinical issues and educational issues. She expressed the hope that funding would increase for educational research.

A National League for Nursing (NLN) task group worked for 7 years to compile research in nursing education and to publish a book on their results (Schultz, 2009). Some of the studies reviewed concerned learner developmental stages, aptitude, motivation, and learning styles. The taskforce concluded that more research is needed on effective teaching and that there is a need to build a science of nursing education.

Replication studies should be a high priority for nursing research. **Replication studies** involve repeating a study with all the essential elements of the original study held intact. Different samples and settings may be used. Replication studies in nursing have not been numerous, and the lack of these studies has hindered the development of a cumulative body of nursing knowledge. This type of study is of particular importance in clinical nursing research. Because of the small nonrandom samples used in many studies, nurses need to conduct many similar studies on the same topic to allow for generalization of findings. Nursing studies have typically been one of a kind. The results of a single study rarely provide enough evidence for making decisions about nursing practice. An example of a replication study is presented in Chapter 5.

NATIONAL INSTITUTE OF NURSING RESEARCH

The National Institute of Nursing Research (NINR) was officially established within the National Institutes of Health (NIH) on June 10, 1993. It replaced the National Center for Nursing Research (NCNR), which had been established in 1986. It is one of the 27 institutes that comprise the National Institute of Health (NIH). With the creation of the NINR, nursing research received a big boost in respectability. Funding for nursing research has increased a great deal. In 1986 the NCNR had a budget of $16 million. In 1995 the NINR received an appropriation of close to $50 million from Congress. By 2001 funding had been increased to almost $90 million. In 2005 the budget for the NINR was more than $138 million. The 2010 budget allocation was more than $145 million, with the proposed 2011 budget being set at more than $150 million. Information on the National Institute of Nursing Research can be found on the NINR Web site (http://ninr.nih.gov/).

The NINR mission statement indicates support for clinical and basic research and research training on health and illness across the lifespan. Areas of research emphasis are: promoting health and preventing disease, improving quality of life, and eliminating health disparities. The entire mission statement and strategic plans can be found at http://ninr.nih.gov/AboutNINR.

THE COCHRANE COLLABORATION AND THE COCHRANE NURSING CARE FIELD

The Cochrane Collaboration, established in 1993, is an international nonprofit organization of people with the goal of helping health care providers, policy makers, patients, and their advocates and caretakers make well-informed decisions about health care. Visit the Cochrane Web site at http://cochrane.org.

There are more than 27,000 contributors from more than 100 countries. The Collaboration's goals are achieved through the preparation, updating, and promoting of systematic reviews based on research studies. These reviews are accessible online through *The Cochrane Library* (http://cochrane. org). More than 4,000 reviews have been published as of December 2009. These reviews are generally considered, in the health care community, to be the most comprehensive, reliable and relevant source of evidence on which to base health care decisions. Each review addresses a clearly formulated question, such as "Can antibiotics help in alleviating the symptoms of a sore throat?" Stringent guidelines are used to establish whether there is conclusive evidence about a certain treatment or the accuracy of a diagnostic test. The reviews are updated regularly. The Cochrane Collaboration is discussed further in Chapter 18.

The Cochrane Collaboration established a nursing entity in March 2009, titled the Cochrane Nursing Care Network (CNCN). It became one of the 16 fields and networks within the Cochrane Collaboration. The first inaugural CNCN symposium was held in Singapore in October 2009. More than 135 people from 11 countries attended.

The name of the nursing field was officially changed in April 2010 to the Cochrane Nursing Care Field (CNCF). Other existing Cochrane Networks are also now officially called fields. The CNCF is coordinated from Adelaide, Australia.

The CNCF will be developing a number of resources such as nursing care Cochrane Review Summaries, nursing care-relevant podcasts, CNCF news, and online and face-to-face involvement of its members in preparing summaries and other materials. Volunteers are needed to help with all of these projects and are asked to register their interests at the Web site. More information on the CNCF is presented in Chapter 18.

SUMMARY

Nursing research is defined as the systematic, objective process of analyzing phenomena of importance to nursing. It includes studies concerning nursing practice, nursing education, nursing administration, and nurses themselves. **Clinical nursing research** is research that has the potential to affect the care of clients.

Nursing knowledge has come from tradition, authority, trial and error, and scientific research. Scientific research uses **empirical data** (data gathered through the senses) and is a systematic, orderly, and objective method of seeking information.

Basic research is concerned with generating new knowledge; **applied research** seeks solutions to immediate problems. Most nursing studies have been applied research. Many studies, however, contain elements of both basic and applied research.

The most important goal for conducting nursing research is the promotion of evidence-based nursing practice. **Evidence-based nursing practice** (EBNP) means that nurses make clinical decisions based on the best research evidence, their clinical expertise, and the health care preferences of their patients/clients. Other goals for research are to ensure credibility of the nursing profession, provide accountability for nursing practice, and document the cost effectiveness of nursing care.

Quantitative research is concerned with objectivity, tight controls over the research situation, and the ability to generalize findings. **Qualitative research** is concerned with the subjective meaning of an experience to an individual. **Outcomes research** focuses on measurable outcomes of interventions with certain patient populations.

Nurses act as principal investigators, members of research teams, identifiers of researchable problems, evaluators of research findings, users of research findings, patient/client advocates during studies, and subjects/participants in research.

Research utilization focuses on the implementation of findings from specific research studies. Because nurses were not prepared, at the time, to conduct research, members of other disciplines conducted many of the early nursing studies. Some of these studies, such as the Goldmark Report in 1923 and the Brown Report in 1948, contributed important information about nursing and nursing education. As nurses began to receive advanced degrees, these degrees were generally in the field of education. Many of the studies conducted by the first nurse researchers in this country were in the area of nursing education. Florence Nightingale recommended clinical nursing research in the mid-1800s, but this type of research was scarce until the 1970s. Many nursing organizations have identified clinical nursing research priorities for the future. Also, replication studies are needed in nursing. **Replication studies** involve repeating a study with all the essential elements of the original study held intact.

The National Institute of Nursing Research (NINR) was established in 1993. Funding by Congress has increased from $16 million in 1986 to the National Center for Nursing Research, the precursor to the NINR, to more than $145 to NINR in 2010.

The Cochrane Nursing Care Network (CNCN) was registered in March 2009 as one of the Fields and Networks within the Cochrane Collaboration. The name was changed in April 2010 to the Cochrane Nursing Care Field (CNCF).

NURSING RESEARCH ON THE WEB

For additional online resources, research activities, and exercises, go to **www.mynursingkit.com.** Select Chapter 1 from the drop-down menu.

GET INVOLVED ACTIVITIES

1. Divide into two debate teams. One team will be *for* the issue, "Nearly all nursing research should be *clinical* research." The other team will be *against* the issue.
2. Think of three methods of sharing research findings with colleagues at school or at work.
3. Express to your peers your greatest fears about critiquing research articles.
4. Develop a statement to present to a group of hospital administrators that would focus on the need to increase funding for nursing research in their institution.
5. A philanthropist puts a note on the bulletin board at your school or work setting. She wrote that she is willing to fund a $200,000 nursing study in the name of her deceased mother who was cared for by "wonderful nurses." She is asking for suggestions. What *one* study would you suggest?
6. Go to the Cochrane Nursing Care Field (CNCF) Web site (http://cncf.cochrane.org/) and familiarize yourself with plans for the future. Discuss these with your colleagues.

SELF-TEST

Circle the letter before the *best* answer.

1. The most objective means of obtaining nursing knowledge is through
   A. trial and error.
   B. tradition.
   C. scientific research.
   D. authority.
2. The general public
   A. has little knowledge about nursing research.
   B. is able to distinguish between medical and nursing research.
   C. is not interested in nursing research.
   D. asks nurses to explain nursing research to them.
3. Which of the following statements concerning nursing research is true?
   A. The scientific base for nursing practice expanded greatly in the first half of the 20th century.
   B. The majority of nursing studies before 1950 focused on clinical problems.
   C. Many studies have focused on nurses themselves.
   D. The first nursing investigations were conducted in the United States.
4. The major reason for conducting nursing research is to
   A. promote evidence-based care for patients/clients.
   B. promote the growth of the nursing profession.
   C. document the cost effectiveness of nursing care.
   D. ensure accountability for nursing practice.
5. Which of the following is generally true concerning the knowledge base for nursing?
   A. Most of the knowledge that has been used by nurses was developed by nurses.
   B. Much of the knowledge that has been used by nurses was developed by members of other disciplines.
   C. Nurses have used knowledge developed by nurses and by members of other disciplines in even proportions.
6. As nurses first began to receive advanced educational preparation and became qualified to conduct research, many of their studies concerned
   A. nursing education.
   B. characteristics of nurses.
   C. nursing administration.
   D. nursing care.
7. The first journal devoted primarily to the publication of nursing research was
   A. *Nursing Research.*
   B. *Research in Nursing and Health.*
   C. *Applied Nursing Research.*
   D. *American Journal of Nursing.*
8. Nursing leaders have called for research focusing on which of the following topics? Choose all that apply.
   A. quality of life
   B. patient safety

C. living with a chronic illness

D. end-of-life care

9. Which of the following agencies is most influential, at the present time, in funding nursing research?

A. American Nurses Association

B. National Center for Nursing Research

C. National Institute of Nursing Research

D. Sigma Theta Tau International, Honor Society for Nursing

10. All nurses should be able to

A. identify researchable problems for nursing research studies.

B. explain the details of a medical research study to potential participants.

C. determine when most study findings are ready for use in nursing practice.

D. critique, with confidence, the majority of published nursing research studies.

REFERENCES

Abdellah, F. G., & Levine, E. (1965). *Better patient care through nursing research.* New York: Macmillan.

Association of Community Health Nursing Educators (ACHNE) Research Committee. (2010). Research priorities for public health nursing. *Public Health Nursing, 27,* 94–100. doi: 10.1111/j.1525-1446.2009.00831.x

Bayley, E. W., MacLean, S. L., Desy, P., & McMahon, M. (2004). ENA's Delphi study on national research priorities for emergency nurses in the United States. *Journal of Emergency Nursing, 30,* 12–21.

Berger, A. M., Berry, D. L., Christopher, K. A., Greene A. L., Maliski, S., Swenson, K. K., . . . Hoyt, D. R. (2005). Oncology Nursing Society year 2004 research priorities survey. *Oncology Nursing Forum, 32,* 281–290.

Blackledge, H. A. (2009). ANF 2009 nursing research review chair exemplifies leadership. *The American Nurse, 41,* 15.

Brooten, D., Kumar, S., Brown, L. P., Butts, P., Finkler, S. A., Bakewell-Sachs, S., . . . Deliveria- Papadopoulos, M. (1986). A randomized clinical trial of early hospital discharge and home follow-up of very-low-birth-weight infants. *New England Journal of Medicine, 315,* 934–939.

Burns, N., & Grove, S. K. (2009). *The practice of nursing research: Appraisal, synthesis, and generation of evidence* (6th ed.). St. Louis, MO: Saunders Elsevier.

Doorenbos, A. Z., Berger, A. M., Brohard-Holbert, C., Eaton, L. Kozachik, S., Lo Biondo-Wood, G., . . . Varricchio, C. (2008). 2008 ONS research priorities survey. *Oncology Nursing Forum, 35,* E100–107.

Dougherty, M. D. (2010). Evidence-based practice and nursing research [Editorial]. *Nursing Research, 59,* 1.

Habel, M. (2005, March 14). Can you answer patients' questions about clinical trials? *NurseWeek—South Central Edition,* pp. 23–25.

Henderson, V. (1956). Research in nursing practice—when? *Nursing Research, 4,* 99.

Kerlinger, F. (1986). *Foundations of behavioral research* (3rd ed.). New York: Holt, Rinehart & Winston.

Knox, T., & Davie, J. (2009). Nasogastric tube feeding—which syringe size produces lower pressure and is safest to use? *Nursing Times, 105,* 24–33.

Lake, E. T. (2006). Multilevel models in health outcomes research: Part I. Theory, design, and measurement. *Applied Nursing Research, 19,* 51–55.

Marvin, M. (1927). Research in nursing. *American Journal of Nursing, 27,* 331–335.

Massive nurses' health study in seventh year, reports first findings on disease links in women. (1983). *American Journal of Nursing, 83,* 998–999.

McIlrath, C., Keeney, S., McKenna, H., & McLaughlin, D. (2010). Benchmarks for effective primary case-based nursing services for adults with depression: A Delphi study. *Journal of Advanced Nursing, 66,* 269–281.

Oman, K. S., Krugman, M. E., & Fink, R. M. (2003). Nursing research secrets. Philadelphia: Hanley & Belfus.

Polit, D. F., & Beck, C. T. (2008). *Nursing research: Generating and assessing evidence for nursing practice* (8th ed.). Philadelphia: Lippincott Williams & Wilkins.

Pullen, L., Tuck, I., & Wallace, D. C. (1999). Research priorities in mental health nursing. *Issues in Mental Health Nursing, 20,* 217–227.

Rittenmeyer, P. (1982). The evolution of nursing research. *Western Journal of Nursing Research, 4,* 223–225.

Sabourin, H. (2009). The last word: Getting on with the job of supporting research. *Canadian Nurse, 105,* 40.

Salmond, S. W. (1994). Orthopaedic nursing research priorities: A Delphi study. *Orthopaedic Nursing, 13,* 31–45.

Schultz, C. M. (Ed.). (2009). *Building a science of nursing education: Foundations for evidence-based teaching–learning.* New York: National League for Nursing.

Sedlak, C., Ross, D., Arslanian, C., & Taggart, H. (1998). Orthopaedic nursing research priorities: A replication and extension. *Orthopaedic Nursing, 17*(2), 51–58.

Simmons, L. W., & Henderson, V. (1964). *Nursing research—A survey and assessment.* New York: Appleton-Century-Crofts.

Tingen, M. S., Burnett, A. H., Murchison, R. B., & Zhu, H. (2009). The importance of nursing research. *Journal of Nursing Education, 48,* 167–170.

Tucker-Allen, S. (2003). Nursing education as a respected area of research [Editorial]. *The Association of Black Nursing Faculty Journal, 14,* 115.

CHAPTER 2

Ethical Issues in Nursing Research

OUTLINE

OBJECTIVES

On completion of this chapter, you will be prepared to:
1. Discuss some of the unethical studies that have been documented in the literature
2. Trace the development of ethical codes and guidelines
3. Appreciate the role of institutional review boards
4. Identify the elements of informed consent
5. Recognize unethical research
6. Act as a patient advocate during research investigations
7. Critique the ethical aspects of a study

NEW TERMS DEFINED IN THIS CHAPTER

The ethical aspects of a proposed research study take precedence over any other areas of the study. The rights of study participants must be protected in all research studies. Why, then, can everyone reading this book probably recall hearing about some unethical research?

During 1942 and 1943, World War II prisoners' wounds were deliberately infected with bacteria. Infection was caused by forcing wood shavings and ground glass into the wounds. Sulfanilamide was then given to these prisoners to determine the effectiveness of this drug. Some subjects died and others suffered serious injury. The so-called subjects for these experiments were prisoners in the German concentration camps. Many nurses participated in these unethical experiments; others found ways to avoid participation, such as becoming pregnant or asking for transfers to other assignments (Bonifazi, 2004).

Between June and September 1944, photographs and body measurements were taken of 112 Jewish prisoners. They were then killed, and their skeletons defleshed. One purpose of this study was to determine if photographs from live human beings could be used to predict skeletal size. The skeleton collection was to be displayed at the Reich University of Strasbourg (Nuremberg Military Tribunals, 1949).

How could such atrocities be committed in the name of science? Some of these studies were based on the rationale that the victims were not "real" people like the Germans. The German race was viewed as superior, and it was believed that this race would one day rule the world.

Widespread knowledge about unethical research conducted in Germany was obtained immediately after World War II. However, it was not until the early 1980s that the public became informed about the atrocities committed in Japan during that same period. It appears that a conspiracy between U.S. government leaders and the Japanese prevented this material from being made public (Shearer, 1982). To obtain the results of the Japanese experiments, immunity was granted to Shiro Ishii, commander of the Japanese biological warfare unit, and his subordinates. The silence was first broken in 1975 when a Japanese film producer, Haruko Yoshinaga, tracked down 35 people involved in the incidents. Japanese and American writers then began demanding information from the Pentagon under the Freedom of Information Act. Shearer revealed some of these horrible experiments:

1. Infecting women prisoners with syphilis, having them impregnated by male prisoners, then dissecting the live babies and mothers.
2. Draining the blood from prisoners' veins and substituting horse blood.
3. Exploding gas gangrene bombs next to prisoners tied to stakes.
4. Vivisecting prisoners to compile data on the human endurance of pain. (p. 10)

In 1995 six former members of the Japanese biological warfare unit published a book, *The Truth About Unit 731*, to tell about the atrocities that they had seen or heard about ("Japanese Book Details Scientific Atrocities," 1996).

Because the United States has a strong Judeo-Christian background, it may seem unlikely that such heinous research could ever be conducted in this country. However, the following examples of research were, in fact, carried out in the United States.

One of the most widely known unethical studies was carried out in 1932 in Macon County, Alabama by the U.S. Public Health Service. The study was titled "Tuskegee Study of Untreated Syphilis in the Negro Male." Of the 600 black male subjects, 399 had syphilis, and 201 did not have the disease. Subjects with active cases were given *no* treatment. All subjects were given free medical exams, free meals, and burial expenses (Centers for Disease Control and Prevention, 2010). Even after penicillin was accepted as the treatment of choice for syphilis in 1945, subjects were still given no treatment. This unethical study became common knowledge 40 years after it was begun. On May 16, 1997, President Bill Clinton made a public apology on behalf of the nation.

It is common knowledge that smallpox is no longer a threat to the world. Few people remember, or even know, that Edward Jenner deliberately exposed an 8-year-old child to cowpox to try out his new vaccine for smallpox (Hayter, 1979).

From 1963 to 1966, a group of children diagnosed with mental retardation were deliberately exposed to infectious hepatitis in Willowbrook State Hospital on Staten Island, New York (Krugman, Giles, & Hammond, 1971). The children were deliberately injected with the hepatitis virus. The researchers defended the project by proposing that the vast majority of the children would acquire the infection anyway while at Willowbrook and that it would be better for them to acquire the disease under carefully controlled conditions. They then tried to treat them with gamma globulin.

In July 1963 doctors at the Jewish Chronic Disease Hospital in Brooklyn, New York injected live cancer cells into 22 elderly patients. The study was designed to measure patients' ability to reject foreign cells. The patients were told that they were being given skin tests (Katz, 1972).

In Los Angeles, California, between 1989 and 1991 approximately 900 children, who were mostly black or Hispanic, were given an experimental measles vaccine called EZ ("Measles Mistake," 1996). The researchers never told the parents about the experiment because the vaccine was unlicensed. Kaiser Permanente and the Centers for Disease Control and Prevention (CDC), sponsors of the study, said the drug was safe, but agreed that they should have notified parents about the status of the drug.

A similar situation occurred in 1991 at the Standing Rock Sioux Reservation in the Dakotas ("Parents Say Government Quiet," 1996). A group of American Indian children were given a vaccine for hepatitis A. Parents were never told their children were part of a research project and that the vaccine had not been approved at that time. The study was sponsored by the CDC and the Indian Health Service.

In 2005 it was revealed that government-funded researchers tested experimental AIDS drugs on hundreds of foster children without providing these children with an independent advocate (Solomon, 2005). These children, who were mostly poor or from minority groups, received cutting-edge treatments at the government's expense. In some cases, their lives were extended. However, many children experienced side effects, such as rashes, vomiting, and sharp drops in infection-fighting blood cells. They had no advocate to weigh the advantages and disadvantages of their participation in research.

In 2007 newly discovered documents revealed that Indian soldiers were deliberately exposed to mustard gas during World War II to test their reaction to this chemical ("Indian Troops were part of WWII Gas Tests," 2007). Documents in Britain's National Archives describe the experiments carried out at a remote British base in what is now Pakistan. Troops were marched into the gas chambers. They usually wore gas masks, but on one occasion masks were not used to determine the effect of the gas on their eyes.

In a 2009 article in *Clinical Nurse Specialist* titled "A Case of Scientific Misconduct," Patricia O'Malley describes shredding a manuscript she had written and then tossing it in the trash can. She discovered, to her disbelief, that several published papers that she had used as references had been retracted. The reason was falsified data. The manuscript discussed a relabeled agent and multimodal analgesia that she believed would have implications for CNS practice.

DEVELOPMENT OF ETHICAL CODES AND GUIDELINES

The need for ethical guidelines becomes clear after reading these accounts of unethical research projects. The development of appropriate guidelines is not simple. Ethics is concerned with rules and principles of human behavior. Because human behavior is very complex, rules to govern the actions of human beings are difficult to formulate. Studies of recorded history show that people have always been interested in this topic. The biblical Ten Commandments is one example of a code of conduct that has endured through the centuries. Ethical principles frequently change with time and the development of new knowledge.

The present ethical standards used in nursing research, and in research conducted by other disciplines, are based on the guidelines developed after World War II. The atrocities committed in the German prison camps led to the Nuremberg Trials after the war. The 1947 Nuremberg Code resulted from the revelations of unethical human behavior that occurred during the war. This code seeks to ensure that several criteria for research are met including the following:

1. Potential subjects must be informed about the study.
2. The research must be for the good of society.
3. Animal research should precede research on humans, if possible.
4. An attempt must be made by the researcher to avoid injury to research subjects.
5. The researcher must be qualified to conduct research.
6. Subjects or the researcher can stop the study if problems occur.

Many other ethical codes have been developed since the Nuremberg Code. On December 10, 1948, the General Assembly of the United Nations adopted the Universal Declaration of Human Rights (http://www.un.org/en/documents/udhr).

The World Medical Association adopted the Declaration of Helsinki in 1964. Revised several times, the sixth revision came in 2008 (http://wma.net/en/30publications/10policies/b3/index.html).

In 1978 The National Commission for the Protection of Human Subjects of Biomedical and Behavioral Research was formed. The goals of this commission were to (a) identify basic ethical principles that should guide the conduct of research involving human subjects and (b) develop guidelines based on principles that had been identified. The report titled "Ethical Principles and Guidelines for the Protection of Human Subjects of Research," published by this commission in 1979, was titled *The Belmont Report*, named after the Belmont Conference Center where the document was drafted. It identified three basic principles related to research subjects:

1. Respect for Persons—research subjects should have autonomy and self-determination
2. Beneficence—research subjects should be protected from harm
3. Justice—research subjects should receive fair treatment

The U.S. Department of Health, Education and Welfare (HEW), now the Department of Health and Human Services (DHHS), published general guidelines for research in 1981. These have been revised several times. Also, special guidelines exist for research with vulnerable groups such as children, the mentally retarded, and prisoners. Any institution that receives federal money for research must abide by the DHHS guidelines or risk losing federal money.

The federal government guidelines resulted in the creation of institutional review boards (IRBs). These review boards are given various names, such as Human Research Committee, Human Subjects Committee, and Committee for the Protection of Human Subjects. Every agency or institution that receives federal money for research must have an IRB to review research proposals. The federal government, through the Office of Protection from Research Risk (OPRR), oversees IRBs.

Some institutions have nursing research committees specifically concerned with research conducted by nurses. Research policies and procedures vary from agency to agency. Therefore, nurse researchers should become informed about the requirements of specific institutions that will be used for data collection.

Permission for nurse researchers to conduct research may take some time. Weierbach, Glick, and Fletcher (2010) discussed this process in an article in *Journal of Nursing Administration*. Approval for their study was needed from both the community hospital IRB where they were going to conduct their study and the university committee IRB where they were employed. The approval process took 7 months.

Researchers must also be aware of the Health Insurance Portability and Accountability Act (HIPAA), which was implemented on April 14, 2003. Known as the HIPAA Privacy Rule, this act protects an individual's health information. It was designed to protect the unauthorized use and disclosure of a person's medical and health information. Authorization for use and disclosure must be obtained in writing from the person involved. This requirement pertains both to health care and to research conducted in a health care setting. Researchers may be required to obtain the person's signature on a separate document or integrate the information into the research informed consent document that potential research subjects must sign (Arford, 2004).

RESEARCH GUIDELINES FOR NURSES

In 1968 the American Nurses Association Research and Studies Commission published a set of guidelines for nursing research. These guidelines, revised in 1975 and 1985, are titled *Human Rights Guidelines for Nurses in Clinical and Other Research.* They address the rights of research subjects and nurses involved in research. Subjects must be protected from harm, their privacy should be ensured, and their dignity preserved. Nurses who are asked to participate in research should be fully informed about the research, and be included on the IRBs that review research proposals. The American Nurses Association published another set of guidelines in 1995. This document is titled *Ethical Guidelines in the Conduct, Dissemination, and Implementation of Nursing Research* (Silva, 1995). Although much of this document covers the same material as the earlier sets of guidelines, it emphasizes research integrity and the reporting of suspected, alleged, or known incidents of scientific misconduct in research.

MISCONDUCT IN RESEARCH

The Office of Research Integrity (ORI) is supported by the U.S. Public Health Services (PHS). This organization promotes integrity in biomedical and behavioral research at about 4,000 institutions worldwide. Although findings of scientific misconduct are not common, the ORI investigates approximately 200 cases a year of suspected misconduct by researchers who have received federal funding. Tracking began in 1989. The ORI received 201 allegations of research misconduct in 2008, (Office of Research Integrity Annual Report, 2008, available at http://ori.dhhs.gov/).

Since 1993, nursing research studies have been cited by the ORI several times. In 2008 final action was taken against a master's prepared, advanced practice nurse who falsified data that were reported to the National Surgical Adjuvant Breast & Bowel Project (NSABP) and Cancer and Leukemia Group B (CALGB) cooperative research groups. He was found to have falsified data on a patient's CT scan report and performance status records. He also falsified patients' hematology and chemistry reports (http://ori.hhs.gov/misconduct/cases/). In January 2010 a former nursing professor was issued a final notice of debarment based on falsified data on a research study that involved an intervention to reduce sexual risk behaviors in high risk, impaired populations of homeless men with mental illness (http://ori.hhs.gov/misconduct/cases/).

An issue facing nurse researchers is the sources of funding for their research. Private foundations and the federal government provide much of the money for nursing research projects. However, many nurse researchers are turning to industry as another source of funding. In this day of managed care, corporations may be interested in certain projects that may match their companies' interests and products, particularly in the area of health promotion, which is of prime importance to nursing. Erlen (2000) cautioned that "conflicts of interest" may occur when nurse researchers accept funds and enter into financial relationships with industry.

ELEMENTS OF INFORMED CONSENT

The principal means for ensuring that the rights of research subjects are protected is through informed consent. **Informed consent** concerns subjects' participation in research in which they have full understanding of the study before the study begins. The major elements of informed consent are:

1. Researcher is identified and credentials presented.
2. Subject selection process is described.
3. Purpose of study is described.
4. Study procedures are discussed.

5. Potential risks are described.

6. Potential benefits are described.

7. Compensation, if any, is discussed.

8. Alternative procedures, if any, are disclosed.

9. Anonymity or confidentiality is assured.

10. Right to refuse to participate or to withdraw from study without penalty is assured.

11. Offer to answer all questions is made.

12. Means of obtaining study results is presented.

Researcher Is Identified and Credentials Presented

The researcher must identify himself or herself and present qualifications to conduct the study. If a sponsor or sponsoring agency is involved, subjects should be given this information. Frequently, a sentence such as the following will be included in the study explanation: "I am a nursing student at _____ University and am conducting a research study as part of the requirements for _____."

Nurse researchers in clinical practice must take extra precautions to inform clients that they are acting in their capacity as researchers and not as nurses. Potential subjects may not be able to differentiate when the nurse is acting as a caregiver or as a researcher.

Subject Selection Process Is Described

Note that the use of the term research *subjects* is decreasing. In today's literature, you may see the terms *participants, respondents, and informants.* The term *subjects* is still used often in this text because it remains prominent in the literature. Also, "subjects' rights" is a very important issue. (The term *informants' rights* just does not seem to carry the same meaning. An informant sounds more like someone who is providing information to the police department!)

One of the primary goals of all researchers is to choose an unbiased sample. Chapter 11 discusses sampling procedures to enhance the selection of such a sample; the focus here is the ethical nature of selecting a sample.

The subjects should be told how they were chosen to participate in the study. If subjects were randomly selected, they should be provided with this information. If they must meet certain criteria to be eligible, these criteria should be presented early in the request for their participation.

As most of you know, research has been conducted most often with white men. This practice can no longer continue. In the past, women were not included in research. The rationale was that women's biological rhythms might "mess up the results."

Public Law 103-4, passed in 1993, requires that researchers recruit women and minorities for their studies. In 1994 NIH officials revised their gender and minority inclusion policy to meet the requirements of this law (the policy was revised again in 2001). Researchers applying to the NIH for funding are required to include plans for the recruitment of women, men, and ethnic or racial groups. Harden and McFarland (2000) wrote that adequate gender and minority representation is "crucial to ensure that the research has relevance to all segments of the diverse U.S. population" (p. 86).

The inclusion of women in nursing research was examined by Crane, Letvak, Lewallen, Hu, and Jones (2004). They examined research studies conducted between 1995 and 2001 that were published in five nursing journals: *Nursing Research, Research in Nursing & Health, Western Journal of Nursing Research, Applied Nursing Research,* and *Journal of Nursing Scholarship.* Of the 139 studies that met their criteria for inclusion in their research, 117 included women. Crane et al. conceded that the majority of the studies included women, but called for continuing efforts to include sufficient numbers of women in research studies.

Polit and Beck (2009) studied gender bias in nursing research. Approximately 71% of participants were females in 834 studies published in eight English language nursing research journals in

2005–2006. This bias was strong in the United States and Canada, but many female participants were found also in studies from European countries, Asian countries, and in Australia.

Jacobson, Chu, Pascucci, and Gaskins (2004) analyzed studies published in four major nursing research journals from 1992 to 2000. They examined these studies to determine race, ethnicity, and culture of subjects in nursing research studies. Results showed that nurse researchers are being responsive to the need for more research on various racial, ethnic, and cultural groups. The most striking finding concerned the number of nonwhites in the samples.

The National Institute of Nursing Research (NINR) has committed a large amount of its funding for minority health issues. In the NINR Strategic Plan for 2006–2010 (http://ninr.nih.gov. AboutNINR), one of the areas of research emphasis is "Eliminating Health Disparities." According to the Strategic Plan, this emphasis "dovetails with a period of growing national and international recognition of the impact of race, gender, socioeconomic status, ethnic origin, geography, and culture on the health of individuals and groups." The proposed 2011 budget for the NINR (http://ninr.nih. gov.AboutNINR) mentions recent efforts that explore novel approaches to improving self-management of diabetes in minority and underserved populations. Also mentioned is a project to study biobehavioral mechanisms underlying preterm birth in minority women and a plan to develop an intervention to promote physical activity in Latinas.

Purpose of Study Is Described

The purpose or objectives of the study should be clearly presented. The material should be in the potential subject's preferred language and all printed material at the subject's reading level.

The researcher should be honest and open in presenting the purpose of the study. It is not always necessary, however, to describe the entire nature of the study. For example, if a study were being conducted to determine the difference between patients' satisfaction with nursing care given under a primary nursing or team nursing approach, subjects might be told that the study was examining patients' satisfaction with the type of nursing care that they were receiving. It would not be necessary to describe primary nursing and team nursing to the potential subjects. Ask yourself what information you would want to receive, or would want a close relative to receive, to make an informed decision about participation in a study.

Study Procedures Are Discussed

All aspects of the study should be fully explained. This includes telling the potential subjects when the study will take place and where. The researcher must emphasize the subjects' time involvement and all activities that the subjects must perform. This aspect of informed consent is particularly important in experimental studies in which people will receive some type of treatment. Sometimes a so-called cover story is presented to subjects rather than the true explanation of the study. Deliberate deception of this sort is unethical. Even if subjects are later told of the deception, the use of false information is unethical.

One frequently cited study by Milgram (1963) examined obedience to authority. The study was done in a laboratory setting and described to potential subjects as a learning experiment. Subjects were told to administer electrical shocks when the so-called learners gave incorrect responses, but the learners were actually actors. These actors, who were out of sight, groaned and screamed during the experiment. Twenty-six of the subjects, or 65% of the group, continued to administer shocks throughout the experiment, even when they thought they were administering lethal shocks. Responses of discomfort among the subjects who were administering the supposed electrical shocks included sweating, trembling, and stuttering. One subject had a convulsive seizure. This study demonstrates severe deception by the researcher.

If it is necessary to withhold information about a study from potential subjects, they must be informed of this before the study, and a debriefing session held afterward. **Debriefing** involves a meeting with research participants that ensures their understanding of the reasons and justification for the procedures that were used in the study. It is the researcher's responsibility to ensure that no more than minimal risks are involved in the study.

In a study where it is not desirable to inform subjects fully before it begins, subjects have the right to be fully informed at the conclusion of the study and be given an opportunity to withdraw consent for their data to be included in the study results. Many researchers prefer not to conduct studies in which the researcher is not completely candid with subjects before the beginning of the study.

Potential Risks Are Described

Subjects must be told of any possible discomforts, either physical or psychological, that might occur as a result of participation. Any invasion of privacy must also be discussed. It is difficult at times for the researcher to identify all of the potential risk factors because of the variations in human responses to different situations. The investigator is obligated to try to identify all possible risks that would surely influence the subjects' decision to participate. Many questions arise about what constitutes a risk. If a study is being conducted in which healthy volunteers will be involved in mild exercise, should these subjects be informed explicitly that they could experience a "heart attack" or a "stroke" during the exercise? The researcher might scare off all prospective subjects! Consultation with experts in the research area should be held and then discretion exercised in presenting risks to potential subjects. One of the roles of IRBs is to assess the adequacy of consent forms.

Potential Benefits Are Described

The Nuremberg Code set the requirement that research must be for the good of society. All research, even basic research that is conducted primarily to obtain new knowledge, must have the potential to benefit society.

In describing benefits to potential subjects, the investigator should describe both those applicable to the people involved in the study as well as how the results could benefit others. In a study (Simpson, 1985) involving the use of play therapy before physical examinations of preschool children, the mothers of the potential subjects were told that the potential benefits included possible reductions in anxiety of the children during the physical examinations; better cooperation during the procedures, and, therefore, more accurate results from the examinations. Mothers also were told that these results would help nurses in the future to better prepare preschool children for physical examinations. Appendix A includes a copy of the consent form for this study.

Compensation, If Any, Is Discussed

Monetary compensation or any other type of compensation should be described to potential subjects. Any time compensation is being provided in a study, the possibility exists that biased results may be obtained. Subjects may try to "perform" in a manner that they believe will fulfill the researcher's expectations. Nevertheless, researchers frequently use small monetary incentives as enticements for potential subjects. One good example of this is seen in the various types of market research that are conducted around the country. To control for biased responses, participants are usually not told which of the comparison products is the focus of the study. In nursing research, the researcher should avoid monetary compensation, if possible. Subject "compensation" should come from those items listed under "potential benefits." The researcher, however, should cover the cost of such items as laboratory tests and travel expenses for the subjects.

Occasionally, the nurse researcher has the obligation to offer services in the event that potential risks materialize into actual risks. In one study, a researcher presented an anxiety management seminar to nurses to help them control anxiety in their work settings. One of the risks involved a potential rise in anxiety levels, rather than the intended decrease in anxiety, as a result of attending the anxiety seminar. The researcher informed subjects that she was experienced in psychotherapy and would be available if their anxiety levels rose during the study.

Alternative Procedures, If Any, Are Disclosed

Potential subjects should be informed of any alternative procedures that may be followed, such as "You may fill out the questionnaire here or take it home." More importantly, they must be given an explanation of alternative procedures or treatments that may be received by others. For example, a control group of subjects in an experimental study must be made aware that other subjects will be receiving some type of treatment. If potential subjects have a choice of groups, this option must be presented to them. The Hawthorne effect (see Chapter 9) can bring about changes in subjects because they are aware that they are participants in a study. For this reason, it is becoming increasingly common to provide some type of alternative activity for the control group to make them feel they are actually study participants. Frequently, as part of the explanation given before the study, the researcher tells the control group that the experimental treatment will be available to them on completion of the study. If the control group is really a comparison group, in that these subjects are receiving some alternative or routine treatment, the subjects in the experimental group could also be offered this alternative or routine treatment at the conclusion of the study.

Anonymity or Confidentiality Is Assured

Anonymity occurs when no one, including the researcher, can link subjects with the data they provide. If subjects can be linked to data, the researcher has the obligation to address confidentiality. **Confidentiality** involves protection of the subjects' identities by the researcher. In many studies, it is not possible to maintain anonymity. The researcher will usually come face to face with subjects in an experimental study. To maintain confidentiality, data are coded and subjects' names and code numbers are kept in a separate location that is accessible only to the researcher or members of the research team. Any list that links subject names with data should be destroyed at the conclusion of the study.

To assure anonymity or confidentiality, subjects and the site where the study was conducted should be described in general terms in the description of the sample and the setting. If either the subjects or the study location can be identified by this general description, confidentiality has been violated. For example, the setting might be identified as a 1,000-bed psychiatric institution in a small southwestern city. If there is only one such institution in that area, you have identified the institution as surely as if you had included the name. Identity of hospitals, schools, and other institutions should be kept confidential, unless these agencies have given permission to be identified in the study.

Confidentiality can be assured by the deletion of any identifying information that would allow subject identification. Subjects should always be assured that they are free to omit information from their responses if they believe the data will identify them in any way. If subjects are being assured of anonymity, which is frequently done in survey research, instructions should clearly inform subjects to refrain from including their names or other identifying information on the questionnaires.

Right to Refuse to Participate or to Withdraw from Study Without Penalty Is Assured

All participation in nursing research *must* be voluntary. Even if a random sampling procedure is used to obtain participants, these people must be given the opportunity to decide if they wish to participate. No form of coercion should be involved. There must be no penalty involved for nonparticipation. For example, patient care should not be affected by patients' participation or nonparticipation in a study. Students' grades in a course should not be influenced by research participation.

Beginning researchers frequently have difficulty separating the role of researcher from practitioner. A nurse might decide to conduct a study in which his or her "own" patients will be the subjects or the patients' charts will be used for data collection. In such an instance, the researcher must approach the research setting as if he or she were a complete stranger. If research is being conducted, permission must be obtained to use patients' records, even if the nurse has full access to these records in clinical practice.

Potential research subjects must be informed that they may withdraw from a study at any time and for any reason. This is particularly important in experimental studies in which a treatment is involved. As you may remember, the Nuremberg Code stated that a subject might withdraw from a study if any problem occurred. Today, subjects may withdraw for *any* reason.

Offer to Answer All Questions Is Made

Potential subjects must always be given the opportunity to ask any questions they may have about the study. It is almost impossible for the researcher to include every aspect of the study in a verbal or written explanation. Subjects frequently have questions about the study, and an opportunity should be presented for these questions during the verbal explanation of the study. The researcher is obligated to be available (by phone, postal mail, or e-mail) if questions arise at a later time or if subjects have questions when reading the written explanation of a study.

Means of Obtaining Study Results Is Presented

Many potential research subjects are concerned with the use of study findings. Will their employers get a copy of the results? Will the study results be published? How can they find out the results? Although the researcher probably does not know for sure if the study results will ever be published, the researcher's publication plans (and desires) must be indicated. Research subjects should always be given the opportunity to obtain the study results. This does not mean that a copy must be sent to all participants. In fact, many participants are not interested in the results. It is, therefore, appropriate for the researcher to place some of the responsibility for obtaining results on the study subjects. A comment such as the following may be included in the consent information: "A copy of the study results may be obtained by writing or calling the researcher." Of course, this would necessitate the inclusion of a phone number or a mailing address or e-mail address where the researcher could be reached at the conclusion of the study. The approximate date when results will be available should also be provided.

DOCUMENTATION OF INFORMED CONSENT

The researcher must document that informed consent was obtained. If self-report questionnaires are used, a statement should be included on the questionnaire, in capital letters, similar to the following: RETURN OF THIS QUESTIONNAIRE WILL INDICATE YOUR CONSENT TO PARTICIPATE IN THIS STUDY. In other types of studies, consent is obtained in written form, stating that the subject has willingly given permission and is aware of the risks and benefits. Oral permission may be obtained but must be witnessed by a third person. If the subject is a minor or is not able to give informed consent because of mental or physical disability, the consent of a legally authorized representative, such as a child's parent, must be obtained. As previously mentioned, Appendix A includes an example of a consent form.

All information on a consent form must be understandable to the subject or the subject's representative. This means that the oral or written explanation must be in the subject's native language or preferred language and be at the subject's reading level. Nurses are aware that many forms signed by patients have not represented informed consent, and they must assure that this practice is rectified.

THE NURSE RESEARCHER AS A PATIENT ADVOCATE

The nurse researcher has the responsibility to protect the privacy and the dignity of the people involved in the research and to protect them from harm. Even if study subjects willingly and knowingly were to agree to participate in a study involving undue physical risks or psychological risks, the researcher has an obligation to refrain from conducting such research. The nurse researcher must assume responsibility for study conditions and avoid undue physical or psychological risks to the subjects.

Nurses should be able to answer patients' questions about research studies, particularly clinical trials (Habel, 2005). **Clinical trials** are research studies conducted to evaluate new treatments, new drugs, and new or improved medical equipment. Thousands of people participate in clinical trials each year in the United States. These studies are sponsored and funded by a number of organizations, such as medical institutions. Their purpose is to answer questions about how to cure or control disease. Nurses should familiarize themselves with any clinical trials that are being conducted in their work setting. Then they should be willing to answer any questions that patients may have before, during, or after these studies.

Certain special groups of people are considered particularly vulnerable research subjects because they are either unable to give informed consent or because the likelihood of coercion to participate is strong. These groups include children, geriatric clients, prisoners, people with AIDS, the homeless, and unconscious or sedated patients. Special precautions must be taken to ensure that the study has a low risk potential for these vulnerable people. When children are younger than 7 years, parental consent is sufficient. If a child is older than 7 years, not only must the parent consent to the child's participation, but the child must also agree to be in the study by giving assent to participate. **Assent** means that an underage child or adolescent freely chooses to participate in a study.

CRITIQUING THE ETHICAL ASPECTS OF A STUDY

It may be difficult to critique the ethical aspects of a research report. Little space is usually given to this part of the study in published reports. Most journal articles contain one or two sentences that mention subjects' rights were protected and informed consent was obtained. It is understandable that little is printed about the ethical issues of the study. Much of this information would be repeated in each study report that is published. However, the reader of a research report may be able to determine the ethical nature of the study. For example, if the report states that permission to conduct the study was obtained from an IRB, the subjects' rights were likely protected. Also, if the study has been funded, there is some assurance that the researcher had to provide evidence of protection of subjects' rights before funds were awarded. Box 2–1 lists guidelines for critiquing the ethical aspects of a study.

Box 2–1 Guidelines for Critiquing the Ethical Aspects of a Study

1. Was the study approved by an Institutional Review Board (IRB)?
2. Was informed consent obtained from the subjects?
3. Is there information about provisions for anonymity or confidentiality?
4. Were vulnerable subjects used?
5. Does it appear that subjects might have been coerced into acting as subjects?
6. Is it evident that the benefits of participation in the study outweighed the risks involved?
7. Were subjects provided the opportunity to ask questions about the study and told how to contact the researcher if other questions arose?
8. Were the subjects told how they could obtain the results of the study?

SUMMARY

Many unethical studies were conducted during World War II, particularly in the prison camps in Germany. Unethical research studies have also been revealed here in the United States.

Because of the public outcry against the atrocities committed in Germany in the 1940s, the Nuremberg Code was developed in 1947. This code calls for voluntary subjects and qualified researchers. Other ethical codes have been formulated since World War II. Many professional groups have developed codes for their members.

The federal government developed research guidelines in the early 1970s, and these guidelines have been revised several times. The original guidelines called for the creation of institutional review boards (IRBs) to be established in all agencies that receive federal money for research. IRBs review research proposals and set standards for research conducted in their agencies.

In 1968 the American Nurses Association developed a set of guidelines for nursing research. These guidelines, *Human Rights Guidelines for Nurses in Clinical and Other Research,* were revised in 1975 and 1985. The American Nurses Association published another set of guidelines in 1995, *Ethical Guidelines in the Conduct, Dissemination, and Implementation of Nursing Research.*

The principal means for ensuring the rights of research subjects is through informed consent. **Informed consent** means that subjects agree to participate in studies about which they have complete understanding before the study begins. The major elements of informed consent concern the researcher's qualifications, subject selection process, purpose of the study, study procedures, potential risks and benefits to subjects, compensation, alternative procedures, anonymity and confidentiality, right to refuse to participate, offer to answer questions, and means of obtaining study results. **Debriefing** involves a meeting with research participants after the study is completed. The purpose is to ensure subjects' understanding of the reasons and the justification for the procedures used in the study.

Anonymity means that no one can identify the subjects in a study. **Confidentiality** means that the researcher will protect the subjects' identities.

The nurse researcher must act as a patient advocate, particularly in **clinical trials.** This advocacy involves protecting patients' privacy and dignity and ensuring that there are no undue physical or psychological risks to subjects. Particular attention should be given to the rights of certain vulnerable groups, such as children, geriatric clients, prisoners, and unconscious or sedated patients. If a child is older than 7 years, the child must give **assent** to participate in a study.

NURSING RESEARCH ON THE WEB

For additional online resources, research activities, and exercises, go to **www.mynursingkit. com.** Select Chapter 2 from the drop-down menu.

GET INVOLVED ACTIVITIES

1. Prior to your next class, peruse the newspapers or periodicals to see if there is any report of an unethical study.
2. Ask your colleagues at work or your family or friends to tell you about some unethical research that they have seen or heard about.
3. Imagine that you are trying to obtain a 10-year-old child's assent to participate in a study. Outline a procedure that would ensure the child was making his or her own decision to participate.
4. Read the following explanation of a study and try to determine if all of the elements of informed consent are present. Use the 12 elements of informed consent presented in this chapter as your criteria.

Students,

You are being invited to participate in a research project concerning assertiveness levels and locus of control. Participation in this project is strictly voluntary, and your grade in this class will not be influenced by your failure to participate in this study. You may choose to write a short research paper to earn the equivalent class credit.

Your participation in this study will require approximately 30 minutes of class time and will involve completion of two questionnaires. There are no risks involved in this study other than the uncomfortable feelings that may arise when reading the questions. There are several potential benefits of participating in this study. You may learn more about yourself and also learn about the research process. Additionally, the knowledge gained from this study will help nurse educators to predict assertiveness levels and locus of control levels of nursing students in the future.

Answers will remain anonymous. Please do not put your name or any identifying information on the questionnaires. If you have any questions, please feel free to ask them. Results will be available on completion of the study.

SELF-TEST

Circle the letter before the *best* answer.

1. A questionnaire is being used to gather data on the study sample. Identification numbers on the corner of the questionnaires correspond to the researcher's master list of names and numbers. Respondents are assured that this information will not be shared with anyone. The researcher is trying to ensure
   A. informed consent.
   B. anonymity.
   C. data security.
   D. confidentiality.

2. Study participants are asked to complete a questionnaire before and after a relaxation session. One potential participant asks how confidentiality will be assured. The researcher states:
   A. Participants will place *only* their first names on the questionnaires.
   B. An identification number will be placed on the questionnaire that corresponds to the researcher's master list of names and numbers.
   C. It is very difficult to assure confidentiality in research involving questionnaires, but an effort will be made to assure confidentiality.
   D. Participants will be asked to place their names on the questionnaire, but only the researcher will have access to the questionnaires.

3. If an individual volunteers to participate in a study, he or she is *always* guaranteed that which of the following will be done?
   A. Anonymity will be provided.
   B. Confidentiality will be provided.
   C. Informed consent will be obtained.
   D. Protection from psychological stress will be assured.

4. An institutional review board is required in which type of agency or institution?
   A. all agencies and institutions
   B. all agencies and institutions that receive federal money for research
   C. federal agencies
   D. health care agencies and institutions

5. Which of the following is "least" likely to be provided for subjects?
   A. informed consent
   B. anonymity
   C. confidentiality
   D. privacy

6. What is the name of the process used to obtain a child's agreement for participation in a study?
   A. assent
   B. consent of a minor
   C. minor agreement
   D. informed consent

7. A friend of yours has agreed to participate in a research study. However, she is upset that she has to contact the researcher to obtain a copy of the study results. She thinks she should automatically be sent a copy. You tell her:
   A. The researcher *should* automatically send a copy of the study results to all participants.
   B. Researchers are required, by federal guidelines, to send a copy of the study results to all participants.
   C. Study participants should be provided with information that will allow them to contact the researcher if a copy of the study results is desired.
   D. A copy of the study abstract should be mailed to all participants within 6 weeks of completion of the study.

Write T (True) or F (False) beside the following statements:

_____ 8. Once a subject signs an informed consent form, he or she is agreeing to remain in the study until it is completed.

_____ 9. All study subjects *must* be guaranteed anonymity.

_____ 10. Access to the results of a study in which they have participated is the right of all participants.

_____ 11. In a study in which confidentiality is guaranteed, anonymity is usually guaranteed also.

_____ 12. Debriefing means that the researchers meet and discuss problems that occurred in a study.

REFERENCES

Arford, P. H. (2004). Working with human research protections. *Journal of Nursing Scholarship, 35*, 265–271.

Bonifazi, W. L. (2004, November 1). Cruelty and courage: Nurses in the Nazi era. *Nurseweek*, pp. 24– 26.

Centers for Disease Control and Prevention. (2010). The Tuskegee timeline. Retrieved on April 10, 2010 from http://cdc.gov/nchstp/od/tuskegee/time.htm

Crane, P. B., Letvak, S., Lewallen, L., Hu, J., & Jones, E. (2004). Inclusion of women in nursing research. *Nursing Research, 53*, 237–232.

Erlen, J. A. (2000). "Conflict of interest": An ethical dilemma for the nurse researcher. *Orthopaedic Nursing, 19*, 74–77.

Habel, M. (2005, March 14). Can you answer patients' questions about clinical trials? *Nurseweek*, pp. 23–25.

Harden, J. T., & McFarland, G. (2000). Avoiding gender and minority barriers to NIH funding. *Journal of Nursing Scholarship, 32*, 83–86.

Hayter, J. (1979). Issues related to human subjects. In F. Downs & J. Fleming (Eds.), *Issues in nursing research* (pp. 107–147). New York: Appleton-Century-Crofts.

Indian troops were part of WWII gas tests. UPI.com (2007, Sept. 1). Retrieved on April 7, 2010 from http://upi.com/Top_News/2007/09/01Indian-troops-were-part-of-WWII-gas-tests/UPI-81141188677473

Jacobson, S. F., Chu, N. L., Pascucci, M. A., & Gaskins, S. W. (2004). Characteristics of nursing research on race, ethnicity, and culture. *Journal of Multicultural Nursing & Health, 10*(3), 6–12.

Japanese book details scientific atrocities. (1996, February 5). *Dallas Morning News*, p. 24A.

Katz, K. (1972). *Experimentation with human beings*. New York: Russell Sage.

Krugman, S., Giles, J., & Hammond, J. (1971). Viral hepatitis, type B (MS-2 strain): Studies on active immunization. *Journal of the American Medical Association, 217*, 41-45.

Measles mistake. (1996, June 20). *USA Today*, p. 1D.

Milgram, S. (1963). Behavioral study of obedience. *Journal of Abnormal and Social Psychology, 67*, 371–378.

Nuremberg Military Tribunals. (1949). *Trials of war criminals before the Nuremberg Military Tribunals under Control Council Law No. 10* (Publication No. 1949–841584, Vol. 2). Washington, DC: U.S. Government Printing Office.

O'Malley, P. (2009). A case of scientific misconduct. *Clinical Nurse Specialist, 23*, 265–267.

Parents say government quiet on vaccine testing. (1996, December 22). *Dallas Morning News*, p. 6A.

Polit, D. F., & Beck, C. T. (2009). International gender bias in nursing research, 2005–2006: A quantitative content analysis. *International Journal of Nursing Studies, 46*, 1102–1110.

Shearer, L. (1982, October 17). Now it can be told. *Dallas Morning News*, pp. 10–11.

Silva, M. C. (1995). *Ethical guidelines in the conduct, dissemination, and implementation of nursing research*. Washington, DC: American Nurses Association.

Simpson, M. (1985). *Therapeutic play and cooperation of preschoolers during physical examinations*. Unpublished master's thesis, Texas Woman's University, Denton.

Solomon, J. (2005, May 5). AIDS researchers used foster children who lacked advocates. *Dallas Morning News*, p. 12A.

Weierbach, F. M., Glick, D. F., & Fletcher, K. (2010). Nursing research and participant recruitment. *Journal of Nursing Administration, 40*, 43–48.

CHAPTER 3

An Overview of Quantitative Research

OUTLINE

Steps in Quantitative Research
- Identify the Research Problem
- Determine the Purpose of the Study
- Formulate the Research Question
- Review the Literature
- Develop a Theoretical/Conceptual Framework
- Identify the Study Assumptions
- Acknowledge the Limitations of the Study
- Formulate the Hypothesis
- Define the Study Variables/Terms
- Select the Research Design
- Identify the Population

- Select the Sample
- Conduct a Pilot Study
- Collect the Data
- Organize the Data for Analysis
- Analyze the Data
- Interpret the Findings
- Communicate the Findings
- Utilize the Findings

Summary
Nursing Research on the Web
Get Involved Activities
Self-Test

OBJECTIVES

On completion of this chapter, you will be prepared to:
1. List the steps in conducting quantitative research
2. Discuss the steps in quantitative research

NEW TERMS DEFINED IN THIS CHAPTER

W hat is nursing research? What is it all about? How do you do it? This chapter helps answer some of your questions about quantitative nursing research. At this point, try to get a general, overall picture of this type of research. Although quantitative research is not completely unbiased, it "provides a level of objectivity that increases our confidence in the conclusions we draw with regard to scientific facts and existing scientific principles" (Giuliano & Polanowicz, 2008, p. 222).

Most quantitative studies follow almost the same steps. As you progress through this book, you will find that these steps will become clearer. Each of the steps in conducting a quantitative study is elaborated on in other chapters in this book. Chapter 4 presents an overview of qualitative research.

STEPS IN QUANTITATIVE RESEARCH

Nearly every author refers to the identification of the problem as the first step, and the communication of research findings or the utilization of research findings as the final step, in scientific quantitative research. There is some variation in the other steps. Some authors combine several steps into one step, which accounts for the smaller numbers of steps identified by some sources. Macnee and McCabe (2008) list 5 steps in the research process. Stommel and Wills (2004) identify 9 steps. Houser (2008) also presents 9 steps. Burns and Grove (2009) list 17 steps. Polit and Beck (2008) enumerate 18 steps. The current edition of this textbook discusses 19 steps. The last step, "Utilize the findings," was added in the last edition of the book.

There can be some overlapping of the steps in the research process and some shifting back and forth between the steps. In general, however, the scientific research process proceeds in an orderly fashion and consists of the steps identified in Table 3–1.

Identify the Research Problem

The first step, and one of the most important steps, in the research process is to clearly identify the problem that will be studied. In a nursing study, the **research problem** is an area where knowledge is needed to advance the practice of nursing. Generally, a broad topic area is identified, and then the topic is narrowed down to a specific problem to be studied. This step of the research process may be the most difficult of all and may take a great deal of time.

TABLE 3–1 Steps in the Research Process

Identify the research problem
Determine the purpose of the study
Formulate the research question
Review the literature
Develop a theoretical/conceptual framework
Identify the study assumptions
Acknowledge the limitations of the study
Formulate the hypothesis
Define the study variables/terms
Select the research design
Identify the population
Select the sample
Conduct a pilot study
Collect the data
Organize the data for analysis
Analyze the data
Interpret the findings
Communicate the findings
Utilize the findings

Study problems can be identified from suggestions published in the literature, from recommendations made following previous studies, through the testing of theories, or from personal experiences. The problem should be of interest to the researcher and be significant to nursing. Chapter 5 further discusses the identification of nursing research problems.

An example of a problem area is "the anxiety levels of women before hysterectomy surgery." The researcher has observed this anxiety in her area of practice, and recognizes that a number of measures might be used to reduce anxiety. She wonders whether a back rub might be helpful. So, the specific problem to be studied concerns anxiety levels of women about to undergo a hysterectomy and ways to reduce this anxiety. In an introductory section, such as "Background" or "Literature Review," there would probably be a broad discussion of the problem area, including the number of women who undergo hysterectomies each year, and then a narrowing down to the specific area of study.

There is some confusion in the literature about the terms "goals," "objectives," "problem area," "problem statement," "purpose," and "research question." The phrase "problem statement" indicates *one* sentence. However, typically there are several sentences at the beginning of a research report that describe the problem of the study.

Kerlinger (1986) stated that a research problem is an interrogative sentence or statement that asks: "What relation exists between two or more variables?" (p. 16). Grammatically, a statement and an interrogatory sentence are not compatible, which has always presented a problem for this author! However, questions do demand answers more than declarative statements. In their research textbook, Polit and Beck (2008) discuss the use of research questions and assert, "Questions invite an answer and help to focus attention on the kinds of data that would have to be collected to provide that answer" (p. 89). They stated that some research reports contain research questions and omit a problem statement or a statement of the study purpose. Each of the Cochrane Reviews (see Chapter 1) addresses a clearly stated question, such as "Can antibiotics help in alleviating the symptoms of a sore throat?" (http://cochrane.org/cochrane-reviews). Therefore, in this text, all examples of research problems are written in the interrogative form, as research questions.

Determine the Purpose of the Study

Although the term *purpose* is often used interchangeably with *problem,* a distinction can be made between these two terms. The research problem addresses *what* will be studied; the purpose provides *why* the study is being done. In most published nursing research studies, the purpose of the study is presented rather than a problem statement or a research question. All articles in *Nursing Research* contain a purpose statement. The following is an example of a purpose statement for the study concerning anxiety levels of women about to undergo a hysterectomy: "This study will try to determine whether a back rub is an effective means of reducing anxiety levels of women who are about to undergo a hysterectomy."

Formulate the Research Question

A **research question** is the specific question that the researcher expects to be answered in a study. The research question should specify the variables and the population that are being studied. A **variable** is a characteristic or attribute that differs among the persons, objects, events, and so forth being studied (e.g., age, blood type). The population is the group that will be studied. An example of a research question follows: "Is there a difference in anxiety levels of women about to undergo a hysterectomy between those women who receive a back rub and those who do not receive a back rub?"

Review the Literature

Research should build on previous knowledge. Before beginning a quantitative study, it is important to determine what knowledge exists of the study topic. There are few topics about which there is no existing knowledge base. There are many routes of access to the published literature. Literature sources can be located through indexes, abstracts, and computer-assisted searches. Chapter 6 presents material on reviewing the literature.

Besides determining the extent of the existing knowledge related to the study topic, the review of the literature also helps develop a theoretical or conceptual framework for a study. Finally, the review of the literature can help the researcher plan study methods. For example, instruments or tools may be discovered that can be used to measure the study variables. By reviewing the literature, a researcher will be able to profit from the successes and failures of other researchers.

The review should be continued during the course of the investigation until the time of data collection. This ensures the researcher that she or he has as much information as possible and the most up-to-date information on the study topic.

Occasionally, the initial review of the literature may actually precede the identification of the problem. The problem area may be determined from the suggestions or recommendations of researchers who have conducted previous studies in the area of interest.

Develop a Theoretical/Conceptual Framework

The goal of research is to develop scientific knowledge. Research and theory are intertwined. Research can test theories as well as help develop and refine theories. Thus, theoretical frameworks are a valuable part of scientific research (see Chapter 7). The theoretical or conceptual framework assists in the selection of the study variables and in defining them. The framework also directs the hypothesis(es) and the interpretation of the findings. In a classic editorial in *Nursing Research*, Florence Downs (1994) stated that a "study that lacks a theoretical rationale lacks substance and fails to answer the 'so what' question" (p. 195).

Some research of a purely descriptive nature may not require a theoretical framework. Most nursing studies can profit, however, from the identification of a framework for the study. An examination of recently published nursing studies reveals that increasing numbers of these studies are based on a clearly identified theoretical framework. Research conducted within the context of a theoretical framework, compared to research that is not theory based, is more valuable in providing understanding and knowledge that can be used in the future. Research without theory provides a set of isolated facts.

Nursing is viewed as an applied science and has oftentimes relied on the theories of other disciplines. However, nurse researchers have developed theories and are building a body of nursing knowledge (see Chapter 7). Because the process is evolving, nurses continue to use many theories from other disciplines.

Identify the Study Assumptions

Assumptions are beliefs that are held to be true but have not necessarily been proven. Each scientific investigation is based on assumptions. These assumptions should be stated explicitly. Frequently, however, the assumptions are implicit. This means that the study was based on certain assumptions, but the researcher did not openly acknowledge or list these assumptions.

Assumptions are of three types: universal assumptions, assumptions based on theory or research findings, and common sense assumptions that are necessary to carry out the study. Universal assumptions are beliefs that are assumed to be true by a large percentage of society, such as, "All human beings need love." Assumptions also can be derived from theory or previous research. If a study is based on a certain theory, the assumptions of that theory become the assumptions of the study based on that particular theory. In addition, the results of previous studies can form the basis for assumptions in the present research investigation. Finally, certain common sense assumptions must be made to carry out a study. For example, if an investigator were conducting a study to examine behaviors of fathers toward their children, it would be necessary to assume that the men in the study were actually the fathers of the children in the study.

Consider an example in which nurses are trying to determine the most appropriate means to teach patients to operate an insulin pump. A universal assumption might be that uncontrolled diabetes is a threat to the physical well-being of individuals. An assumption based on research might be that the insulin pump is an effective means of delivering medication to diabetics. Finally, a commonsense assumption might be made that the subjects are interested in controlling their diabetes and that they have the mental capacity to understand the material being taught.

Acknowledge the Limitations of the Study

The researcher should try to identify study limitations or weaknesses. **Limitations** are uncontrolled variables that may affect study results and limit the generalizability of the findings. In nearly every research study, including nursing studies, there are variables over which the researcher either has no control or chooses not to exercise control. These variables are called *extraneous variables*. For example, the educational level of subjects would be a study limitation if the researcher could not control this variable and thought that it might influence the study results. In experimental studies, uncontrolled variables are referred to as threats to internal and external validity (see Chapter 9).

The researcher should openly acknowledge the limitations of a study, as much as possible, before data are collected. Other limitations may occur while the study is in progress (such as malfunctions of equipment and subject dropout). The limitations must be taken into consideration when the conclusions of a study are formulated and when recommendations are made for future research.

Formulate the Hypothesis

A researcher's expectation about the results of a study is expressed in a hypothesis. A **hypothesis** predicts the relationship between two or more variables. The hypothesis furnishes the predicted answer to the research question. The hypothesis contains the population and variables, just as does the research question. In addition, the hypothesis proposes the relationship between the independent and the dependent variables. In experimental studies, the **independent variable** is the "cause" or the variable thought to influence the dependent variable. The **dependent variable** is the "effect" or the variable influenced by the researcher's manipulation (control) of the independent variable. A hypothesis must be testable or verifiable empirically, which means that it must be capable of being tested in the real world by observations gathered through the senses.

Consider the research question: Is there a correlation between body image and self-esteem levels of women who have experienced a mastectomy? After the review of the literature on the topic, a theory might be located that predicts a positive relationship between body image and self-esteem levels. The following hypothesis might then be formulated: The more positive the body image of women who have experienced a mastectomy, the higher is their self-esteem level. This type of hypothesis is referred to as a *directional research hypothesis*. It contains the direction of the researcher's expectations for the study results.

Although the null hypothesis (which predicts that no relationship exists between variables) is tested statistically, the directional research hypothesis is the preferred type for nursing studies. This type of hypothesis is derived from the theoretical/conceptual framework for the study and should, therefore, indicate the expected relationship between variables.

Experimental, comparative, and correlational studies call for hypotheses. In qualitative studies and some descriptive studies, a hypothesis is not needed. In those studies that do not require hypotheses, the research is guided by the research question(s). The following are examples of research questions that would not call for hypotheses: "What are the adjustment behaviors of family members when the husband/father has experienced a myocardial infarction?" "Do family members become closer or more distant in their interpersonal relationships with each other?" "What is the greatest adjustment difficulty reported by family members?" "Do different families report similar or dissimilar adjustment problems?"

Define the Study Variables/Terms

The variables and terms contained in the study hypothesis or research question need to be defined so their meaning is clear to the researcher and to the reader of a research report. Terms should be defined both conceptually and operationally. A **conceptual definition** is a dictionary definition or theoretical definition of an abstract idea that is being studied by the researcher. An **operational definition** indicates how a variable will be observed or measured. Operational definitions frequently include the instrument that will be used to measure the variables. If anxiety were being measured, the theoretical definition might be taken from a certain theorist's description of anxiety. The operational definition would then be indicated by the identification of the tool or behavior that would be used to measure anxiety.

The operational definition allows replication of a study. If a researcher would like to replicate a study, using another group of subjects or another setting, it would be necessary to know exactly how the variables were measured in the previous study.

Besides defining the variables in a hypothesis or research question, the population for the study should be defined or narrowed down to the specific group that will be studied. If the population were identified as myocardial infarction patients, this group could be further defined as men between the ages of 35 and 55 years who have experienced a first myocardial infarction and are patients in a large teaching hospital in the northeastern United States.

Select the Research Design

The **research design** is the plan for how the study will be conducted. It is concerned with the type of data that will be collected and the means used to obtain these data. For example, the researcher must decide if the study will examine cause-and-effect relationships or only describe existing situations. The researcher chooses the design that is most appropriate to test the study hypothesis(es) or answer the research question(s).

Research designs can be categorized as quantitative or qualitative. They also can be categorized as experimental or nonexperimental. Experimental designs can be further divided into true experimental, quasi-experimental, and pre-experimental designs. Nonexperimental designs include survey studies, correlational studies, comparative studies, and methodological studies. Research designs are discussed in Chapters 9 and 10.

In experimental research, the investigator plays an active role and has more control over the research situation than in a nonexperimental study. More control can be exercised over the extraneous variables that might influence research results. In experimental nursing studies, a nursing intervention is usually introduced. The nurse researcher manipulates this variable by deciding who will and will not receive an intervention. Frequently, one group receives the usual intervention, while another group receives some new intervention that is hoped to be more effective. In nonexperimental research, the investigator collects data without actively manipulating any variable. It is appropriate to discuss cause-and-effect relationships only when experimental designs are used. It is sometimes difficult because of ethical reasons, however, to conduct experimental research with human beings. For this reason, many nursing research investigations have been of the nonexperimental type.

Identify the Population

The **population** is a complete set of individuals or objects that possess some common characteristic of interest to the researcher. The researcher must specify the broad population or group of interest as well as the actual population that is available for the study. The first type of population is identified as the target population, and the second type is called the accessible population (see Chapter 11). The **target population,** also called the *universe,* is made up of the group of people or objects to which the researcher wishes to generalize the findings of a study. The **accessible population** is the group that is actually available for study by the researcher. The term *population* does not always mean that human beings will be studied. A nurse researcher might study a population of charts or a population of blood pressure readings, for example.

By identifying the population, the researcher makes clear the group to which the study results can be applied. Scientific research is concerned with generalizing research results to other subjects and other settings. Populations are always of interest in scientific research, even when only a small group of subjects is being studied. Otherwise, the research becomes problem solving.

Although the researcher would like to assert that the study results apply to a wide target population, this population must be similar to the accessible population for such an assertion to be made. For example, the accessible population might be pregnant women in one clinic setting. These women are primigravidas and their ages vary from 25 to 35 years. The target population would be 25- to 35-year-old primigravidas. It might also be necessary to further delineate the target population according to ethnicity or income levels of the accessible population in the clinical setting of the study. In other words, the target population to which the researcher wishes to generalize study results must be similar to the accessible population.

Select the Sample

Although researchers are always interested in populations, usually a subgroup of the population, called a **sample,** is studied. The sample is chosen to represent the population and is used to make generalizations about the population. Obtaining data from an entire population is costly and time consuming, and it may even be impossible, at times, to contact or locate every member of a given population. If the sample is carefully selected, the researcher can make claims about the population with a certain degree of confidence. The method of selecting the sample determines how representative the sample is of the population.

Probability samples are those chosen by a random selection process in which each member of the population has a chance of being in the sample. Chapter 11 discusses different types of probability sampling methods. If nonprobability sampling is used, the researcher has less confidence that the sample is representative of the population. The investigator cannot estimate the probability that each element of the population has a chance of being selected for the sample, and the possibility of a biased sample is great. The researcher must determine which sampling method to use, after considering the advantages and disadvantages of the various types of probability and nonprobability sampling methods.

Nursing research is generally conducted with human beings; therefore, subjects' rights must be considered and the proper permissions secured before subjects are approached to participate in a study. All research with humans must involve voluntary participation of the subjects. Even in studies that use a random selection process, the sample may not be truly random, unless all selected subjects actually agree to participate in the study.

Conduct a Pilot Study

It is advisable to conduct a pilot study before the study subjects are approached and the actual study is carried out. A **pilot study** involves a miniature trial version of the planned study. People are selected for the pilot study who have similar characteristics to those of the sample that will be used for the actual study. Stommel and Wills (2004) called pilot studies "building blocks" to larger studies. A pilot study can prevent the researcher from conducting a large-scale study that might have little value. Some researchers have come to this conclusion when it is too late!

According to Jairath, Hogerney, and Parsons (2000), there are several reasons for conducting a pilot study. The major objectives are to examine issues related to the design, sample size, data collection procedures, and data analysis approaches.

A pilot study can be used to test a new instrument or to evaluate an existing instrument that has been altered. The researcher may think that the questionnaire is so simple that a 10-year-old could fill it out but finds out in a pilot study that 30-year-olds have great difficulty in understanding several of the questions. The pilot study also can be used to evaluate the study procedures and, in general, help to get the "bugs" out before the actual study is conducted. Factors can be examined, such as how long it will take to conduct the data collection and how subjects can be expected to respond to the data collection methods.

After the pilot study is conducted, necessary revisions should be made. It may be advisable to carry out another pilot study if changes have been made in the instrument(s) or the research procedures.

Collect the Data

The **data** are the pieces of information or facts that are collected in scientific investigations. Although the data-collection step of the research process may be very time consuming, it is sometimes considered the most exciting part of research.

The variable or variables in a study must be measured. This is carried out through the data-collection procedures. Data collection should be a systematic process. These questions must be answered: Who will collect the data? When will the data be collected? Where will the data be collected? What data will be collected? How will the data be collected? Use the acronym WWWWH (Who–When–Where–What–How).

A multitude of data-collection methods are available to nurse researchers. The choice of methods is determined by the study hypothesis(es) or the research question(s), the design of the study, and the amount of knowledge available about the study topic. Many research projects use more than one data-collection method. Some of these methods and the various instruments appropriate for nurse researchers are discussed in Chapters 12 and 13.

Organize the Data for Analysis

After the data are collected, it is necessary to organize the data for tabulation and evaluation. This task can be overwhelming at times. Actually, this step of the research process should have been planned long before the data were collected. The researcher should have prepared dummy tables and graphs that could then be filled in with the data once they are obtained.

If questionnaires have been used, it will be necessary to determine if they have been completed correctly. Decisions will have to be made about missing data. If interviews have been recorded, the tapes will have to be analyzed and data then placed in some kind of written form.

A statistician should be consulted in the early phase of the research process, as well as in the data analysis phase of the study. Just as plans for organizing the data should be made before data collection begins, plans for analyzing the data also should be made before obtaining the data. It is frustrating for a statistician to be approached by a researcher with a mound of data and the plea "What should I do with this stuff?" The statistician can help determine what data are needed for a study and what statistical procedures will be appropriate to analyze the data.

Analyze the Data

This stage of the research process—analyzing the data—may make some of you cringe, for you can quickly ascertain that statistics may be involved. After reviewing statistical concepts in Chapters 14 and 15, you will realize that an understanding of difficult mathematical principles is not necessary to conduct research or evaluate research results.

Data analysis has been greatly simplified today because of computer programs. When data had to be analyzed by hand, or even when pocket calculators became available, data analysis was very time consuming. Now a researcher can sit at a computer terminal and input large amounts of data and receive the results of the analysis almost instantaneously.

Interpret the Findings

After the data are analyzed, the findings should be interpreted in light of the study hypothesis(es) or research question(s). If a hypothesis was tested, a determination is made as to whether the data support the research hypothesis. Also, the framework for the study is discussed in light of the findings. If the data support the research hypothesis, then the theoretical or conceptual framework is also supported. Conversely, if the research hypothesis is not supported, the framework for the study is also not supported. Of course, the researcher should discuss any problems incurred in the course of the study or any limitations of the design that may have influenced the study results.

The results of the present study are compared with those of previous studies that investigated the same or similar variables; thus, the researcher is able to contribute to the existing body of knowledge on the study topic.

After the findings are interpreted, the researcher should indicate the implications for nursing. A consideration is made of changes that might be called for in nursing practice, nursing education, or nursing administration as a result of the study findings. Finally, recommendations for future research are proposed.

Communicate the Findings

This step of the research process may be the most important one for nursing. No matter how significant the findings may be, they are of little value to the rest of the nursing profession if the researcher fails to disseminate these results to other colleagues. The results of many nursing studies never get published or shared with other nurses.

Research findings can be communicated through many different mediums. The most effective method of reaching a large number of nurses is through publication in research journals such as *Applied Nursing Research, Biological Research for Nursing, Clinical Nursing Research, Journal of Advanced Nursing, Nursing Research, Research in Nursing and Health,* and *Western Journal of Nursing Research.* Research results also may be published in clinical journals such as *Heart & Lung, Issues in Mental Health Nursing,* and *Journal of Obstetric, Gynecologic, and Neonatal Nursing.* Chapter 17 lists additional journals. Nurses should also present their research results in person to colleagues at national, regional, state, and local gatherings of nurses.

An exciting method of presenting research results at meetings is through poster sessions. Posters are prepared that describe the major areas of the research, such as the problem area, hypotheses, and findings. Posters, as a communication medium, permit results of many studies to be disseminated to interested research consumers. The number of oral presentations that can be attended in a given day is quite limited, but many research posters can be viewed in a short time. Generally, the investigator is present at least part of the time that the poster session is being held to answer questions about the study. Poster presentations are further discussed in Chapter 17.

Utilize the Findings

The first four editions of this book did not identify "Utilize the Findings" as the final step in the research process. Utilization of research findings was discussed, but not in relation to the researcher who conducted the study. As the 5th edition was being prepared, the decision was made that the researcher *should* get involved in implementing the findings of his or her study. This might seem a little unfair to you. After all, the researcher did all of the work in conducting the study. Shouldn't someone else see that the findings are integrated into nursing practice? However, who knows the most about the research study? After answering this question, it began to seem logical that this person should get involved in seeing that the study findings are used in practice. The researcher may not actually implement the findings, but he or she can make recommendations about how the findings could be integrated into nursing practice. For example, the researcher could act as a consultant to nurses in health care agencies who want to use the study findings. Additionally, the researcher is actually helping promote utilization of study findings by disseminating these findings in as many ways as possible.

SUMMARY

In general, quantitative research proceeds in an orderly fashion. The first step is to clearly identify the problem that will be studied. In a nursing study, the **research problem** is an area where knowledge is needed to advance the practice of nursing. The researcher should also clearly identify the specific purpose of the study. A **research question** is the specific question that the researcher expects to be answered in a study. The research question specifies the variables and the population that are being studied. A **variable** is a characteristic or attribute that differs among the persons, objects, or events that are being studied.

The literature is reviewed to determine the existing knowledge on the study topic. A theoretical/conceptual framework is developed to guide the research. The **assumptions** on which the study is based are clearly identified, and the **limitations** or weaknesses of the study are acknowledged.

Next, the researcher states the study expectations in the form of a **hypothesis.** The hypothesis links the **independent variable** (cause) with the **dependent variable** (effect).

The variables and terms in the study hypothesis or research question need to be defined. A **conceptual definition** is a clearly stated meaning or example of an abstract idea or concept that is being studied by the researcher. An **operational definition** indicates how the concept will be measured in a particular study. The **research design** is the plan for how the study will be conducted. A design is selected that is most appropriate to test the study hypothesis(es) or answer the research question(s). Research designs can be classified as quantitative or qualitative. They also can be classified as experimental or nonexperimental.

The **population** or group of interest is identified. A **target population** is a group to which the researcher wishes to generalize the study findings. An **accessible population** is the group that is actually available for study by the researcher. The **sample** is a subgroup that is chosen to represent the population.

It is advisable to conduct a **pilot study**, or miniature trial version of a study, before the actual data are collected. **Data** are the pieces of information collected during the study. After data are collected, they are organized, analyzed, interpreted, and communicated. Finally, the last phase of a study involves the utilization of the results.

NURSING RESEARCH ON THE WEB

For additional online resources, research activities, and exercises, go to **www.mynursingkit.** **com.** Select Chapter 3 from the drop-down menu.

GET INVOLVED ACTIVITIES

1. Identify several topics that you believe are important for future nursing research studies. Have group members discuss which topics would be most appropriate for quantitative research studies.

2. Ask for two volunteers to debate which step of the quantitative research process is the *most* important one. Allow these two people to make their own choice about which step is most important. Other individuals will be allowed to provide input.

3. Select a research article that will be read by the entire group. Identify the number of steps of the research process that can be clearly identified in the article.

4. Develop a research proposal, using all of the steps outlined in this chapter. Start with a problem area and write a research question. The topic can be something humorous that

is specific to your group, such as, "Is there a difference in the average number of movies seen in the past year by married nurses compared to single nurses?" Proceed through the rest of the steps of the research process. You may want to collect data, have some person or persons analyze it, and bring the results to the group the next time it meets. Using a trivial topic like this may make the research process seem less formidable.

5. Divide into two teams and debate the value of adding this final step to the research process: utilization of research findings. One team would support adding this step by tak-

ing the position that it is the responsibility of the researcher to see that research findings are implemented. The other team would oppose adding this step to the research process by supporting the position that implementation of research is the responsibility of other people at a later time.

6. Determine an appropriate publication source that could be used to communicate the results of a study topic that the group decides on or to communicate the results of the study that the group has proposed in Activity 4. Who would be interested in the results of this study?

SELF-TEST

Circle the letter before the *best* answer.

1. All authors agree on the following number of steps in conducting quantitative research:
   A. 10
   B. 15
   C. 18
   D. There is no set number of steps.

2. Which of the following answers is true concerning quantitative research?
   A. The steps always proceed in the same way in each study.
   B. There may be some shifting back and forth between the steps.
   C. The most important step is to identify the study hypotheses.
   D. The steps are never carried out in an orderly fashion.

3. One of the main purposes of conducting a review of the literature before carrying out a research project is to
   A. determine existing knowledge on the topic.
   B. help select an optimum sample size.
   C. discover an instrument for data collection that has been used many times.
   D. prevent duplication of research.

4. Which of the following is *true* concerning assumptions?
   A. Assumptions are beliefs that have been found to be true.
   B. Researchers' false beliefs are often called assumptions.
   C. Expectations for study results are presented in the form of assumptions.
   D. All studies are based on assumptions.

5. The plan for how a study will be conducted is called the
   A. design.
   B. hypothesis.
   C. data-collection method.
   D. research process.

6. The small group selected from a larger group to participate in a study is known as the
   A. study population.
   B. sample population.
   C. sample.
   D. element.

7. At what point in the research process should a statistician be consulted initially?
   A. early in the research project
   B. immediately before data are collected
   C. after data have been collected
   D. before the data have been analyzed

8. A friend asks you to explain the difference between a conceptual definition and an operational definition of anxiety. You help her to understand these concepts by providing her with the following operational definition of anxiety:
   A. an overwhelming feeling of uneasiness
   B. a score above 40 on the Nieswiadomy Anxiety Inventory
   C. discomfort at the highest level
   D. pulse rates

9. The final step of the research process, for the researcher, is to
A. analyze the data.
B. interpret the findings
C. communicate the findings.
D. utilize the findings.

10. Which of the following communication mediums is the most efficient means of presenting research findings?
A. books
B. journals
C. research seminars
D. poster sessions

REFERENCES

Burns, N., & Grove, S. K (2009). *The practice of nursing research: Appraisal, synthesis, and generation of evidence* (6th ed.). St. Louis, MO: Saunders Elsevier.

Downs, F. S. (1994). Hitching the research wagon to theory [editorial]. *Nursing Research, 45,* 195.

Giuliano, K. K., & Polanowicz, M. (2008). Interpretation and use of statistics in nursing research. *AACN Advanced Critical Care, 19,* 211–222.

Houser, J. (2008). *Nursing research: Reading, understanding, creating evidence.* Sudbury, MA: Jones and Bartlett Publishers.

Jairath, N., Hogerney, M., & Parsons, C. (2000). The role of the pilot study: A case illustration from cardiac nursing research. *Applied Nursing Research, 13,* 92–96.

Kerlinger, F. (1986). *Foundations of behavioral research* (3rd ed.). New York: Holt, Rinehart & Winston.

Macnee, C. L., & McCabe, S. (2008). *Understanding nursing research: Using research in evidence-based practice* (2nd ed.). Philadelphia: Lippincott Williams & Wilkins.

Polit, D. F., & Beck, C. T. (2008). *Nursing research: Principles and methods* (8th ed.). Philadelphia: Lippincott Williams & Wilkins.

Stommel, M., & Wills, C. E. (2004). *Clinical research: Concepts and principles for advanced practice nurses.* Philadelphia: Lippincott Williams & Wilkins.

CHAPTER 4

An Overview of Qualitative Research

OUTLINE

OBJECTIVES

On completion of this chapter, you will be prepared to:

1. Differentiate between qualitative and quantitative research
2. Recall the types of qualitative research
3. List the overall steps in qualitative research
4. Discuss each step in qualitative research
5. Identify two of the most common data collection methods used in qualitative research
6. Recognize reliability and validity issues in qualitative research
7. Discuss the complexity of analyzing qualitative data
8. Identify sources for the presentation of qualitative research studies
9. Determine the benefits of combining quantitative and qualitative research methods
10. Recognize the issues that may arise when combining quantitative and qualitative research methods

NEW TERMS DEFINED IN THIS CHAPTER

content analysis, pg. 50
focus group, pg. 49
interview, pg. 49
mixed methods research, pg. 52

participant observation, pg. 49
saturation, pg. 48
triangulation, pg. 53

Are you more interested in individuals and their subjective feelings than you are in objective data obtained from groups of people? If your answer is "Yes," you may like this chapter.

Nurse researchers have conducted quantitative research for many years and have demonstrated their expertise in this methodology. They have revealed the usefulness of this type of research for the nursing profession and our patients/clients. However, for many years, nurses have begun to question the appropriateness of using only this approach to examine some of the phenomena of interest to nursing.

Nursing has traditionally focused on the individual and the holistic nature of the person. This value system is more consistent with qualitative research philosophy than with quantitative research philosophy. In qualitative research, the individual's perspective is very important, whereas in quantitative research, the focus is on the group or population of interest, rather than on the individual.

Interest in qualitative research in nursing grew in the United States during the last few decades of the 20th century. DeSantis and Ugarriza (2000) wrote that during the 1990s, "qualitative methodology surged to the forefront of nursing research" (p. 351). The interest seems to still be vibrant in the 21st century. Here is a list of some of the qualitative studies published in 2009 and 2010:

"An In-depth Exploration of Information-seeking Behavior among Individuals with Cancer" (Lambert, Loiselle, & Macdonald, 2009)

"The Exploration of the Lived Experience of the Graduate Nurse Making the Transition to Registered Nurse During the First Year of Practice" (Zinsmeister & Schafer, 2009)

"The Impact of HIV Education on the Lives of Ugandan Nurses and Nurse-midwives" (Harrowing, 2009)

"Maintaining the Balance: Older Adults with Chronic Health Problems Manage Life in the Community" (Jacelon, 2010)

"Online Fathering"(Schachman, 2010)

"Parents' Experiences in Decision Making with Childhood Cancer Clinical Trials" (Woodgate & Yanofsky, 2010)

Were you able to detect that these studies were qualitative based on the wording in some of the titles? Such terms as "The Exploration of the Lived Experience of the Graduate Nurse . . ." and "Parents' Experiences in Decision Making . . ." provide clues that these articles would present the results of qualitative studies.

A number of books devoted to qualitative nursing research are available. Several are listed on the Amazon.com Web site. The most recent one listed (as of July 2010) is *Qualitative Research in Nursing and Healthcare* by Holloway and Wheeler (2009). One book listed, *Advanced Qualitative Research for Nursing* by Joanna Latimer (2003), is available for use with Kindle, the wireless reading device developed by Amazon. So, a reader can learn about qualitative research anywhere he or she goes!

There has been some concern in nursing that the interest in evidence-based practice will decrease the number of qualitative studies. Sandelowski (2004) addressed this issue by calling for qualitative researchers to focus more on the usefulness of their findings to the evidence-based practice movement. She contended that the findings of qualitative studies should be part of the evidence in evidence-based practice. She wrote that qualitative health research "is the best chance for evidence-based practice to realize the ideal of using the best evidence to create the best practices for individuals" (p. 1382). She further called for qualitative researchers to "take more stock of our stories: to showcase what and how they reveal, clarify, distill, elaborate, extend, complicate, confirm, refute, explain, reframe, personify, individualize, specify, sensitize, persuade, evoke, and provoke" (p. 1382).

COMPARISON OF QUALITATIVE AND QUANTITATIVE RESEARCH

Quantitative research is based on the concepts of manipulation and control of phenomena and the verification of results, using empirical data gathered through the senses. Qualitative research focuses on gaining insight and understanding about an individual's perception of events. Morse (2005b)

TABLE 4–1 Comparison of Qualitative and Quantitative Research

Qualitative	Quantitative
Subjective data	Objective data
Discovery	Explanation
Whole is greater than the parts	Parts are equal to the whole
Multiple truths	One truth
Small sample sizes	Large sample sizes
Deliberately selected samples	Random samples
Participants/informants	Subjects
Results presented as narrative data	Results presented as numbers/statistics
Researcher part of the study	Researcher separate from the study

asserted that qualitative research is a way of thinking, seeing, and conceptualizing. Verification of results through the senses is not called for. The individual's interpretation of events or circumstances is of importance, rather than the interpretation made by the researcher. Table 4–1 compares some characteristics of qualitative and quantitative research.

According to Porter (1989), "while the qualitative researcher attempts to obtain rich, real, deep and valid data, the quantitative researcher aims for hard, replicable and reliable data" (p. 98). Streubert and Carpenter (2002) asserted that the inability of researchers to measure certain phenomena quantitatively and the dissatisfaction with the results of measurement of other phenomena has led to the acceptance of qualitative research approaches to gain knowledge. Chamberlain (2009) pointed out that there are "parts of the human system that are not amenable to quantitative measurement" (p. 52). She contended that qualitative research methods were designed to address this issue.

Qualitative research is concerned with in-depth descriptions of people or events, and data are collected through such methods as unstructured interviews and participant observation. Nurses should be comfortable with these two methods of data collection because of their nursing educational preparation and clinical experiences (Connelly & Yoder, 2000).

In qualitative research, the researcher searches for patterns and themes in the data, rather than focusing on the testing of hypotheses. The qualitative researcher is not limited by existing theories but rather must be open to new ideas and new theories.

At first glance, it might appear that qualitative research would be easier to conduct than quantitative research. The researcher need not be as concerned with numbers and complicated statistical analyses. However, qualitative research is not recommended for the beginning researcher. The guidelines for this type of research are not as clear-cut and easy to follow as the guidelines for conducting quantitative research. The beginning qualitative researcher should seek a mentor.

TYPES OF QUALITATIVE RESEARCH

There are many different qualitative research traditions or approaches. Streubert and Carpenter (2002) discuss five: phenomenology, grounded theory, ethnography, historical, and action research. Burns and Grove (2009) list six approaches to qualitative research: phenomenological, grounded theory, ethnographic, historical, philosophical inquiry, and critical social theory methodology. Polit and Beck (2008) present 11 qualitative research traditions: ethnography, ethnoscience, phenomenology, hermeneutics, ethology, ecological psychology, grounded theory, ethnomethodology, semiotics, discourse analysis, and historical analysis. Table 4–2 lists some of the types of qualitative research.

Qualitative research traditions or types are discussed in this book as qualitative research designs. Chapter 10 reviews some common qualitative research designs and excerpts are provided from recent research studies in which these designs were used.

TABLE 4–2 Types of Qualitative Research

Action research	Ethnography	Grounded theory
Case study	Ethnology	Hermeneutics
Critical social inquiry	Ethnomethodology	Historical
Discourse analysis	Ethnonursing	Phenomenology
Ecological psychology	Ethnoscience	Philosophical inquiry
Ethical inquiry	Feminist inquiry	Symbolic interaction

STEPS IN QUALITATIVE RESEARCH

Identify the Problem of the Study

Just as the identification of the problem is the first step in quantitative research studies, the identification of the problem or phenomenon of the study is also the first step in the qualitative research process. In quantitative research, the researcher generally begins with a broad general area of study and then narrows the focus to a small area of study before data collection begins. In qualitative research, the problem area or phenomenon of study may remain general until the researcher actually enters the field setting. Then, the topic area may be narrowed down.

The problem to be examined in a qualitative study may indicate the general nature of the phenomenon to be studied and the group or community that will be studied.

State the Purpose

In an article reporting on a qualitative study, the reader might see a one-sentence statement of purpose. For example, a purpose statement might be, "To describe the experiences of Haitians who survived a 7.0 earthquake in January 2010."

Select the Research Design

The research design in a qualitative study depends on the phenomenon that will be studied. For example, in a purpose statement about the Haitian earthquake survivors, the researcher would be interested in a description of what people experienced during that earthquake. This study would probably call for a phenomenological approach to data collection. If the researcher were interested in the steps that the survivors went through to resolve their crisis, a grounded-theory approach might be used to gather the data. If the researcher were interested in how nurses worked with earthquake survivors to reach a resolution of the crisis situation, an action research approach might be used.

Review the Literature

Qualitative researchers debate about this step. Some believe that a cursory review of the literature prior to conducting research may help focus the study, but many qualitative researchers do not begin with a review of the literature. In discussing phenomenology, Chamberlain (2009) stated: "Only after the study is complete is the literature review conducted" (p. 52).

In quantitative research, the researcher always begins with a review of the literature. It helps the researcher determine what is already known about the study topic. The quantitative researcher seeks information on what type and how many studies have been conducted in the past on this topic. Also, the researcher may discover a theory that will help guide the proposed study, obtain information on research methodology, or locate an instrument or instruments to assist in data collection.

Qualitative researchers, in contrast, generally do not begin with an extensive review of the literature. Many qualitative researchers believe that reviewing the literature before conducting a qualitative study, particularly a phenomenological study, will bias the study results. They do not want to know what other researches think or believe about the phenomenon of interest prior to collecting their own data.

Do not get the impression that some qualitative researchers disregard the review of the literature entirely. They just believe that the review of the literature should be conducted at the conclusion of the study. The purpose of the literature, then, is to obtain information that will enable researchers to inform readers of their research study results and how the findings of their particular study fit into the existing body of knowledge on the topic of interest.

Select the Sample

One of the criticisms of qualitative studies is that sample sizes are generally smaller than in quantitative studies. There are no set rules about the necessary sample size for a qualitative study. Sandelowski's (1995b) article "Sample Size in Qualitative Research" is an excellent source on this topic. She claims that the quality of information obtained from each respondent is more important than the amount of data obtained. She stated that samples may be "too small to support claims of having achieved either informational redundancy or theoretical saturation, or too large to permit the deep, case-oriented analysis that is the raison d'être of qualitative inquiry" (p. 179).

Frequently, sample sizes are quite small in qualitative research. In a study by Furness and Garrud (2010), five facial cancer surgery patients were asked to record their experiences, thoughts, and feelings for up to 1 year, as they underwent and recovered from their surgery. Brethauer and Carey (2010) described the experiences of six mothers who had infants with neonatal jaundice. Zinsmeister and Schafer (2009) interviewed nine graduate nurses in their study of the lived experience of graduate nurses during their first 6 months to 1 year of nursing practice.

Saturation is a concept in qualitative studies regarding sampling. **Saturation** occurs when the researcher hears a repetition of themes or salient points as additional participants are interviewed. No new information is obtained; the data become redundant. This can happen after interviewing 10 people, or not until after 100 are interviewed. Brethauer and Carey (2010) asserted that saturation occurred after they had interviewed six mothers of infants who had experienced neonatal jaundice.

Saturation

A group of researchers in Sweden studied the needs of spouses of patients with complications of heart failure after cardiac surgery (Ågren, Frisman, Berg, Svedjeholm, & Strömberg, 2009). Thirteen spouses (10 women and 3 men) were interviewed. The core category of *confirmation* was identified as describing the individual needs of the spouses. This core category combined three underlying subcategories: *security, rest for mind and body,* and *inner strength*. After 12 interviews, saturation was reached. One more interview was performed to confirm that saturation had been reached.

Gain Entry to the Research Site

In quantitative research, the researcher spends time locating a place to conduct a study. Frequently, permission must be obtained from a health care agency and the IRB (see Chapter 2) in that agency. Quantitative researchers may complain about the time involved in obtaining permission to conduct a study.

Qualitative researchers conduct their research in the field or place where the research participants live or work. However, before approaching potential research participants, the researcher must obtain permission from the IRB where she or he is employed. Additionally, to receive research funding, the researcher has to demonstrate that the study proposal has been approved by an IRB.

Generally, the qualitative researcher tries to contact key people in the area of interest. In ethnographic research, these individuals are called *key informants* (see Chapter 10). They may be able to help the researcher get in touch with potential research participants who would be able to provide valuable insight into the phenomenon of interest.

Protect the Rights of Participants

In qualitative research, the researcher interacts very closely with the study participants. Therefore, ethical issues may be even more important in qualitative research than in quantitative research. Because of the close relationship between the researcher and the study participants, these people tend to share very personal and private information with the researcher.

Anonymity is generally not a consideration in qualitative research because the researcher knows the identity of the study participants. However, confidentiality is a very important issue. The researcher must take particular care to protect the identity of study participants. The sample size is usually very small and, because of the rich descriptive information presented in study results, it might be easy to identify study participants. The researcher may have to omit the usual demographic information that is presented on study subjects in a quantitative research report. For example, the qualitative researcher may want to omit such information as the age, educational level, and occupation of study participants.

Collect the Data

Interview is probably the most common type of data-collection method used in qualitative studies. An **interview** is a method of data collection in which an interviewer obtains responses from a subject in a face-to-face encounter or through a telephone call. The interviews used in qualitative research are generally semistructured rather than structured, as might be the case in quantitative research. According to Donalek (2005), an interview in qualitative research is a "shared journey." She asserted that it is important for the novice interviewer to practice the method repeatedly, preferably under the guidance of an experienced interviewer. Chapter 13 discusses interviews.

Another common type of data-collection method in qualitative research is participant observation. **Participant observation** involves the direct observation and recording of information and requires that the researcher become a part of the setting in which the person, group, or culture is being observed. Observation data methods are discussed in Chapter 13.

Interviews and observation allow for the flexibility that is needed in qualitative research. Other types of data-collection methods include open-ended questionnaires, diaries, life histories, official documents, letters, and photographs.

In qualitative research, the amount of time for data collection is generally not specified when a study begins. In some types of qualitative research, such as grounded theory methodology, data collection continues until the data are saturated (Thomas, 1990.) Even considering the small number of participants, the amount of data is usually voluminous.

The use of focus groups has increased in nursing studies. A **focus group** consists of a small group of individuals meeting together and being asked questions, by a moderator, about a certain topic or topics. The advantage of this approach is that it is a time-saver compared to individual interviews. However, there may not be equal participation by group members. Some people may be reluctant to express their views to others in a group setting.

Côté-Arsenault and Morrison-Beedy (2005) noted in an article in *Research in Nursing & Health* that the cornerstones for successful focus groups are a well-defined purpose, carefully planned environment, and well-trained personnel. Many examples are found in the literature in which a focus group has been used. Redmon and Curtis (2009) claim that focus groups are a respected qualitative methodology and that their use is growing.

Focus Group

A study was conducted to determine health professionals' perspectives on assisting low-income mothers with infant feeding (Olson, Horodynski, Brophy-Herb, & Iwanski, 2010). Five focus groups were held for 36 health professionals (pediatricians, nurses, WIC professionals, and Cooperative Extension nutrition educators). Interviews were audio taped, transcribed, and analyzed. Six major content categories were identified. The researchers asserted that they had identified information needed by these mothers, which will lead to improved communication between mothers and health professionals.

The reliability and validity of research findings are of great importance in all studies. Although the methods may vary according to the type of study, both qualitative and quantitative researchers are interested in the credibility of their findings. Reliability in qualitative research can be defined as the "repeatability of scientific observations, and sources that could influence the stability and consistency of those observations" (Hinds, Scandrett-Hibden, & McAulay, 1990, p. 431). Validity means that the findings "reflect reality, and the meaning of the data is accurately interpreted" (Hinds et al., 1990, p. 431).

The rigor and objectivity of the methods and the desire for generalizability of findings of qualitative studies are not present to the same extent as in quantitative studies. Replication of a study is very desirable in quantitative research. However, qualitative studies are generally not replicated because knowledge of the findings of one study could bias the results of another study (Porter, 1989). Additionally, Leininger (1985) likened qualitative research to the detective studying for clues. Each situation is unique.

Rather than discussing the strict rigor and objectivity of their research, qualitative researchers often mention the relevance of their study findings. The subjects themselves are frequently considered as the persons most knowledgeable about the topic. Therefore, the researcher often returns to the subjects for their assessment of the accuracy of the researcher's interpretation of the data.

One of the ways that the rigor of a qualitative study is considered is through the long period of time spent collecting data. Data are generally collected until it becomes clear that no new information is being collected. Also, multiple sources of data are frequently used, which provides a check for both reliability and validity. Both the large amount of data collected and the length of time spent collecting data helps increase the reliability and validity of qualitative study findings.

Analyze the Data

Thomas (1990) compared the analysis of quantitative and qualitative data. She likened quantitative analysis to grading multiple-choice or true-false questions. Qualitative analysis is like grading essay questions. Essay questions may be easier to write, but they are much harder to grade.

According to Jacelon and O'Dell (2005), data analysis in qualitative research begins once data collection begins. Data analysis is generally not a distinct step in qualitative studies as it is in quantitative studies. In many qualitative studies, the researcher begins interpreting data as data are collected.

There are no universally accepted rules for analyzing qualitative data. Analysis of data in qualitative studies usually involves an examination of words rather than numbers, as is the case in quantitative studies. Generally, a large number of direct quotes made by the participants are included in study reports. The task of analyzing all of these data can be overwhelming. One large study might involve the analysis of several thousand pages of notes! Qualitative researchers may spend months analyzing their data.

All qualitative studies involve content analysis procedures in one form or another (McLaughlin & Marascuilo, 1990). In general, **content analysis** involves creating categories of data and developing rules for coding data into these categories. The use of content analysis varies according to the type of qualitative study that is conducted. Grounded theory, ethnography, and phenomenological research are based on the specific techniques developed from the three disciplines that developed these methods: sociology, anthropology, and psychology, respectively. More information on specific content analysis methods can be found in other sources.

Coding is the basic data analysis tool of qualitative researchers. Statements made by study participants are grouped and given a code. Coded data are clustered together into themes. The qualitative researcher is then presented with the challenge of conveying the study findings to the reader. Jacelon and O'Dell (2005) proposed that the qualitative researcher must become a "storyteller."

Data can be analyzed manually or through the aid of computer software programs. With the advent of these software programs, data analysis has been greatly enhanced for qualitative researchers. Qualitative data analysis software (QDAS) can store data, edit data, retrieve segments of text, and assemble data according to themes or categories.

A number of software programs are helpful in analyzing qualitative data. These include ATLAS.ti, Ethnograph, HyperRESEARCH, and NVivo.

The NVivo7 software program was used to help analyze data in a study that asked the question, "What is the impact of an HIV/AIDS education program on the lives of a group of Ugandan nurses and nurse-midwives?" (Harrowing, 2009). Tapes and field notes were transcribed and entered in NVivo7. Thematic coding occurred simultaneously with data collection.

Sandelowski (1995a) issued a caution about the use of computer technology in the analysis of qualitative data. She wrote that this type of technology is changing the "look and feel" of qualitative research and that computer printouts of data give the information a "veneer" of objectivity. She jokingly wrote that even "soft" data could be considered as "hard" data when it is produced by "hardware." Sandelowski expressed a fear that the art of qualitative work will be adversely affected by this technology. In examining a number of recently published reports of qualitative research studies, only a few mentioned the use of qualitative data software programs.

Interpret the Data

The qualitative researcher must interpret the study data, just as the quantitative researcher must interpret the data. However, in a qualitative study this step is not as clear-cut as in a quantitative study.

Interpretation of the data frequently occurs simultaneously with data collection. Researchers pour over their data again and again, trying to obtain "meaning" from the data. They "immerse" themselves in the data, constantly searching for patterns and themes. Although qualitative researchers generally do not try to make generalizations from their findings, they do try to determine how their study results can be applied and usually address this issue at the end of their study reports.

Communicate the Study Results

Where and how do qualitative researchers present their study results? Research findings can be communicated through many different mediums. It is very common today for qualitative research study results to be published. Most nursing research journals contain reports of this type of research. When you scan the research article titles on the covers or inside pages of research journals, frequently it is evident which title is associated with a qualitative study and which title is associated with a quantitative study.

The best way for researchers to contact a large number of nurses is through publication in research journals such as *Qualitative Health Research* and *Nursing Research.* Other journals that report the results of qualitative research include *Applied Nursing Research, Journal of Advanced Nursing, Research in Nursing and Health,* and *Western Journal of Nursing Research.* Research results can also be published in clinical journals such as *Issues in Mental Health Nursing, Journal of Obstetric, Gynecologic, and Neonatal Nursing,* and *Urological Nursing.*

Nurses who conduct qualitative research should personally present their research results, just as quantitative researchers do, to colleagues at national, regional, state, and local gatherings of nurses. Posters are a very effective means of presenting quantitative findings, and qualitative researchers may also present their results on posters. However, it is a little more difficult for qualitative researchers than quantitative researchers because qualitative findings usually contain examples of statements made by the study participants. Verbatim transcript data may take up a lot of poster space.

Utilize the Study Results

The findings of qualitative research should be used in nursing practice, just like the results of quantitative studies. Implications for nursing practice are usually included at the end of a qualitative research report, just as is found in quantitative reports.

Zinsmeister and Schafer (2009) examined the experience of graduate nurses making the transition to the registered nurse role, using a phenomenological research approach. Five factors were revealed that contributed to a positive transition experience. At the end of their article in *Journal for Nurses in Staff Development*, they called for organizations to provide the opportunities and resources to educate and socialize new nurses for the "promotion of professional growth, empowerment, and autonomy of all staff . . ." (p. 33).

There is some confusion about the implementation of the results of qualitative studies. Finfgeld-Connett (2010) contend that findings from many qualitative studies have had little impact on clinical practice. In her article in *Journal of Advanced Nursing*, she asserted that single qualitative study findings are not directly applicable to clinical practice. She stated, "methods for systematically compiling and synthesizing qualitative findings have just recently been developed in nursing" (p. 246). She called for nurse researchers to conduct well-designed meta-synthesis investigations (see Chapter 15) that will help generate findings applicable to clinical practice and policy formation.

COMBINING QUALITATIVE AND QUANTITATIVE METHODS

Many nurse researchers have recommended the use of both qualitative and quantitative research methods in a single study. Ford-Gilboe, Campbell, and Berman (1995) called for nurse researchers to combine "numbers and stories." Combining both qualitative and quantitative methods increases the researcher's ability to rule out rival explanations for phenomena (Hinds, 1989). Field and Morse (1985) asserted that the strongest research findings are found in studies that use both research methods. These two authors described the sequential and simultaneous use of the two methods. In the sequential use of the methods, the qualitative method might be used initially, until hypotheses emerge. Then, the hypotheses might be tested using a quantitative method.

Myers and Haase (1989) indicated that the integration of quantitative and qualitative approaches is inevitable and essential for nursing research. However, for the two approaches to be combined, the researcher must value both approaches. Haase and Myers (1988) indicated that merely including open-ended questions in a study does not indicate a true combination of the two research approaches. Using a qualitative approach, the researcher must search for the underlying meanings in the data, rather than just identifying and counting the frequency of surface themes.

Many textbooks and articles discuss the issues involved in combining qualitative and quantitative research methods. Sandelowski (2000) has written a very good article on this topic. She discusses how confusion still exists about how to accomplish "mixed-method" studies. She places particular focus on sampling, data collection, and data analysis. Morse (2005a) wrote in an editorial in *Qualitative Health Research* that the "faddishness" of mixed-method design brings many unanswered questions. She stated that many methodological issues need to be resolved. She, too, voiced concerns about data collection and sample sizes.

Two terms found in the nursing research literature refer to combining methods or procedures in research studies: "mixed methods research" and "triangulation." Although much has been written on these two topics, there is still disagreement about their meaning and use in nursing research. Generally speaking, **mixed methods research** involves the combination of quantitative and qualitative methods in one study. **Triangulation** most often indicates the use of two or more different sampling strategies, data collectors, data collection procedures, or theories in one study. In trigonometry and geometry, triangulation is the process of determining the location of a point, indirectly, by measuring angles to it from known points. The term triangulation is used in many fields such as surveying and navigation. In the social sciences, it is used to indicate that an investigator is using more than one means of gaining understanding about the phenomenon under study.

Combining Quantitative and Qualitative Methods

Strategies to manage dyspnea by elders with end-stage chronic obstructive pulmonary disease (COPD) were identified in a study by Thomas (2009). Quantitative and qualitative data were gathered. The Treatment for Breathing Problems (TBP) questionnaire generated quantitative data; a written open-ended question provided qualitative data. When the two sets of data were compared, 10 of the 11 topmost strategies identified on the TBP agreed with one of the four themes identified through the qualitative data.

SUMMARY

Interest in qualitative research continues in the nursing profession. However, there is some concern that the focus on evidence-based practice may decrease the interest in qualitative research.

Quantitative research is based on the concepts of manipulation and control, whereas qualitative research focuses on gaining insight and understanding. In qualitative research, the individual's interpretation of events or circumstances is of utmost importance.

The many types of qualitative research include: ethnography, grounded theory, phenomenology, historical research, case studies, and action research.

Steps in qualitative research include (a) identify the problem of the study, (b) state the purpose, (c) select the research design, (d) review the literature, (e) select the sample, (f) gain entry to the research site, (g) protect the rights of participants, (h) collect the data, (i) analyze the data, (j) interpret the data, (k) communicate the study results, and (l) utilize the study results.

The most commonly used method of data collection in qualitative research is the **interview**. **Participant observation** is another widely used method of data collection. **Focus groups** consist of small groups of individuals meeting together and being asked questions, by a moderator, about a certain topic or topics.

Saturation occurs when the researcher is hearing a repetition of themes or salient points as additional participants are interviewed; data collection ceases at that time. Sample sizes may be quite small in qualitative research.

The reliability and validity of qualitative studies are determined differently than in quantitative studies. Qualitative studies are considered valid if the findings "reflect reality" from the point of view of the subject. Both the large amount of data collected and the length of time spent collecting data help increase the reliability and validity of qualitative data.

Qualitative studies produce large amounts of data. The data generally consist of words rather than numbers. Data analysis usually occurs throughout the course of the study, rather than at its completion. Data can be analyzed manually or through the aid of computer software programs. **Content analysis** involves creating categories of data and developing rules for coding data into these categories.

Many nurse researchers have recommended the use of both qualitative and quantitative research methods in a study. **Mixed methods research** indicates that quantitative and qualitative research methods have been used in the same study. **Triangulation** involves the use of two or more different sampling strategies, data collectors, data collection procedures, or theories in one study.

NURSING RESEARCH ON THE WEB

For additional online resources, research activities, and exercises, go to **www.mynursingkit. com.** Select Chapter 4 from the drop-down menu.

GET INVOLVED ACTIVITIES

1. Divide into pairs. Choose a topic for which you think only a qualitative design would be appropriate to study the phenomenon. Share these topics with the entire group.
2. Stay in the same pairs. Choose a topic for which you think either a qualitative or quantitative design would be appropriate to study a particular phenomenon. Share these topics with the entire group.
3. Remain with your partner from Activity 2. Write a problem statement or purpose statement for either the qualitative study or quantitative study proposed in Activity 2.
4. As a group, identify potential funding sources for a qualitative research study. What approach or techniques would you use to convince the funding source of the value of your proposed study?
5. Debate, with the entire group, what you believe to be the future direction of nursing research. Will quantitative or qualitative research become the dominant research method?

SELF-TEST

Write T (True) or F (False) beside the following statements:

_____ 1. Qualitative research has been the type of research chosen by most nurse researchers in the past.

_____ 2. The researcher exerts tight controls over the research situation in qualitative research.

_____ 3. There has been an increase in the number of qualitative studies conducted in the past few years.

_____ 4. Many nurses are calling for a combination of both qualitative and quantitative methods in research.

_____ 5. Qualitative researchers are very concerned with the generalizability of their study findings.

_____ 6. The number of subjects is generally larger in qualitative research than in quantitative research.

_____ 7. Qualitative research is less common today than it was 20 years ago.

Circle the letter before the *best* answer.

8. Which of the following statements is true when comparing qualitative research to quantitative research?
   A. Qualitative research is easier to conduct than quantitative research.
   B. The amount of data to be analyzed is usually greater in qualitative studies than in quantitative studies.
   C. The amount of time needed to conduct a qualitative study is usually less than in a quantitative study.
   D. Qualitative research most frequently uses a deductive approach, whereas

quantitative research uses an inductive approach.

9. If a researcher were planning a qualitative study, which of the following data-collection methods do you think would *most* likely be considered?
   A. closed-ended questions and nonparticipant observations.
   B. participant observations and semistructured interviews.
   C. structured interviews and physiological measures.
   D. closed-ended questions and structured interviews.
   E. all of these data collections methods would probably be considered.

10. When both qualitative and quantitative research methods are used simultaneously in the same study, this procedure is called
   A. mixed methods.
   B. meta-analysis.
   C. multitrait/multimethod.
   D. methodological plurality.

REFERENCES

Ågren, S., Frisman, G. H., Berg, S., Svedjeholm, R., & Strömberg, A. (2009). Addressing spouses' unique needs after cardiac surgery when recovery is complicated by heart failure. *Heart & Lung: Journal of Acute & Critical Care, 38*, 284–291. doi:10.1016/j.hrtlng.2008.10.002

Brethauer, M., & Carey, L. (2010). Maternal experience with neonatal jaundice. *Maternal Child Nursing, 35*, 8–14.

Burns, N., & Grove, S. K. (2009). *The practice of nursing research: Appraisal, synthesis, and generation of evidence* (6th ed.). St. Louis, MO: Saunders Elsevier.

Chamberlain, B. (2009). Phenomenology: A qualitative method. *Clinical Nurse Specialist, 23*, 52–53.

Connelly, L. M., & Yoder, L. H. (2000). Improving qualitative proposals: Common problem areas. *Clinical Nurse Specialist, 14*, 69–74.

Côté-Arsenault, D., & Morrison-Beedy, D. (2005). Focus on research methods. Maintaining your focus in focus groups: Avoiding common mistakes. *Research in Nursing & Health, 28*, 172–179.

DeSantis, L., & Ugarriza, D. N. (2000). The concept of theme as used in qualitative nursing research. *Western Journal of Nursing Research, 22*, 351–372.

Donalek, J. G. (2005). The interview in qualitative research. *Urologic Nursing, 25*, 124–125.

Field, P. A., & Morse, J. M. (1985). *Nursing research: The application of qualitative approaches.* Rockville, MD: Aspen.

Finfgeld-Connett, D. (2010). Generalizability and transferability of meta-synthesis research findings. *Journal of Advanced Nursing, 66*, 246–254. doi:10.1111/j.1365-2648.2009.05250.x

Ford-Gilboe, M., Campbell, J., & Berman, H. (1995). Stories and numbers: Coexistence without compromise. *Advances in Nursing Science, 18*, 14–26.

Furness, P. J., & Garrud, P. (2010). Adaptation after facial surgery: Using the diary as a research tool. *Qualitative Health Research, 20*, 262–272. doi: 10.1177/1049732309357571

Haase, J. E., & Myers, S. T. (1988). Reconciling paradigm assumptions of qualitative and quantitative research. *Western Journal of Nursing Research, 10*, 128–136.

Harrowing, J. N. (2009). The impact of HIV education on the lives of Ugandan nurses and nurse-midwives. *Advances in Nursing Science, 32*. E94–E108

Hinds, P. S. (1989). Method triangulation to index change in clinical phenomena. *Western Journal of Nursing Research, 11*, 440–447.

Hinds, P. S., Scandrett-Hibden, S., & McAulay, L. S. (1990). Further assessment of a method to estimate reliability and validity of qualitative research findings. *Journal of Advanced Nursing, 15*, 430–435.

Jacelon, C. S. (2010). Maintaining the balance: Older adults with chronic health problems manage life in the community. *Rehabilitation Nursing, 35*, 16–22; 40.

Jacelon, C. S., & O'Dell, K. K. (2005). Case and grounded theory as qualitative research methods. *Urologic Nursing, 25*, 49–52.

Lambert, S. D., Loiselle, C. G., & Macdonald, M. E. (2009). An in-depth exploration of information-seeking behavior among individuals with cancer. *Cancer Nursing, 32*, 11–23.

Leininger, M. M. (Ed.). (1985). *Qualitative research methods in nursing.* Orlando, FL: Grune & Stratton.

McLaughlin, F. E., & Marascuilo, L. A. (1990). *Advanced nursing and health care research: Quantification approaches.* Philadelphia: Saunders.

Morse, J. M. (2005a). Evolving trends in qualitative research: Advanced in mixed-method design [Editorial]. *Qualitative Health Research, 15*, 583–585.

Morse, J. M. (2005b). Fostering qualitative research [editorial]. *Qualitative Health Research, 15*, 287–288.

Myers, S. T., & Haase, J. E. (1989). Guidelines for integration of quantitative and qualitative approaches. *Nursing Research, 38*, 299–301.

Olson, B. H., Horodynski, M. A., Brophy-Herb, H., & Iwanski, K. C. (2010). Health professionals' perspectives on the infant feeding practices of low income mothers. *Maternal Child Health Journal, 14*, 75–85. doi: 10.1007s10995-008-0425-2

Polit, D. F., & Beck, C. T. (2008). *Nursing research: Principles and methods* (8th ed.). Philadelphia: Lippincott Williams & Wilkins.

Porter, E. J. (1989). The qualitative-quantitative dualism. *Image: Journal of Nursing Scholarship, 21*, 98–102.

Redmond, R. A., & Curtis, E. A. (2009). Focus groups: Principles and process. *Nurse Researcher, 16*(3), 57–69.

Sandelowski, M. (1995a). On the aesthetics of qualitative research. *Image: Journal of Nursing Scholarship, 27*, 205–209.

Sandelowski, M. (1995b). Sample size in qualitative research. *Research in Nursing & Health, 18*, 179–183.

Sandelowski, M. (2000). Combining qualitative and quantitative sampling, data collection, and analysis techniques in mixed-method studies. *Research in Nursing & Health, 23,* 246–255.

Sandelowski, M. (2004). Using qualitative research. *Qualitative Health Research, 14,* 1366–1386.

Schachman, K. A. (2010). Online fathering. *Nursing Research, 59,* 11–17. doi: 10.1097/nnr.0b013e3181c3ba05

Streubert, H. J., & Carpenter, D. R. (2002). *Qualitative research in nursing: Advancing the humanistic imperative* (3rd ed.). Philadelphia: Lippincott Williams & Wilkins.

Thomas, B. S. (1990). *Nursing research: An experiential approach.* St. Louis, MO: Mosby.

Thomas, L. A. (2009). Effective dyspnea management strategies identified by elders with end-stage chronic obstructive pulmonary disease. *Applied Nursing Research, 22,* 79–85. doi:10.1016/j.apnr.2007.04010

Woodgate, R. L., & Yanofsky, R. A. (2010). Parents' experiences in decision making with childhood cancer clinical trials. *Cancer Nursing, 33,* 11–18.

Zinsmeister, L. B., & Schafer, D. (2009). The exploration of the lived experience of the graduate nurse making the transition to registered nurse during the first year of practice. *Journal for Nurses in Staff Development, 25,* 28–34.

CHAPTER 5

Identifying Nursing Research Problems

OUTLINE

OBJECTIVES

On completion of this chapter, you will be prepared to:

1. Identify sources of nursing research problems
2. Determine factors to be considered when choosing an appropriate topic for a research study
3. List the criteria to be considered when writing a research question
4. Discuss the format for writing a research question
5. Write research questions for proposed nursing studies
6. Critique problem statements, purpose statements, and research questions in published research reports and articles

NEW TERMS DEFINED IN THIS CHAPTER

bivariate study, pg 64   univariate study, pg 63
multivariate study, pg 64

Many beginning researchers believe that all the important nursing research studies have already been conducted. This is not true. Most of the studies that have been conducted have raised further questions that need answers.

How does a nurse determine what to study? Some nurse researchers have a clearly identified research problem area from the beginning of their research projects, but this usually is not the case. It is difficult to narrow down the broad problem area to a feasible study. A mistake of beginning researchers (and some experienced ones) is to try to examine too much in one study. The belief seems to be "If a little data are good, a lot of data are even better." It would be much more beneficial to nursing for a researcher to conduct a well-designed small study rather than a poorly designed large study.

Sharts-Hopko (2000) called for nurses to identify the problems or issues that come up repeatedly in their practice areas. She asked nurses to consider problems that take up staff time or cause frustration to staff. With the advent of advanced practice nursing, there are even more possibilities for research studies. Pierce (2009) suggested that nurses ask research questions that they "passionately want answered" (p. 156). She furthered called for narrowing down the focus of a study and determining its feasibility before the study begins.

The number of potential nursing studies is infinite. In the first chapter of this book, you read about some research priorities identified by various nursing leaders and nursing organizations. The excuse of "I can't think of anything to study" is not an acceptable reason for failing to conduct research.

The first step and one of the most important requirements of the research process is to be able to delineate the study area clearly and state the research problem concisely. This is also one of the most difficult tasks of the researcher, especially for the beginning researcher. Many hours may be spent on this part of the research project.

One of the expectations of undergraduate nursing students is that they will be able to identify problems that are appropriate for nursing research studies. Therefore, this chapter helps you determine how to identify a researchable problem and how to write a clear and concise research question. Also, information is provided on how to critique the problem statements, purpose statements, and research questions in research articles.

SOURCES OF NURSING RESEARCH PROBLEMS

The sources for generating appropriate nursing research problems are numerous. Four of the most important ones are discussed here: personal experiences, literature sources, existing theories, and previous research.

Personal Experiences

There probably is not a nurse or nursing student among us who has not observed something in nursing practice that was a source of concern. You may have wondered why nurses dislike working with clients with a history of alcoholism or why some nurses seem to make patients feel like criminals when pain medications are requested. You may also have experienced a nagging doubt about why a procedure is done in a certain manner. On the positive side, you may have observed that clients who are allowed unrestricted visiting hours seem to adjust better to hospitalization and that allowing patients to select special foods from a hospital menu seems to decrease their complaints about hospital food. Thus, from your personal experiences and observations, you may identify a topic for study.

Literature Sources

The existing nursing literature is an excellent source of ideas for research. Nearly every published study concludes with recommendations for further studies. Unpublished theses and dissertations also contain suggestions for studies. Turn to the last page of the final chapter, and you probably will find the researcher's suggestions and pleas for needed research. Responses to these suggestions could positively influence the direction of nursing research.

The call for future research is not limited to recommendations at the end of published and un-published studies. Contemporary nursing leaders continually plead for nursing research in articles and books. Many speakers at nursing conventions and conferences address the need for specific areas of nursing research. Chapter 1 discussed priorities for nursing research that have been offered by various nursing groups.

Existing Theories

One type of research that is desperately needed in nursing is the type that tests existing theories. Research is a process of theory development and testing. Nurses use many theories from other disciplines in their practice. Are these theories always appropriate for nursing? For example, is change theory as applicable in a hospital as it is in a manufacturing company? Are learning theories as predictive of the behavior of sick people as they are for the behavior of well people? For instance, my father was an independent man from strong German ancestry. He was a take-charge kind of person. However, when you put him in a health care setting, such as a hospital or a doctor's office, he became as timid as a young child. My mother had to ask all of the questions of the health care personnel. Now, imagine if you tried to use a traditional learning theory while trying to teach my father about some aspect of his health care. You might say to yourself, "This is an independent man who likes to take control." So, you might try to get him to direct his own learning. Wrong approach! He needed to be told, retold, and have demonstrated what he was supposed to do. As you can see, theories may need to be adapted for patients/clients in health care settings.

If an existing theory is used in a research study, a specific propositional statement or statements from the theory must be isolated. Generally, an entire theory is not tested; only a part or parts of the theory are subjected to testing in the clinical situation. For example, a learning principle from a theory of Carl Rogers (1969) might be chosen to guide a patient education program. This learning principle would be transformed into a propositional statement. Later, a hypothesis would be formulated from the propositional statement. Rogers has asserted that learning is facilitated when the student participates responsibly in the learning process. He calls for students to contract with the teacher about what the student should do in the pursuit of knowledge. The researcher would then ask, "Given this proposition from Rogers's theory, what hypothesis or research question would be needed to study this proposition?" You might hypothesize that "Nursing students who contract for a specific grade are more likely to obtain that grade than nursing students who do not contract for a specific grade."

The testing of an existing theory, or deductive research, is definitely needed in nursing. Most researchers, however, begin with a problem that has personal relevance in their immediate work environment. This is understandable because the motivation to conduct research is usually higher if the researcher feels some personal involvement and interest in the results of the study.

Previous Research

One disadvantage in using personal experiences as the source of research problems is that this practice frequently leads to a large number of small, unrelated studies, in which there is limited generalizability of study results. Although "doing your own thing" is important in the motivation of researchers to conduct studies, the nursing profession needs researchers who are willing to replicate, or repeat, studies of other researchers. A body of knowledge should be developed on a sound foundation of research findings. If nursing practice is to be guided by research, the results of studies must be verified. Hypotheses must be tested and retested on adequate sample sizes. Replication studies, therefore, are needed. As stated in Chapter 1, replication studies involve repeating a study with all the essential elements of the original study held intact. Different samples and settings may be used. Replication studies in nursing have not been numerous, and the lack of these studies has hindered the development of a cumulative body of nursing knowledge. A cursory review of the literature in 2010 uncovered few replications studies by nurses.

For some reason, the idea of replication seems to carry a negative connotation. Students have asked, "Can a person 'copy' someone else's study? Isn't that like cheating?" During the formative years in educational settings, the dire consequences of plagiarism are continually stressed. It is quite possible that nurses' reluctance to replicate studies is related to this earlier socialization process.

The value of replication studies needs to be emphasized to beginning researchers and to experienced researchers as well. A researcher who avoids replication studies needs to ask the question, "Would I have more confidence in the results of a single study conducted with 30 subjects in one setting or the results of several similar studies using many subjects in different settings?" Fahs, Morgan, and Kalman (2003) have made a strong call for replication studies.

In addition to exact replication studies, investigations are needed that address the shortcomings of previous research. Different instruments may be used, refinements may be made in the experimental treatments, or more appropriate outcome measures may be identified.

Replication Study

Participants in a study were randomly assigned to be shown images of a nurse who was either overweight or weight appropriate (Hicks et al., 2008). They were asked to rate their confidence in the health teaching provided by that nurse. This study replicated one done in 2006 by Wells, Lever, and Austin. Results of the two studies were similar. Members of the public have higher confidence in the ability of normal-weight nurses to teach about diet and exercise in comparison to overweight nurses.

RESEARCH PROBLEM CONSIDERATIONS

Many factors should be considered when trying to decide if a certain topic is appropriate for a scientific investigation. Some of these factors include ethical issues, significance of the study for nursing, personal motivation of the researcher, qualifications of the researcher, and feasibility of the study.

Ethical Issues

One of the most important considerations in a study concerns the ethical aspects of the project. Everyone is familiar with the terrible atrocities of World War II in which prisoners were subjected to many types of inhumane treatment under the guise of research. Although ethical guidelines for research were developed after World War II, many unethical studies have been conducted since then and continue today. Some of these studies were discussed in Chapter 2.

It is the responsibility of researchers to guarantee, to the best of their ability, that their research is ethical. Investigators must be familiar with ethical guidelines of the federal government, professional organizations, and specific institutions where research is to be conducted.

Significance to Nursing

Every nursing study should have significance for nursing. This does not mean that the findings must have the capability of transforming the entire nursing profession and nursing practice. However, it may well be a nonsignificant piece of research if a common question is, "How would the results of this study influence my practice?"

The researcher should ask questions such as these: Will clients or health care professionals benefit from the findings of this study? Will the body of nursing knowledge be increased as the result of this study? Can nurses use the results? If the answers to these questions are "Yes," the problem has significance for nursing.

Personal Motivation

Personal motivation may not be the single most important deciding factor in a researcher's decision to conduct a study, but it certainly ranks high on the priority list. If a person is not interested in the problem to be investigated, it will be difficult to work up enthusiasm for the project and conduct a worthwhile study. Remember the statement by Pierce (2009) presented earlier in this chapter: Nurses should choose research questions that they "passionately want answered" (p. 156).

Without personal interest, the research process may become very tedious, and the study may never be completed. But if a researcher is intrigued and curious about the problem, research can become fascinating. The steps can become a treasure hunt. When the data are being prepared for analysis, the excitement grows and the adrenaline flows. At this stage in your understanding and familiarity with the research process, you may be having difficulty believing this. Speak with a nurse who has conducted research. Even if his or her study was conducted as a course requirement and enthusiasm was not great at the beginning of the project, it is quite likely that excitement and curiosity increased as the study progressed.

Think of questions that have arisen during your clinical experiences. Also, you may have become intrigued by something you have read about in a professional journal or textbook. Many areas in nursing need further research. It is hoped that in the near future you will find an area that is not only significant to nursing but of personal interest to you.

Researcher Qualifications

Not every nurse is qualified to conduct research. Caution must be exercised when research skills are not well developed. Inappropriate designs may be chosen and inadequate data-collection methods used.

Research is generally conducted by nurses who have received advanced educational preparation concerning research methodology. However, beginning research skills should be learned at the undergraduate level. A class research project may be conducted in which the students design a survey study and act as the subjects. Enthusiasm for research seems to rise during the course of a class project. If several sections of a research course are being taught during the same semester, the students in the various sections may want to compare their results. A spirit of healthy competition may be fostered. If clinical research is planned, the beginning researcher should collaborate with a more experienced researcher, such as a faculty member or an advanced practice nurse.

Feasibility of Study

Feasibility is an essential consideration of any research project. The researcher needs to be reasonably sure that the study can actually be carried out. Many questions need to be answered. How long will the project take? Are appropriate instruments available? Can subjects be obtained? What is the cost? Does the researcher have support for the project?

Time

A nurse might be interested in studying sibling relationships among quintuplets. Knowledge of the incidence of quintuplet births would certainly discourage anyone considering research on this particular population unless the researcher planned to make this a lifetime project! Time is always a factor to be considered. It is wise to allow more time than seems to be needed because unexpected delays frequently occur.

Cost

All research projects cost money; some studies are much more expensive than others. The researcher must consider, realistically, the financial resources available. Many sources of outside funding exist, but not nearly enough to cover all of the needed research. Some of the various sources of funding are discussed in Chapter 17.

Equipment and Supplies

"The best laid plans of mice and men oft times go astray," according to a line in Robert Burns's poem *To a Mouse.* This saying is certainly true in the research situation. The researcher can devise a study that is significant to nursing and appears feasible to conduct, and suddenly find out that there is no equipment to measure the research variables accurately. Even if equipment is available, it may not be in proper working condition. All research projects require some type of resources. Make an accurate determination of the needed equipment and supplies before making the final decision to conduct a study.

Some questions that should be asked (and answered) before beginning a research project are:

1. What equipment will be needed?
2. Is this equipment available and in proper working order?
3. Is there a qualified operator of the equipment?
4. Are the necessary supplies available or can they be obtained?

Some of the more common pieces of equipment that are used in nursing research are physiological data-gathering devices such as thermometers and stethoscopes. Also, office equipment such as computers and photocopy machines may be needed. Access to a computer is nearly always needed today, even if the amount of data is rather small. Hardly any researcher hand analyzes data today. If the researcher takes into consideration equipment and supplies in the early phases of a research project, there is less likelihood that the project will have to be revised or discarded later because of equipment or supply problems.

Administrative Support

Many research projects require administrative support. Nurses working in health care institutions, such as hospitals, may seek released time to conduct research or ask for funds to support a proposed project. Research requires time, money, and supplies. The nurse researcher will find it very difficult to conduct research independently.

Faculty research expectations and support for research by faculty members varies among educational institutions. Not only is financial support helpful, but also, in many cases, psychological support from the administration is even more helpful. Knowing that your superiors support your research efforts can be a very powerful motivating force.

Peer Support

We never outgrow our need for peer support. Many research ideas have never been developed because potential researchers received no support for their ideas from their peers. A comment such as, "Why would you want to conduct a study like that?" could discourage a researcher from proceeding with a study. One of the best ways a nurse researcher can determine a researchable problem is through interactions and discussions with other nurses. This collegial relationship is very important for the researcher, especially for the beginning researcher who has not yet developed confidence in his or her research skills. A climate of shared interest in nursing research is essential among the members of the nursing profession.

Availability of Subjects

A researcher may believe that study subjects are readily available and anxious to participate in a proposed study. Much to the researcher's surprise, this may not be the case. Potential subjects may not meet the study criteria, be unwilling to participate, or already be participating in other studies.

RESEARCH QUESTION CRITERIA

The important criteria for writing a research question are that it (a) is written in interrogative sentence form, (b) includes the population, (c) includes the variable(s), and (d) is empirically testable.

Written in Interrogative Sentence Form

The use of a question format to narrow down the research problem seems to be the clearest way to identify the problem area of a study. When questions are asked, answers are sought. If a declarative sentence is used to describe the problem area, the desire to seek an answer to the problem does not seem as clear-cut.

Consider the following two ways of expressing the same study problem:

- **Declarative form:** This study examines the relationship between the number of hours that baccalaureate nursing students have studied and their anxiety levels before the midterm examination.

- **Interrogative form:** Is there a correlation between the number of hours that baccalaureate nursing students have studied and their anxiety levels before the midterm examination?

The question format seems to demand an answer more than the declarative form. However, many problem statements in the literature are written in the declarative form.

A research question should always be stated in a complete and grammatically correct sentence. It should be stated in such a manner that the research consumer can read it, understand it, and respond to it. To get all necessary information into the research question, the sentence may become rather long. Students have made comments such as "You are asking me to write a run-on sentence" and "My English teacher would have given me a failing grade on a sentence like that." Although the research question may be long in some instances, it should always be grammatically correct. Otherwise, confusion will arise, and the research problem may be unclear.

Includes the Population

The population should be delimited (narrowed down) to the main group of interest. A population such as "nurses," "students," or "patients" is too broad to be examined. It would be better to identify these populations as "neonatal intensive care unit nurses," "baccalaureate nursing students," and "patients with a recent diagnosis of diabetes." This narrowing down of the population in the research question still does not identify the specific study population. The specific population needs to be discussed in detail in another area of the research proposal or research report. This information is usually found in the "Methods" section.

Includes the Variable(s)

The research question should contain the variable(s) to be studied. There may be one, two, or many variables examined in a study.

One-Variable Studies

When a study is of an exploratory nature and contains only one variable, it may be called a **univariate study**. An example of a research question for such a study might be "What sources of work stress are identified by thoracic intensive care unit nurses?" The single variable in this question is "sources of work stress." It is considered a variable because it is expected that the reported sources of stress will vary among the different nurses surveyed. Single-variable, or univariate, studies are frequently the beginning step in a research project. In the example just given, sources of stress might be identified in a univariate study. Another study might then be conducted to determine if a correlation exists between the number of reported sources of stress and the nurses' desire to leave the thoracic intensive care unit as a place of employment. A further study might be conducted in which one of the common stressors was controlled to determine if the desire to leave thoracic intensive care nursing would differ between the experimental group members and the control group members. These last two study suggestions each focus on two variables.

Two-Variable Studies

Generally, nursing research is concerned with more than one variable. It would be interesting to know what sources of stress are identified by thoracic intensive care unit nurses. However, it would be more important to know how these stressors affect these nurses and whether anything could be done to decrease the stressors or reduce their impact on the nurses.

Research in nursing, as well as in other disciplines, is frequently concerned with two variables. When two variables are examined, the study may be called a **bivariate study**. Generally, one of the variables is called the independent and one the dependent variable. Consider the example concerning stress among nurses in the thoracic intensive care unit. The research question might be "Is there a correlation between the number of sources of stress reported by nurses in a thoracic intensive care unit and the nurses' desire to leave employment in the thoracic intensive care unit?" In this question, the independent variable is "the number of reported sources of stress," and the dependent variable is "the desire to leave employment in the thoracic intensive care unit."

Also, consider the previous example of the study in which an attempt might be made to control or decrease one of the stressors identified by thoracic intensive care unit nurses, to determine if their desire to leave this area of employment would decrease. The identified stressor might be the nurses' unfamiliarity with the equipment in the unit. The research question might be "Is the level of desire to leave thoracic intensive care unit nursing different between a group of thoracic nurses who have attended a workshop on thoracic intensive care unit equipment and a group of thoracic nurses who have not attended the workshop?" Although the sentence is wordy, it is better to repeat words than to create any misunderstanding about what is being compared. The independent variable in this problem statement is "attendance or nonattendance at a workshop on thoracic intensive care unit equipment," and the dependent variable is "desire to leave thoracic intensive care unit nursing."

Occasionally, in a correlational study, an independent and dependent variable are not identifiable because it is not possible to determine which variable is influencing the other variable. For example, if you were examining the relationship between students' scores on a psychology test and their scores on a math test, it would not be appropriate to identify one as the independent and one as the dependent variable. You would not be able to label one of these variables as the "cause" and the other variable as the "effect."

Multiple-Variable Studies

Whenever more than two variables are examined in a study, the research can be considered as a multiple-variable, or **multivariate study**. Multiple-variable research is becoming increasingly common in nursing. Frequently, it is the interaction of variables that is of interest. For example, a researcher might conduct a study to determine why clients do not take their medications as directed after they are discharged. Educational levels might be considered as the influential factor, and the researcher may believe that the patients with high levels of education will be more compliant with the medical regimen than patients with low levels of education. Quite likely the results of the study will not support this belief. Why? Many factors may be influencing the person's medication compliance behavior. People may consider themselves as "weak" and lacking control over their bodies if they have to take medications. Also, a relative of the client may view the medicine favorably or unfavorably. The medication may be expensive. The likelihood exists that a variety of factors may be influencing the client's compliance behavior.

Why do nursing students pass or fail the national licensing examination? Is there just one factor involved, such as grade-point average? Or could many factors be influential, such as the amount of time studied, the motivation to be a nurse, and the amount of time slept the night before the examination?

Empirically Testable

Testable research questions contain variables that can be measured by the researcher. For a research question to be empirically testable, empirical data must be available about the variable(s) of interest. As you remember, empirical data consist of data gathered through the sense organs. These data consist of observations that are made through hearing, sight, touch, taste, or smell. Additional equipment to aid our senses also may be used. This equipment might be thermometers, scales, or stethoscopes.

Ethical and value issues, or "right" and "wrong" decisions, are not appropriate for scientific research. Consider these research questions: "Should patients be allowed to have an unlimited number of visitors?" "What is the best way to teach nursing students about the research process?" These are not researchable questions. Scientific studies do not concern values or ethical issues. A good way to detect a value question is to look for words like "should" and "better." The two previous examples could be changed to testable research questions in the following manner: "Is there a difference in the anxiety levels of patients between those who are allowed an unlimited number of visitors and those who are allowed visitors only at specified visiting hours?" and "Is there a difference between the final examination scores of nursing research students who are taught by a lecture method and those who are taught by a seminar method?"

It is also better to avoid words like "cause" and "effect." Rather than writing a research question that says, "What is the effect of room temperature on the oral temperature measurements of children?" change this question to, "Is there a difference in the oral temperature measurements of a group of children in a room where the temperature is kept at 65°F in comparison to the oral temperature measurements of this same group of children when the room temperature is kept at 75°F?" Although investigators are interested in cause-and-effect relationships, causality is difficult to prove and, therefore, it is better to avoid using this word or similar words in the research question statement or hypothesis of a study.

RESEARCH QUESTION FORMAT

The following material is presented to help you learn how to write research questions. Please do not consider these examples as the *only* way to present research questions. These examples are a combination of my ideas and thoughts about research and other researchers' ideas and beliefs. Some of my students have called me the "Research Guru." I am not! You are reading my ideas and thoughts about research in this textbook, but others have ideas and beliefs that are equal or superior to mine.

Research questions for studies that examine more than one variable are usually written as correlational statements or comparative statements.

I. **Correlational Statement**

Format: Is there a correlation between X (independent variable) and Y (dependent variable) in the population?

Example: Is there a correlation between *anxiety* and *midterm examination scores* of baccalaureate nursing students?

II. **Comparative Statement**

A. Descriptive Study

Format: Is there a difference in Y (dependent variable) between people in the population who *have X* characteristic (independent variable) and those who *do not have X* characteristic?

Example: Is there a difference in *readiness to learn about preoperative teaching* between preoperative patients who *have high anxiety levels* compared to preoperative patients who *have low anxiety levels*?

B. Experimental Study

Format: Is there a difference in *Y* (dependent variable) between Group A who *received X* (independent variable) and Group B who *did not receive X*?

Example: Is there a difference in the *preoperative anxiety levels* of patients who were *taught relaxation techniques* compared to those patients who were *not taught relaxation techniques*?

Practice substituting other variables for the *X* and *Y* in the examples. You will soon be able to formulate research questions with greater ease.

It may appear that there are two independent variables in the research question for the descriptive and experimental studies. Both of these research questions have only *one* independent variable, but the independent variable has two levels or subdivisions. In the descriptive study, the two levels of the independent variable are "high anxiety" and "low anxiety." In the experimental study, the two levels of the independent variable are "taught relaxation techniques" and "not taught relaxation techniques."

As you may have noticed, these research questions are written in a neutral, nonpredictive form. The descriptive study question could have been written, "Are preoperative patients who have high anxiety levels less ready to learn about preoperative teaching than preoperative patients who have low anxiety levels?" There are several reasons for leaving the research question neutral or nonpredictive. The researcher may have very little information about the study area or little knowledge about the possible results of a study when the research question is written. It is advisable to conduct a review of the literature and then develop a theoretical or conceptual framework for the study. With this background, a hypothesis can then be written that predicts the expected study results. The prediction should be put in the hypothesis, not in the research question.

CRITIQUING PROBLEM STATEMENTS, PURPOSE STATEMENTS, AND RESEARCH QUESTIONS

The initial task of the reader of a research article is to determine the problem of the study. The reader will need to locate the problem statement, purpose statement, or research question. The research report may also contain study objectives or goals. This information should be presented at the beginning of a research report. It is often found in the abstract, but also should be presented in the body of the article, usually at the end of the introductory section. If the problem statement, purpose statement, or research question is not clearly stated early in the research report, it will be difficult for the reader to proceed further in evaluating the study.

Purpose statements and research questions are easily identifiable in a research report because they are labeled as such. As mentioned in Chapter 3, all recent research articles in *Nursing Research* contain a purpose statement. Problem statements may not be as easy to locate. A more general statement about the study problem may be located, such as this statement found in a study report by Roos, Kärner, and Hallert (2009): "Uncertainty exists as to whether GI symptoms may explain the poorer treatment outcome of women with CD (celiac disease)" (p. 196).

Once information about this area of a research report is located, certain guidelines may be used for evaluation purposes. First, the reader should determine if there is a problem statement, purpose statement, or research question early in the research report, and is the problem area narrowed down in one of these statements or questions? The scope of the problem is also considered. Is the problem area too narrow or too broad? It may appear that the researcher tried to study too many variables in one study. The problem statement, purpose statement, or research question should contain both the population and the variable(s) that will be studied. It should be apparent that the study was either quantitative or qualitative. The possibility of gathering empirical data on the topic of interest should be evident. Determination should then be made about the ethical nature of the study. Next, the reader must consider the significance of the problem area to nursing. Box 5–1 lists the questions to be asked while evaluating this area of a research report.

**Box 5–1. Guidelines for Critiquing Problem Statements,
Purpose Statements, and Research Questions**

Based on the problem statement, purpose statement, or research question:

1. Is the research problem area clear?
2. Is their a succinct problem statement, purpose statement, or research question?
3. Are the study variables and the population included?
4. Can a determination be made as to whether the study was a quantitative or qualitative study?
5. Can a decision be made that empirical data were gathered on the topic of interest?
6. Does it appear that the study was ethical?
7. Is the feasibility of the study evident?
8. Is the significance of the study to nursing apparent?

SUMMARY

The selection of a research problem is probably the most important and most difficult step in the research process. Some of the most common sources of research ideas are personal experiences, literature sources, existing theories, and previous studies. Nurses need to conduct replication studies based on previous nursing research investigations.

Several criteria should be considered in determining a problem to study. First, ethical issues must be considered. Second, the problem should be significant to nursing. Third, personal motivation to conduct the study should be present. Fourth, the researcher's qualifications must be considered. Finally, the feasibility of the study must be considered. How long will the project take? How much will it cost? Can the needed equipment and supplies be obtained? Does the researcher have administrative and peer support for the project? Is a study sample available?

The research problem area should be narrowed down to a research question. The question should contain the population and variables that are being studied, and be empirically testable. The use of a question format is a clear way to identify the problem area for a study. Questions demand answers. Another way to make a research question concise is by delimiting or narrowing down the population for the study. Also, the variables under study must be clearly identified. One, two, or many variables may be studied.

Studies may be referred to as **univariate, bivariate,** or **multivariate** studies, according to whether one, two, or many variables are being studied. There is an increasing emphasis on multivariate research because nursing is concerned with the relationships between many combinations of variables. Testable research questions contain variables that can be measured empirically. Empirical data consist of data gathered through the sense organs. Scientific research questions do not concern value or ethical issues. Research problems that examine more than one variable are usually written in the form of a correlational statement or comparative statement.

NURSING RESEARCH ON THE WEB

For additional online resources, research activities, and exercises, go to **www.mynursingkit.com.** Select Chapter 5 from the drop-down menu.

GET INVOLVED ACTIVITIES

1. Gather in groups of four to six people and practice writing research questions. Place the research questions on the blackboard and take turns presenting them to the rest of the group.
2. Bring in research articles that contain problem statements/purpose statements/research questions. Have volunteers read their statements. Pick the most appropriate statement.
3. Are more of the statements written as problem statements, purpose statements, or as research questions?
4. Rewrite, in interrogatory form, some of the declarative problem statements/purpose statements that were brought to the group.
5. Think of a problem to address that is not appropriate for research because it is an ethical or value issue (such as "Should all nurses work 12-hour shifts?").
6. Change the problem area of Activity 5 into a researchable problem area.

SELF-TEST

Evaluate the following research questions. Select answer A, B, C, or D according to the presence of the necessary elements of an acceptable research question.

A. The population is missing.
B. The dependent variable is missing.
C. The independent variable is missing.
D. All elements are present.

____ 1. Is there a correlation between fathers' heights and their sons' heights?

____ 2. Is there a difference in the level of assertiveness between men and women?

____ 3. Is there a difference in anxiety levels after a relaxation exercise?

____ 4. Is there a correlation between exercise and weight loss?

____ 5. Is there a relationship between the self-concept of baccalaureate nursing students and their level of career aspirations?

____ 6. Is there a difference in pregnant women who attend prenatal classes and those who do not attend prenatal classes?

____ 7. Is there a difference in the anxiety levels of preoperative patients after practicing relaxation exercises?

____ 8. Is there a correlation between anxiety levels and pulse rates?

____ 9. Is there a difference in people who have exercised and those who have not exercised?

____ 10. Is there a difference in the birth weight of infants?

REFERENCES

Fahs, P. S., Morgan, L. L., & Kalman, M. (2003). A call for replication. *Journal of Nursing Scholarship, 35*, 67–71.

Hicks, M., McDermott, L. L., Rouhana, N., Schmidt, M., Seymour, M. W., & Sullivan, T. (2008). Nurses' body size and public confidence in ability to provide health education. *Journal of Nursing Scholarship, 40*, 349–354.

Pierce, L. L. (2009). Twelve steps for success in the nursing research journey. *The Journal of Continuing Education in Nursing, 40*, 154–161.

Rogers, C. (1969). *Freedom to learn.* Columbus, OH: Charles E. Merrill.

Roos, S., Kärner, A., & Hallert, C. (2009). Gastrointestinal symptoms and well-being of adults living on a gluten-free diet. *Gastroenterology, 32*, 196–201.

Sharts-Hopko, N. C. (2000). *Journal of the Association of Nurses in AIDS Care, 11*, 86–88.

Wells, M., Lever, D., & Austin, E. N. (2006). The effect of the nurse's body size on client confidence in the nurse's ability to provide health education on diet and exercise. Unpublished manuscript, State University of New York, Binghamton.

CHAPTER 6

Review of the Literature

OUTLINE

OBJECTIVES

On completion of this chapter, you will be prepared to:

1. Determine the purposes for the literature review
2. Recognize the need for becoming familiar with the library's services
3. Distinguish between primary and secondary sources in research literature
4. Recognize the importance of grey literature
5. Discuss print resources that may be used in locating literature references
6. Discuss electronic sources that may be used in locating literature references
7. Compare electronic sources that are useful for nurses when conducting a literature review
8. Obtain references from online journals
9. Conduct a literature search on a given topic
10. Extract pertinent information from literature sources
11. Critique the literature review section of research articles

NEW TERMS DEFINED IN THIS CHAPTER

abstracts, pg 72

e-journals, pg 77

e-zines, pg 77

grey literature, pg 72

indexes, pg 72

primary source, pg 71

secondary source, pg 71

Writing about reviewing the literature is a challenge; the information becomes somewhat outdated almost as soon as you read it. With the help of a librarian friend, I have tried to bring the information up to date, as of May 2010.

This chapter presents information on the purposes of a literature review, use of the library, primary and secondary reference sources, grey literature, print sources, electronic sources, online databases, online journals, and how to obtain information from literature sources. This textbook presents more information on electronic sources than in previous editions. The Internet has made conducting a literature review much more manageable than when this author was a student. At that time, hours were spent in the library perusing printed copies of journal articles and books; many more hours were spent copying material from these sources. With the advent of the Internet, libraries are as close as your computer.

The Internet, as you know, is a connection of millions of computers around the world. Information travels over the Internet through a variety of languages, known as protocols. The World Wide Web (WWW), or the Web, is a part of the Internet. It is a collection of media resources accessible through the Internet. The Web uses the hypertext transfer protocol (HTTP). Browsers are used to connect to the Web. Throughout this chapter, the term Web is used rather than Internet because you are referred to specific sites on the Web. Remember, however, that the Web is ever changing. A site that you visit today may be totally different (or disappear) in a short period of time. Apologies are given to you today for any sites that you cannot access on the date that you try to obtain information from them.

The material here is presented as if you were preparing to conduct a literature review for a proposed study. However, the information may be used to conduct a review of the literature for any paper you might write or project you might conduct. The chapter closes with a section on how to critique the literature review section of a research article.

PURPOSES OF THE LITERATURE REVIEW

There are many purposes for reviewing the literature before conducting a research study. The most important one is to determine what is already known about the topic that you wish to study. Research is an ongoing process that builds on previous knowledge. There are very few topics so rare that they have never been investigated.

The researcher generally begins the literature review with a study topic in mind. Occasionally, a literature source serves as the basis for the study topic. Many published studies contain recommendations for future research; therefore, the idea for a study may actually be formed while reading a published study report. Regardless of the basis for the topic, existing knowledge of the topic is determined by a review of the literature. A search is made to locate previous studies in that area. If previous research is found, the researcher must decide whether to replicate a study or examine another aspect of the problem. The review of the literature is necessary, therefore, to narrow the problem to be studied. As you may recall from Chapter 4, the review of the literature may not be conducted at the beginning of some qualitative studies.

Once the researcher is familiar with the existing literature, a framework must be established in which to place the study results. In a quantitative study, this involves locating theoretical or conceptual formulations that will help guide the study. The research hypotheses or questions will be based on the theoretical or conceptual framework of the study, and the research findings will be interpreted in light of the study framework. Therefore, the literature review can help locate a framework for the proposed study.

Another purpose of the review of the literature is to help plan the study methodology. Appropriate research methods and research tools for the study may be selected after reading the accounts of other studies. The researcher may be able to capitalize on the successes as well as the failures of other investigators.

Nurses in the United States are particularly fortunate because of the vast amount of published material in the field of nursing. When conducting a review of the literature, nurses may wish there were not so much material! However, nurses in many countries are envious of our resources because they have only a few nursing journals published in their native language.

USE OF THE LIBRARY

As time passes, fewer and fewer nurses and nursing students are making use of libraries. Even though the Internet and Web are absolutely astounding in their ability to retrieve information, please don't give up your trips to the library! Libraries contain a wealth of information. There is a feeling that you get in a library that you probably will not experience in any other location. It is almost like a place of reverence!

If you are unfamiliar with a particular library to which you have access, acquaint yourself with that library's facilities and holdings. Tour the library and consult the staff. Librarians are usually delighted to familiarize you with the use of the card catalog (generally online), numerous databases, and various search strategies. The librarian can inform you about hours of operation, photocopy services, checkout policies, and interlibrary loan materials available from other cooperating libraries.

Librarians are trained professionals who locate and assess information, and the libraries where they work often hold valuable resources (Hallyburton & St. John, 2010). Librarians can help you locate millions of items that you might not find, even with the best Internet search engine (Wink, 2009). If you are searching for a health science library in your area, http://nnlm.gov is a Web site that provides locations for these libraries.

Collaboration between clinicians and librarians is particularly important in this day of evidence-based practice. According to Vrabel (2005), the librarian may be very helpful when you are searching for high levels of evidence such as controlled trials and systematic reviews. Librarians can also help nurses find practice guidelines. Billings and Kowalski (2009) wrote that librarians can provide a great deal of help in locating information that is pertinent for clinical nursing practice. As Arndt and McGowan (2009) stated, "Librarians are aware of the differences that exist between surfing the Web and searching a database" (p. 360). Krom, Batten, and Bautista (2010) discussed collaboration among a clinical nurse specialist, health science librarian, and staff nurse on an evidence-based practice (EBP) initiative carried out in a hospital in Connecticut. The health science librarian was considered an expert in retrieving information from the literature. This collaborative project was successful, and a suggestion was made to use it in other medical facilities seeking to educate staff nurses about EBP.

PRIMARY AND SECONDARY SOURCES

Literature sources may be classified as primary or secondary sources. A **primary source** in the research literature is a description of a research study written by the original investigator(s). A **secondary source** is a summary or description of a research study written by someone other than the study investigator(s).

Primary sources for studies are frequently found in journal articles. For example, the journal *Nursing Research* publishes research study results written by the original investigator(s). Other journals that contain primary sources for nursing studies include *Advances in Nursing Science, Applied Nursing Research, Biological Research for Nursing, Clinical Nursing Research, Nursing Science Quarterly, Research in Gerontological Nursing, Research in Nursing and Health, Western Journal of Nursing Research, and Worldviews on Evidence-Based Nursing.* Many clinical journals, such as *Heart & Lung: The Journal of Acute and Critical Care* and *Pediatric Nursing,* also contain research reports. Chapter 17 lists additional journals.

The beginning researcher may be tempted to rely on secondary sources. Oftentimes, summaries of studies or theories are quicker to read and easier to understand than the original works. Secondary sources may provide valuable insight into the material, but it is the original or primary source that should be read, when possible. There is always a danger that the author of a secondary source may misinterpret information or leave out important information that might be valuable to the reader.

Try to begin your search with the most recent primary sources. Read the abstract or summary of the study to determine if the source should be read in depth. These primary sources will frequently contain reference citations for earlier research reports that may be relevant to your proposed study.

GREY LITERATURE

Grey literature, also called *gray* literature, can be defined as any document that is not commercially published and is not usually indexed or made available in the major databases. Grey literature generally includes conference proceedings, dissertations, theses, technical reports, and unpublished research reports. Many research reports never get published because there were no significant findings. Researchers are reluctant to submit a manuscript for this type of study because journal reviewers are unlikely to recommend publication of these manuscripts. Finally, journal editors are less likely to publish non-significant findings than significant findings. Because of this publication bias, grey literature has become increasingly important, particularly in systematic reviews and meta-analysis studies. Some Web sites assist individuals who are searching for grey literature. The New York Academy of Medicine Library provides a bimonthly report of grey literature in health services research and certain public health topics (http://nyam.org/library/pages/grey_literature_report).

PRINT SOURCES

Although print sources are being accessed less often than in the past, all nurses need to be familiar with these sources. Some literature can be obtained only through the print format because the information has not yet been included in an electronic form. Two types of print sources are indexes and abstracts.

Indexes contain reference materials on periodicals and some books. Printed indexes are library resources that provide assistance in obtaining journal articles and other publications related to a topic of interest.

The *Cumulative Index to Nursing & Allied Health Literature* (CINAHL) was first published in 1961. It covers nursing and allied health journals, including the fields of dental hygiene, medical records, nutrition and dietetics, occupational therapy, physical therapy, physician's assistant, and respiratory therapy. The title of the index was *Cumulative Index to Nursing Literature* until 1977, when the decision was made to include allied health literature and, thus, change the name of the index. Nurses used the print version of this database for many years. These indexes were called "the red books," for an obvious reason. Print indexes are rarely used today. Recently, a library posted an advertisement asking for someone to take some issues of their print collection off of their hands because it was taking up too much space! There are now several online versions of this index (*CINAHL® Database, CINAHL® Plus; CINAHL® with Full Text, CINAHL® Plus with Full Text* (see the Online Databases section).

Index Medicus is a well-known index of medical literature. It includes nursing and some other allied health fields. It was first published in 1879. After 1997, use of the print index decreased rapidly. The print version was discontinued in 2004. This database can be searched online through MEDLINE.

Abstracts contain brief summaries of articles. Research abstracts contain the purpose, methods, and major findings of studies. By reading abstracts of studies, the researcher can determine whether to obtain a copy of the entire research study.

From 1960 to 1978, *Nursing Research Abstracts* were published in the bimonthly issues of *Nursing Research.* Each November/December issue contained an author and subject guide to the abstracts published during the previous year in *Nursing Research.*

The American Psychological Association has published *Psychological Abstracts* since 1927. It covers abstracts dating from 1973 and covers 1,300 professional journals. These abstracts cover material in the field of psychology and related disciplines and include certain psychologically-oriented articles from nursing journals. The abstracts include summaries of journal articles, technical reports, and books. Many libraries carry the CD-ROM version of *PsychLIT*®—a two-CD set that is updated quarterly and includes more than 670,000 records.

A comprehensive abstracting source for doctoral dissertations, *Dissertation Abstracts International* (DAI) has been published since 1938. The authors of the dissertations write their own abstracts, and all abstracts written since 1980 are approximately 350 words each.

Master Abstracts International (MAI) contains author-written 150-word abstracts of master's theses. Because master's abstracts are submitted voluntarily, only a small percentage of abstracts from U.S. master's theses appear in MAI.

Previous editions of this textbook gave fairly detailed descriptions of the printed indexes and abstracts that were most important to nurses. However, nurses seldom use these printed sources of literature information today because of the availability of electronic sources.

ELECTRONIC SOURCES

As previously mentioned, electronic sources have become the preferred format for accessing the literature. Electronic communication is changing how information is retrieved and disseminated, and it is also impacting the communication of research results. Electronic sources include online catalogs and online databases.

Online Catalogs

In most libraries, that wonderful old piece of furniture called the "card catalog" has disappeared. It has been replaced with computer terminals. Users are able to determine the holdings of their particular library (as well as other libraries) through this medium. The online catalog contains an alphabetical listing of books under several different categories such as title, author, subject heading, and keyword. A keyword search finds the word(s) anywhere in the item record; this type of search is much broader than a subject heading search. The records obtained in a keyword search are usually arranged by relevance rather than alphabetically.

For some time, libraries have been aware that they cannot function as independent units and still provide optimum service to their clientele. No one library can afford all of the holdings that might be desired. Library networks help librarians determine whether to purchase certain books and also allow them to inform library users of the location of reference materials.

A listing of books held by libraries throughout the world may be obtained through the Online Computer Library Center (OCLC). OCLC is a nonprofit, membership computer library service and research organization that was founded in 1967 by university presidents for the purpose of sharing library resources, and, therefore, reducing costs. An online-shared cataloging system has been available since 1971. The OCLC Interlibrary Loan service allows libraries to borrow and lend through an online network of libraries. The services of OCLC are not available directly to individuals. These services must be accessed through libraries.

The OCLC database contained more than 1.5 billion records in May 2010 (http://oclc.org/us/en/worldcat/statistics/default.htm). A record is added every 10 seconds. These records are received from more than 72,000 libraries. WorldCat holds tens of millions of bibliographic records that represent more than 1 billion items, and covers hundreds of languages. WorldCat is a unique database because most of the content is input by librarians around the world whose home institutions are part of the OCLC membership.

One of the more recent innovations in accessing books is called e-books. Check with your local library to determine what services they offer concerning e-books. Some of the vendors for these books include NetLibrary and Ebrary. You may also want to search Google Scholar to discover the location of scholarly books and how they can be accessed.

Online Databases

For those who own personal computers, it is possible to access databases without using the physical resources of the library. If you are a student, you will probably be able to use a microcomputer at home to tie in with the online services at your university. Some universities allow students to have free accounts that provide access to the Web. Many health care institutions also provide this type of service for their employees. You might also purchase online services yourself through a commercial vendor. The numbers of online databases that are free to the public, such as PubMed and ERIC, are increasing each year.

The Web is a massive collection of files. These files are called pages. A browser is needed to access these pages. Popular browsers are Internet Explorer, Chrome, and Firefox. If you are unsure of the source you wish to access, you need to use a search engine, such as Yahoo, Google, Lycos, WebCrawler, AltaVista, Excite, Scirus, or Google Scholar to search the Web for you. You may want to use more than one search engine because no engine indexes all of the material on the Web. Megasearch engines, such as Bing, Comodo Dragon, Dogpile, Mamma, Metacrawler, and SurfWax, have been developed. These megasearch engines combine results from many search engines.

If you know exactly where you wish to go on the Web, you need to enter the URL (Uniform Resource Locator) of the source. These usually begin with http (HyperText Transfer Protocol). It is generally not necessary to type the http part of the URL. The browser automatically assumes that the URL begins with http. Some URLs are case sensitive, so be aware of the need for capital letters for some addresses. One part of the URL indicates the domain name. Three initials at the end of the URL, after the dot, are used to designate the various domains. For example, "com" is used for commercial organizations, "edu" is used for educational institutions, "gov" denotes government institutions, "org" is used for such agencies as professional societies and charities, and "mil" indicates military sites. There were six domains in 1987; today, the number of domains is in the hundreds. In March 2010, Wikipedia listed 21 top-level domains. Because of the huge amount of material on the Web, new domains have been developed, and more are being proposed. Two fairly new domains are "museum" and "travel."

Before beginning a computer-assisted search, the researcher must define and narrow the topic. A well-designed search strategy will result in more relevant "hits" on the Web. Searches, however, for a variety of reasons, may not provide the desired references. Many search engines now have advanced search tools or terms that can be used in a search. These include limiters such as "and/or/not/," "as a phrase," "without the word," "date limiters," and "language limiters."

Finding information on the Web may be time consuming and unpredictable because there are so many sites and Web pages. Currently, there is no official gatekeeper for the Web. Therefore, care must be exercised when accessing information from this medium.

As of May 2010, there were 206,026,787 sites (http://Netcraft.com). Netcraft is an Internet services company based in Bath, England that conducts monthly surveys of sites. Although the number of sites has continued to increase nearly every year since 1995, there was a slight decrease in sites between February 2010 and May 2010 (207,316,960 to 206,026,787).

Specific online databases are discussed next. There are many online databases that are reliable and accurate. Some of those considered to be most useful to nurses are described here. In contrast to the print versions of these databases, the online versions contain abstracts for most of the entries and full-text versions for an increasing number of journal articles.

Note that it is wise to search in more than one database. If the identical search term is used when exploring two different databases, you may obtain quite different results. A group of researchers conducted a literature search for references on alcohol consumption and the risk of breast cancer and large bowel cancer (Lemeshow, Blum, Berlin, Stoto, & Colditz, 2005). They had to search many databases before they obtained most of the sources that they believed were relevant. They searched these databases: MEDLINE, Embase, Biosis, DISSERTATION ABSTRACTS ONLINE, ETOH, and SCI EXPANDED-SSCI. They also conducted hand searches of the reference lists of sources that they located.

CINAHL Databases

There are four CINAHL online databases. These databases provide records from journals as well as from books, book chapters, pamphlets, audiovisuals and educational software, nursing dissertations, conference proceedings, and standards of professional practice. Check with the library of your academic or health care institution to determine which databases are available to you. These databases are made accessible through commercial vendors who use Internet "platforms" to transmit information. EBSCO Publishing provides services through EBSCO*host* and Wolters Kluwer Health provides services through *Ovid*.

Subjects may be searched via the CINAHL Subject Heading List. These subject headings follow the structure of the Medical Subject Headings (MeSH) used by the National Library of Medicine (NLM). However, many individuals try to type in a key term or phrase and see what happens (this author is guilty!).

The following information on the four CINAHL databases was obtained on March 22, 2010 from EBSCO*host* (http://www.ebscohost.com/academic).

CINAHL® Database   The *CINAHL Database* is the basic CINAHL database. This database indexes more than 2,980 journals, dating back to 1981, and contains more than 2 million records. It provides more than 70 full-text journals and also contains clinical innovations, critical paths, drug records, research instruments, and clinical trials.

CINAHL® Plus   The *CINAHLPlus* database contains every feature of the basic database. Coverage dates back to 1937, rather than 1981. The database has more than 4,300 indexed journals, and provides access to nearly 80 full-text journals. Evidence-Based Care Sheets are also available in full-text format.

CINAHL® with Full Text   Just like the basic database, the *CINAH with Full Text* database indexes more than 2,980 journals. However, this database provides full text for more than 600 journals. Citations date back to1981.

CINAHL® Plus with Full Text   One of the newest databases relevant to nursing is the *CINAHL Plus with Full Text* database. This database contains material similar to *CINAH Plus*. It indexes more than 4,300 journals and provides access to more than 760 full-text journals. Records date back to 1937. Many libraries are acquiring this database because of its superiority to the other CINAHL databases.

Registry of Nursing Research

Sigma Theta Tau International Honor Society of Nursing makes this database available through its Virginia Henderson International Nursing Library. Access to the database has been made easy for users to obtain evidence and scientific findings from abstracts of research studies, conference presentations, practice innovations, and evidence-based projects. The research abstracts can be found through several search fields: title of the study, last name of the primary investigator, and key word(s) in the abstract. Free access to this database can be found at http://nursinglibrary.org/.

MEDLINE Databases

The following three MEDLINE databases are discussed: *MEDLINE®*, *MEDLINE® with Full Text*, and *Medline® Plus.*

MEDLINE®   (Medical Literature Analysis and Retrieval System Online) This database provides access to journals in the life sciences, with a concentration on biomedicine. It also includes information from nursing, dentistry, veterinary medicine, and pharmacy. *MEDLINE* became available in 1971. Material is available for more than 5,400 biomedical journals published in the United States and 80 other countries. Although coverage is worldwide, most records are obtained from English-language sources or have abstracts in English. Thousands of records are added each Tuesday through Saturday.

MEDLINE is available through the National Library of Medicine (NLM). This free database is accessible through PubMed. You may access Pub Med directly at http://pubmed.gov. This retrieval system was developed by the National Center for Biotechnology Information (NCBI) at the NLM.

A search of *MEDLINE* can be done using the MeSH (Medical Subject Headings) controlled vocabulary or by author name, title word, text word, journal name, phrase, or any combination of these. The search provides a citation that includes authors, title, and source. An abstract is often included. Full-text is available for some articles.

MEDLINE® with Full Text   *MEDLINE with Full Text* is the world's most comprehensive source for full-text articles from medical journals. It provides full text for more than 1,450 journals indexed in *MEDLINE*. Coverage dates back to 1949, with full-text material back to 1965.

Medline® Plus   *MedlinePlus* is the NLM's free Web site for consumer health information. This database became operational in 1998. It covers more than 800 topics of interest to health care consumers, and new links are added continually. It is available at http://www.nlm.nih.gov/medlineplus/. Material is available in more than 40 languages. You can find the most comprehensible material in the "Easy-to-Read" area of the Web site. Go to the site, click on "Health Topics," then click on "Easy-to-Read." This takes you to "Easy-to-Read beginning with A." The topics are in alphabetical order. Materials are usually written at the 5th to 6th grade reading level.

Cochrane Database of Systematic Review

The Cochrane Reviews database is available directly from the Cochrane Library at http://www.cochrane.org/reviews/. The database is published by the Cochrane Collaboration, which is an international network of individuals and institutions that prepare, maintain, and disseminate systematic reviews of the effects of health care. More than 4,000 reviews are available.

The Cochrane Collaboration was established in 1993 and named after Archie Cochrane (1909–1988), a British epidemiologist. Cochrane suggested that because health care resources would always be limited, we should use treatments that have been shown to be effective. He stressed the importance of using evidence from randomized controlled trials (RCTs).

Once you access this database, you will probably go back many times. Cochrane reviews examine the best evidence that is available in the literature about health care interventions. These reviews examine the evidence for and against the effectiveness of certain treatments (medications, surgery, education, etc.) for many health care problems such as breast cancer. Abstracts are available free of charge on the Cochrane Library Web site. Data from studies are often combined statistically in a meta-analysis. A meta-analysis statistically combines the results of several studies that have examined the same topic (see Chapter 15).

When the Cochrane database was accessed on May 5, 2010, a recent review was found that examined the difference in smoking cessation rate between individuals who gradually reduced smoking and those who quit abruptly. The review included results from 10 studies and a total of 3,760 participants. Now, maybe your curiosity is aroused enough for you to go to the Web site and see if you can find the results!

ERIC

The ERIC database is the world's largest source of education information. It is sponsored by the Institute of Education Sciences (IES) of the U.S. Department of Education. ERIC provides a comprehensive, easy-to-use, Internet-based bibliographic and full-text database of education research and education-related information. This database contains more than 1.3 million bibliographic records (March 2010) of journal articles and other education-based material, as well as some links to full-text articles. Hundreds of records are added each week. Free public access to this database is available at http://eric.ed.gov/.

PsycINFO

The American Psychological Association prepares the PsycINFO database. It covers literature from psychology and related disciplines, one of which is nursing. It now contains quite a few nursing journals, such as *Advances in Nursing Science, Cancer Nursing, Clinical Nursing Research, Journal of Nursing Measurement, Journal of Nursing Scholarship,* and *Nursing Research.* This database contains more than 2.8 million records dating from the 1800s to the present and is updated weekly. Records are selected from nearly 2,457 journals, as of March 2010. You will probably be able to access this database through your school or health care institution. Individuals may also purchase a 24-hour search, which cost $11.95 in October 2010. This service is available at http://apa.org/pubs/databases/access/direct.aspx.

Dissertation Abstracts Online
DISSERTATION ABSTRACTS ONLINE is produced by ProQuest Information and Learning. Degree-granting institutions submit copies of dissertations and theses to University Microfilms International (UMI). Citations for these dissertations and theses are included in the online database and in four UMI print publications: *Dissertation Abstracts International* (DAI), *American Doctoral Dissertations* (ADD), *Comprehensive Dissertations Index* (CDI), and *Masters Abstracts International* (MAI). A search can be done by subject, title, or author to nearly every American dissertation accepted at an accredited institution since 1861. It contains more than 2.2 million records. Selected master's theses have been included since 1962. Abstracts are included for doctoral dissertations from July 1980 and for master's theses from January 1988.

ProQuest Nursing & Allied Health Source™
ProQuest Nursing & Allied Health Source provides reliable health care information that covers nursing, allied health, and alternative and complementary medicine. This database meets the needs of researchers at health care facilities, as well as academic institutions for nursing and allied health programs. Abstracting and indexing are provided for more than 850 titles, with 715 titles in full text.

Other Online Databases
Many other online databases can be searched for free by nurses. These include the following:

AIDS*info* (HIV/AIDS Information) (http://aidsinfo.nih.gov/)

Haz-Map (Hazardous Agents) (http://hazmap.nlm.nih.gov/)

ClinicalTrials (database on access to clinical trials) (http://clinicaltrials.gov)

TOXNET (Toxicology Data Network) (http://toxnet.nlm.nih.gov/)

Online Journals

An increasing number of journals are available both in print and online. Some are available only online. Online journals are often called **e-journals**. Online magazines are called **e-zines**. An e-journal is a digital periodical published on the Internet or Web. E-journals are becoming a means of meeting the increased demands for immediate knowledge dissemination. The process of preparation and review of manuscripts is essentially the same as with print journals; it is the means of submission and dissemination that is different. A fee is usually charged for online access to full-text articles. Knowing that many financially strapped students are reading this textbook, Table 6–1 presents *free* online journals. Each issue of *OJIN* (*Online Journal of Issues in Nursing*) is made available to members of the American Nurses Association first. All viewers are then able to read a particular issue when the next issue of the journal is posted. For example, the January issue of *OJIN* is made available to all viewers in May of that year.

At http://nursingcenter.com you can view the table of contents of the most current issue of more than 50 nursing journals. Also, a sample of the content of the journal articles is available if you click on the individual articles in the table of contents. Some of the journals available are *American Journal of Nursing, Advances in Nursing Science, Cancer Nursing, Dimensions of Critical Care Nursing, Holistic Nursing Practice, Journal of Cardiovascular Nursing, Journal of Hospice and Palliative Nursing, Journal of Nursing Administration, MCN: The American Journal of Maternal Child Nursing, Nursing*

TABLE 6–1 Free Online Journals/Magazines

Journal/Magazine	URL
Imprint (magazine for nursing students)	http://www.nsna.org (click on Publications)
Internet Journal of Advanced Nursing Practice	http://ispub.com
Journal of Undergraduate Nursing Scholarship	http://juns.nursing.arizona.edu
Online Journal of Issues in Nursing	http://nursingworld.org/ojin
Online Journal of Nursing Informatics	http://ojni.org
Online Journal of Rural Nursing and Health Care	http://www.rno.org/journal
Southern Online Journal of Nursing Research	http://snrs.org/publications/journal.html

Management, and *Nursing Research.* Some of these journals allow full access to articles that are set up for continuing education (CE) credit.

Over the next few years, articles from many medical journals will be available online and free of charge. These articles will be made available immediately and up to several months or years after their original publication date. The unrestricted access to scientific knowledge is becoming a new standard in publishing. Participating journals include the *Journal of the American Medical Association* (JAMA), *New England Journal of Medicine,* and *Annals of Internal Medicine.* Some articles from back issues of these journals are already available. For more information, visit http://freemedicaljournals.com.

OBTAINING INFORMATION FROM LITERATURE SOURCES

After literature sources are located, pertinent material must be extracted from these sources. This can be a formidable task. Some people try to avoid this task as long as possible by printing every article on a certain topic. However, the researcher must finally read the literature sources and decide what material is appropriate for the study under consideration.

Before recording bibliographic material such as the author's name or title of the report, determine the requirement for reference citations in your particular school or class. The American Psychological Association (APA) (2010) format has become quite popular in the nursing literature, and many nursing education programs use APA style.

A great deal of psychological pain will be avoided if complete reference material is recorded for each literature source. It is frustrating to have to return to the library or go back on the Web to search for missing items (such as volume numbers). You may discover that some part of the reference citation is missing as you are hurrying to complete your paper at 2 A.M. in the morning before the paper is due. The motto is "Record references accurately" (RRA). If you use direct quotations, copy this material very carefully, word for word. Use quotation marks to indicate the quoted material. Be very careful to write down the page number for the quotation (or another trip to the library or Web site will be necessary!). For references obtained from the Web, provide the date when you viewed the page as well as its location on the Web.

In taking notes, be as brief as possible, but do not omit important information. It is better to have too much information from a source rather than not enough. For relevant research articles, you will probably want to record information on the problem of the study, hypotheses, methodology, type of sample, findings, and conclusions.

CRITIQUING THE LITERATURE REVIEW SECTION OF RESEARCH ARTICLES

It is difficult to critique a literature review section of a research article if you are not familiar with the literature on the study topic. For example, you will not be able to determine if the researcher has included classic sources and the most recent sources. However, there are many aspects of the literature review that you will be able to evaluate even if you are not an expert in the content area.

You may not be able to determine if the most recent references have been included. However, if all sources appear to be older than 5 years, you might wonder if some recent references may have been omitted. Also, if the topic is one that you know has been studied for many years, such as preoperative teaching, you would expect to see older studies cited as well as recent studies.

The literature review should contain mostly paraphrases, rather than direct quotes. However, remember to reference the writings of others even if paraphrases are used. Sources should be critically appraised, and the relevance of the sources should be clear. The review should be concise and to the point.

Determine if the researcher is citing primary sources or secondary sources when reporting results of studies conducted in the past. Although it may not always be possible for you to determine if a source is a primary one, an examination of the reference list at the end of the article will provide some clues. If most of the references are from research journals, you will be more confident that the sources are primary ones. If the reference list contains book chapters and literature reviews on a certain topic, it is likely that some secondary sources are being cited. The only way to make a definite determination of the type of source would be to locate each reference yourself, which may not be practical.

If a theorist has been cited, the reference list should contain that theorist's name as the author of the cited material. If, for example, Maslow's theory is being discussed in the article you are critiquing, expect to see a reference that shows Maslow as the author.

Determine if the researcher has presented both supporting and opposing literature. Are there studies in which support for the theory was *not* demonstrated? If this is the case, the researcher should present this information in the literature review section. Sometimes the discerning reader will find opposing studies included in the discussion section of the article and it may appear to the reader that the researcher went back to the library and hunted for new sources to support nonsignificant findings!

It is not uncommon for journal article reference lists to have errors. Oermann, Mason, and Wilmes (2002) examined reference lists in the *American Journal of Nursing*, *Nursing Outlook*, and *RN*. Of the 130 references they examined, 33 (25%) contained errors. Serious errors (errors that would hamper document retrieval) were found in 19% of the references. Most of these errors were related to mistakes in issue numbers or missing issue numbers (in those journals where each issue begins with Page 1). In 2005, the *Oncology Nursing Forum* staff began an initiative to verify every reference in every article because of the number of reference errors that they had encountered in the past (Amen, King, & Rieger, 2005).

Box 6–1 presents guidelines for critiquing the literature review section of a research article.

Box 6–1. Guidelines for Critiquing the Literature Review

1. Is the literature review comprehensive?
2. Is the literature review concise?
3. Does the review flow logically from the purposes(s) of the study?
4. Are all sources relevant to the study topic?
5. Are sources critically appraised?
6. Are both classic and current sources included?
7. Are paraphrases or direct quotes used most often?
8. Are both supporting and opposing theory and research presented?
9. Can a determination be made if sources are primary or secondary?
10. Are all sources that are cited in the article on the reference list?
11. Do the references appear to be free of citation errors?

SUMMARY

The most important reason for reviewing the literature before conducting a research study is to determine what is already known about the study topic. Previous studies are located, and a theoretical or conceptual basis for the study is sought in the literature.

Literature sources may be classified as primary or secondary. A **primary source** in the research literature is a description of a study written by the original researcher(s). A **secondary source** provides a summary or description of a research study written by someone other than the original study investigator(s). **Grey literature** can be defined as any document that is not commercially published and is not indexed or made available in the major databases.

Literature sources can be located through print sources and electronic sources. Print sources include indexes and abstracts. **Indexes** are used to obtain references to periodical articles. **Abstracts** contain brief summaries of articles and contain the purpose, methods, and major findings of studies. Electronic sources include online catalogs and online databases. Online journals and magazines, called **e-journals** and **e-zines**, are becoming popular.

Accuracy in recording bibliographic material is essential. Direct quotations must be recorded word for word and the page number indicated. Even paraphrases must be referenced.

NURSING RESEARCH ON THE WEB

For additional online resources, research activities, and exercises, go to **www.mynursingkit. com.** Select Chapter 6 from the drop-down menu.

GET INVOLVED ACTIVITIES

1. Choose a topic (such as cancer, teenage pregnancy, or social support) on which you wish to obtain information from an online database. Do a search of that particular database. Record the number of "hits" you receive. Then, carry out the same process with one other online database. Was there any difference in the number of "hits" you received?
2. Examine the reference lists of two research articles. Are you able to determine the number of references that appear to be primary sources and the number of references that appear to be secondary sources?
3. Examine these same reference lists again and try to determine if the researcher has used classical sources and current sources.
4. Conduct a search for nursing-related articles that are free online. Make a listing of Internet sites and share them with your colleagues.
5. Access the Cochrane Library and find a summary of a systematic review. Share your results with your colleagues.

SELF-TEST

Circle the letter before the *best* answer.

1. Which of the following is the *most* important reason for conducting a review of the literature before conducting a research study?
   A. The research design can be copied from a previous study.
   B. A determination will be made about the existing knowledge in the identified problem area.
   C. An instrument may be uncovered that will be appropriate for the proposed study.
   D. The feasibility of the study can be determined.

2. A primary source for a nursing research study is
   A. the retrieval mechanism that is first used in locating the research study.
   B. an index that directs the reader to the research study.
   C. a description of the study written by the researcher who conducted the study.
   D. a summary of research on the study topic.

3. How can you best determine if primary sources are listed on the reference list of an article?
   A. Access each reference yourself
   B. Primary sources are usually listed first on the reference list
   C. The reference list contains articles from research journals
   D. Make a personal contact with the primary author

4. Most research articles that appear in the journal *Nursing Research* are examples of
   A. primary sources.
   B. secondary sources.
   C. meta-analysis studies.
   D. systematic reviews.

5. Which of the following databases is available only through a library?
   A. WorldCat
   B. Haz-Map
   C. MEDLINE
   D. TOXNET

6. If you wanted to obtain the most comprehensive study results on a particular health care intervention, you would want to access which of the following databases?

   A. MEDLINE®
   B. CINAHL® Database
   C. CINAHL® Plus
   D. Cochrane Database of Systematic Reviews

7. Which of these printed indexes *does not* have an online version?
   A. *Cumulative Index to Nursing & Allied Health Literature*
   B. *Index Medicus*
   C. *Nursing Studies Index*

8. Which of the following sources should be searched for a 1980 article published in the *American Journal of Nursing*?
   A. *CINAHL® Database*
   B. *CINAHL® Plus*
   C. *Medline® Plus*
   D. *Cochrane Database of Systematic Reviews*

9. In conducting a literature review, the reader is *least* interested in which of the following information about a research study?
   A. research study results
   B. opinions about the research study
   C. how the research variables were operationally defined
   D. research study methodology

10. Which of the following statements is true about online databases?
    A. No online databases are available to the general public.
    B. Some online databases are available to the general public.
    C. Most people are not interested in online databases.
    D. Other sources of obtaining information are more valuable than online databases.

REFERENCES

Arndt, R. M., & McGowan, N. (2009). Library and information literacy. *Journal of Emergency Nursing, 35,* 360–362.

Amen, K., King, C. R., & Rieger, P. T. (2005). The bane of accurate referencing: How to achieve "Perfection." *Oncology Nursing Forum, 32,* 734–736.

American Psychological Association. (2010). *Publication manual of the American Psychological Association* (6th ed.). Washington, DC: Author.

Billings, D. M., & Kowalski, K. (2009). Nurses working with librarians. *The Journal of Continuing Education in Nursing, 40,* 16–17.

Hallyburton, A., & St. John, B. (2010). Partnering with your library to strengthen nursing research. *Journal of Nursing Education, 49,* 164–167. doi: 10.3928/01484834-20091118-04

Krom, Z. R., Batten, J., & Bautista, C. (2010). A unique collaborative nursing evidence-based practice initiative using the Iowa model. *Clinical Nurse Specialist, 24,* 54–59.

Lemeshow, A. R., Blum, R. E., Berlin, J. A., Stoto, M. A., & Colditz, G. A. (2005). Searching one or two databases was insufficient for meta-analysis of observational studies. *Journal of Clinical Epidemiology, 58,* 867–873.

Oermann, M. H., Mason, N. M., & Wilmes, N. A. (2002). Accuracy of references in general readership nursing journals. *Nurse Educator, 27,* 260–264.

Vrabel, M. (2005). Searching for evidence: The value of a librarian-clinician collaboration—the librarian's role. *Home Health Care Management & Practice, 17,* 286–292.

Wink, D. (2009). Teaching with technology: Finding information on the Internet. *Nurse Educator, 34,* 51–53.

CHAPTER 7

Theory and Nursing Research

OUTLINE

OBJECTIVES

On completion of this chapter, you will be prepared to:

1. Define theory, concept, construct, proposition, empirical generalization, model, and conceptual models
2. Discuss four nursing conceptual models
3. Distinguish between theoretical and conceptual frameworks
4. Describe deductive and inductive reasoning processes in theory generation and development
5. Identify theories used in nursing
6. Identify the steps used in testing a theory
7. Critique the study framework section of research reports

NEW TERMS DEFINED IN THIS CHAPTER

concept, pg 84
conceptual framework, pg 87
conceptual models, pg 85
construct, pg 84
deductive reasoning, pg 88
empirical generalization, pg 84
grand theories, pg 89

inductive reasoning, pg 88
middle-range theories, pg 89
model, pg 85
propositional statements, pg 84
theoretical framework, pg 87
theory, pg 84

Y ou stop at a gas station to fill up your tank. The price of a gallon of gas makes you cringe. A small meal probably wouldn't cost any more! You pay for the gasoline, get back in your car, and head for home. What could be causing this high price for gasoline? Could it be the theory of supply and demand? The demand for gasoline continues to increase. Therefore, suppliers are able to charge higher prices.

As you drive down the freeway in the busy afternoon traffic, you notice the discourtesy of the drivers and the continual honking of horns. Many drivers appear tense and impatient. You think about the problems these people may have encountered during the day as well as the added inconvenience of the traffic congestion. Without a conscious awareness, you may be considering a stress theory as the explanation for the behaviors that you have observed.

People use theories to explain happenings in their lives and in their environments. Nurses also use theories to explain happenings of significance to nursing. Nursing research and nursing practice should be based on theory. When research is guided by a theoretical framework, the theory guides the research process from the beginning to the end—that is, from the identification of the research problem to the formulation of the study conclusions. You may ask, where does a researcher find a theory for a study or determine which theory would be most appropriate? This chapter helps answer these questions and, it is hoped, helps you to recognize the value of theory-based nursing research.

THEORY TERMINOLOGY

Many nurses experience confusion when confronted with the terms in this chapter. There is no absolute or correct definition for many of these terms. The lack of agreement in terminology sometimes leaves you wondering which definition to use. It is more important for you to gain a basic understanding of the terminology than to memorize definitions. You will be in a better position to recognize the terms when you encounter them in the research literature. Rather than memorizing one correct definition of the word *theory,* for example, try to gain an understanding of what a theory is and how it is useful in nursing.

Some definitions and explanation of terminology are presented first to help you understand the content of this chapter. These definitions and explanations were generated after reviewing the latest literature on the use of theory in nursing.

Theory

One of the most commonly quoted definitions of a theory was formulated by Kerlinger (1973): "A theory is a set of interrelated constructs (concepts), definitions, and propositions that present a systematic view of phenomena by specifying relations among variables, with the purpose of explaining and predicting the phenomena" (p. 9). Polit and Beck (2008) have defined a theory as "a systematic, abstract explanation of some aspect of reality" (p. 57). Burns and Grove (2009) described a theory as "an integrated set of defined concepts and propositions that present a view of a phenomenon and can be used to describe, explain, predict, or control the phenomenon" (p. 39). A more easily understood (although not as comprehensive) definition used in this book is that a **theory** is a set of related statements that describes or explains phenomena in a systematic way. Theories explain why one event is associated with another event or what causes an event to occur. Theories are composed of concepts and the relationships between these concepts. Relationships between concepts are presented in theoretical statements, called **propositional statements**. These propositional statements are connected in a logical system of thought.

Theory development is the basic aim of science (Kerlinger, 1986). Theories make scientific findings meaningful and generalizable. The facts that are derived from many separate and isolated investigations take on meaning when placed within a theoretical context.

Theory comes from the Greek word *theoria*, which means a beholding, spectacle, or speculation. *Speculation* is an appropriate word to use when discussing theories. Theories are always speculative and never considered to be true or proven. They provide description and explanation of the occurrence of phenomena and are always subject to further development or revision. Theories may even be discarded, if not supported by empirical evidence.

Concept

Concepts are the building blocks of theory. A **concept** is a word picture or mental idea of a phenomenon. Concepts are words or terms that symbolize some aspect of reality. The meaning of a concept is conveyed by the use of a definition and examples of instances of the concept. A concept may be very concrete, such as the human heart, or very abstract, such as love. Concrete concepts may be specified and defined more easily than abstract concepts.

Construct

A highly abstract, complex phenomenon (concept) is denoted by a made-up, or constructed, term. **Construct** is the term used to indicate a phenomenon that cannot be directly observed but must be inferred by certain concrete or less abstract indicators of the phenomenon. Examples of constructs are wellness, mental health, self-esteem, and assertiveness. Each of these constructs can be identified only through the presence of certain measurable concepts. Wellness might be inferred through laboratory data or clinical observation. The laboratory data would be a very objective indicator of wellness, whereas the clinical observation would be a less objective indicator of wellness.

Propositional Statements

A propositional statement asserts the relationship between concepts. Propositional statements are derived from theories or from generalizations based on empirical data. A propositional statement may indicate the relationship between concepts in several ways. A propositional statement may assert simply that two events or phenomena tend to vary together. For example, "There is a relationship between pulse rates and respiration rates." Propositional statements may also assert that one variable causes another variable. For example, "Bacteria cause disease."

Empirical Generalization

When a similar pattern of events is found in the empirical data of a number of different studies, the pattern is called an **empirical generalization** (Reynolds, 1971). Empirical generalizations summarize the results of several empirical studies. Burns and Grove (2009) asserted that empirical generalizations are "statements that have been repeatedly tested and have not been disproved" (p. 140). Many studies have shown that women attend church more often than men. The empirical generalization can, therefore, be made that women are more frequent church attendees than men.

Hypothesis

The term *hypothesis* was defined in Chapter 3. A hypothesis predicts the relationship between two or more variables. Hypotheses present the researcher's expectations about the outcome of a study.

Through hypotheses, theoretical propositions are tested in the real world. The investigator can then advance scientific knowledge by supporting or failing to support the tested theory.

Model

The more complex the issues, the greater is the need to "create order out of chaos" by constructing models (Blackwell, 1985, p. 169). A **model** is a symbolic representation of some phenomenon or phenomena. Bush (1979) wrote that a model "represents some aspect of reality, concrete or abstract, by means of a likeness which may be structural, pictorial, diagrammatic, or mathematical" (p. 16). Probably the most common usage of the term model is when discussing structural types of models, such as model trains, model airplanes, and models of the human heart. The types of models that nurses are interested in when conducting nursing research are generally of the structural or diagrammatic form. A diagram or a picture can portray a theory in a fashion that clearly demonstrates the structure and parts of the theory. Whereas a theory focuses on statements or explanations of the relationships between phenomena, a model focuses on the structure or composition of the phenomena.

Conceptual Models

Conceptual models are made up of concepts and propositions that state the relationship between the concepts. These concepts are generally very abstract and not readily observable in the empirical world. Conceptual models in nursing present broad general concepts of interest to nursing. Common concepts identified in nearly all of the nursing models are person, environment, health, and nursing (Fawcett, 1995; Fitzpatrick & Whall, 1996; George, 1995). Each nursing model addresses these elements in a unique fashion.

NURSING CONCEPTUAL MODELS

Several nurse theorists have developed conceptual models concerned with the phenomena of importance to nursing. These theorists include Dorothea Orem, Martha Rogers, Callista Roy, and Betty Neuman. A brief overview of the models introduced by these four nurse theorists is presented next.

Orem's Self-Care Model

Dorothea Orem has been developing her ideas about self-care since the early 1950s. Concepts in her model are self-care, self-care agency, self-care demand, self-care deficit, nursing agency, and nursing system. Three theories have been derived from Orem's self-care model: theory of nursing systems, theory of self-care deficit, and theory of self-care. Modifications of her original ideas are found in the sixth edition of her text *Nursing: Concepts of Practice* (2001).

Orem's model is particularly appropriate today with the general public's increased interest in self-care. An article published in *Nursing Science Quarterly* in April 2000 (Taylor, Geden, Isaramalai, & Wongvatunyu, 2000) identified 66 published research studies that had used components of Orem's theories. Many recent studies have also used her theories.

Orem's Nursing Systems Theory

Orem's Theory of Nursing Systems was the framework for a study that evaluated the usefulness and usability of follow-up telehealth medication counseling among a sample of community-based patients with Parkinson's disease (Fincher, Ward, Dawkins, Magee, & Willson, 2009). A self-care standardized medication educational session lasting 20 to 30 minutes was conducted, and patients and nurses evaluated the usefulness of this intervention.

Rogers's Science of Unitary Human Beings

One of the most unique conceptual models in nursing is that proposed by Martha Rogers. She first presented her science of unitary human beings in her 1970 book, *An Introduction to the Theoretical Basis of Nursing*. By the time she died in 1994, her ideas had made a great impact on nursing and probably will continue to do so for many years to come. Much of Rogers's work is contained in the book *Martha E. Rogers: Her Life and Her Work* by Malinski and Barrett (1994). The book was released shortly after Rogers's death.

Rogers continually refined her model, and when she spoke to groups of nurses (including this author), she frequently asked that they discuss her most current ideas rather than those presented in her 1970 book (which she called "the purple book"). Just as she viewed humans as continually evolving, her ideas were continually evolving. She originally used the term *man* in her writings. After 1983, she used the term *unitary human beings*. Her latest ideas were published in *Nursing Science Quarterly* in the article "Nursing Science and the Space Age" (Rogers, 1992).

Humans and their environment are viewed as two energy fields that are always open to each other. Each human field is unique, and change is always toward increasing complexity and diversity. Aging is viewed as a "creative process directed toward growing diversity of field pattern and organization" (Rogers, 1980, p. 336).

Rogers's model is unique in that the person is viewed as a unified whole. No parts or subsystems are separated out. Although other models propose to present a holistic view of people, this view is often contradicted by the models' examination of the parts or subsystems of people.

Rogers's Science of Unitary Human Beings

Farren (2010) used Rogers's Science of Unitary Human Beings to study the relationships among power, uncertainty, self-transcendence, and quality of life in breast cancer survivors. The researcher concluded that there are "complex and synergistic relations among the cluster of field pattern manifestations that contribute to quality of life in breast cancer survivors" (p. 63).

Roy's Adaptation Model

Roy first published her ideas about adaptation as a framework for nursing in a 1970 article in *Nursing Outlook*. She has continued to publish extensively on her model. A thorough presentation of her ideas is found in the second edition of her text *Introduction to Nursing: An Adaptation Model* (1984). Refinements of her model are found in the second edition of *The Roy Adaptation Model* by Roy and Andrews (1999) and in the third edition published in 2008.

Roy has pointed out that nursing focuses on the person as a total being, whereas medicine focuses on the patient's disease process. Humans are considered to be biopsychosocial beings in constant interaction with the changing environment. People are viewed as adaptive systems with cognator and regulator coping mechanisms that act to maintain adaptation in four response modes: physiological, self-concept, role function, and interdependence.

Roy's Adaptation Model

Roy's Adaptation Model (RAM) was the theoretical framework used to study quality of life (QOL) as perceived by lung transplant candidates and their caregivers (Lefaiver, Keough, Letizia, & Lanuza, 2007). The adaptive modes of the caregiver and lung transplant candidate were measured with the Quality of Life Index (QLI). The researchers pointed out parallels between the RAM adaptive modes and the elements of the QLI.

Neuman's Systems Model

The Neuman model first appeared in a 1972 article in *Nursing Research*. It was also outlined in Riehl and Roy's *Conceptual Models for Nursing Practice* (in both the 1974 and 1980 editions). The first edition of her book, *The Neuman Systems Model*, was published in 1982. Refinements were presented in the 1989, 1995, and 2002 editions. The fifth edition was published in March 2010, with a 2011 copyright date. Jacqueline Fawcett co-authored this edition of the book with Neuman. According to Günüsen, Üstün, and Gigiotti (2009), more than 200 studies based on Neuman's system model have been published in articles and book chapters.

Neuman has proposed a model that focuses on the total person. The person or client system (individual, group, community) is subject to environmental stressors that are intrapersonal, interpersonal, and extrapersonal. The client system is composed of physiological, psychological, sociocultural, developmental, and spiritual variables. The client is protected from stressors by a flexible line of defense that is dynamic. The next barrier to stressors is the person's normal line of defense that has been built over time. When this defense is penetrated, the internal lines of resistance are activated to stabilize the client system.

Nursing interventions may occur at the primary, secondary, or tertiary levels of prevention. Primary prevention is appropriate before reaction to a stressor has occurred. Secondary prevention is used when reaction to a stressor has already occurred. Tertiary prevention is used to foster rehabilitation and a return to wellness. The nursing process is divided into three steps: nursing diagnosis, nursing goals, and nursing outcomes.

Neuman's Systems Model

Neuman's Systems Model was used as the conceptual framework to study stress in a group of critical care nurses in South Africa (Moola, Ehlers, & Hattingh, 2008). Study results presented perceptions and experiences about stressful events and factors contributing to stress in the critical care environment, as well as the nurses' needs for support systems.

THEORETICAL AND CONCEPTUAL FRAMEWORKS

A framework for a research study helps organize the study and provides a context for the interpretation of the study findings. Either a theoretical or a conceptual framework should be used in all quantitative studies. Theoretical and conceptual frameworks are often used interchangeably in the literature. The two frameworks are similar in that both provide a background or foundation for a study. However, there are differences in these two types of frameworks.

A **theoretical framework** presents a broad, general explanation of the relationships between the concepts of interest in a research study; it is based on *one* existing theory. When using a theoretical framework, each main study concept is related back to a concept from an existing theory. A proposition from the selected theory will be tested in any study based on that particular theory.

Suppose a teacher wanted to know if contracting for grades would motivate students to earn higher grades. After exploring different theories, she might decide to test a proposition from Carl Rogers's (1969) theory of learning. One of Rogers's propositions is that learning is facilitated when the student participates responsibly in the learning process. The two theory concepts are "learning" and "participates responsibly in the learning process." The two study concepts that can be matched up with these two theory concepts are "earn higher grades" (which would match up with "learning") and "contracting for grades" (which would match up with "participates responsibly in the learning process"). Thus, based on the stated proposition from Rogers's theory, the researcher would be able to predict that students who contract for grades would earn higher grades than students who do not contract for grades.

If there is no existing theory that fits the concepts to be studied, the researcher may construct a conceptual framework to be used in the proposed research study. A **conceptual framework** helps explain the relationship between concepts, but rather than being based on one theory, this type of framework links concepts selected from several theories, from previous research results, or from the researcher's own experiences. The researcher relates the concepts in a logical manner. A conceptual framework is a less well-developed structure than a theoretical framework but may serve as the impetus for the formulation of a theory.

A graduate nursing student decided to examine nurses' job satisfaction levels and their levels of empathy in their interactions with patients. After searching the literature, she was able to find an empathy theory and a job satisfaction theory. However, she could locate no theory that combined these two concepts. Therefore, she constructed a conceptual framework using these two theories. Based on the empathy theory, she reasoned that being empathetic requires being satisfied with self. She further reasoned that if people are happy in their jobs, they will be satisfied with themselves. Therefore, she proposed that job satisfaction and empathy are positively related.

The findings of a study should be related back to the study framework. Otherwise, numerous isolated findings would exist for each study. The concrete findings are linked to the abstract ideas of the theory or to the propositions proposed by the researcher in the conceptual framework. Thus, an explanation for the study findings is presented, and the body of knowledge on the study topic is increased.

THEORY GENERATION AND DEVELOPMENT

Researchers are concerned with both theory generation and the development of theories. The two activities go hand in hand. Figure 7–1 shows the processes of theory generation and the development of theories through testing. As you can see, theory generation and development involve both inductive and deductive reasoning processes. **Deductive reasoning** proceeds from the general (theory) to the specific (empirical data). **Inductive reasoning,** in contrast, proceeds from the specific (empirical data) to the general (theory).

The deductive process moves from a general abstract explanation to a specific event in the real world. A hypothesis is deduced from a theory, and the hypothesis is empirically tested in a real-life situation. The researcher asks the question, "If this theory is valid, what kind of behavior or event would I expect to find in my study?" For example, you might test a propositional statement from Maslow's (1970) theory of motivation that states "If a person's safety needs are not met, safety needs will take precedence over self-esteem needs." If this statement is valid, you would expect to find that people are more concerned about receiving the correct medications than they are about being told they are "good" patients.

When an inductive process is used, data are gathered from a real-life situation and the researcher tries to derive a general explanation of this behavior or event. The question is asked, "How can I explain what I have been observing?" For example, you might observe that patients who are occupied in

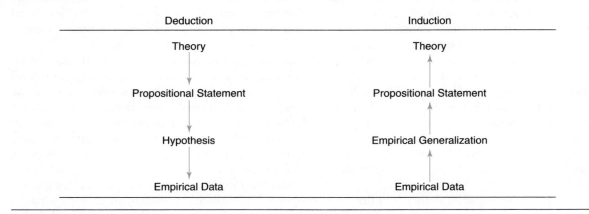

▶ FIGURE 7–1   Deductive and inductive processes in theory generation and development

some activity, such as watching television, seem to be less anxious than patients who are not involved in a specific activity. You continue to observe many patients and find that this pattern seems to hold true for most of the patients on the unit where you work. Your explanation for this phenomenon would involve an inductive reasoning process. An existing anxiety theory might provide an explanation for the phenomenon just discussed. If no existing theory can be located that explains this phenomenon, the researcher may start the process of generating a new theory. After empirical data are gathered on a number of occasions, empirical generalizations are made. The next step is to develop propositional statements. Finally, the propositional statements are logically related to form a theory.

TYPES OF THEORIES

Theories can be described according to the range of phenomena they describe and explain. Two types of theories are grand theories and middle-range theories. There is lack of consensus among nursing experts about the definition and scope of these two types of theories. Generally, **grand theories** address a broad range of phenomena in the environment or in the experiences of humans. **Middle-range theories** have a much more narrow focus; they are concerned with only a small area of the environment or of human experiences and incorporate a small number of concepts.

Grand theories are important in every discipline. According to Fitzpatrick and Whall (1996), a grand theory "serves as a guiding light, as a historical holder of disciplinary beliefs, and as a provider of visions of the future" (p. 2). Although grand theories are revered by many nurses, middle-range theories have been found to be more valuable to nursing research than have grand theories. The works of many of the nurse theorists have been identified as conceptual models at the grand-theory level. Some nurses have contended that these models do not drive research (Tripp-Reimer, Woodworth, McCloskey, & Bulechek, 1996).

As you may recall, the nurse theorists have broadly discussed health, environment, person, and nursing. It is difficult to isolate a propositional statement from these broad concepts that can then be tested in a research study. For example, if a nurse wanted to find out if back rubs promote sleep in hospitalized patients, a middle-range theory, probably one that focuses on a proposition from a relaxation theory, would be needed to guide the study.

One of the shortcomings of the use of middle-range theories appears to be that most of them are from other disciplines. Examples of these theories include social support, coping, anxiety, adult learning, body image, stress, and helplessness. Although knowledge does not belong to any one discipline, each discipline looks at phenomena from a different perspective. Few disciplines are concerned with people who are ill. For example, learning theories that may be useful with well people may not be appropriate for sick people, who not only are ill but under a great deal of stress. An individual whose normal preferred learning mode is auditory may need a totally different approach when hospitalized. This person may now need visual as well as auditory learning signals, and the signals may need to be repeated several times. One cannot assume that a theory used in one discipline should be transferred directly over for use in another discipline. Modifications may be needed, or the theory may be deemed inappropriate for use in nursing.

SOURCES OF THEORIES FOR NURSING RESEARCH

Nurses have available to them a wealth of theories on which to base their research. These theories have been developed in nursing and in many other disciplines. At the present time, nurses continue to use many theories from other disciplines.

Theories From Nursing

Although there are a number of nursing conceptual models, only a few theories have been derived from these models. Additionally, relatively few studies have tested nursing theories.

Rosemarie Parse, editor of *Nursing Science Quarterly,* reported on a meeting of doctoral faculty from various schools of nursing around the country (Parse, 2003). Some of the faculty contended that if a nurse conducted a study, it would be considered nursing research. Others disagreed and asserted that for a study to be classified as nursing research, the inquiry must advance nursing knowledge through the use of nursing frameworks and theories. Parse, herself, made a strong plea in 2000 for the use of nursing theories in nursing research. In an editorial in *Nursing Science Quarterly,* Parse (2000) strongly argued that a nursing research study must use a nursing framework or theory. Fawcett (2000) wrote a similar editorial in the *Western Journal of Nursing Research.* The following month Brink (2000) published an editorial in the same journal and disagreed with Fawcett's position. She asserted that any research that has a direct bearing on nursing practice is considered nursing research. She further claimed that nursing is an applied discipline and draws knowledge from many sources. She asserted that if we were to ignore factual data simply because it came from another discipline, we would have to redo a lot of previous research or admit to "culpable ignorance."

Although nurse researchers have generally used theories that were not developed by nurses, the literature has many examples of studies that relied on the theoretical work of nurses. Examples of studies that used the models of Orem, Rogers, Roy, and Neuman were presented earlier in this chapter. Additional theories developed by nurses may be identified in published studies. Some of these include Benner's (1984) model on novice to expert, Cox's (1982) interaction model of client health behavior (IMCHB), King's (1981) theory of goal attainment, Mishel's (1981, 1990) uncertainty in illness theory, Peplau's interpersonal theory (1988), Pender's (1996) health promotion model, and Watson's (2005) theory of human caring.

Mishel's Uncertainty in Illness Theory

Mishel's Uncertainty in Illness theory was used in a study to evaluate the psychometric properties of a new instrument developed to measure uncertainty in children and adolescents (8–17 years) with cancer (Stewart, Lynn & Mishel, 2010). The instrument is called Uncertainty Scale for Kids (USK). The USK demonstrated strong reliability and preliminary evidence for construct and discriminant validity. The researchers contend that these results show promise for further research on uncertainty in illness in children with cancer.

Pender's Health Promotion Model

A tailored intervention based on Pender's Health Promotion Model (HPM) was compared to a generic intervention in a study that sought to increase physical activity and healthy eating among rural women (Walker et al., 2009). Perceived benefits, barriers, self-efficacy, and interpersonal influences were cognitions selected from the HPM in designing the tailored intervention. Although both groups showed gains in physical activity and healthy eating, a higher proportion of the HPM intervention group met the Healthy People 2010 criteria for moderate or greater intensity activity, fruit and vegetable servings, and percentage of calories from fat at 12 months post intervention.

Watson's Theory of Human Caring

Jean Watson's Theory of Human Caring directed a study by Pipe, Bortz, and Dueck (2009) that evaluated a brief stress management intervention for nurse leaders. Nurse leaders (n = 33) were randomly assigned to a brief mindfulness meditation course (MMC) or a leadership course (control). Mindfulness meditation course participants self-reported the most improvement in stress symptoms. Mindfulness "was conceptualized as a way of caring/nurturing the self so that one's leadership could be more caring and effective by extension. (p. 131).

Sometimes nurse researchers combine two nursing theories in their studies. The following example uses Orem's self-care agency, a component of her self-care deficit theory, and Pender's revised health belief model for health promotion.

Combining Two Nursing Theories

Youngkin and Lester (2010) studied the accuracy of a home self-test system for bacterial vaginosis (BV) in women. Orem's self-care agency concept was used to teach women how to understand the disease, assess for BV, and record their findings. The researchers believed that Pender's health promotion model guided the nurses as they helped women to modify their health behaviors through self-care interventions. The goal of secondary prevention in health promotion is health protection, which should decrease the risks of undiagnosed progression of BV.

Theories From Other Disciplines

Nursing is referred to as a practice discipline. It has been said frequently that nursing, as a practice discipline, has borrowed knowledge from other disciplines, such as chemistry, biology, sociology, psychology, and anthropology. Levine (1995) has opposed the use of the term "borrowed." She said it indicates that something needs to later be "returned." Levine wrote, "The fruits of knowledge are not the private domain of one discipline, to be returned like a borrowed cup of sugar to a neighbor" (p. 12).

The use of knowledge from other disciplines is necessary, but frequently this knowledge is not suitable to the needs of the nursing profession. Nurses must find ways to adapt the numerous theories from other disciplines. Once these theories have been adapted, they should be considered as shared knowledge rather than as borrowed theories (Stevens, 1979). Table 7–1 lists theories from other disciplines that are used to explain phenomena in nursing. These theories concern concepts

TABLE 7–1 Theories From Other Disciplines

1. Adult learning theory: Knowles (1990)
2. Anxiety: Spielberger (1972)
3. Body image: Schilder (1952)
4. Change theory: Lewin (1951)
5. Cognitive dissonance: Festinger (1957)
6. Coping: Lazarus and Folkman (1984)
7. Crisis: Caplan (1964)
8. Developmental theory: Piaget (1926); Freud (1938); Erikson (1950) Havighurst (1952)
9. Family communication theory: Satir (1967)
10. Family theory: Minuchin (1974); Duvall (1977)
11. Health behaviors: Becker (1985)
12. Helplessness: Seligman (1975)
13. Job satisfaction: Herzberg (1966)
14. Moral reasoning: Kohlberg (1978)
15. Motivation: Maslow (1970)
16. Pain: Melzack and Wall (1983)
17. Relaxation: Benson (1975)
18. Role theory: Mead (1934); Biddle (1986)
19. Social learning theory: Bandura (1985); Rotter (1954)
20. Stress: Selye (1976)
21. Transtheoretical model of behavior change: Prochaska & DiClemente (1983)

such as social learning, adult learning, role socialization, stress, helplessness, cognitive dissonance, human development, motivation, crisis, relaxation, pain, anxiety, body image, job satisfaction, family interactions, communication, coping, moral reasoning, health behaviors, and change.

The gate control theory of pain by Melzack and Wall (1983) served as the framework for Hatfield's (2008) study of sucrose use to decrease infant biobehavioral responses to immunizations. Sheenan (2009) used Prochaska and DiClemente's (1983) transtheoretical model (TTM) in her study of knowledge of prostate cancer and prostate cancer screening among a group of men at average risk of developing cancer. Bandura's (1985) self-efficacy theory was used in a simulation study as a teaching–learning method to increase self-efficacy of nursing students during their first clinical course (Bambini, Washburn, & Perkins, 2009). Lazarus and Folkman's (1984) theory of stress, appraisal, and coping was used in a study by Song and Nam (2010) to examine coping strategies, physical function, and social adjustment in people with spinal cord injury. The adult learning theory of Malcom Knowles (1990) was used by Schneiderman, Corbridge, and Zerwic (2009) in a study of the effectiveness of a self-directed online learning module for arterial blood gas interpretation.

Combining Theories From Nursing and Other Disciplines

In some studies, nurse researchers have determined that a combination of theories from nursing and other disciplines would guide their research more appropriately than a theory from only one discipline.

Combining Nursing and Non-nursing Theories

Hoffman et al. (2009) combined the middle-range nursing theory of unpleasant symptoms (TOUS) by Lentz et al. (1997) with Bandura's (1997) self-efficacy theory. The researchers contended that the TOUS helps to understand the multidimensional nature and impact of symptoms, whereas Bandura's theory demonstrates how a persons' belief in his or her ability to self-manage symptoms actually influences that person's performance of corresponding behaviors.

THEORY TESTING IN NURSING RESEARCH

In the early stages of a research project, the researcher should consider the theoretical or conceptual framework for the study. This framework is usually determined after a thorough review of the literature. If nursing is to build a scientific knowledge base, nursing studies should be based on a theoretical or conceptual framework so that the findings may be placed within the existing knowledge base for the profession. The most efficient way to obtain a body of knowledge for nursing is to build on the work of other researchers who have used the same theoretical base. Even a small research project becomes quite important when the findings of the study can be added to those of others who have used the same theoretical frame of reference.

Many studies are conducted in which a researcher wishes to study a particular problem but has no theory in mind that will be tested. In such cases, an attempt should be made to select a theory that will be useful in guiding the study. Sometimes more than one theory might be appropriate, but the researcher should choose the one that seems to describe and explain the relationship between the study variables more clearly and succinctly than other available theories. Choosing a theory for a study may be a difficult task, especially for the beginning researcher. To choose an appropriate theory, a familiarity with various theories is necessary. Descriptions of theories may be obtained through many sources. Various books and articles contain information about theories.

Once a theory has been selected, it is wise to consult the original or primary source of the theory. For example, if information is sought on Maslow's theory of motivation, Maslow's (1970) book should be read. By using a primary source, the researcher will gain the most accurate description of the theory as presented by the theorist.

The chosen theory should be considered throughout the research process. A step-by-step use of the chosen theory requires that the researcher:

1. Review various theories that may be appropriate to examine the identified problem.
2. Select a theory to be tested in the study.
3. Review the literature on this theory.
4. Develop study hypothesis(es) or research questions based on a propositional statement or statements from the theory.
5. Define study variables, using the selected theory as the basis of the theoretical definitions.
6. Choose study instruments that are congruent with the theory.
7. Describe study findings in light of the explanations provided by the theory.
8. Relate study conclusions to the theory.
9. Determine support for the theory based on study findings.
10. Determine implications for nursing based on the explanatory power of the theory.
11. Make recommendations for future research concerning the designated theory.

Theory generation and building through research are essential to the development of scientific knowledge. Because the nursing profession is very concerned at present with the need for nursing knowledge, it can be seen that an understanding and use of theory are critical for all nurses. Theory is of little benefit to the profession if it is deemed unimportant by the rank-and-file members. It is hoped you will become convinced of the value of theory that has been tested through research. You can help spread the message to your nursing colleagues.

CRITIQUING THE STUDY FRAMEWORK

Many nursing studies that are published today contain a clearly identified theoretical or conceptual framework for the study. Other studies do not. Therefore, the first determination to make is whether or not the researcher identified a framework for the study. Sometimes, the research report contains a heading for this section of the study. Other times, the discussion of the theoretical or conceptual framework is included in the introductory section or the review of literature section. The important point is to determine if a framework is clearly identified by the researcher.

If a theoretical or conceptual framework has been clearly identified in the report, the next evaluation step concerns the basis for the framework. Is it based on a nursing theory or a theory from another discipline? At the present time, many nursing studies are based on concepts and theories from other disciplines.

The reader then evaluates the appropriateness of the framework for the study. The entire research report must be read before the evaluation of the framework is made. Then, the reader might ask this question: "Would another theory have been more appropriate to guide the study?" There may be several theories that might have been used in any given study. Imagine that, after reading the research report, it appears to you the researcher was interested in helping subjects alter an unhealthy behavior—smoking. The researcher used a learning theory and taught subjects about the dangers of cigarette smoking. Considering the great amount of publicity about the dangers of cigarette smoking, you might wonder if another theory might have been more useful in helping predict a change in an unhealthy behavior. It is possible that the subjects already had knowledge of the dangers of cigarette smoking, but did not perceive themselves as vulnerable: "Cancer won't happen to me." A theory, such as the health belief model, might have been used. The researcher might focus on the concept of perceived susceptibility of the disease when presenting material about the dangers of smoking to the subjects.

You may be thinking, "I don't know that many theories. How can I evaluate this part of a study and decide whether the most appropriate theory was used?" This is a difficult task, but my guess is

Box 7–1. Guidelines for Critiquing the Study Framework

1. Is the framework clearly identified?
2. Is the framework based on a nursing theory or a theory from another discipline?
3. Does the framework appear to be appropriate for the study?
4. Are the concepts clearly defined?
5. Are the relationships among the concepts clearly presented?
6. Is(are) the propositional statement(s) identified that will guide the research question(s) or hypothesis(es)?
7. Are operational definitions provided for the theoretical concepts that will be tested?
8. Does the researcher relate the study findings back to the study framework?
9. Do the study findings provide support for the study framework?

that you know more theories than you think you do. You may not know the name of the theorist, but you are familiar with the ideas in the theory. If you have some nagging doubt when you read the framework section of an article, ask other nurses what they think about the framework.

If you think that the framework seems appropriate for the study, determine if there is a thorough explanation of the concepts and their relationship to each other.

An entire theory is rarely tested in one study. Thus, is a specific propositional statement from the theory identified that will guide the hypothesis(es) or research question(s)? Are operational definitions provided for the concepts that will be measured in the study? Box 7–1 presents guidelines for critiquing the theoretical/conceptual framework of a study.

SUMMARY

An understanding of theory in nursing and the use of theory in research requires familiarity with terms such as *theory, concept, construct, propositional statements, empirical generalization, model, conceptual models, theoretical frameworks,* and *conceptual frameworks.*

A **theory** is a set of statements that describes or explains phenomena in a systematic way. Theories are composed of concepts and the relationship between these concepts. These relationships are presented in propositional statements that are connected in a logical way.

Concepts are the building blocks of theory. A **concept** is a word picture or mental idea of a phenomenon. Concepts may be concrete or abstract.

A **construct** is a phenomenon (concept) that cannot be directly observed, but must be inferred by certain concrete or less abstract indicators of the phenomenon. Examples of constructs are wellness and mental health.

Propositional statements present the relationship between concepts in a theory. All theories contain propositional statements.

An **empirical generalization** is a summary statement of the findings of a number of different studies concerning the same phenomenon.

A **model** is a symbolic representation of phenomena. A model can be structural, pictorial, diagrammatic, or mathematical. Models focus on the structure of phenomena rather than on the relationships between phenomena, as is the case with theories.

Conceptual models are made up of concepts and propositions. The concepts are usually abstract. Conceptual models in nursing identify concepts of interest to nursing such as person, environment, health, and nursing.

A **theoretical framework** differs from a conceptual framework. A theoretical framework is based on propositional statements from one theory, whereas a **conceptual framework** links concepts from several theories, from previous research results, or from the researcher's own experience. In developing a conceptual framework, the researcher relates concepts in a logical manner to form propositional statements.

Researchers are concerned with the generation and development of theories through testing. Both inductive and deductive reasoning processes are used in theory generation and development. **Deductive reasoning** proceeds from the general (theory) to the specific (empirical data). **Inductive reasoning** flows from the specific (empirical data) to the general (theory).

Two types of theories are grand theories and middle-range theories. **Grand theories** are concerned with a broad range of phenomena in the environment or in the experiences of humans; **middle-range theories** are concerned with only a small area of the environment or human experiences.

Nurses have used theories from nursing and from other disciplines when conducting nursing research. These theories from other disciplines concern concepts such as social learning, adult learning, role socialization, stress, helplessness, cognitive dissonance, human development, motivation, crisis, relaxation, pain, anxiety, body image, job satisfaction, family interactions, communication, coping, moral reasoning, change, and health behaviors.

A theoretical or conceptual framework should be used in all quantitative research. The framework guides the steps in the research process and is the mechanism through which a generalizable body of knowledge is developed.

NURSING RESEARCH ON THE WEB

For additional online resources, research activities, and exercises, go to **www.mynursingkit. com.** Select Chapter 7 from the drop-down menu.

GET INVOLVED ACTIVITIES

1. Write the name of a theory on the blackboard. No duplicates are allowed, so write your theory on the board as soon as you can!
2. Bring a research article to class that contains a theory. See how many different theories the class has identified in published studies.
3. Using the same articles from Activity 2, try to identify other theories that might have been used as the frameworks for these studies.
4. Identify some specific area where you think an additional theory is needed to guide nursing practice.
5. Based on the idea generated in Activity 4, make up a name for this theory (be creative!).
6. Divide into teams. Each team will choose a nurse theorist. Debate which of these theorists has made the most valuable contributions to nursing research.

SELF-TEST

Match the description of terms in Column B with terms in Column A.

Column A	Column B
1. theory	A. word picture or mental idea of a phenomenon
2. concept	B. contains propositional statements
3. construct	C. a statement that asserts the relationship between concepts
4. proposition	D. highly abstract phenomenon that cannot be directly observed
5. model	E. symbolic representation of some phenomenon or phenomena

Circle the letter before the *best* answer.

6. Nursing research has used which of the following reasoning processes?
   A. inductive
   B. deductive
   C. both inductive and deductive
   D. neither inductive nor deductive

7. Deriving a propositional statement from a theory involves the logical reasoning process called
   A. deduction.
   B. conceptualization.
   C. induction.
   D. critical analysis.

8. Which of the following statements regarding theory is *false*?
   A. It proves the relationship between variables.
   B. It describes the relationship between variables.
   C. It explains the relationship between variables.
   D. It contains propositional statements.

9. Which of the following is *not* one of the common concepts that are included in nearly all of the nursing conceptual models?
   A. person
   B. environment
   C. death
   D. health
   E. nursing

10. You are trying to help a client stop consuming foods that are high in complex carbohydrates. Which of the following model/theory would probably be *most* appropriate?
    A. anxiety theory
    B. adult learning theory
    C. health belief model
    D. health care system model

11. Which of the following theories was developed by a nurse theorist?
    A. social cognitive theory
    B. uncertainty in illness theory
    C. hierarchy of needs theory
    D. job satisfaction theory

REFERENCES

Bambini, D., Washburn, J., & Perkins, R. (2009). Outcomes of clinical simulation for novice nursing students: Communication, confidence, clinical judgment. *Nursing Education Perspectives, 30,* 79–82.

Bandura, A. (1977). *Self-efficacy: The exercise of control.* New York: W. H. Freeman & Co.

Bandura, A. (1985). *Social foundations of thought and action: A social cognitive theory.* Englewood Cliffs, NJ: Prentice-Hall.

Becker, M. H. (1985). Patient adherence to prescribed therapies. *Medical Care, 23,* 539–555.

Benner, P. (1984). From novice to expert: Excellence and power in clinical nursing practice. Menlo Park, CA: Addison-Wesley.

Benson, H. (1975). *The relaxation response.* New York: Morrow.

Biddle, B. J., (1986). Recent developments in role theory. *Annual Review of Sociology, 12,* 67–92.

Blackwell, B. (1985). Models: Their virtues and vices. *Journal of Cardiac Rehabilitation, 5,* 169–171.

Brink, P. J. (2000). A response to Fawcett. *Western Journal of Nursing Research, 22,* 653–655.

Burns, N., & Grove, S. (2009). The practice of nursing research: Appraisal, synthesis, generation of evidence. (6th ed.). St. Louis, MO: Saunders Elsevier.

Bush, H. (1979). Models for nursing. *Advances in Nursing Science, 1*(2), 13–21.

Caplan, G. (1964). *Principles of preventive psychiatry.* New York: Basic Books.

Cox, C. (1982). An interaction model of client health behavior: Theoretical prescription for nursing. *Advances in Nursing Science, 5*(1), 41–56.

Duvall, E. (1977). *Marriage and family development* (5th ed.). Philadelphia: Lippincott.

Erikson, E. (1950). *Childhood and society.* New York: W. W. Norton.

Farren, A. T. (2010). Power, uncertainty, self-transcendence, and quality of life in breast cancer survivors. *Nursing Science Quarterly, 23,* 63–71. doi: 10.1177/0894318409353793

Fawcett, J. (1995). *Analysis and evaluation of conceptual models of nursing* (3rd ed.). Philadelphia: F. A. Davis.

Fawcett, J. (2000). But is it *nursing* research? *Western Journal of Nursing Research, 22,* 524–525.

Festinger, L. (1957). *A theory of cognitive dissonance.* Stanford, CA: Stanford University Press.

Fincher, L., Ward, C., Dawkins, V., Magee, V. & Willson, P. (2009). Using telehealth to educate Parkinson's disease patients about complicated medication regimens. *Journal of Gerontological Nursing, 35*(2), 16–24.

Fitzpatrick, J. J., & Whall, A. L. (1996). *Conceptual models of nursing: Analysis and application* (3rd ed.). Stamford, CT: Appleton & Lange.

Freud, S. (1938). *The basic writings of Sigmund Freud.* New York: Random House.

George, J. B. (1995). *Nursing theories: The base for professional nursing practice* (4th ed.). Norwalk, CT: Appleton & Lange.

Günüsen, N. P., Üstün, B., & Gigiotti, E. (2009). Conceptualization of burnout from the perspective of the Neuman Systems Model, *Nursing Science Quarterly, 22*, 200–204. doi: 10.1177/0894318409338685

Hatfield, L. A. (2008). Sucrose decreases infant biobehavioral pain response to immunizations: A randomized controlled trial. *Journal of Nursing Scholarship, 40*, 219–225.

Havighurst, R. (1952). *Developmental tasks and education.* New York: Longmans, Green.

Herzberg, F. (1966). *Work and the nature of man.* Cleveland: World Publishing.

Hoffman, A. J., von Eye, A., Gift, A. G., Given, B. A., Given, C. W., & Rothert, M. (2009). Testing a theoretical model of perceived self-efficacy for cancer-related fatigue self-management and optimal physical functional status. *Nursing Research, 58*, 32–41.

Kerlinger, F. (1973). *Foundations of behavioral research* (2nd ed.). New York: Holt, Rinehart & Winston.

Kerlinger, F. (1986). *Foundations of behavioral research* (3rd ed.). New York: Holt, Rinehart & Winston.

King, I. M. (1981). *A theory for nursing: Systems, concepts, process.* New York: John Wiley.

Knowles, M. (1990). *The adult learner: A neglected species* (4th ed.). Houston: Gulf Press.

Kohlberg, L. (1978). The cognitive developmental approach to moral education. In P. Scharf (Ed.), *Readings in moral education* (pp. 36–51). Minneapolis: Winston Press.

Lazarus, R. S., & Folkman, S. (1984). *Stress, appraisal, and coping.* New York: Springer.

Lefaiver, C. A., Keough, V., Letizia, M., & Lanuza, D. M. (2007). Using the Roy Adaptation Model to explore the dynamics of quality of life and the relationship between lung transplant candidates and their caregivers. *Advances in Nursing Science, 30*, 266–274.

Lentz, E. R., Pugh, L. C., Milligan, R. A., Gift, A., & Suppe, F. (1997). The middle-range theory of unpleasant symptoms: An update. *Advances in Nursing Science, 19*(3), 14–27.

Levine, M. Y. (1995). The rhetoric of nursing theory. *Image: Journal of Nursing Scholarship, 27*, 11–14.

Lewin, K. (1951). *Field theory in social science.* Westport, CT: Greenwood.

Malinski, V. M., & Barrett, E. A. M. (Eds.). (1994). *Martha E. Rogers: Her life and her work.* Philadelphia: F. A. Davis.

Maslow, A. (1970). *Motivation and personality* (2nd ed.). New York: Harper & Row.

Mead, G. (1934). *Mind, self and society.* Chicago: University of Chicago Press.

Melzack, R., & Wall, P. (1983). *The challenge of pain* (rev. ed.). New York: Basic Books.

Minuchin, S. (1974). *Families and family therapy.* Cambridge, MA: Harvard University Press.

Mishel, M. H. (1981). The measurement of uncertainty in illness. *Nursing Research, 30*, 258–263.

Mishel, M. H. (1990). Reconceptualizatin of the Uncertainty in Illness Theory. *Image: Journal of Nursing Scholarship, 22*, 256–262.

Moola, S., Ehlers, V. J., & Hattingh, S P. (2008). Critical care nurses' perceptions of stress and stress-related situations in the workplace. *Curationis, 32*, 77–86.

Neuman, B. (1972). A model for teaching total person approach to patient problems. *Nursing Research, 2*, 264–269.

Neuman, B. (1974). The Betty Neuman Health-Care Systems Model: A total person approach to patient problems. In J. P. Riehl & C. Roy (Eds.), *Conceptual models for nursing practice* (pp. 99–114). New York: Appleton-Century Crofts.

Neuman, B. (1980). The Betty Neuman Health-Care Systems Model: A total person approach to patient problems. In J. P. Riehl & C. Roy (Eds.), *Conceptual models for nursing practice* (2nd ed., pp. 99–114). New York: Appleton-Century Crofts.

Neuman, B. (1982). *The Neuman systems model.* Norwalk, CT: Appleton-Century-Crofts.

Neuman, B., & Fawcett, J. (2011). *The Neuman system model* (5th ed.) Upper Saddle River, NJ: Prentice Hall.

Orem, D., Taylor, S., & McLaughlin, K. (2001). *Nursing: Concepts of practice* (6th ed.). St. Louis, MO: Mosby Year Book.

Parse, R. R. (2000). Obfuscating: The persistent practice of misnaming. *Nursing Science Quarterly, 13*, 91.

Parse, R. R. (2003). What constitutes nursing research? *Nursing Science Quarterly, 16,* 287.

Pender, N. J. (1996). *Health promotion in nursing practice* (3rd ed.). Norwalk, CT: Appleton & Lange.

Peplau, H. E. (1988). *Interpersonal relations in nursing.* London: Macmillan Education.

Piaget, J. (1926). *The language and thought of the child.* New York: Harcourt, Brace, and World.

Pipe, T. B., Bortz, J. J., & Dueck, A. (2009). Nurse leader mindfulness meditation program for stress management. *JONA, 39*, 130–137.

Polit, D. F., & Beck, C. T. (2008). Nursing research: Generating and assessing evidence for nursing practice (8th ed.). Philadelphia: Lippincott Williams & Wilkins.

Prochaska, J. O., & DiClemente, C. C. (1983). Stages and processes of self-change of smoking: Toward an integrative model of change. *Journal of Consulting Psychology, 52*, 390–395.

Reynolds, P. (1971). *A primer in theory construction.* Indianapolis: Bobbs-Merrill.

Rogers, C. (1969). *Freedom to learn.* Columbus, OH: Charles E. Merrill.

Rogers, M. (1970). *An introduction to the theoretical basis of nursing.* Philadelphia: F. A. Davis.

Rogers, M. (1980). Nursing: A science of unitary man. In J. P. Riehl and C. Roy (Eds.), *Conceptual models for nursing practice* (2nd ed., pp. 329–337). New York: Appleton-Century-Crofts.

Rogers, M. (1992). Nursing science and the space age. *Nursing Science Quarterly, 5*, 27–34.

Rotter, J. (1954). *Social learning and clinical psychology.* Englewood Cliffs, NJ: Prentice-Hall.

Roy, C. (1970). Adaptation: A conceptual framework for nursing. *Nursing Outlook, 18*, 42–45.

Roy, C. (1984). *Introduction to nursing: An adaptation model* (2nd ed.). Englewood Cliffs, NJ: Prentice- Hall.

Roy, C., & Andrews, H. A. (1999). *The Roy adaptation model* (2nd ed.). Stamford, CT: Appleton & Lange.

Roy, C., & Andrews, H. A. (2008). *The Roy adaptation model* (3rd ed.). Upper Saddle River, NJ: Prentice Hall.

Satir, V. (1967). *Conjoint family therapy* (rev. ed.). Palo Alto, CA: Science & Behavior Books.

Schilder, P. (1952). *The image and appearance of the human body.* New York: International University Press.

Schneiderman, J., Corbridge, S., & Zerwic, J. J. (2009). Demonstrating the effectiveness of an online, computer-based learning module for arterial blood gas analysis. *Clinical Nurse Specialist, 33,* 151–155.

Seligman, M. (1975). *Helplessness: On depression, development, and death.* San Francisco: W. H. Freeman.

Selye, H. (1976). *The stress of life* (rev. ed.). New York: McGraw-Hill.

Sheehan, C. A. (2009). A brief educational video about prostate cancer screening: A community intervention. *Urologic Nursing, 29,* 103–111, 117.

Song, H.-Y., & Nam, K. A. (2010). Coping strategies, physical function, and social adjustment in people with spinal cord injury. *Rehabilitation Nursing, 35,* 8–15.

Spielberger, C. (1972). Anxiety as an emotional state. In C. D. Spielberger (Ed.), *Anxiety: Current trends in theory and research* (Vol. 1, pp. 3–47). New York: Academic Press.

Stevens, B. (1979). *Nursing theory.* Boston: Little, Brown.

Stewart, J. L., Lynn, M. R., & Mishel, M. H. (2010). Psychometric evaluation of a new instrument to measure uncertainty in children and adolescents with cancer. *Nursing Research, 59,* 119–125.

Taylor, S. G., Geden, E., Isaramalai, S., & Wongvatunyu, S. (2000). *Nursing Science Quarterly, 13,* 104–110.

Tripp-Reimer, T., Woodworth, G., McCloskey, J. C., & Bulechek, G. (1996). The dimensional structure of nursing interventions. *Nursing Research, 45,* 10–17.

Youngkin, E. Q., & Lester, P. B. (2010). Promoting self-care and secondary prevention in women's health: A study to test the accuracy of a home self-test system for bacterial vaginosis. *Applied Nursing Research, 23,* 2–10.

Walker, S. N., Pullen, C. H, Boeckner, L., Hageman, P. A., Hertzog, M., Oberdorfer, M. K., & Rutledge, M. J. (2009). Clinical trial of tailored activity and eating newsletters with older rural women. *Nursing Research, 58,* 74–85.

Watson, J. (2005). *Caring science as sacred science.* Philadelphia: F. A. Davis.

CHAPTER 8

Hypotheses

OUTLINE

Purposes of Hypotheses

Sources or Rationale for Hypotheses

Classifications of Hypotheses

- Simple and Complex Hypotheses
- Null and Research Hypotheses
- Nondirectional and Directional Research Hypotheses

Hypothesis Criteria

- Written in a Declarative Sentence
- Written in the Present Tense
- Contain the Population
- Contain the Variables

- Reflect the Problem Statement, Purpose Statement, or Research Question
- Empirically Testable

Hypothesis Format

Hypotheses and Theory Testing

Critiquing Hypotheses

Summary

Nursing Research on the Web

Get Involved Activities

Self-Test

OBJECTIVES

On completion of this chapter, you will be prepared to:

1. Determine the purposes of hypotheses in research studies
2. Identify sources or rationale for study hypotheses
3. Describe classifications of hypotheses
4. Distinguish between simple and complex hypotheses
5. Compare null hypotheses and research hypotheses
6. Differentiate nondirectional and directional research hypotheses
7. List the criteria to be considered when formulating a hypothesis
8. Discuss the format for writing hypotheses
9. Recognize the use of hypotheses in the testing of theories
10. Determine the types of studies for which hypotheses are not needed
12. Critique study hypotheses in research reports

NEW TERMS DEFINED IN THIS CHAPTER

complex hypothesis, pg 101

directional research hypothesis, pg 104

interaction effect, pg 103

nondirectional research hypothesis, pg 104

null hypothesis, pg 103

research hypothesis, pg 103

simple hypothesis, pg 101

You wonder why the traffic is moving so slowly. You start thinking of possible reasons. There may have been an accident up ahead. Or maybe a car has stalled and people must switch lanes to get past the stalled car. Yesterday, you read in the paper that road repairs were going to be made on some of the streets in your city, but you cannot remember which streets were going to be repaired. The next thought that comes to mind is there may be a police officer parked on the side of the road just waiting for speeders. Suddenly, you see flashing lights and hear an ambulance siren. Then you see two crumpled cars and people standing around them. Now you know that an accident is the cause of the traffic slowdown. The hunches you had about the reasons for the slow traffic could be considered hypotheses. After the facts were gathered, you find that your first hunch was correct. The accident is the cause of the slow traffic.

In scientific research, hypotheses are intelligent guesses that assist the researcher in seeking the solution to a problem. Kerlinger (1986) has defined a hypothesis as a "conjectural statement of the relations between two or more variables" (p. 17). Polit and Beck (2008) presented a similar definition by calling a hypothesis a "statement of the researcher's expectations about relationships between study variables" (p. 66). As stated in Chapter 3, the following definition of a hypothesis is used in this book: A hypothesis is a statement of the predicted relationship between two or more variables. Research studies may have one or several hypotheses.

The hypothesis links the independent and the dependent variables. Recall that an independent variable is the "cause," and the dependent variable is the "effect" in experimental studies. The researcher manipulates, or controls, the independent variable. In nonexperimental studies, the words *cause* and *effect* are not appropriate because the researcher does not manipulate the independent variable. The researcher, however, may be able to determine which variable might have an influence on the other variable. The direction of influence runs from the independent variable to the dependent variable. A researcher might be trying to examine the relationship between age and the amount of exercise that people perform. The independent variable would be "age" and the dependent variable "exercise performance." It would not be appropriate to say that age is the "cause" of the amount of exercise that one performs although the direction of influence logically flows from age to exercise performance.

Hypotheses should always be written before the study begins and not changed after the study results are examined. This is like changing your choice of who will win a race after you have already watched the race!

PURPOSES OF HYPOTHESES

Hypotheses serve several purposes in research studies. They lend objectivity to scientific investigations by pinpointing a specific part of a theory to be tested. Through hypotheses, theoretical propositions can be tested in the real world. The investigator can then advance scientific knowledge by supporting or failing to support the tested theory. Even when the research hypothesis is not supported, scientific knowledge is gained. Negative findings are sometimes as important as positive ones. Hypotheses also guide the research design and dictate the type of statistical analysis to be used with the data. Finally, hypotheses provide the reader with an understanding of the researcher's expectations about the study before data collection begins. Hypotheses are more important than ever in this day of evidence-based nursing practice. Nurses need to know that their practice is based on research studies in which hypothesis testing has supported certain nursing care practices or interventions.

SOURCES OR RATIONALE FOR STUDY HYPOTHESES

Hypotheses are not wild guesses or shots in the dark. The researcher should be able to state the source or rationale for each hypothesis. This source or rationale for the hypothesis may come from a theory, a previous research study, or personal experience.

The most important source of a hypothesis is the theoretical or conceptual framework developed for the study. This process of hypothesis development involves deductive reasoning. A propositional statement is isolated from the study framework and empirically tested. For example, using Maslow's theory of human needs, you might decide to test the proposition that safety needs take precedence over self-esteem needs. This proposition could then be transferred into a hypothesis to be tested in a research study. You might ask a group of patients to rate a list of nursing actions, and then you could determine if they rated actions that concern patient safety higher than actions that concern meeting their self-esteem needs.

Hypotheses for nursing research studies can also be derived from the findings of other studies. The researcher may test the assumptions of another study or test a hypothesis based on the findings of another study.

Finally, a nurse may have a hunch that comes from personal experiences or observations. For example, you may have noticed that psychiatric patients seem to become more anxious as the time for their discharge approaches. Observations continue to be made. Patients' charts are examined to determine behaviors reported by other staff members. The behaviors recorded on the charts seem to agree with your observations. Thus, an empirical generalization may be made based on these observations: "As the time for discharge draws near, the anxiety levels of psychiatric patients increase." The following hypothesis might then be tested: "The anxiety levels of psychiatric patients are higher immediately before discharge than they are 3 days before discharge." Recall the difference between induction and deduction. This hypothesis was derived through induction. It was based on an empirical generalization derived from your observations as a nurse. Even when a study is based on empirical generalizations from the researcher's own experiences, a review of the literature should be conducted in the study area to determine what is already known on the topic. Then an attempt should be made to find a theoretical explanation for the observed phenomenon.

CLASSIFICATIONS OF HYPOTHESES

Hypotheses can be categorized as simple hypotheses or complex hypotheses. They can also be classified as research hypotheses or null hypotheses. Research hypotheses can be further divided into nondirectional and directional hypotheses.

Simple and Complex Hypotheses

A **simple hypothesis** concerns the relationship between one independent and one dependent variable. Independent and dependent variables were discussed in Chapter 3. If you recall, in experimental studies the independent variable may be considered as the "cause," or reason that a phenomenon occurs, and the dependent variable the "effect," or occurrence of the phenomenon. Independent and dependent variables can also be identified in many nonexperimental studies by examining the direction of the influence of one variable on the other or by determining which variable occurred before the other one. The independent variable occurs first in chronological time (but not necessarily first in the hypothesis statement itself).

A **complex hypothesis** concerns a relationship where two or more independent variables, or two or more dependent variables, or both, are being examined in the same study. A simple hypothesis might be called bivariate and a complex hypothesis multivariate.

Simple hypotheses contain one independent variable and one dependent variable; complex hypotheses contain more than one independent and/or dependent variable. As long as there is more than one independent variable, or more than one dependent variable, or both, the hypothesis is considered complex. Table 8–1 gives examples of simple and complex hypotheses.

Caution should be exercised when using complex hypotheses. It may be better to divide a complex hypothesis into two or more simple hypotheses. Although you may read about "partial support" for a hypothesis, this is inaccurate. If only part of the hypothesis is supported, the researcher is in the partial support crisis. In actuality, a hypothesis is either supported totally or it is not supported. It is like being pregnant. A woman is either pregnant or not pregnant. She cannot be a little bit pregnant!

Consider this hypothesis: A positive relationship exists between patients' perception of pain control and (a) complaints of pain and (b) requests for pain medications. Statistically, two hypotheses will be tested: (a) the relationship between perception of pain control and complaints of pain and (b)

TABLE 8–1 Simple and Complex Hypotheses

Population	Independent Variable	Dependent Variable	Type of Hypothesis	Hypotheses
1. Infants	Level of alcohol use of mothers	Birth weight	Simple	Birth weight is lower among infants of alcoholic mothers than among infants of nonalcoholic mothers.
2. Intensive care unit patients	Sleep deprivation	Anxiety	Simple	The greater the degree of sleep deprivation, the higher the anxiety level of intensive care unit patients.
3. Adults	a. Type of diet b. Exercise	Weight	Complex	Daily weight loss is greater for adults who follow a reduced calorie diet and exercise daily than for those who do not follow a reduced calorie diet and do not exercise daily.
4. Nurse practitioners	Type of nurse practitioner	Job mobility	Simple	The level of job mobility is different for psychiatric nurse practitioners than for medical-surgical nurse practitioners.
5. Women	Method of delivery	a. Postpartum depression b. Feelings of inadequacy	Complex	More postpartum depression and feelings of inadequacy are reported by women who give birth by cesarean delivery than by those who deliver vaginally.
6. Postmyocardial infarction patients	Denial	Anxiety	Simple	There is a negative relationship between denial and reports of anxiety among postmyocardial infarction patients.

the relationship between perception of pain control and requests for pain medications. If a significant relationship is found between perception of pain control and complaints of pain but not between perception of pain control and requests for pain medication, then a *partial* support crisis has occurred. The researcher cannot decide to divide the original hypothesis at this time, but must admit that the research hypothesis has not been supported. This problem could have been solved by writing two simple hypotheses rather than one complex hypothesis.

Sometimes complex hypotheses are necessary. Whenever the researcher wants to examine an interaction effect, a complex hypothesis is called for. An **interaction effect** concerns the action of two variables in conjunction with each other. Consider Hypothesis 3 in Table 8–1. The researcher believes that the combination of diet and exercise is necessary for weight loss.

Null and Research Hypotheses

Those of you who have had a course in statistics will recall that a **null hypothesis** (H_0) predicts that no relationship exists between variables, and it is the null hypothesis that is subjected to statistical analysis. For those of you who have repressed statistics into your unconscious and for those who have not yet taken a statistics course, you need to know that the null hypothesis is tested even when the research hypothesis is stated in the study. A **research hypothesis** or alternative hypothesis (H_1) states the expected relationship between variables. Other names for the research hypothesis are *scientific, substantive,* and *theoretical.* With this type of hypothesis, the reader of a research report can determine exactly what the researcher expects to find when analyzing the data.

Statistical logic requires that a testable hypothesis state the expectation of no correlation between the variables or no difference between groups or sets of data on the variable being measured. If the research hypothesis proposes that a correlation exists between two variables, the null hypothesis states that no correlation exists. If the research hypothesis states that a difference exists between two groups or sets of data, the null hypothesis states that no difference exists.

Although some research studies express hypotheses in the null form, it is generally more desirable to state the researcher's expectations, according to Batey (1977) and Kerlinger (1986). Polit and Beck (2008) have written that they prefer directional hypotheses when there is a reasonable basis for them because these hypotheses "clarify the study's framework and demonstrate that researchers have thought critically about the phenomena under study" (p. 99). A review of the current nursing research journals shows that the research hypothesis has replaced the statistical null hypothesis as the preferred way of expressing the predictions for studies. The use of theoretical frameworks in nursing research has brought about this change. Study predictions should be based on the study framework.

The level of significance for rejecting the statistical null hypothesis should always be stated before data are collected. In nursing, as in many other disciplines, the level of significance is usually set at .05. A significance level of .05 means that the researcher is willing to risk being wrong 5% of the time, or 5 times out of 100, when rejecting the null hypothesis (see Chapter 15). Generally, the aim of the researcher is to reject the null hypothesis because this provides support for the research hypothesis. Sir Ronald Fisher (1951) stated, "Every experiment may be said to exist only in order to give the facts a chance of disproving the null hypothesis" (p. 16).

Occasionally, the null hypothesis and the research hypothesis are the same. The researcher actually expects no correlation between variables or no difference between groups being compared on a certain variable. For example, an in-service educator at a hospital might believe that a certain inexpensive teaching program is as effective as an expensive teaching program for patients with diabetes. The educator might predict that there would be no difference in patients' knowledge of the subject matter when the two different teaching programs are used. Usually, the researcher *does* expect to find a difference or a correlation; otherwise, the study would not have been conducted.

Null Hypotheses

A null hypothesis was tested in a study (Harrison, Speroni, Dugan, & Daniel, 2010) that compared the quality of blood specimens drawn on one group of patients (N = 200) by Emergency Medical Services (EMS) staff versus specimens obtained on another group (N = 200) by Emergency Department (ED) staff when the patients reached the emergency department. One aspect of the study examined redraw rates. Study results showed no statistically significant differences in redraw rates between the two groups. The null hypothesis was not rejected.

Polit and Beck (2009) studied gender bias in nursing research. They tested the null hypothesis that males and females are represented equally as participants in nursing research studies. The null hypothesis was rejected. Overall, in 834 studies published in eight English-language nursing research journals in 2005–2006, approximately 71% of participants were females. This bias was strong in the United States and Canada; many female participants were also found in studies conducted in Europe, Asia, and Australia.

As you can see, the null hypothesis was *not* rejected in the study by Harrison et al, but *was* rejected in the Polit and Beck study. Female participants were more numerous than male participants, which is rather surprising. In the past, many research studies were conducted only on men.

Nondirectional and Directional Research Hypotheses

Research hypotheses may be described as being nondirectional or directional. In a **nondirectional research hypothesis**, the researcher merely predicts that a relationship exists. The direction of the relationship is not presented.

Nondirectional Research Hypothesis

The safety and effectiveness of three types of large-volume enema solutions were compared in healthy subjects by Schmeltzer, Schiller, Meyer, Rugari, and Case (2004). The nondirectional hypothesis predicted: "There are differences between tap water, soapsuds, and PEG-ES [polyethylene glycol-electrolyte] enema solutions in (1) net output, (2) rectal mucosal irritation, and (3) subjective discomfort." The researchers actually found that soapsuds and tap water enemas produced significantly greater returns than the PEG-ES but were more uncomfortable. Rectal biopsies showed surface epithelium loss after soapsuds and tap water but not after PEG-ES. Schmeltzer et al. called for more research.

You may have noticed that this nondirectional research hypothesis example comes from a 2004 reference. An examination of recently published studies did not reveal any nondirectional hypotheses. Of course, not all published studies were reviewed!

In the **directional research hypothesis,** the researcher predicts the type of relationship that is expected. Directional hypotheses have several advantages: They make clear the researcher's expectation, allow more precise testing of theoretical propositions, and allow the use of one-tailed statistical tests. Statistical significance is more easily achieved when one-tailed tests are used (see Chapter 15).

Directional Research Hypothesis

Teng et al. (2009) studied the professional commitment of nurses in Taiwan in regard to patient safety and patient-perceived care quality. These researchers predicted in their two hypotheses that professional commitment enhances (a) patient safety and (b) care quality. Both of their hypotheses were supported by the data.

When a study is not based on a theory or the findings of related studies are contradictory, the investigator may decide to use a nondirectional hypothesis. Examine the hypotheses in Table 8–1. Try to determine the directional and nondirectional hypotheses. Only one of them is a nondirectional hypothesis. Did you discover which one?

HYPOTHESIS CRITERIA

A hypothesis should:

1. be written in a declarative sentence.
2. be written in the present tense.
3. contain the population.
4. contain the variables.
5. reflect the problem statement, purpose statement, or research question.
6. be empirically testable.

Written in a Declarative Sentence

Hypotheses should always be written in declarative sentences. Whereas the research question inquires about some phenomenon or phenomena of interest in the study, the hypothesis presents an answer to the question in the form of a declarative statement.

Written in the Present Tense

Hypotheses found in the published research reports may be written in the future tense. However, hypotheses are tested in the present and should be written in the present tense.

- **Future tense:** There *will* be a positive relationship between the number of times children have been hospitalized and their fear of hospitalization (incorrect format).
- **Present tense:** There *is* a positive relationship between the number of times children have been hospitalized and their fear of hospitalization (correct format).

Contain the Population

The population needs to be specifically identified in the hypothesis, just as it is in the problem statement, purpose statement, or research question. If the research question identifies the population as "middle-aged (40–55 years old) women who are about to undergo a hysterectomy," these same terms should be contained in the hypothesis. It would not be correct to identify the population in the hypothesis only as "hysterectomy patients."

Contain the Variables

Notice that the word *variable* is written as a plural noun in the heading for this paragraph. In the identification of the study problem section of Chapter 5, this same heading was written as variable(s). In the problem statement or research question, you might have only one variable. A univariate research problem statement or research question is acceptable. Remember, however, a scientific hypothesis contains at least two variables, one independent and one dependent, which are linked in the hypothesis.

Frequently, the hypothesis contains the instrument or tool that will be used to measure the dependent variable. This instrument links the hypothesis more closely to the actual data-gathering procedure and helps operationalize the dependent variable. Here is an example of two ways to write the same hypothesis:

- Anxiety levels are lower for preoperative hysterectomy patients who have practiced relaxation exercises than for preoperative hysterectomy patients who have not practiced relaxation exercises.
- Anxiety levels, as measured by the state anxiety scale of Spielberger's State-Trait Anxiety Inventory, are lower for preoperative hysterectomy patients who have practiced relaxation exercises than for preoperative hysterectomy patients who have not practiced relaxation exercises.

As you can see, the second example contains the instrument that will be used to measure the dependent variable. The hypothesis will still need further clarification, however, before it is ready to be tested. For example, relaxation exercises would have to be operationally defined before the study could actually be conducted.

Reflect the Problem Statement, Purpose Statement, or Research Question

To reemphasize the point, the hypothesis should contain essentially the same material as the problem statement, purpose statement, or research question. Occasionally, you read a research report in which it appears that one person wrote the purpose statement and another person wrote the hypothesis without ever reading the purpose statement. For example, the purpose statement might indicate "depression" as the dependent variable, whereas the hypothesis contains "sadness" as the dependent variable. Congruency is a must!

Empirically Testable

The ability to obtain empirical data should have been determined as the research problem was formalized. If there is no possibility of obtaining empirical data, it will not be possible to conduct a quantitative study. A hypothesis that cannot be empirically tested has no scientific merit. Ethical and value issues are two areas that are inappropriate for hypothesis testing because data cannot be obtained that can be empirically verified. Consider the following hypothesis: "Nurse practitioners are better health care providers than physicians." This hypothesis is not empirically testable because *better* is a value word. You could, in fact, change the wording of this hypothesis to make it empirically testable: "Nurse practitioners spend more time teaching their clients about preventative health care practices than do physicians." The term *time* could be measured empirically.

HYPOTHESIS FORMAT

Research questions that examine more than one variable are usually written in the form of a correlational statement or comparative statement. The same holds true for hypotheses. The issue of correlations and comparisons becomes very important when the data are submitted for statistical analysis. Statistical tests are basically designed to examine correlations between variables or comparisons among sets of data. One study might compare the average pulse rates of *two* different groups, whereas another study might examine the correlation between pulse rates and respirations in *one* group of subjects. A different statistical test would be needed to analyze the data from these two studies.

A directional research hypothesis should contain a predictive term like *less, greater, decrease in*, or *negative correlation*. Let us examine some examples of research questions and corresponding hypotheses. The predictive terms in the two hypotheses are in italics.

* **Research Question:** Is there a correlation between anxiety levels and midterm examination scores of baccalaureate nursing students?
* **Hypothesis:** There is a *negative correlation* between anxiety levels and midterm examination scores of baccalaureate nursing students.
* **Research Question:** Is there a difference in readiness to learn about preoperative teaching between preoperative patients who have high anxiety levels compared with preoperative patients who do not have high anxiety levels?
* **Hypothesis:** Readiness to learn about preoperative teaching is *less* among preoperative patients who have high anxiety levels compared with preoperative patients who do not have high anxiety levels.

HYPOTHESES AND THEORY TESTING

Chapter 15 discusses the statistical testing of a hypothesis. It seems important at this point, however, to mention hypothesis testing and its relation to theory. A hypothesis usually tests only one proposition from a theory, not an entire theory.

Hypotheses are never proved or disproved. Novice researchers can be spotted easily if they discuss trying to "prove" their hypotheses. Remember, neither theories nor hypotheses are proved. In my research classes, a student has to bring cookies to the next class if he or she says the word *prove* out loud in a class discussion. I even have to bring cookies if I slip and say the "p" word myself.

If the null hypothesis is rejected, the research hypothesis is supported. If the research hypothesis is supported, the theory from which the hypothesis was derived will also be supported. Likewise, if the research hypothesis is not supported, the theory is also not supported. When the data fail to support the theory, a critical reexamination of the theory is needed. Beginning researchers frequently have difficulty in explaining their findings when these findings fail to support the tested theory. In some cases, the researcher points out all of the limitations of the study and intimates that the theory is probably valid. The researcher then points out that the study results failed to support the theory because of design or methodology problems that are the fault of the researcher. It is possible that study limitations may have, in fact, influenced the results of the study, but it is also possible that the theory is not valid. In some studies where hypotheses are tested, questions may also be posed. These questions may relate to the hypotheses. For example, suppose a researcher is testing a new intervention for weight loss. The hypothesis might be "People who are overweight and allowed to eat a candy bar each day as part of their diet lose more weight over a 6-week period than those who are not allowed to eat a candy bar." (Note: This is my kind of diet!) The researcher might also ask such questions as "Which type of candy bars do people choose?" "How many calories are in the candy bars that are chosen?" "What percentage of their daily calories is consumed in the candy bars?" My father worked for a candy factory for 50 years before he retired. Although we did not have many material possessions when I was growing up, we always had candy! The neighborhood children were jealous. I must acknowledge that mother allowed only small amounts of candy in our house, and only on special occasions.

CRITIQUING HYPOTHESES

First, the evaluator of a research report determines if the report contains a hypothesis or hypotheses. Optimally, a section heading clearly labels the hypotheses. If the study contains no hypotheses, a determination should be made as to whether or not the study is appropriate for hypothesis testing.

If the study report contains a hypothesis or hypotheses, a number of factors must be considered. Box 8–1 presents the criteria for evaluating study hypotheses.

Box 8–1 Guidelines for Critiquing Hypotheses and Research Questions

1. Does the study contain a hypothesis or hypotheses?
2. Is each hypothesis clearly worded and concise?
3. Is the hypothesis written in a declarative sentence?
4. Is each hypothesis directly tied to the study problem?
5. If there is a clearly identified study framework, is each hypothesis derived from this framework?
6. Does each hypothesis contain the population and at least two variables?
7. Is each hypothesis stated as a directional research hypothesis? If not, is the rationale given for the type of hypothesis that is stated?
8. Is it apparent that each hypothesis can be empirically tested?
9. Does each hypothesis contain only one prediction?

Hypotheses should be clear and concise declarative sentences and written in the present tense. Hypotheses should reflect the problem statement, purpose statement, or research question and be derived from the study framework if there is a clearly identified study framework. If there is no identified study framework, the source or rationale for each hypothesis should be apparent to the person critiquing the research report. For example, a hypothesis might be based on previous research findings. The preferred type of hypothesis is a directional research hypothesis. It is easy to determine that the hypothesis is directional if it contains a word or phrase such as "greater than," "increase in," or "negative correlation." The hypothesis should contain the population and study variables. Each hypothesis should be empirically testable and contain only one prediction. The hypothesis may contain the name of the specific research instrument(s) that will be used to measure the study variables. If not, the research report should contain an operational definition of each of the study variables.

It is not uncommon for a study to have tested many more hypotheses than are stated. This fact may be discovered when examining the statistical results. For every statistical test result and accompanying probability value (p), the researcher has tested a hypothesis, whether or not the hypothesis was actually stated. Frequently, after eyeballing the data, the researcher may decide to make some additional statistical analyses. For example, suppose a determination was being made about the effectiveness of preoperative relaxation exercises in controlling postoperative anxiety. The study results indicate that the postoperative anxiety levels of subjects are not significantly different between those who practiced relaxation preoperatively and those who did not. However, when the researcher looked over the data, it appeared that the relaxation exercises might have been effective for women, but not for men. An additional statistical comparison might be made between the women who practiced relaxation and those who did not. This type of statistical analysis is labeled a post hoc (after the fact) comparison.

SUMMARY

A hypothesis is a statement of the predicted relationship between two or more variables. Hypotheses allow theoretical propositions to be tested in the real world, guide the research design, dictate the type of statistical analysis for the data, and provide the reader with an understanding of the researcher's expectations about the study before data collection begins.

The rationale or sources of hypotheses can come from theories, previous research studies, or the researcher's own personal experiences. Nursing research involves both inductive and deductive means of formulating hypotheses.

Hypotheses can be categorized as simple or complex. **Simple hypotheses** contain one independent and one dependent variable; **complex hypotheses** contain two or more independent variables, or two or more dependent variables, or both. An **interaction effect** concerns the action of two variables in conjunction with each other.

Hypotheses may also be classified as statistical null hypotheses or research hypotheses. The **null hypothesis** states that no difference exists between groups or sets of data or that there is no correlation between variables. The **research hypothesis** states that a difference or correlation does exist. Research hypotheses can be divided into nondirectional and directional hypotheses. The **nondirectional research hypothesis** indicates that a difference or correlation exists, but does not predict the type. The **directional research hypothesis** states the type of correlation or difference that the researcher expects to find. The directional research hypothesis is the preferred type for nursing research studies, unless the study is not based on theory or if previous studies in the area have demonstrated contradictory findings.

A hypothesis should (a) be written in a declarative sentence, (b) be written in the present tense, (c) include the population, (d) include the variables, (e) reflect the problem statement, purpose statement, or research question, and (f) be empirically testable.

The results of statistical analysis will either support or fail to support the hypothesis. Hypotheses are never proved or disproved. If the null hypothesis is rejected, then the research hypothesis is supported. Thus, if a theoretical proposition is being tested and support is found for the research hypothesis, the theory is also supported.

NURSING RESEARCH ON THE WEB

For additional online resources, research activities, and exercises, go to **www.mynursingkit. com.** Select Chapter 8 from the drop-down menu.

GET INVOLVED ACTIVITIES

1. Each person will bring a research article that contains a hypothesis and share it with his or her colleagues. Critique as many of the hypotheses as time allows. Approximately how many research studies did you have to examine to find one that contained a hypothesis?
2. Rewrite one of these hypotheses found in the literature that does not meet the criteria for an acceptable hypothesis.
3. Divide into groups and practice writing hypotheses. Each group will write two hypotheses. In the first one, use the word *headache* as an independent variable, and in the second one, use *headache* as the dependent variable.
4. Write questions that the researcher might ask in a study that are related to one of the hypotheses developed in class.
5. Propose two study examples in which hypotheses would not be needed.
6. Suggest reasons why many published research studies do not contain hypotheses.

SELF-TEST

Identify the independent variable(s) and dependent variable(s) in the following hypotheses.

1. Male appendectomy patients request more pain medication on the first postoperative day than do female appendectomy patients.
2. There is an inverse relationship between the number of prenatal classes attended by pregnant women and their degree of fear concerning labor and delivery at the time of delivery.
3. Unmarried pregnant teenagers report a less positive body image than do married pregnant teenagers.
4. There is an inverse relationship between postoperative hysterectomy patients' anxiety levels and their requests for pain medication.
5. There is a higher incidence of marijuana usage among first-year high school students than among high school seniors.
6. Older adults demonstrate a lower self-image after retirement than before retirement.
7. The job turnover rate and job dissatisfaction levels of graduate nurses who have worked less than 2 years is higher than for those graduate nurses who have worked 2 or more years.

Evaluate the following hypotheses using the criteria presented in this chapter; identify any errors that exist in the hypotheses.

8. Baccalaureate-prepared nurses provide for more of the psychosocial needs of clients.
9. Is there a difference in the anxiety levels of cardiac patients who are taught guided imagery techniques compared to cardiac patients who are not taught guided imagery techniques?
10. Depression levels decrease as the amount of interactions with a pet increases.
11. Nurses provide better health teaching instructions to clients than do doctors.
12. There is a positive relationship between nurses' job autonomy levels and their reported job satisfaction levels.

REFERENCES

Batey, M. (1977). Conceptualization: Knowledge and logic guiding empirical research. *Nursing Research, 26,* 324–329.

Fisher, R. (1951). *The design of experiments* (6th ed.). New York: Hafner.

Harrison, G., Speroni, K. G., Dugan, L., & Daniel, M. G. (2010). A comparison of the quality of blood specimens drawn in the field by EMS versus specimens obtained in the emergency department. *Journal of Emergency Nursing, 36,* 16–20. doi:10.1016/j.jen.2008.11.001

Kerlinger, F. (1986). *Foundations of behavioral research* (3rd ed.). New York: Holt, Rinehart & Winston.

Polit, D. F., & Beck. C. T. (2008). *Nursing research: Principles and methods* (8th ed.). Philadelphia: Lippincott Williams & Wilkins.

Polit, D. F., & Beck, C. T. (2009). International gender bias in nursing research, 2005–2006: A quantitative content analysis. *International Journal of Nursing Studies, 46,* 1102–1110.

Schmeltzer, M., Schiller, L. R., Meyer, R., Rugari, S. M., & Case, P. (2004). Safety and effectiveness of large-volume enema solutions. *Applied Nursing Research, 17,* 265–274.

Teng, C. I., Dai, Y. T., Shyu, Y. I. L., Wong, M. K., Chu, T. L., & Tsai, Y. H. (2009). Professional commitment, patient, safety, and patient-perceived care quality. *Journal of Nursing Scholarship, 41,* 301–309. doi:10.1111/j.1547-5069.2009.01289.x

Quantitative Research Designs

OUTLINE

OBJECTIVES

On completion of this chapter, you will be prepared to:
 1. Identify criteria for exploratory, descriptive, and explanatory studies
 2. Define experimental research
 3. Differentiate between internal and external validity in experimental designs

4. Identify six threats to internal validity
5. Identify three threats to external validity
6. Distinguish among true experimental, quasi-experimental, and pre-experimental designs
7. Describe three true experimental designs
8. Describe two quasi-experimental designs
9. Describe two pre-experimental designs
10. Discuss four types of nonexperimental research designs
11. Recognize two types of settings in which research is conducted
12. Identify factors that influence the choice of research designs
13. Critique the design section of quantitative studies

NEW TERMS DEFINED IN THIS CHAPTER

attrition, pg 116
cause-and-effect relationship, pg 114
comparative studies, pg 125
comparison group, pg 119
control group, pg 119
correlation, pg 124
correlation coefficient, pg 125
correlational studies, pg 124
descriptive studies, pg 113
double-blind experiment, pg 117
experimenter effect, pg 117
explanatory studies, pg 113
exploratory studies, pg 113
ex post facto studies, pg 126
external validity, pg 114
extraneous variable, pg 114
field studies, pg 127
Hawthorne effect, pg 117
history, pg 115
instrumentation change, pg 116
internal validity, pg 114
laboratory studies, pg 127
manipulation, pg 119
maturation, pg 115
methodological studies, pg 126

mortality, pg 116
negative relationship, pg 125
nonequivalent control group design, pg 121
one-group pretest-posttest design, pg 123
one-shot case study, pg 123
positive relationship, pg 125
posttest-only control group design, pg 120
pre-experimental designs, pg 122
pretest-posttest control group design, pg 119
prospective studies, pg 126
quasi-experimental designs, pg 121
random assignment, pg 118
reactive effects of the pretest, pg 117
retrospective studies, pg 126
Rosenthal effect, pg 117
secondary analysis studies, pg 127
selection bias, pg 115
simulation studies, pg 127
Solomon four-group design, pg 121
study limitations, pg 114
survey studies, pg 124
testing, pg 116
time-series design, pg 122
true experimental designs, pg 119

Do you sew? Do you cook? If so, you probably use patterns and recipes. Do you shop? (silly question!) Before you go shopping, do you make a plan about which shops you will visit and in what order? These patterns, recipes, and shopping plans provide guidelines that help you construct a beautiful piece of clothing, cook a delicious meal, or have a successful shopping trip.

This chapter introduces the concept of research design, which is the pattern, recipe, or plan, as it were, for a research study. The choice of a research design concerns the overall plan for the study. It is concerned with the type of data that will be collected and the means used to obtain the needed data. The researcher must decide if the study will try to determine causative factors, explore relationships, or examine historical data, for example. The design is not concerned with the specific data-collection methods, such as questionnaires or interviews, but with the overall plan for gathering data. The design must be appropriate to test the study hypothesis(es) or answer the research question(s). General guidelines for critiquing a quantitative design are presented at the end of this chapter.

EXPLORATORY, DESCRIPTIVE, AND EXPLANATORY STUDIES

The amount of existing knowledge about the variable(s) can be used as the criterion for classifying research as exploratory, descriptive, or explanatory. Although there can be an overlap between the first two categories, it is helpful to examine them separately.

Exploratory studies are conducted when little is known about the phenomenon of interest. For instance, you might decide to examine the needs of family members of a patient who will be receiving antibiotics at home by the IV push method. Patients and their caregivers are being taught how to give medications via IV push. Shortened hospital stays and cost-cutting measures have brought about this change. To determine what questions need to be asked, you would conduct a review of the literature. It is likely that you would find little written on this topic. An exploratory research study would, therefore, be appropriate.

A flexible approach rather than a structured approach to data collection would be used. In exploratory studies, there is interest in examining the qualitative aspects of the data as well as the quantitative aspects. Hypotheses are generally not appropriate for these types of studies. Although there is interest in qualitative data, this type of study would not be classified as a qualitative study because the researcher would be interested in gathering data that could be grouped, categorized, and eventually generalized to other groups of patients and their caregivers.

In **descriptive studies**, phenomena are described or the relationship between variables is examined. A descriptive study is similar to an exploratory study. However, the two categories can be distinguished by considering the amount of information that is available about the variable(s) under investigation. As previously stated, exploratory studies are appropriate when little is known about the area of interest. When enough information exists to examine relationships between variables, descriptive studies may be conducted in which hypotheses are tested.

By the time you read this material, IV antibiotic push therapy at home will probably be commonplace. Therefore, enough information might be available to conduct a descriptive study on this topic. You might try to determine which of the new antibiotics causes the most venous spasm during IV push therapy at home.

Explanatory studies search for causal explanations and are much more rigorous than exploratory or descriptive studies. This type of research is usually experimental. Enough knowledge exists about the variables of interest that the investigator is able to exercise some degree of control over the research conditions and manipulate one or more of the variables. This will become clearer as you read more about experimental research in this chapter.

In returning to the home IV antibiotic example, you may now have enough information to design an explanatory study. You might design an intervention to help patients and their caregivers reduce the incidence of venous spasm.

In summary, exploratory and descriptive studies describe phenomena and examine relationships among phenomena, whereas explanatory studies help provide explanations for the relationships among phenomena. Many nursing studies have been exploratory or descriptive in nature. A large number of explanatory studies have also been reported in the nursing literature.

RESEARCH DESIGNS

Although the terms *exploratory, descriptive,* and *explanatory research* can be used to indicate the type of study being conducted, these terms do not clearly indicate the study plan or specific design. There are several ways to classify research designs. This text presents designs under the two broad categories of

TABLE 9–1 Quantitative Research Designs

Experimental Designs	Nonexperimental Designs
True experimental designs	Action studies
Pretest-posttest control group	Comparative studies
Posttest-only control group	Correlational studies
Solomon four-group	Evaluation studies
Quasi-experimental designs	Meta-analysis studies
Nonequivalent control group	Metasynthesis studies
Time-series	Methodological studies
Pre-experimental designs	Secondary analysis studies
One-shot case study	Survey studies
One-group pretest-posttest	

quantitative and qualitative designs. As mentioned earlier in this textbook, some studies combine aspects of quantitative and qualitative research in the same study.

Quantitative designs are discussed in this chapter, and qualitative designs are presented in the next chapter. Quantitative designs are divided into experimental and nonexperimental designs. Table 9–1 presents some of the various experimental and nonexperimental designs.

EXPERIMENTAL RESEARCH

Experimental research is concerned with cause-and-effect relationships. A **cause-and-effect relationship** occurs when one thing or event makes some other thing or event happen. For example, obesity could be considered an *effect* of overeating (cause).

All experimental studies involve manipulation or control of the independent variable (cause) and measurement of the dependent variable (effect). Although experimental research designs are highly respected in the scientific world, causal relations are difficult to establish, and, as discussed in the previous chapter, researchers should avoid using the word *prove* when discussing research results. Controls are difficult to apply when experimental research is conducted with human beings. This is one of the reasons that many nursing studies have employed nonexperimental designs.

VALIDITY OF EXPERIMENTAL DESIGNS

In experimental studies, as well as in other types of research, the researcher is interested in controlling extraneous variables that can influence study results. **Extraneous variables** are those variables the researcher is not able to control, or does not choose to control, and which can influence the results of a study. Other names for extraneous variables are *confounding* and *intervening*. These variables are also called *study limitations*. The researcher acknowledges these study limitations in the discussion section of a research report. The extraneous variables, or competing explanations for the results, in experimental studies are labeled threats to internal and external validity (Campbell & Stanley, 1963).

In an experimental study, the researcher is trying to establish a cause-and-effect relationship. The **internal validity** of an experimental design concerns the degree to which changes in the dependent variable (effect) can be attributed to the independent variable (cause). Threats to internal validity are factors other than the independent variable that influence the dependent variable. These factors constitute rival explanations or competing hypotheses that might explain the study results.

External validity concerns the degree to which study results can be generalized to other people and other settings. These kinds of questions should be answered about external validity: With what degree of confidence can the study findings be transferred from the sample to the entire population? Will these study findings hold true with other groups in other times and places?

Internal and external validity are related in that as the researcher attempts to control for internal validity, external validity is usually decreased. Conversely, when the researcher is concerned with external validity or the generalizability of the findings to other settings and other people, the strict control necessary for high internal validity may be affected. Therefore, the researcher must decide how to balance internal and external validity.

Threats to internal and external validity are addressed before the discussion of the types of experimental designs so that you can better determine the strengths and weaknesses of the various designs as you read about them in this chapter.

Threats to Internal Validity

Campbell and Stanley (1963) and Cook and Campbell (1979) have identified threats to the internal validity of a study. Six of these threats are discussed in this chapter: selection bias, history, maturation, testing, instrumentation change, and mortality.

Selection Bias

The **selection bias** threat occurs when study results are attributed to the experimental treatment or the researcher's manipulation of the independent variable when, in fact, the results are related to subject differences before the independent variable was manipulated. This selection threat should be considered in experimental studies when subjects are not randomly assigned to experimental and comparison groups. For example, suppose the researcher decides to offer a seminar to help people stop cigarette smoking. Fifteen volunteers are obtained who indicate they would like to stop smoking. This group is designated as the experimental group. Fifteen other people are recruited who have not shown a desire to stop smoking. This group becomes the control group. The 15 subjects in the experimental group may have been more motivated to stop smoking before the treatment than the 15 subjects in the control group. The selection process for the groups may, therefore, have biased the eventual results of the study.

History

The threat of **history** occurs when some event besides the experimental treatment occurs during the course of a study, and this event influences the dependent variable. A researcher might be interested in determining the incidence of breast self-examination (BSE) among women after attending a 3-week teaching program on BSE. During the time the study is being conducted, an article is published in the newspaper concerning the rise in the number of women with breast cancer. This "history" event could result in an increase in the incidence of BSE behaviors. At the conclusion of the study, the researcher would not be able to determine if the teaching program (independent variable) was the reason for the increase in the incidence of BSE (dependent variable) or if the newspaper article was the impetus for an increase in BSE among the study subjects.

History is controlled by the inclusion of at least one simultaneous control or comparison group in a study. Additionally, random assignment of subjects to groups helps control the threat of history. Environmental events (history) would, therefore, be as likely to occur for subjects in one group as in another. If a difference is found between the groups at the conclusion of the study, the researcher is much more confident that the manipulation of the independent variable is the cause of this difference.

Maturation

Maturation becomes a threat when changes that occur within the subjects during an experimental study influence the study results. People may become older, taller, or sleepier from the time of the pretest to the posttest. If a school nurse was interested in the weight gain of children who receive a hot breakfast at school each day, she would have to keep in mind that changes may occur in these children during the course of the study that are not related to the experimental treatment. The children will probably gain some weight as they eat more and grow older regardless of whether they eat a hot breakfast at school or not. Again, a comparison group of similar children helps control for this threat. Maturation processes are then as likely to occur in one group as in another.

Testing

The testing threat may occur in studies where a pretest is given or where subjects have knowledge of baseline data. **Testing** refers to the influence of the pretest or knowledge of baseline data on the posttest scores. Subjects may remember the answers they put on the pretest and put the same answers on the posttest. Also, subjects' scores may be altered on the posttest as a result of their knowledge of baseline data. For example, if subjects were weighed and told their weight before an experimental weight reduction program, these subjects might make some effort on their own to lose weight because they have discovered they are overweight. This knowledge of baseline data could be considered a pretest.

Testing Threat

Brandon, Schuessler, Ellison, and Lazenby (2009) studied hospital readmissions, quality of life, and self-care behaviors of patients with heart failure following a telephone intervention by advanced practice nurses. They pointed out that testing might have been a limitation in their study because participants were given a pretest and a posttest. Knowing the purpose of the study, some participants may have adjusted their posttest answers in a particular direction or unintentionally reported inaccurate information.

Instrumentation Change

When mechanical instruments or judges are used in the pretest and posttest phases of a study, the threat of instrumentation must be considered. **Instrumentation change** involves the difference between the pretest and posttest measurement caused by a change in the accuracy of the instrument or the judges' ratings, rather than as a result of the experimental treatment. Judges may become more adept at the ratings or, on the contrary, become tired and make less exact observations. Training sessions for judges and trial runs to check for fatigue factors may help control for instrumentation changes. Also, if mechanical instruments are used, such as sphygmomanometers, these instruments should be checked for their accuracy throughout the study.

Mortality

The **mortality** threat occurs when the subjects do not complete a study. **Attrition** or dropout may occur in any research study. However, the term *mortality* is reserved for experimental studies in which the dropout rate is different between the experimental and the comparison groups. The observed effects may occur because the subjects who dropped out of a particular group are different from those who remained in the study. For example, if a large number of experimental group subjects who scored very high on an anxiety pretest dropped out of the study, the average anxiety scores on the posttest for the experimental group might be deceivingly low. The researcher might falsely conclude that the treatment really worked well! There is no research design that will control for mortality because, for ethical reasons, participants can never be forced to remain in a study.

The longer a study lasts, the more likely that subject dropout will occur. Fogg and Gross (2000) pointed out that if subjects dropped out of a study at random, the problem might not be so bad, However, the reasons that people drop out could make the resultant two groups quite different than they were at the beginning of the study. For example, if the dependent variable was depression, it is possible that people with the highest or lowest levels of depression would be the ones to drop out of the study.

Subject mortality is a problem that plagues nurse researchers in nearly all clinical studies. To control for this threat, the researcher should try to establish a relationship with the study participants and help them recognize the importance of their continued participation in a particular study.

Threats to External Validity

Campbell and Stanley (1963) have identified 4 threats to external validity, and Bracht and Glass (1968) delineated 10 threats to the external validity of a study. Three threats are discussed in this chapter: the Hawthorne effect, the experimenter effect, and the reactive effects of the pretest.

Hawthorne Effect

The **Hawthorne effect** occurs when study participants respond in a certain manner because they are aware that they are being observed. This term came about as the result of the studies on worker productivity at the Hawthorne plant of the Western Electric Company. Working conditions were varied, such as changing the length of the working day. Worker productivity was found to increase no matter what changes were made. The increase in productivity was finally determined to be the result of the subjects' knowledge that they were involved in a research study and that someone was interested in them.

Hawthorne Effect

Sheenan (2009) studied men at average risk of developing prostate cancer. The men were shown a 6-minute video on prostate cancer and prostate cancer screening. These participants scored higher on knowledge of prostate cancer screening and rated their own risk of prostate cancer more accurately after watching the video. Sheenan acknowledged that a possible limitation of her study was the Hawthorne effect. The men may have answered differently than they usually would because they knew their answers were being observed and recorded.

The Hawthorne effect may also be considered a threat to internal validity. It might be possible to control this threat by using a double-blind experiment. In a **double-blind experiment**, neither the researcher nor the research participants are aware of which participants are in the experimental group and which participants are in the control group.

Experimenter Effect

The **experimenter effect** is a threat to study results that occurs when researcher characteristics or behaviors influence subject behaviors. Examples of researcher characteristics or behaviors that may be influential are facial expressions, clothing, age, gender, and body build. Although the term *experimenter effect* is appropriate to use only when discussing experimental research, a term with a similar meaning is used in nonexperimental research. The **Rosenthal effect**, named after the person who identified this phenomenon, is used to indicate the influence of an interviewer on respondents' answers. It has been shown that researcher characteristics such as gender, dress, and type of jewelry may influence study participants' answers to questions in nonexperimental studies.

Reactive Effects of the Pretest

When a pretest and a posttest are used in an experimental study, the researcher must be aware not only of the internal validity threat that may occur, but also of the external validity threat that may exist. The **reactive effects of the pretest** occurs when subjects have been sensitized to the treatment because they took the pretest. This sensitization may affect the posttest results. People might not respond to the treatment in the same manner if they had not received a pretest. The pretest does not have to be a paper-and-pencil test. As mentioned previously, if study participants were told their weight prior to a weight reduction study, this knowledge of baseline data would be considered a pretest.

You might say, "I still don't see how this threat is different from the internal validity threat of "testing." The internal validity threat occurs if the pretest or knowledge of baseline data is the *cause* of the results on the posttest, and an external validity threat occurs if the pretest acts as a *catalyst* in bringing about the results on the posttest. In this situation, the pretest is not the direct cause of the change in the posttest measurements; it is the indirect cause.

Are you ever going to know for sure if the pretest threat has occurred? Probably not. Just remember that there is a possibility this threat may occur if a pretest is given in a study or if subjects have knowledge of their baseline data (such as their cholesterol levels) that will then be compared to posttest results (their decrease or increase in cholesterol levels). You may want to read this section several times. This material gives my students a headache!

SYMBOLIC PRESENTATION OF RESEARCH DESIGNS

Research designs are often easier to understand when seen in a symbolic form. The symbols used to depict the designs in this chapter are based on the notation scheme of Campbell and Stanley (1963).

R = random assignment of subjects to groups
X = experimental treatment or intervention
O = observation or measurement of dependent variable

The Xs and Os on one line apply to a specific group. The time sequence of events is read from left to right. If an X appears first and then an O, this means the intervention occurred first and then an observation was made. If a subscript appears after an X or O (X_1; X_2; O_1; O_2), the numbers indicate the first treatment, second treatment, first observation, second observation, and so forth.

$R\ O_1\ X\ O_2$ (Experimental group)
$R\ O_1\ \ \ O_2$ (Comparison group)

This example has two groups, both of which were formed through random assignment (R) of subjects to groups. **Random assignment** is a procedure that ensures that each subject has an equal chance of being assigned or placed in any of the groups in an experimental study. Both groups in the example were measured or given a pretest (O_1) on the phenomenon of interest (dependent variable). The experimental group was exposed to an experimental treatment (independent variable); the comparison group was not exposed to this treatment. Then, both groups were again measured or given the posttest (O_2) on the phenomenon of interest (dependent variable).

There are a number of ways of carrying out random assignment. Today it is often done through a computer-generated process.

Random Assignment

In McCaffrey's (2009) study she asked: Is there a difference in cognitive function in older adults who listen to music following hip or knee surgery when compared to those who do not listen to music? Participants were assigned to the experimental or control group by choosing 1 of 22 slips of paper. Eleven of the slips contained an "E" for experimental; 11 contained a "C" for control group. Sampling was discontinued after 22 participants had been selected.

TYPES OF EXPERIMENTAL DESIGNS

The three broad categories of experimental research designs are true experimental, quasi-experimental, and pre-experimental. The distinction between these designs is determined by the amount of control the researcher is able to exercise over the research conditions.

True Experimental Designs

The **true experimental designs** are those in which the researcher has a great deal of control over the research situation. Threats to the internal validity of the study are minimized. Only with the use of true experimental designs may causality be inferred with any degree of confidence. With these types of designs, the researcher has some confidence that the independent variable was the cause of the change in the dependent variable. A true experimental design has three criteria:

1. The researcher manipulates the experimental variable(s).
2. At least one experimental and one comparison group are included in the study.
3. Subjects are randomly assigned to either the experimental or the comparison group.

The first criterion for a true experimental design is manipulation of the independent variable. Sometimes, there is a misunderstanding of the term *manipulation* as it is used in experimental studies. The concept of manipulation might bring to mind the picture of puppets on a string; however, in research the term **manipulation** means that the independent, or experimental, variable is controlled by the researcher. The researcher has control over the type of experimental treatment administered and who will receive the treatment.

The experimental treatment in nursing research usually concerns some type of nursing intervention. The researcher manipulates the independent variable, or nursing intervention, by administering it to some subjects and withholding it from others. The dependent variable, or the effects of the nursing intervention, is then observed. For example, a nurse researcher might implement a new, structured, preoperative teaching program with a group of preoperative patients and use the routine teaching program with another group of preoperative patients. The anxiety levels of both groups of patients might be the dependent variable that was observed.

The second criterion for a true experimental design is the use of a comparison or control group. The term *control group* is seen more frequently in the literature than the term *comparison group.* A **control group** usually indicates a group in an experimental study that does not receive the experimental treatment. In nursing research, the withholding of a treatment may be unethical. In the previous example concerning preoperative patients, the withholding of preoperative teaching would not be considered ethical. In many nursing studies, therefore, a comparison group is used rather than a control group that receives no intervention. The comparison group usually receives the "normal" or routine intervention. The term **comparison group** is used in this text to indicate any group in an experimental study that either receives no treatment or a treatment that is not thought to be as effective as the experimental treatment.

Finally, the third criterion for true experimental studies is the random assignment of subjects to groups. As previously mentioned, random assignment ensures that each subject has an equal chance of being placed into any of the groups in an experimental study. Keep in mind that random sampling and random assignment are two entirely different concepts. These concepts are discussed further in Chapter 11. At this point, be aware that random assignment concerns the equality of groups in experimental studies. The random assignment of subjects to groups eliminates selection bias as a threat to the internal validity of the study.

The following sections discuss three types of true experimental designs: pretest-posttest control group design, posttest-only control group design, and Solomon four-group design.

Pretest-Posttest Control Group Design

The **pretest-posttest control group design** is probably the most frequently used experimental design. In this design, (a) the subjects are randomly assigned to groups, (b) a pretest is given to both groups, (c) the experimental group receives the experimental treatment and the comparison group receives the routine treatment or no treatment, and (d) a posttest is given to both groups.

$$R \; O_1 \; X \; O_2 \; \text{(Experimental group)}$$
$$R \; O_1 \qquad O_2 \; \text{(Comparison group)}$$

The researcher is able to determine if the groups were equal before the treatment was administered. If the groups were not equivalent, the posttest scores may be adjusted statistically to control for the initial differences between the two groups that were reflected in the pretest scores.

A nurse researcher might be interested in the usefulness of a diabetic teaching film. A group of clients with diabetes are randomly assigned to the experimental or comparison group. Both groups are then pretested on their knowledge of diabetes. Members of the experimental group watch the diabetic teaching film. Members of the comparison group are asked to read printed material that is similar to the information covered in the teaching film. Both groups are then posttested on their knowledge of diabetes. Finally, the difference between the posttest scores of the two groups is compared.

The pretest-posttest control group design controls for all threats to internal validity. The disadvantage of this design concerns the external threat of the reactive effects of the pretest. The results of the study can be generalized only to situations in which a pretest would be administered before the treatment.

Pretest-Posttest Control Group Design

Kimball et al. (2010) used a pretest-posttest control group design to study various teaching methods used with rehabilitation patients being discharged from the hospital. Patients or family members were randomly assigned to three teaching methods: (a) geragogy format plus scheduled time for teaching, (b) geragogy format alone, and (c) standard teaching method. Geragogy involves adult teaching principles and strategies designed for use with geriatric patients. Based on a comparison of pretest and posttest scores, the teaching method did not have a significant effect on medication knowledge ($p = .65$) or confidence for administering medications ($p = .73$).

Posttest-Only Control Group Design

In the **posttest-only control group design**, (a) subjects are randomly assigned to groups, (b) the experimental group receives the experimental treatment, and the comparison group receives the routine treatment or no treatment, and (c) a posttest is given to both groups.

$$R \; X \; O_1 \; \text{(Experimental group)}$$
$$R \quad O_1 \; \text{(Comparison group)}$$

The posttest-only control group design is easier to carry out and superior to the pretest-posttest design. The researcher does not have to be concerned with the reactive effects of the pretest on the posttest. The generalizability of the results would be more extensive. A study similar to the example described regarding the pretest-posttest control group design could be developed. The only difference would be that the two groups would not receive a pretest on their knowledge of diabetes.

Random assignment of subjects into groups in the posttest-only control group design helps ensure equality of the groups. The use of a large sample size will increase the effectiveness of random assignment. Although random assignment should ensure equality of groups, researchers seem to be fearful that the groups may not, in fact, be similar. They, therefore, sometimes choose to administer a pretest.

The posttest-only control group design should be used when it is not possible to administer a pretest or when it would not make sense to administer a pretest.

Posttest-Only Control Group Design

Cason, Kardong-Edgren, Cazzell, Behan, and Mancini (2009) randomly assigned groups of nursing students to three methods of teaching cardiopulmonary resuscitation skills: (a) traditional classroom instruction, (b) group learning, and (c) self-directed learning. Self-directed learning was found to be as effective or better on most of the items on the skills checklist than the more resource- and time-consuming traditional classroom method.

In this study by Cason et al., it would not have been appropriate to administer a pretest because the students had little or no knowledge about cardiopulmonary resuscitation skills. Thus, the researchers used a posttest-only design.

Solomon Four-Group Design

In the **Solomon four-group design**, (a) subjects are randomly assigned to one of the four groups; (b) two of the groups, experimental group 1 and comparison group 1, are pretested; (c) two of the groups, experimental group 1 and experimental group 2, receive the experimental treatment, whereas two of the groups, comparison group 1 and comparison group 2, receive the routine treatment or no treatment; and (d) a posttest is given to all four groups.

$$R\ O_1\ X\ O_2\ \text{(Experimental group 1)}$$
$$R\ O_1\quad O_2\ \text{(Comparison group 1)}$$
$$R\quad X\ O_2\ \text{(Experimental group 2)}$$
$$R\quad\quad O_2\ \text{(Comparison group 2)}$$

The Solomon four-group design is considered to be the most prestigious experimental design (Campbell & Stanley, 1963) because it minimizes threats to internal and external validity. This design not only controls for all of the threats to internal validity, but also controls for the reactive effects of the pretest. Any differences between the experimental and the comparison groups can be more confidently associated with the experimental treatment. Unfortunately, this design requires a large sample, and statistical analysis of the data is complicated. Only one Solomon four-group design could be located in the nursing literature during the past 5 years.

Solomon Four-Group Design

A Solomon four design was used to measure the impact of a pretest on the posttest knowledge scores of prostate screening among a sample of 198 African American men (Weinrich et al., 2007). Two types of information brochures were used. The men were randomly assigned to four groups; two received a pretest and two did not. It was hypothesized that posttest scores would be higher in men who had completed a pretest than in men who had not completed a pretest. Study results supported this hypothesis, and the suggestion was made that a pretest might enhance patient education. Also, the contention was made that researchers may not be able to generalize study results to a clinical setting where a pretest is usually not administered.

Quasi-Experimental Designs

Sometimes researchers are not able to randomly assign subjects to groups, or for various reasons no comparison group is available for an experimental study. **Quasi-experimental designs** are those in which there is either no comparison group or subjects are not randomly assigned to groups. The researcher uses existing, or intact, groups for the experimental and comparison groups. Although the researcher does not have as much control in a quasi-experimental study as in a true experiment, there are some advantages to the use of quasi-experimental designs. By conducting experiments with naturally occurring groups, the real world is more closely approximated than when subjects are randomly assigned to groups.

Many different designs fall into the category of quasi-experimental designs. Two of these are discussed next: nonequivalent control group design and time-series design.

Nonequivalent Control Group Design

The **nonequivalent control group design** is similar to the pretest-posttest control group design except there is no random assignment of subjects to the experimental and comparison groups.

$$O_1 \ X \ O_2 \ \text{(Experimental group)}$$
$$O_1 \quad O_2 \ \text{(Comparison group)}$$

A researcher might choose a group of patients with diabetes on one hospital floor for the experimental group and a group of patients with diabetes on another floor for the comparison group. The experimental treatment would be administered to the experimental group; the comparison group would receive the routine treatment or some alternative treatment.

Threats to internal validity controlled by the nonequivalent control group design are history, testing, maturation, and instrumentation change. The biggest threat to internal validity is selection bias. The two groups may not have been similar at the beginning of the study. It is possible, however, to test statistically for differences in the groups. For example, it could be determined if the ages and educational backgrounds of the subjects in both groups were similar. If the groups were similar at the beginning of the study, more confidence could be placed in a cause-and-effect relationship between variables. A statistical test called analysis of covariance (ANCOVA) (see Chapter 15) can be used to help control for differences that might have existed, through chance, between the experimental and control groups at the beginning of the study.

Nonequivalent Control Group Design

Health-related quality of life (HRQOL) is considered a goal of care for the elderly. Residents in a nursing home in Hong Kong were assigned as an intact group to either the experimental (Tai Chi) or control conditions (usual daily activities). The researchers (L. Lee, D. Lee, & Woo, 2009) contended that this design controlled for variations that might have been present if individuals from different groups were compared to each other rather than to individuals in the same group. Results showed a significant improvement in HRQOL after residents practiced Tai Chi.

Time-Series Design

In a **time-series design**, the researcher periodically observes or measures the subjects. The experimental treatment is administered between two of the observations.

$$O_1 \ O_2 \ O_3 \ X \ O_4 \ O_5 \ O_6$$

A researcher might assess the pain levels of a group of clients with low back pain. After 3 weeks of pain assessment (O_1, O_2, O_3), subjects could be taught a special exercise to alleviate low back pain. During the next 3 weeks, pain levels would again be measured (O_4, O_5, O_6). The results of this study would help the researcher determine if low back pain persists, if a specific exercise is effective in reducing low back pain, and if the effectiveness of the exercise persists.

The time-series design with its numerous observations or measurements of the dependent variable helps strengthen the validity of the design. The greatest threats to validity are history and testing.

Pre-experimental Designs

Pre-experimental designs is the name applied by Campbell and Stanley (1963) to experimental designs that are considered very weak and in which the researcher has little control over the research. Sometimes these types of designs are discussed to provide examples of how not to do research! The two pre-experimental designs discussed here are the one-shot case study and the one-group pretest-posttest design.

One-Shot Case Study

In a **one-shot case study**, a single group is exposed to an experimental treatment and observed after the treatment.

$$X O$$

A group of patients with diabetes might attend a diabetic education class (X) and be tested on their knowledge of diabetes (O) after the class is completed. This design does not call for any comparisons to be made. There is no way to determine if the level of knowledge about diabetes was the result of the class. The patients could have already possessed this knowledge before the class.

Threats to internal validity are history, maturation, and selection bias. The threats of testing and instrumentation change would not be applicable in this design. Selection bias would be a very serious threat in this particular design. The one-shot case study is the weakest of all the experimental designs because it controls for no threats to internal validity. No example of this type of study was found in the recent nursing literature.

One-Group Pretest-Posttest Design

The **one-group pretest-posttest design** provides a comparison between a group of subjects before and after the experimental treatment.

$$O_1 X O_2$$

A group of patients with diabetes could be given a pretest of their diabetes knowledge (O_1). This group would then attend a diabetic education class (X) and be posttested (O_2) at the end of the class.

Threats to internal validity would be history, maturation, testing, and instrumentation change. Note that this design has two threats that were not applicable in the last design. Because of the existence of a pretest and posttest, testing and instrumentation change now become threats to internal validity.

One Group Pretest-Posttest Design

A one-group pretest-posttest design was used to study perception of symptoms and quality of life following ablation in patients with supraventricular tachycardia (SVT) (Wood, Stewart, Drew, Scheinman, & Froëlicher, 2010). In comparison to patients' baseline reported data, their posttest data revealed decreases in frequency and duration of SVT episodes, number of symptoms, and the impact of SVT on their routine activities.

NONEXPERIMENTAL RESEARCH

Nurse researchers have made great use of the nonexperimental research designs. Many times, experimental research cannot be conducted with human beings because of ethical reasons. At other times, nonexperimental research is the most proper type of research to obtain the needed data. In trying to determine clients' perceptions of pain, the only way to obtain this information would be to ask these clients about their pain. An experimental study would not be appropriate. All nonexperimental research is descriptive because there is no manipulation or control of variables, and the researcher can describe the phenomenon only as it exists. Although the researcher cannot talk about a cause-and-effect relationship in nonexperimental research, it is important to obtain valid study results in this type of research. The researcher must attempt to control for extraneous variables through such means as careful selection of the study sample. Threats to internal validity and external validity are terms that are reserved for use in discussing experimental studies. However, in nonexperimental research, extraneous variables or study limitations must also be considered.

TYPES OF NONEXPERIMENTAL DESIGNS

Table 9–1 lists nine types of nonexperimental research; five of these designs are discussed in the following sections: survey, correlational, comparative, methodological, and secondary analysis studies.

Survey Studies

Survey studies are investigations in which self-report data are collected from samples with the purpose of describing populations on some variable(s) of interest. Surveys have probably been conducted as long as humankind has been in existence. Accounts of surveys are recorded in the Bible and in other historical books. Probably everyone who is reading this material has been involved in some type of survey. Two of the more common public opinion surveys conducted in the United States are the Gallup and Harris polls. These national polls use scientific sampling techniques to obtain information about large groups of people through the sampling of a small percentage of the total groups.

The control exercised by the researcher in survey research lies in the sampling technique. The ability to generalize sample results to the population of interest depends on the sampling method. Probability sampling techniques and adequate sample sizes (see Chapter 11) are very important in survey research.

Many disciplines, especially the social sciences, have used survey research. Surveys generally ask subjects to report their attitudes, opinions, perceptions, or behaviors. A nurse researcher might use a survey to gather data on the health needs of clients, their sleep patterns, or their perceptions of the nursing care they have received.

Surveys may be conducted by phone, mail, the Internet, or through personal contact with the subjects. The most common data collection techniques used in survey research are questionnaires and interviews. In surveys, participants may be studied using a cross-sectional or a longitudinal approach (see Chapter 11). In a cross-sectional survey, subjects are studied at one point in time. Longitudinal surveys follow subjects over an extended period of time.

One of the chief virtues of survey research is its ability to provide accurate information on populations, using relatively small samples. Another advantage of survey research concerns the large amount of data that can be obtained rather quickly and with minimal cost. However, self-report responses may be unreliable because people may provide socially acceptable responses.

Survey Study

Jones (2010) examined registered nurses' attitudes and degrees of comfort in regard to providing patient education in rural community hospitals. A survey was sent to 412 registered nurses in five rural community hospitals in Maryland; 273 surveys were returned. Experienced nurses and those with advanced degrees were more comfortable teaching patients about diagnoses and treatments.

Correlational Studies

In **correlational studies**, the researcher examines the strength of relationships between variables by determining how changes in one variable are associated with changes in another variable. A **correlation** indicates the extent to which one variable (X) is related to another variable (Y). As X increases, does Y increase or decrease? In a simple correlational study, one group of subjects is measured on two variables (X and Y) to determine if there is a relationship between these variables. Other correlational studies may examine the relationship among more than two variables.

The magnitude and direction of the relationship between two variables is indicated by a **correlation coefficient**. Correlation coefficients may be positive (+) or negative (−) and range from −1.00 (perfect negative correlation) to 1.00 (perfect positive correlation). If the correlation coefficient has no sign in front of it (e.g., .80), a positive relationship is indicated. A negative correlation coefficient is preceded by a negative sign (e.g., −.80). A correlation coefficient of .00 indicates no relationship between variables. Correlation coefficients are reported through various statistics such as the Pearson's product-moment correlation (more commonly called the Pearson r) and the Spearman rho (see Chapter 14).

A **positive relationship**, or direct relationship, means that as the value of one variable increases, the value of the other variable increases. A **negative relationship**, or inverse relationship, means that as the value of one variable increases, the value of the other variable decreases. Suppose data are gathered on age and assertiveness levels of registered nurses. A correlation coefficient of .80 would indicate a fairly strong positive relationship between age and assertiveness levels of registered nurses. The older the nurse, the more assertive she or he is. Conversely, a correlation coefficient of −.80 would indicate a strong negative relationship. The older the nurse, the less assertive she or he is.

The identification of an independent and a dependent variable may not be appropriate in some correlational studies. Generally, however, the independent variable is that variable that comes first in chronological order and that influences the other variable. For example, if you were trying to determine if there is a correlation between age and assertiveness levels, the independent variable would be age, and the dependent variable would be assertiveness levels. The subject's age is a nonmanipulated, inherent variable that exists in time, or chronological order, before the variable of assertiveness. Even if a strong correlation were found between these two variables, the researcher should not conclude that age *causes* assertiveness. There may, in fact, be some other variable(s) that bring about the assertiveness levels of people. For example, you would probably find a strong positive relationship between the number of churches in a city and the number of people who dine out each week. Do you think the number of churches would be the *cause* of the large number of people who dine out in a week? No, the probable causative factor is the number of people who live in that city. A large city will probably have more people and more churches than a small city. Therefore, if a city has a large population, there is probably going to be a large number of people who dine out each week.

Correlational Study

Song and Nam (2010) conducted a correlational study in South Korea to examine the relationships among coping strategies, physical function, and social adjustment in people with spinal cord injury. No coping strategy was significantly correlated with physical function. However, significant positive associations (<.01) were found between seven out of eight coping strategies (planful problem solving, positive reappraisal, confrontive coping, accepting responsibility, distancing, self-controlling, seeking social support) and social adjustment. Escape-avoidance was the only coping strategy that was not significantly associated with social adjustment.

Comparative Studies

Comparative studies examine the differences between intact groups on some dependent variable of interest. This description may sound like the aim of many experimental studies. The difference between comparative studies and experimental studies lies in the researcher's ability to manipulate the independent variable. In comparative studies, there is no manipulation of the independent variable. Frequently, the independent variable is some inherent characteristic of the subjects, such as personality type, educational level, or medical condition.

There are many reasons for the choice of a comparative research design. One reason involves the ethics of research. When human subjects are studied, the manipulation of the independent variable may not be possible. A researcher could not examine child abuse as an independent variable in an experimental study. It would not be ethical to select one group of children who would receive abusive treatment and another group of children who would not receive abusive treatment. However, the researcher could choose a group of children who had experienced abuse during their life and compare them with a group of children who had not been abused. The dependent variable might be self-esteem.

Comparative studies are frequently classified as retrospective or prospective. In **retrospective studies**, the dependent variable (effect) is identified in the present (a disease condition, for example), and an attempt is made to determine the independent variable (cause of the disease) that occurred in the past. In **prospective studies**, the independent variable or presumed cause (high cholesterol blood levels, for example) is identified at the present time, and then subjects are followed in the future to observe the dependent variable (incidence of coronary artery disease, for example).

Retrospective studies are frequently called ex post facto. In **ex post facto studies**, data are collected "after the fact." Variations in the independent variable are studied after the variations have occurred, rather than at the time of the occurrence. For example, a researcher might be interested in the fear responses of children during physical examinations. A study might be conducted to examine previous unpleasant experiences during physical exams that might have influenced the children's present behaviors. These previous experiences might be considered the "cause," and the present fear responses might be the "effect."

Comparative Study

A study conducted by Lee (2009) sought to describe and compare the health promotion behaviors (HPBs) used by older rural (n = 33) and urban women (n = 39) providing care for spouses. These women completed The Health Promoting Lifestyle Profile II (HPLP-II). The most frequently reported HPBs concerned interpersonal relations, spiritual growth, and stress management; the least frequently reported HPBs involved physical activity. No significant differences were found between the scores of the two groups.

A retrospective study starts by examining an effect and then looks back in time to determine the cause; a prospective study starts with the determination of a cause and then looks forward in time to determine the effect on subjects. An example of prospective research is the well-publicized study concerning Agent Orange and Vietnam veterans. During the war in Vietnam, many American servicemen were exposed to the chemical defoliant Agent Orange. After years of examining the effects of this chemical on veterans and their offspring, the Air Force finally issued a report in 1984 that revealed some of the problems linked with exposure to the herbicide Agent Orange, which was named after the color-coded bands on storage drums. Among the problems found were high rates of benign skin lesions, liver disorders, leg pulses that could indicate hardening of the arteries, and minor birth defects in their children ("Agent Orange Study," 1984). Recently, more diseases have been added to the list: Parkinson's, hairy-cell leukemia, and ischemic heart disease (Dao, 2009). It will now be easier for thousands of veterans and their dependents to receive disability checks.

Prospective studies may use an experimental approach, whereas retrospective studies would never use this type of design. In prospective studies, the researcher might manipulate the independent variable, or the cause, and then observe study participants in the future for the dependent variable, or the effect. Prospective studies are costly, and subject dropout may occur. These types of studies are less common than retrospective studies.

Methodological Studies

Nurse researchers must be sure to use instruments in research projects that are valid and reliable measures of the variables of interest. **Methodological studies** are concerned with the development, testing, and evaluation of research instruments and methods. There is a growing interest in methodological research.

Nurses frequently use tools developed by researchers in other disciplines. If these tools are appropriate for nursing research, they definitely should be used. Frequently, however, tools are used because of their availability rather than for their appropriateness to measure the variables of the study.

More methodological studies are now appearing in the nursing literature, which is a positive trend. Nurses will, thus, develop a stockpile of research instruments to measure nursing phenomena. A cursory review of the issues of *Nursing Research* in the last few years revealed that at least one methodological study was included in each issue. As further evidence of the importance of measurement in nursing research, the Jo*urnal of Nursing Measurement* began publication in 1993.

Methodological Study

The Nursing Teamwork Survey (NTS) is an instrument that measures nursing teamwork in acute care hospital settings at the patient unit level (Kalisch, Lee, & Salas, 2010). The researchers tested for content, concurrent, contrast, and convergent validity. The instrument was found to have good psychometric properties.

Secondary Analysis Studies

Sometimes researchers gather a lot of data in a study. They may not actually analyze all of the data that were gathered. In **secondary analysis studies**, data are analyzed that were gathered in a previous study. Researchers may test new hypotheses or ask new research questions. This type of study is efficient and economical, according to Polit and Beck (2008), because data collection is usually the most expensive and time-consuming part of a study.

Secondary Analysis Study

Wyatt, Sikorski, Wills, and An (2010) conducted a secondary analysis of data that were obtained in a previous study. In the original study, data were obtained from a group of women who received either the standard care or a targeted nursing care intervention in their homes during the first two postoperative weeks after breast surgery. Data were obtained on the participants' use of complementary and alternative medicine (CAM) therapies. In the secondary analysis of the data, the CAM data were analyzed in relation to the specific CAM therapies used, number of treatments, and spending. A majority of women (58.6%) used at least one CAM therapy. Vitamins, massage, and homeopathy were the most frequently used therapies, with an average spending of between $19.78 and $38.54.

SETTINGS FOR RESEARCH

Research may be classified as laboratory or field studies, according to the setting in which the study is conducted. In **laboratory studies**, subjects are studied in a special environment created by the researcher. Although laboratory studies are not always highly standardized, the investigator usually attempts to control the research environment as much as possible. **Field studies** are conducted "in the field," or in a real-life situation, where not as much control can be maintained.

Simulation studies are considered to be laboratory studies. In a simulation study, the researcher might measure subjects' responses to descriptions of case studies that are intended to represent real-life situations. The control of the environment in this situation is through the researcher's descriptions of the events in the case studies.

Simulation Study

Two groups of nursing students in Pennsylvania were taught about care of patients with acute coronary syndrome and with acute ischemic stroke (Howard, Ross, Mitchell, & Nelson, 2010). Some participants were taught using a human patient simulator and others using interactive case studies. Students in the human patient simulator group scored higher on the posttest than students in the interactive case studies group. The researchers concluded that students responded favorably to human patient simulators as a teaching method.

A research study receives the classification of *field* study when conducted in a real-life setting. Phenomena are studied in the natural environments in which they occur. Most nursing research has been conducted in the field. The field approach is particularly appropriate for the nurse researcher because nursing is a practice discipline.

CRITIQUING QUANTITATIVE RESEARCH DESIGNS

It may be very difficult for the reader to determine if an appropriate design has been used in a study. As said previously, critiquing is not easy! Advanced research knowledge may be necessary to make an accurate determination of the appropriateness of a study design. However, the beginning researcher or critic can make some overall evaluations of the design section of a research report. Box 9–1 presents criteria for evaluating quantitative research designs.

The entire research report must be read before a determination can be made of whether the research design is appropriate for the study. The major consideration when critiquing a study design concerns the ability of the study design to test the hypothesis(es) or answer the research question(s). Is the researcher trying to determine a cause-and-effect relationship or describe a phenomenon from the point of view of the research subject?

The research design determines how much control the researcher has over the research situation. In some studies, very tight controls are needed; in other studies tight controls would inhibit the collection of valid data. Therefore, the reader of a research report must determine the purpose of the study and what the researcher hoped to add to the body of knowledge on the selected phenomenon or phenomena.

Box 9–1. Guidelines for Critiquing Quantitative Research Designs

1. Is the design clearly identified and described in the research report?
2. Is the design appropriate to test the study hypothesis(es) or answer the research question(s)?
3. If the study used an experimental design, was the most appropriate type of experimental design used?
4. If the study used an experimental design, what means were used to control for threats to internal validity? External validity?
5. Was assignment of subjects to the experimental and control group clearly described?
6. Does the research design allow the researcher to draw a cause-and-effect relationship between the variables?
7. If a nonexperimental design was used, would an experimental design have been more appropriate?
8. What means were used to control for extraneous variables, such as subject characteristics, if a nonexperimental design was used?

SUMMARY

Exploratory, descriptive, and explanatory studies are classified according to the amount of knowledge about the variable(s) of interest. **Exploratory studies** are conducted when little is known about the topic of interest. In **descriptive studies**, the phenomenon of interest may have already been studied in the past, and there is enough information to ask questions about the relationship between variables. **Explanatory studies** search for causal explanations. The researcher exercises control over the research situation by manipulating one or more of the variables and examining the influence of this manipulation on another variable(s).

Experimental research is concerned with **cause-and-effect relationships**. All experimental studies involve manipulation of the independent variable (cause) and measurement of the dependent variable (effect).

Extraneous variables, also called *study limitations, confounding variables,* and *intervening variables,* are uncontrolled variables that may influence study results. In experimental studies, these extraneous variables are called threats to internal and external validity. **Internal validity** concerns the degree to which changes in the dependent variable (effect) can be attributed to the independent variable (cause). **External validity** concerns the degree to which study results can be generalized to other people and settings.

Six threats to internal validity are selection bias, history, maturation, testing, instrumentation change, and mortality. **Selection bias** occurs when study results are attributed to the experimental treatment when, in fact, the results occur because of subject differences before the treatment. **History** occurs when some event other than the experimental treatment occurs during the course of the study, and this event influences the dependent variable. **Maturation** is a threat to internal validity when changes that occur within the subjects during an experimental study influence the study results. The **testing** threat involves the influence of the pretest on the posttest scores. **Instrumentation change** concerns the difference between the pretest and posttest measurements related to a change in the accuracy of the instrument or judges' ratings. The **mortality** threat occurs when the subject dropout rate is different between the experimental and comparison groups, and this difference influences the posttest results. **Attrition**, or dropout, may occur in any research study. However, the term mortality is reserved for experimental studies in which the dropout rate is different between the experimental and the comparison groups.

Three threats to external validity are the Hawthorne effect, the experimenter effect, and the reactive effects of the pretest. The **Hawthorne effect** occurs when study participants respond in a certain manner because they are aware that they are being observed. In a **double-blind** experiment, neither the researcher nor the research participants know who is in the experimental and control groups. A researcher's behavior that influences subject behavior is called the **experimenter effect**. In a nonexperimental study, the influence of the interviewer on the respondents is called the **Rosenthal effect**. The **reactive effects of the pretest** threat occurs when subjects' responses to the experimental treatment are indirectly influenced by the pretest.

Random assignment is a procedure that ensures that each subject has an equal chance of being assigned or placed into any of the groups in an experimental study.

The three broad categories of experimental research designs are true experimental, quasi-experimental, and pre-experimental. **True experimental designs** are determined by three criteria: the researcher manipulates the experimental variable, at least one experimental and one **comparison group** or **control group** are included in the study, and subjects are randomly assigned to either the experimental or comparison group. **Manipulation** means that the independent variable is controlled by the researcher. Three types of true experimental designs are the **pretest-posttest control group design**, the **posttest-only control group design**, and the **Solomon four-group design**.

Quasi-experimental designs have either no comparison group or no random assignment of subjects to groups. Two quasi-experimental designs are the **nonequivalent control group design** and the **time-series design**.

Pre-experimental designs are those in which the researcher has little control over the research. Two types of pre-experimental designs are the **one-shot case study** and the **one-group pretest-posttest design**. There are many different types of nonexperimental designs. **Survey studies** obtain data from samples on certain variables to determine the characteristics of populations on those same variables.

Correlational studies examine the strength of relationships between variables. A **correlation** indicates the extent to which one variable (X) is related to another variable (Y). The magnitude and direction of the relationship between two variables is indicated by a **correlation coefficient**. These coefficients may be positive (+) or negative (−) and range from −1.00 (perfect negative correlation) to 1.00 (perfect positive correlation). A **positive relationship** (direct) means that as the value of one variable increases, the value of the other variable increases. A **negative relationship** (inverse) means that as the value of one variable increases, the value of the other variable decreases.

Comparative studies examine the difference between intact groups on some dependent variable of interest. Many comparative studies are called **ex post facto studies** because the variation in the independent variable has already occurred, and the researcher, "after the fact," tries to determine if the variation that has occurred in the independent variable has any influence on the dependent variable that is being measured in the present. Ex post facto studies may also be called **retrospective studies**. **Prospective studies** are comparative studies in which the independent variable is identified in the present and the dependent variable is measured in the future.

Methodological studies are concerned with the development, testing, and evaluation of research instruments and methods. A growing number of instruments have been developed to measure the specific phenomena of interest to nurses.

In **secondary analysis studies**, a researcher analyzes data gathered in a previous study. The purpose may be to test new hypotheses or answer new research questions.

Research may be conducted in a laboratory or field setting. **Laboratory studies** are conducted in a special environment created by the researcher. **Simulation studies** are a type of laboratory study. **Field studies** are conducted in real-life settings. Most experimental studies in nursing research have been field studies.

NURSING RESEARCH ON THE WEB

For additional online resources, research activities, and exercises, go to **www.mynursingkit. com**. Select Chapter 9 from the drop-down menu.

GET INVOLVED ACTIVITIES

1. Examine the first five research studies that you can locate. Identify the number of studies that used a quantitative design.
2. Using a computerized database, type in "experimental design" and see how many nursing studies in the last 10 years have used an experimental design.
3. Bring a research article to be discussed. Determine the design that was used. Share this information with your peers. Decide if the design appears to be the most rigorous one that could have been used for the study.
4. Divide into groups and develop an idea for a study that would require a quantitative design. Decide on the specific design that your group thinks is most appropriate. Then, exchange your ideas among groups and see if other groups chose the same design as your group. All groups should give the rationale for the design selected.
5. Try to identify limitations in the design that your group has selected.

SELF-TEST

Each item in Column A represents a statement by a subject in a research study. Match the statements on the left with the threats to internal and external validity listed in Column B.

Column A	Column B
1. "It's a good thing I'm in this new diet study. I couldn't believe it when that researcher told me that I was 10 pounds overweight."	A. Hawthorne effect
2. "Aren't we lucky to be part of this experiment?"	B. selection bias
3. "That researcher scares me. I guess I'd better act like he wants me to act."	C. history
4. "I volunteered to be in the experimental group."	D. experimenter effect
5. "I watched this show about lung cancer. It made me realize that I really should try to stop smoking while I'm in this smoking cessation study."	E. testing

Circle the letter before the *best* answer:

6. Which of the following items distinguishes true experimental research from quasi-experimental research?
   A. size of sample
   B. use of a nonprobability sample
   C. random assignment of subjects to groups
   D. introduction of an experimental treatment

7. Which of the following designs would be most appropriate to use in trying to determine if clients' low back pain changes after they were taught an exercise to help correct back alignment?
   A. one-group pretest-posttest design
   B. posttest-only control group design
   C. one-shot case study
   D. pretest-posttest control group design

8. Which of the following designs controls for the sensitization of subjects to a pretest?
   A. pretest-posttest control group design
   B. Solomon four-group design
   C. one-shot case study
   D. time-series design

9. A researcher is studying the use of a new realistic model of the heart to teach people what happens during a heart attack. Two weeks later she will test their recall of the information taught. Which of the following situations that might occur *during* the study would concern the researcher *most* about the validity of her study?
   A. A television celebrity had a heart attack and later announced on television that it is important for people to understand how their heart functions.
   B. Two of the study participants drop out of the study.
   C. The researcher has just learned that the new realistic heart model has increased in price.
   D. The CDC released a report that the number of heart attacks has increased slightly in the last 5 years.

10. A researcher wants to use a true experimental design in her study. However, which of the following circumstances would require the use of a quasi-experimental design rather than a true experimental design?
    A. The researcher is going to administer a pretest to study participants.
    B. It will not be possible for the researcher to use random sampling to obtain study participants.
    C. The health care agency will not allow the researcher to assign study participants to groups randomly.
    D. The study will use a longitudinal design.

REFERENCES

Agent orange study finds health problems. (1984, February 25). *Dallas Morning News*, pp. 1A, 5A.

Bracht, G., & Glass, G. (1968). The external validity of experiments. *American Educational Research Journal, 5*, 437–474.

Brandon, A. F., Schuessler, J. B., Ellison, K. J., & Lazenby, R. B. (2009). The effects of an advanced practice nurse led telephone intervention on outcomes of patients with heart failure. *Applied Nursing Research, 22*, e1–e7.

Campbell, C., & Stanley, J. (1963). *Experimental and quasi-experimental designs for research.* Chicago: Rand McNally.

Cason, C. L., Kardong-Edgren, S., Cazzell, M., Behan, D., & Mancini, M. E. (2009). Innovations in basic life support education for healthcare providers. *Journal for Nurses in Staff Development, 25* (3), E1–E13.

Cook, C., & Campbell, D. (1979). *Quasi-experimentation: Design and analysis issues for field settings.* Chicago: Rand McNally.

Dao, J. (2009, October 12). Door opens to health claims tied to Agent Orange. *The New York Times*, p. 14.

Fogg, L., & Gross, D. (2000). Threats to validity in randomized clinical trials. *Research in Nursing & Health, 23*, 79–87.

Howard, V. M., Ross, C., Mitchell, A. M., & Nelson, G. M. (2010). Human patient simulators and interactive case studies. *CIN: Computers, Informatics, Nursing, 28*, 42–48.

Jones, R. A. (2010). Patient education in rural community hospitals: Registered nurses' attitudes and degrees of comfort. *The Journal of Continuing Education in Nursing, 41*, 41–48. doi:10.3928/00220124-20091222-07

Kalisch, B. J., Lee, H., & Salas, E. (2010). The development and testing of the nursing teamwork survey. *Nursing Research, 59*, 42–50.

Kimball, S., Buck, G., Goldstein, D., Largaespada, E., Logan, L., Stebbins, D.,...Kalman-Yearout, K. (2010). Testing a teaching appointment and geragogy-based approach to medication knowledge at discharge. *Rehabilitation Nursing, 35*, 31–49.

Lee, C. J. (2009). A comparison of health promotion behaviors in rural and urban community-dwelling spousal caregivers. *Journal of Gerontological Nursing, 35*, 34–40.

Lee, L. Y. K., Lee., D. T. F., & Woo, J. (2009). Tai Chi and health-related quality of life in nursing home residents. *Journal of Nursing Scholarship, 41*, 35–43.

McCaffrey, R. (2009). The effect of music on acute confusion in older adults after hip or knee surgery. *Applied Nursing Research, 22*, 107–112. doi: 10.1016/j.apnr.2007.06.004

Polit, D. F., & Beck, C. T. (2008). *Nursing research: Principles and methods* (8th ed.) Philadelphia: Lippincott Williams & Wilkins.

Sheenan, C. A. (2009). A brief educational video about prostate cancer screening: A community intervention. *Urologic Nursing, 29*, 103–111, 117.

Song, H.-Y., & Nam, K. A. (2010). Coping strategies, physical function, and social adjustment in people with spinal cord injury. *Rehabilitation Nursing, 35*, 8–15.

Weinrich, S. P., Seger, R., Curtsinger, T., Pumphrey, G., NeSmith, E. G., & Weinrich, M. C. (2007). Impact of pretest on posttest knowledge scores with a Solomon four research design. *Cancer Nursing, 30*, E16–E28.

Wood, K. A., Stewart, A. L., Drew, B. J., Scheinman, M. M., & Froëlicher, E. S. (2010). Patient perception of symptoms and quality of life following ablation in patients with supraventricular tachycardia. *Heart & Lung, 39*, 12–20. doi:10.1016/j.hrtlng.2009.04.001

Wyatt, G., Sikorski, A., Wills, C. E., & An, H. S. (2010). Complementary and alternative medicine use, spending, and quality of life in early stage breast cancer. *Nursing Research, 59*, 58–66.

CHAPTER 10

Qualitative Research Designs

OUTLINE

OBJECTIVES

On completion of this chapter, you will be prepared to:

1. Discuss six common types of qualitative research designs
2. Describe the most important features of these six types of designs
3. Recall the disciplines associated with some of the various qualitative research designs
4. Identify the most common qualitative designs reported in the nursing research literature
5. Recall some of the reasons that nurse researchers are using qualitative designs in their studies
6. Critique the design sections of qualitative research studies

NEW TERMS DEFINED IN THIS CHAPTER

action research, pg 140
bracketing, pg 134
case studies, pg 139
constant comparison, pg 136
content analysis, pg 139
ethnographic studies, pg 135
external criticism, pg 138

grounded theory studies, pg 136
historical studies, pg 137
internal criticism, pg 138
key informants, pg 135
participatory action research, pg 140
phenomenological studies, pg 134

Y ou are glancing through an issue of a research journal and see the following title: "Experiencing a Earthquake—Up Close and Personal." As this chapter is being written (January 2010), a 7.0 earthquake has just devastated Haiti. You might decide to read such an article because the title indicates you will be reading a first-person account of the experiences of people who survived that terrible earthquake. Were you able to tell that you would probably be reading a qualitative research article?

According to Chamberlain (2009), many scientists believe that quantitative randomized control studies are the only true type of scientific inquiry. She disagreed and contended some phenomena about human beings are not suitable for quantitative study and measurement. She wrote that qualitative research is time consuming and requires extensive resources, but that the outcome may uncover a phenomenon "that is new to all of us" (p. 53). She asked for readers to "give it a try!" Donalek (2004) wrote that conducting qualitative research is "a challenging, exciting, and at times, exhaustive process" (p. 517). However, she asserted that the final research product might be very satisfying for the researcher. Volante (2008) proposed that qualitative research is dynamic and characterized by diversity in its purposes, methodology, and practices.

Chapter 4 presented an overview of qualitative research. Table 4–2 lists some of the different types of qualitative research. As you can see in Table 4–2, there are many different types of qualitative research. Try to gain an overall understanding of these different approaches to qualitative research. Do not be discouraged if you feel you do not quite understand all of the information or have difficulty in distinguishing between the various designs. Just try to gain an appreciation of the value of qualitative research to the nursing profession. At some later time, you may be interested in learning more about one or more types of qualitative research. The words *approaches, types,* and *designs* are used interchangeably here in discussing qualitative research.

QUALITATIVE RESEARCH DESIGNS

Six common qualitative designs are described in this chapter: phenomenological, ethnographic, grounded theory, historical, case study, and action research. Excerpts from published nursing studies are presented for each of these six types of qualitative research.

Phenomenological Studies

Phenomenological studies examine human experiences through the descriptions provided by the people involved. These experiences are called *lived experiences.* The goal of phenomenological studies is to describe the meaning that experiences hold for each subject. This type of research is used to study areas in which there is little knowledge (Donalek, 2004). Jones et al. (2010) studied the meaning of surviving cancer for Latino adolescents and emerging young adults. She claimed that phenomenology enables us to understand "meaning and lived experience of populations that are understudied or marginalized" (p. 74).

In phenomenological research, respondents are asked to describe their experiences, as they perceive them. They may write about their experiences, for example in diaries, but information is generally obtained through interviews.

To understand the lived experience from the vantage point of the subject, the researcher must take into account her or his own beliefs and feeling. The researcher must first identify what she or he expects to discover and then deliberately put aside these ideas; this process is called **bracketing**. Only when the researcher puts aside her or his own ideas about the phenomenon is it possible to see the experience from the eyes of the person who has lived the experience. Phenomenologists generally do not conduct a review of the literature at the beginning of their studies (Chamberlain, 2009).

Phenomenological research would ask a question such as, "What is it like for a mother to live with a teenage child who is dying of cancer?" The researcher might perceive that she, herself, would feel very hopeless and frightened. These feelings would need to be identified and then put aside to listen to what the mother is saying about how she is living through this experience. It is possible that this mother has discovered an important reason for living, whereas previously she had not felt needed anymore by her teenage child.

Parse, Coyne, and Smith (1985) wrote that the analysis of data from these types of studies requires that the researcher "dwell with the subjects' descriptions in quiet contemplation" (p. 5). The researcher then tries to uncover the meaning of the lived experience for each subject. Themes and patterns are sought in the data. Data collection and data analysis occur simultaneously.

Phenomenological research methods are very different from the methods used in quantitative research. Mariano (1990) asserted that phenomenology could be difficult to understand, particularly if a person has had a limited background in philosophy. Although phenomenological research has sometimes been viewed as so-called soft science, Streubert and Carpenter (2002) contended that this research method is rigorous, critical, and systematic. They called for the beginning researcher to seek a mentor who has experience in phenomenological research.

Phenomenological Study

Zinsmeister and Schafer (2009) examined the experience of graduate nurses making the transition to registered nurse, using a phenomenological research approach. Interviews revealed five factors that contributed to a positive transition experience: supportive work environment, positive preceptor experience, comprehensive orientation process, sense of professionalism, and clarity of role expectation.

Ethnographic Studies

Ethnographic studies involve the collection and analysis of data about cultural groups. According to Leininger (1985), ethnography can be defined as "the systematic process of observing, detailing, describing, documenting, and analyzing the lifeways or particular patterns of a culture (or subculture) in order to grasp the lifeways or patterns of the people in their familiar environment" (p. 35). Cameron (1990) wrote that ethnography means "learning from people" (p. 5). Barton (2008) stated that a well-designed ethnographic study enables the researcher to "provide insightful descriptions, test established social and cultural theories, or develop new theory" (p. 8).

In ethnographic research, the researcher frequently lives with the people and becomes a part of their culture. The researcher explores with the people their rituals and customs. An entire cultural group may be studied, or just a subgroup. The term *culture* may be used in the broad sense to mean an entire tribe of Indians, for example, or in a more narrow sense to mean one nursing care unit or one group of nurses.

Ethnographic Study

Harrowing (2009) used an ethnographic research approach to study the impact of HIV education on the lives of 24 Ugandan nurses and nurse midwives. Data were gathered through semistructured interviews. The researcher also observed (a) counseling sessions between participants and their clients, (b) participants engaged in their duties at work sites, and (c) participants in group meetings. Findings revealed that these nurses saw themselves as holistic and collaborative caregivers after receiving their HIV education.

Ethnographers interview people who are most knowledgeable about the culture. These people are called **key informants**. Data are generally collected through participant observation and interviews. As discussed under phenomenological studies, researchers bracket, or make explicit, their own personal biases and beliefs, set them aside, and then try to understand the daily lives of individuals as they live them. Data collection and analysis occur simultaneously. As understanding of the data occurs, new questions emerge. The end purpose of ethnography is the development of cultural theories.

Key Informants

A study by Clark, Bunik, and Johnson (2010) used a "key informant." They focused on the role of curanderos (lay healers used by Latinos in the greater southwestern United States) in addressing childhood obesity in Latino families. A Latina colleague of the researchers identified a person who was thought to be a "credible and locally accomplished curandero." This key informant consulted with the research team, reviewed and helped to revise the interview plans and protocol, and referred the researchers to other curanderos.

Although ethnography is relatively new to nurse researchers, the method has been used in anthropological research for a long time. Margaret Mead (1929) used it to study the Samoans. Ethnography has been the principal method used by anthropologists to study people all over the world. Ethnographers study how people live and how they communicate with each other.

Use of the ethnographic method in nursing research began in the 1960s. Ethnography is useful in nursing because this research method enables nurse researchers to view nursing and health care in the context in which it occurs.

Grounded Theory Studies

Grounded theory is a qualitative research approach developed by two sociologists, Glaser and Strauss (1967). **Grounded theory studies** are studies in which data are collected and analyzed, and then a theory is developed that is *grounded* in the data. Some of the terms used by Glaser and Strauss are difficult for nurses to understand. In 1980 Madeline Leininger began to translate their terms into what she called "standard English" (Leininger, 1985).

The grounded theory method uses both an inductive and a deductive approach to theory development. According to Field and Morse (1985), "constructs and concepts are grounded in the data and hypotheses are tested as they arise from the research" (p. 23). These authors argued that given the state of development of nursing theories, theory generation is more critical than theory testing for the development of nursing knowledge.

According to Jacelon and O'Dell (2005), grounded theory is an excellent method for understanding the processes through which patients learn how to manage new or chronic health problems. Each individual may manage the health problem in a different way. For example, a nurse researcher might be interested in how young women deal with premenstrual syndrome (PMS). In talking to a group of these women, one woman might seem to be distressed at the mention of PMS and not want to discuss it at all. Another woman might seem embarrassed, but is willing to ask questions of the researcher. A third young woman might seem to be perfectly comfortable talking about PMS and is willing to share her experiences with the other women. Each of these women has responded to the topic in a unique way.

Rather than using probability sampling procedures, purposeful sampling is used (see Chapter 11). The researcher looks for certain subjects who will be able to shed new light on the phenomenon being studied. Diversity rather than similarity is sought in the people who are sampled.

Data are gathered in naturalistic settings (field settings). Data collection primarily consists of participant observation and interviews, and data are recorded through handwritten notes and tape recordings. Data collection and data analysis occur simultaneously. A process called **constant comparison** is used, in which data are constantly compared to data that have already been gathered. Pertinent concepts are identified and assigned codes. These codes are constantly reviewed as new interpretations are made of the data. The researcher keeps an open mind and uses an intuitive process in interpreting data. Once concepts have been identified and their relationships specified, the researcher consults the literature to determine if any similar associations have already been uncovered. Consulting the literature for the first time at this stage of a research project is quite different from quantitative methods in which the literature is always consulted early in the research process. Leininger (1985) asserted that a prestudy literature search could lead to "premature closure." This means that the researcher would go into the research setting expecting to find what is reported in the literature. When an instance is found that is similar to that reported in the literature, the researcher would say, "Yes, that's it!" and go home and write the same thing.

Despite the great diversity of the data that are gathered, the grounded theory approach presumes it is possible to discover fundamental patterns in all social life. These patterns are called *basic social processes.*

Grounded theory is more concerned with the generation rather than the testing of hypotheses. The theory that is generated is self-correcting, which means that as data are gathered, adjustments are made to the theory to allow for the interpretation of new data that are obtained.

Although the grounded theory approach was developed by two sociologists, Glaser and Strauss, to study questions in the discipline of sociology, the approach seems quite appropriate to nurse researchers. Nursing is very concerned with social interactions.

Grounded Theory

McLaughlin, Moutray, and Moore (2010) used grounded theory methodology to study the career motivation of 68 nursing students. The participants provided answers to essay questions such as "Please tell me your reasons for entering the nursing profession." The essays were read and reread, and themes were highlighted. Altruism was a major theme, but the opportunities available in nursing also influenced their career decision. Family members who were in the health care profession were viewed as great sources of emotional and instrumental support.

Historical Studies

Nurses are increasingly interested in establishing a body of nursing knowledge and defining the role of professional nurses. One means of achieving these aims is to examine the roots of nursing through historical research. **Historical studies** concern the identification, location, evaluation, and synthesis of data from the past. Historical research seeks not only to discover the events of the past, but also to relate these past happenings to the present and to the future. Leininger (1985) wrote, "Without a past, there is no meaning to the present, nor can we develop a sense of ourselves as individuals and as members of groups" (p. 109).

Although historical research is needed in nursing, a limited number of nurse researchers have chosen this type of research. According to the noted nursing historian Teresa Christy (1975), nurses are action oriented and prefer experimental research to historical research. She contended that many nurses think of historical research as more "search than research" (p. 189). But the process of historical research is basically the same as in many other types of scientific research. The problem area or area of interest is clearly identified, and the literature is reviewed. Research questions are formulated. Finally, the data are collected and analyzed.

Historical research may be more difficult to conduct than some of the other types of research. Christy wrote that the historical researcher must develop the "curiosity, perseverance, tenacity and skepticism of the detective" (p. 192).

The data for historical research are usually found in documents or in relics and artifacts. Documents may include a wide range of printed material. Relics and artifacts are items of physical evidence. For example, you might examine the types of equipment used by nurses in another time period. Historical data can also be obtained through oral reports. The material may be found in libraries, archives, or personal collections. Much valuable material has probably been discarded because no one recognized its importance. A book titled *Capturing Nursing History*, edited by Lewenson and Herrmann (2008), is an excellent source of the "collected wisdom" of 18 leading scholars in the history of nursing. Two of these scholars are the editors of that book.

The sources of historical data are frequently referred to as primary and secondary sources. *Primary sources* provide firsthand information or direct evidence. *Secondary sources* are secondhand information (or sometimes third or fourth hand). For example, a letter written by Florence Nightingale about nursing care during the Crimean War would be considered a primary source of data. If a friend summarized the information about nursing care during the Crimean War based on a letter she received from Florence Nightingale, this source of information would be considered a secondary source.

Primary sources should be used in historical research, when possible. There are many examples of primary sources: oral histories, written records, diaries, eyewitnesses, pictorial sources, and physical evidence. Suppose a nurse researcher wished to examine the practices of nurse midwives during the 1950s. An oral history might be obtained from an older member of the nursing profession who had practiced as a nurse midwife during that time. The researcher might also be able to obtain some of the field notes written by people who had practiced as nurse midwives during the 1950s. Some of the nurses may have kept diary accounts of the events that occurred during that period of their lives. It might also be possible to interview some women who had been cared for by nurse midwives during that time period. These women would be considered eyewitnesses. Some of the women or the nurse midwives might have photographs taken during the birthing events. Finally, it might be possible for the researcher to locate some equipment used by nurse midwives during that period.

The data for historical research should be subjected to two types of evaluation: external criticism and internal criticism. **External criticism** is concerned with the authenticity or genuineness of the data and should be considered first. **Internal criticism** examines the accuracy of the data and is considered after the data are considered to be genuine. Whereas external criticism establishes the validity of the data, internal criticism establishes the reliability of the data.

External criticism would seek to determine if a letter was actually written by the person whose signature was contained in the letter. The writing paper might be examined to determine if that type of paper was in existence during the lifetime of the letter writer. False documents, such as a supposed copy of Adolf Hitler's diary, have been uncovered through the process of external criticism. Various methods, including carbon dating, can be used to determine the age of substances such as paper.

Internal criticism of historical data is more difficult to conduct than external criticism. In the case of a written document, internal criticism would evaluate the material contained in the document. Motives and possible biases of the author must be considered in trying to determine if the material is accurate. It might be fairly easy to determine that a certain person was the writer of a letter being examined. It might not be so easy, however, to determine if the letter contained an accurate recording of events as they actually happened.

Although nurse researchers have conducted only a limited number of historical studies, there seems to be a growing interest in historical research, particularly among doctoral candidates who are writing dissertations. In 1993 the first issue of *Nursing History Review* was published. Members of the American Association for the History of Nursing (AAHN) receive the journal as a benefit of membership in the organization. The URL for the AAHN is http://aahn.org. The Web site states, "Nursing history is not an ornament to be displayed on anniversary days, nor does it consist of only happy stories to be recalled and retold on special occasions. Nursing history is a vivid testimony, meant to incite, instruct and inspire today's nurses as they bravely trod the winding path of a reinvented health care system." The AAHN offers three research awards each year. One award is titled "The Teresa E. Christy Award." This award honors Christy's excellence in historical research. The AAHN will convene its 30th Annual History of Nursing Research Conference in 2013.

Many historical studies have focused on nursing leaders. Few historical studies, however, have been conducted on nursing practice. It is hoped that historical research will expand and nursing be provided with a recorded account of the significant events and developments of nursing practice as well as those of the nursing profession. As interest in historical nursing research increases, nursing archives, which are repositories of nursing memorabilia, are being established throughout the United States. Try to visit one of these storehouses of nursing history.

Historical Study

Hoffart (2009) examined the history of kidney transplant nursing. She analyzed published literature, interviewed early transplant nurses, and studied primary sources such as photos. She described the early clinical practice of transplant nurses between 1950 and 1970. She concluded that transplant nursing practice was greatly influenced by methods of immunosuppression and their associated complications.

Case Studies

Case studies are in-depth examinations of people or groups of people. A case study could also examine an institution, such as hospice care for the dying. The case method has its roots in sociology and has also been used a great deal in anthropology, law, and medicine. In medicine, case studies have frequently been concerned with a particular disease. In nursing, the case study approach might be used to answer a question such as "How do the nurse and patient manage nausea associated with chemotherapy?" Jacelon and O'Dell (2005) have proposed the use of case studies to explore real clinical situations in depth.

A case study may be considered as quantitative or qualitative research, depending on the purpose of the study and the design chosen by the researcher. As is true of other types of qualitative studies, for a case study to be considered as a qualitative study, the researcher must be interested in the meaning of experiences to the subjects themselves, rather than in generalizing results to other groups of people. Case studies are not used to test hypotheses, but hypotheses may be generated from case studies (Younger, 1985).

Patricia Benner is a qualitative researcher who has been interested in how a nurse moves from novice to expert nurse. She has used the case study approach extensively. She contends that case studies help us formalize experiential knowledge and, thus, promote quality nursing care (Benner, 1983).

Data may be collected in case studies through various means such as questionnaires, interviews, observations, or written accounts by the subjects. A nurse researcher might be interested in how people with diabetes respond to an insulin pump. One person or a group of people with diabetes could be studied for a time to determine their responses to the use of an insulin pump. Diaries might be used for the day-to-day recording of information. The nurse researcher would then analyze these diaries and try to interpret the written comments.

Content analysis is used in evaluating the data from case studies. **Content analysis** involves the examination of communication messages. The researcher searches for patterns and themes. After reading the diaries of the individuals who are using insulin pumps, the nurse researcher might come up with themes such as: "freedom from rigid schedule," "more normal life," and "release from self-inflicted pain."

When subjects are chosen for case studies, care must be taken in the selection process. In the previously discussed example, the researcher should avoid choosing only those clients who are expected to respond favorably or unfavorably to the insulin pump.

Case studies are time consuming and may be quite costly. Additionally, subjects may drop out during this type of study. Whenever a study is carried out over an extended period, loss of subjects must be considered. A person may move from the locality or simply decide to discontinue participation in the study.

Case Study

A case study method was used to present the story of one mother concerning her childhood sexual abuse and how it impacted her breastfeeding experiences (Beck, 2009a). Her description vividly presented how breastfeeding brought about panic attacks, dissociation, and flashbacks to the childhood sexual abuse.

Action Research Studies

Action research is a type of qualitative research that seeks action to improve practice and study the effects of the action that was taken (Streubert & Carpenter, 2002). According to Dampier (2009), action research brings about change in the clinical area through an "action-reflection cycle." Solutions are sought to practice problems in one particular hospital or health care setting. There is no goal of trying to generalize the findings of the study, as is the case in quantitative research studies. In action research, the implementation of solutions occurs as an actual part of the research process. There is no delay in implementation of the solutions.

Action research became popular in the 1940s. Kurt Lewin (1946) was influential in spreading action research. He became interested in helping social workers improve their practice. Although many of you may have heard of Lewin and his contribution to change theory, his involvement in action research is not as well known.

Action Research

An action research study was conducted to evaluate a nurse-led unit in a community hospital (Lee, 2009). Participants used group reflection to become involved in the research process. Workshops were held throughout the study to "explore team members' expectations; to identify and discuss the key elements of the study; to explore research methods; to have shared ownership of data collection and analysis; to enhance team members' participation in dissemination of the findings . . ." (p. 31–32).

Participatory action research (PAR) is a special kind of community-based action research in which there is collaboration between the study participants and the researcher in all steps of the study: determining the problem, the research methods to use, the analysis of data, and how the study results will be used. The participants and the researcher are co-researchers throughout the entire research study. According to Kelly (2005), PAR provides an opportunity for involving a community "in the development and assessment of a health program" (p. 65).

CRITIQUING QUALITATIVE RESEARCH DESIGNS

Qualitative studies should not be evaluated with the same set of criteria as quantitative studies. It is more difficult to evaluate qualitative studies using a standard set of criteria. Each qualitative method is unique.

Beck (2009b) asserted that "trustworthiness" is "at the heart" of critiquing qualitative research. She listed five criteria of trustworthiness: (a) credibility—how believable is the data, (b) dependability—how stabile is the data over time and in different situations, (c) confirmability—how much agreement is there between two or more individuals who are reviewing the data for accuracy and meaning, (d) transferability—how applicable are the results to other groups and situations, and (e) authenticity—how closely and faithfully have the researchers described the participants' experiences.

> ## Box 10–1. Guidelines for Critiquing Qualitative Designs
>
> 1. Does the phenomenon lend itself to study by qualitative methods or would a quantitative approach have been more appropriate?
> 2. Does the study focus on the subjective nature of human experience?
> 3. Is the specific qualitative approach named and described?
> 4. Will the study findings have significance for nursing?
> 5. Does the researcher clearly describe how participants were selected?
> 6. How was the sample size determined?
> 7. Is the data collection and recording process fully presented?
> 8. Is it clear how researcher bias in data collection was avoided?
> 9. Is the data analysis method consistent with the purpose and approach of the study?
> 10. Are the study findings clearly presented and study limitations acknowledged?
> 11. Are suggestions made for further research, based on the study findings?

Some general criteria by which qualitative research can be evaluated are found in Box 10–1. You may want to read Chapter 4 again ("Overview of Qualitative Research") before examining the evaluation criteria presented in Box 10–1. These criteria concern not only criteria for evaluating specific designs in qualitative research, but also general criteria for evaluating qualitative research reports. Also, Chapter 20 presents a summary of critiquing guidelines for a qualitative study.

The beginning researcher may be very reluctant to critique qualitative studies. When unfamiliar with the study topic, the reviewer may believe that she or he lacks the expertise to critique the study. However, a determination can be made of how clearly the research report presents the process of data collection and analysis. The most important issue to consider is whether the data are provided to answer the research questions. Are the researcher's conceptualizations clearly based on the data presented? The reviewer should expect to see examples from the data and then make a judgment about how clearly the researcher has presented the interpretation of the data.

SUMMARY

Many nurses are interested in qualitative research. Qualitative research focuses on gaining insight and understanding about an individual's perception of events and circumstances.

Six common types of qualitative research are phenomenological, ethnographic, grounded theory, historical, case study, and action research.

Phenomenological studies examine human experiences through the descriptions that are provided by the people involved. **Bracketing** is the process in which qualitative researchers put aside their own feelings and beliefs about the phenomenon under consideration to keep from biasing their observations.

Ethnographic studies collect data from groups, such as certain cultural groups. Ethnographers frequently live with the people they are studying. Data are collected from **key informants**, who are the people most knowledgeable about the culture.

In **grounded theory studies**, data are collected and analyzed, and then a theory is developed that is *grounded* in the data. A process called **constant comparison** is used, in which data are constantly compared to data that have already been gathered. Pertinent concepts are identified and assigned codes.

Historical studies concern the identification, location, evaluation, and synthesis of data from the past. Historical data should be subjected to both external and internal criticism. **External criticism** is concerned with the authenticity of the data; **internal criticism** is concerned with the accuracy of the data.

Case studies are in-depth examinations of people, groups of people, or institutions. **Content analysis** is the term used to indicate the examination of communication messages obtained in case studies, as well as in other types of qualitative studies.

Action research is a type of qualitative research that seeks action to improve practice and study the effects of the action that was taken. **Participatory action research** (PAR) is a special kind of action research in which there is collaboration between the study participants and the researcher in all steps of the study.

NURSING RESEARCH ON THE WEB

For additional online resources, research activities, and exercises, go to **www.mynursingkit.com.** Select Chapter 10 from the drop-down menu.

GET INVOLVED ACTIVITIES

1. Each person will bring a published article that contains a report of a qualitative study. Using these qualitative research articles located in the literature, determine the specific type of qualitative design that was used.
2. While searching the literature for a qualitative study, make a list of titles that indicate the study might be a qualitative study.
3. Divide into groups and develop an idea for a study in which the grounded theory method or the phenomenological method would be appropriate.
4. Try to obtain a historical research study report that focused on the types of uniforms worn by nurses through the years.

SELF-TEST

Circle the letter before the *best* answer:

1. Which of the following types of studies is considered a qualitative study?
   A. correlational
   B. ethnographic
   C. comparative
   D. methodological
2. Grounded theory research was developed by two
   A. nurses
   B. physicians
   C. psychologists
   D. sociologists
3. Margaret Mead was a researcher from what discipline?
   A. Anthropology
   B. Psychology
   C. Nursing
   D. Sociology

4. Which of the following statements is true concerning the examination of historical research?
   A. Internal criticism should be considered before external criticism.
   B. External criticism should be considered before internal criticism.
   C. Both internal and external criticism should be considered simultaneously.
5. Case studies may concern an in-depth examination of
   A. individuals
   B. groups of peoples
   C. institutions
   D. all of the above
6. Consider this title: "The Lived Experience of Surviving an Earthquake." This title would indicate which of the following types of qualitative research?
   A. ethnographic
   B. phenomenological

C. historical

D. grounded theory

7. The review of the literature in qualitative research is
   A. never conducted prior to the beginning of the study.
   B. sometimes conducted prior to the beginning of the study.
   C. always conducted prior to the beginning of the study.

8. Which type of qualitative research approach would be most appropriate to study nurses' involvement in bringing about a change in the type of forms used to record patient data?
   A. action
   B. ethnographic

C. phenomenological

D. historical

9. Teresa Christy, a nurse, was involved in what type of qualitative research?
   A. action
   B. ethnographic
   C. historical
   D. phenomenological

10. Which type(s) of qualitative research has or have been conducted by nurses?
    A. action
    B. ethnographic
    C. phenomenological
    D. historical
    E. all of the above

REFERENCES

Barton, T. D. (2008). Understanding practitioner ethnography. *Nurse Researcher, 15* (2), 7–18.

Beck, C. T. (2009a). An adult survivor of child sexual abuse and her breastfeeding experience: A case study. *MCN, 34,* 91–97.

Beck, C. T. (2009b). Critiquing qualitative research. *AORN, 90,* 543–554.

Benner, P. (1983). Uncovering the knowledge embedded in clinical practice. *Image: Journal of Nursing Scholarship, 19,* 36–41.

Cameron, C. (1990). The ethnographic approach: Characteristics and uses in gerontological nursing. *Journal of Gerontological Nursing, 16*(9), 5–7.

Chamberlain, B. (2009). Phenomenology: A qualitative method. *Clinical Nurse Specialist, 23,* 52–53.

Christy, T. (1975). The methodology of historical research. *Nursing Research, 24,* 189–192.

Clark, L., Bunik, M., & Johnson, S. L. (2010). Research opportunities with curanderos to address childhood overweight in Latino families. *Qualitative Health Research, 20,* 4–14. doi: 10.1177/1049732309355285

Dampier, S. (2009). Action research. *Nurse Researcher, 16* (2), 4–6.

Donalek, J. G. (2004). Demystifying nursing research: Phenomenology as a qualitative research method. *Urologic Nursing, 24,* 516–517.

Field, P. A., & Morse, J. M. (1985). *Nursing research: The application of qualitative approaches.* Rockville, MD: Aspen.

Glaser, B. G., & Strauss, A. C. (1967). *The discovery of grounded theory: Strategies for qualitative research.* New York: Aldine.

Harrowing, J. N. (2009). The impact of HIV education on the lives of Ugandan nurses and nurse- midwives. *Advances in Nursing Science, 32.* E94–E108.

Hoffart, N. (2009). The development of kidney transplant nursing. *Nephrology Nursing, 36,* 127–138.

Jacelon, C. S., & O'Dell, K. K. (2005). Case and grounded theory as qualitative research methods. *Urologic Nursing, 25,* 49–52.

Jones, B. L., Volker, D. L., Vinajeras, Y., Butros, L., Fitchpatrick, C., & Rossetto, K. (2010). The meaning of surviving cancer for Latino adolescents and emerging young adults. *Cancer Nursing, 33,* 74–81.

Kelly, P. J. (2005). Practical suggestions for community interventions using participatory action research. *Public Health Nursing, 22,* 65–73.

Lee, N.-J. (2009). Using group reflection in an action research study. *Nurse Researcher, 16,* 30–42.

Leininger, M. M. (Ed.). (1985). *Qualitative research methods in nursing.* Orlando, FL: Grune & Stratton.

Lewenson, S. B., & Herrmann, E. K. (Eds). (2008). *Capturing nursing history: A guide to historical methods.* New York: Springer.

Lewin, K. (1946). Action research and minority problems. *Journal of Social Issues, 2*(4), 34–46.

Mariano, C. (1990). Qualitative research: Instructional strategies and curricular considerations. *Nursing & Health Care, 11,* 354–359.

McLaughlin, K., Moutray, M., & Moore, C. (2010). Career motivation in nursing students and the perceived influence of significant others. *Journal of Advanced Nursing, 66,* 404–412. doi: 10.1111/j.1365-2648.2009.05147.x

Mead, M. (1929). *Coming of age in Samoa.* New York: New American Library.

Parse, R. R., Coyne, A. B., & Smith, M. J. (1985). *Nursing research: Qualitative methods.* Bowie, MD: Brady.

Streubert, H. J., & Carpenter, D. R. (2002). *Qualitative research in nursing: Advancing the humanistic imperative* (3rd ed.). Philadelphia: Lippincott Williams & Wilkins.

Younger, J. (1985). Practical approaches to clinical research: The case study. *Pediatric Nursing, 11,* 137.

Volante, M. (2008). Qualitative research. *Nurse Researcher, 16* (1), 4–6.

Zinsmeister, L. B., & Schafer, D. (2009). The exploration of the lived experience of the graduate nurse making the transition to registered nurse during the first year of practice. *Journal for Nurses in Staff Development, 25,* 28–34.

CHAPTER 11

Populations and Samples

OUTLINE

Populations
Samples
Types of Sampling Methods
* Probability Sampling Methods
  – Simple Random Sampling
  – Stratified Random Sampling
  – Cluster Random Sampling
  – Systematic Random Sampling
* Nonprobability Sampling Methods
  – Convenience Sampling
  – Quota Sampling
  – Purposive Sampling

Time Frame for Studying the Sample
Sample Size
Sampling Error and Sampling Bias
Randomization Procedures in Research
Critiquing the Sampling Procedure
Summary
Nursing Research on the Web
Get Involved Activities
Self-Test

OBJECTIVES

On completion of this chapter, you will be prepared to:
1. Define population and sample
2. Distinguish between target and accessible populations
3. Discuss probability and nonprobability sampling procedures
4. Compare four methods of probability sampling
5. Compare three methods of nonprobability sampling
6. Determine which sampling technique to use in various types of research studies
7. Compare longitudinal and cross-sectional studies
8. Enumerate factors to be considered in deciding the size of the sample
9. Discuss sampling error and sampling bias
10. Critique the sampling procedure described in research reports and articles

NEW TERMS DEFINED IN THIS CHAPTER

cluster random sampling, pg 150

cohort study, pg 154

convenience sampling, pg 152

cross-sectional study, pg 154

disproportional stratified sampling, pg 150

element, pg 147

judgmental sampling, pg 154

longitudinal study, pg 154

network sampling, pg 153

nonprobability sampling, pg 152

power analysis, pg 156

probability sampling, pg 147

proportional stratified sampling, pg 150

purposive sampling, pg 154

quota sampling, pg 153

sampling bias, pg 157

sampling error, pg 157

sampling frame, pg 147

simple random sampling, pg 148

snowball sampling, pg 153

stratified random sampling, pg 148

systematic random sampling, pg 151

table of random numbers, pg 148

volunteers, pg 158

Did you check out some new blog site today, or taste a new food, or turn on a different TV program than you have ever watched before? If so, you have been sampling. Sampling is a part of our everyday life. Frequently, decisions in life are made on limited sampling from all of the available options. If you are thinking about going shopping for new clothes today, would you plan to try on all of the clothes in the store before you purchased one item? Probably not, or the store would close before you made your decision!

Researchers also make decisions based on data from samples. However, the consequences of basing decisions on inadequate samples may be much more serious for the researcher than for the shopper. If you chose the wrong size or changed your mind about the style of shoes you bought, you are usually allowed to exchange the shoes or receive your money back. The researcher is not able to change a decision about the selection of a sample for a study once the sample has been chosen. Of course, the safest choice then would be to study total populations. Just as it is unlikely that you would buy a whole "population" of shoes, researchers rarely study entire populations. An understanding of the means of selecting samples for research studies, therefore, is important for nurse researchers.

POPULATION

A population, as mentioned in Chapter 3, is a complete set of persons or objects that possess some common characteristic of interest to the researcher. Quantitative research is very interested in populations. Qualitative research focuses more on individuals, themselves. This chapter focuses on obtaining a sample for a quantitative study. The goal of sampling in quantitative research is to be able to make generalizations about the population from which the sample was drawn.

The population for a study is composed of two groups: the target population and the accessible population. As mentioned in Chapter 3, the target population is composed of the entire group of people or objects to which the researcher wishes to generalize the findings of a study. The target population consists of people or things that meet the designated set of criteria of interest to the researcher. Examples of target populations might be all people who are institutionalized for psychiatric problems in one state or all the charts from well-child clinics for the year 2010. Because the likelihood of being able to obtain a list of these populations is quite low, the researcher usually samples from an available group, called the *accessible population* or *study population*. The need to identify the accessible population is quite important for nurse researchers. By clearly identifying the group from which the study sample was chosen, the investigator enables readers of a research report to come to their own conclusions about the generalizability of the study findings. The conclusions of a research study are based on data obtained from the accessible population, and statistical inferences (see Chapter 15) should be made only to the group from which the sample was randomly selected.

Target and Accessible Populations

A study was conducted on the perceptions of nursing faculty about the importance of instruction in baccalaureate nursing curricula on mass casualty incidents (Whitty & Burnett, 2009). The target population was identified as faculty of accredited baccalaureate nursing programs currently teaching theory or clinical courses or both. The accessible population was nurse educators employed full-time by January 1, 2006 in all accredited baccalaureate nursing programs in Louisiana. This population consisted of 285 educators.

SAMPLES

Although researchers are always interested in populations, an entire population is generally not used in a research study. The researcher probably cannot gain access to a population of potential research participants. Also, the accuracy gained when all members are included is often not worth the time and money involved. In most nursing research studies, a sample or subset of the population is selected to represent the population. When a sample is chosen properly, the researcher is able to make claims about the population based on data from the sample alone. The method of selection and the sample size determine how representative a sample is of the population.

A single member of a population is called an **element**. The terms *population member* and *population element* are often used interchangeably. Elements, or members of a population, are selected from a **sampling frame**, which is a listing of all elements of a population. Sometimes listings of populations, such as membership lists, hospital patient census sheets, and vital statistics listings are readily available. However, it may be necessary for the researcher to prepare the sampling frame by listing all members of the accessible population. This can be a time-consuming task. For example, you might examine a large group of charts and make a list of all patients who were admitted for their second major surgical procedure within the past 2 years.

Although examining each member of a population would generally produce more accurate data, occasionally data obtained from a sample are more exact. For example, in large-scale survey studies in which many interviewers have to be trained, the quality of the interviews would be difficult to control, and a small number of interviews conducted by a well-trained group of interviewers might produce more accurate data than would be produced by a large group of interviewers. Also, when resources are spread thin, a weak study may result.

TYPES OF SAMPLING METHODS

Samples are chosen through two types of sampling procedures: probability and nonprobability. The various types of probability and nonprobability sampling methods are discussed next.

Probability Sampling Methods

Probability sampling, or random sampling, involves the use of a random selection process to obtain a sample from members or elements of a population. The goal of probability sampling is to obtain representative elements of populations.

The term *random* can be confusing to the beginning researcher. The dictionary definition of this word suggests that something occurs haphazardly or without direction. Random sampling, however, is anything but haphazard! It is a very systematic, scientific process. The investigator can specify the chance of any one element of the population being selected for the sample. Each population element has a known chance or probability of being selected for the sample. Selections are independent of each other, and the investigator's bias does not enter into the selection of the sample.

When a random sample is selected, the researcher hopes that the variables of interest in the population will be present in the sample in approximately the same proportions as would be found in the total population. Unfortunately, there is never any guarantee. Probability sampling enables the researcher only to *estimate* the chance that any given population element will be included in the sample. When probability samples are chosen, inferential statistics may be used with greater confidence (see Chapter 15). Without the use of random sampling procedures, the ability to generalize the findings of a study is greatly reduced. Four types of random sampling procedures are examined here: simple, stratified, cluster, and systematic.

Simple Random Sampling

Simple random sampling is a type of probability sampling method that ensures each element of the population has an equal and independent chance of being chosen. This method is generally used in at least one phase of the other three types of random sampling procedures and, therefore, is examined first. Table 11–1 lists the advantages and disadvantages of simple random sampling.

The word *simple* does not mean easy or uncomplicated. In fact, simple random sampling can be quite complex and time consuming, especially if a large sample is desired.

The first step is to identify the accessible population and enumerate or list all the elements of the population. After this sampling frame is developed, a method must be selected to choose the sample. Slips of paper representing each element in the population could be placed in a hat or bowl and the sample selected by reaching in and drawing out as many slips of paper as the desired size of the sample.

Although random sampling can be achieved in this manner, the most commonly used and accurate procedure for selecting a simple random sample is through the use of a **table of random numbers**. A table of random numbers includes a group of numbers that has been generated in such a manner that there is no order or sequencing of the numbers. Each number has an equal chance of following any other number. Tables of random numbers are still found in some research and statistical textbooks. However, today these tables are usually computer-generated. Several Web sites enable you to generate your own table of random numbers. One such site is: http://stattrek.com/Tables/Random.aspx.

Simple Random Sample

A simple random sample of 540 staff nurses who were members of the Ohio Nurses Association were mailed a survey about their beliefs in information systems (IS) (Abdrbo, Hudak, Anthony, & Douglas, 2009). A total of 201 surveys were returned (37.22% response rate). On a scale of 1–5, nurses were found to be satisfied with IS on an average of 3.20, with a range of 1–5.

Stratified Random Sampling

In **stratified random sampling**, the population is divided into subgroups, or strata, according to some variable(s) of importance to the research study. After the population is divided into two or more strata, a simple random sample is taken from each of these subgroups.

Many different characteristics of populations may call for the use of stratified sampling. Subject characteristics, such as age, gender, and educational background, are examples of variables that might be used as criteria for dividing populations into subgroups. For example, a school nurse might be interested in studying marijuana usage among high school students. To determine

TABLE 11-1 Probability Sampling Chart

Type of Sampling	Description of Methodology	Advantages	Disadvantages
A. Simple random	Assign a number to each member of the population. Select the sample through a table of random numbers.	1. Little knowledge of population is needed 2. Most unbiased of probability methods 3. Easy to analyze data and compute errors	1. A complete listing of population is necessary 2. Time consuming 3. Expensive
B. Stratified	Divide population into strata. Determine number of cases desired in each stratum. Random sample these subgroups.	1. Increases probability of sample being representative 2. Assures adequate number of cases for subgroups	1. Requires accurate knowledge of population 2. May be costly to prepare stratified lists 3. Statistics more complicated
1. Proportionate	Determine sampling fraction for each stratum that is equal to its proportion in the total population.		
2. Disproportionate	Sample is drawn in manner to ensure that each stratum is well represented. Used when strata are very unequal.		
C. Cluster	Groups rather than people are selected from population. Successive steps of selection are done (state, city, county). Then sample is randomly selected from clusters.	1. Saves time and money 2. Arrangements made with small number of sampling units 3. Characteristics of clusters as well as those of population can be estimated	1. Larger sampling errors than other probability samples 2. Requires assignment of each member of population uniquely to a cluster 3. Statistics are more complicated
D. Systematic	Obtain listing of population. Determine sample size. Determine sampling interval ($k = N/n$). Select random starting point. Select every kth element.	1. Easy to draw sample 2. Economical 3. Time-saving technique	1. Samples may be biased if ordering of population is not random 2. After the first sampling element is chosen, population members no longer have equal chance of being chosen

if marijuana usage is different among freshmen, sophomores, juniors, and seniors, the total high school population could be stratified into four separate sampling units and a random sample selected from each grade. If a simple random sample technique is used, the four grades might not be represented in large enough numbers to make valid comparisons. Generally, there are more freshmen in a school than there are seniors. Some dropout occurs as students progress through high school. By dividing the total population into the four grades, the school nurse would be more certain that sufficient numbers of students from all four grades will be selected for inclusion in the study.

After dividing the population into subgroups, the researcher must decide how large a sample to obtain from each of these strata. Two approaches may be used. The first is called **proportional stratified sampling** and involves obtaining a sample from each stratum that is in proportion to the size of that stratum in the total population. If there were 400 freshmen, 300 sophomores, 200 juniors, and 100 seniors (highly unlikely!) in a total high school population of 1,000 students, the size of the sample from each of these groups should be freshmen, 40%; sophomores, 30%; juniors, 20%; and seniors, 10%. If a sample of 100 students was desired, the selection should include 40 freshmen, 30 sophomores, 20 juniors, and 10 seniors.

What if the school nurse decided that 10 seniors was not a large enough sample to get a clear picture of marijuana usage among that group? She might decide to choose 25 subjects from each class. The selection of members from strata in which the number of members chosen from each stratum is not in proportion to the size of the stratum in the total population is called **disproportional stratified sampling**. Whenever disproportional sampling is used, an adjustment process known as *weighting* should be considered. This process involves simple computations that are described in many texts on sampling procedures. These adjustments allow a better estimate of the actual population values.

As previously mentioned, simple random sampling is used to obtain the sample elements from each stratum when a stratified random sampling method is used. Table 11–1 lists the advantages and disadvantages of stratified sampling.

Stratified Random Sample

Teng et al. (2009) studied the professional commitment of nurses in Taiwan in regard to patient safety and patient-perceived quality of care. Nurses were chosen from two medical centers in northern Taiwan, one privately owned and the other government owned. Stratified random sampling of the ward units was done in an attempt to ensure that the sample would be proportionate across the units. The sampled nurses worked in more than 80 hospital units. Study results revealed that professional commitment positively influenced patient safety and patient-perceived quality of care.

Cluster Random Sampling

In large-scale studies in which the population is geographically spread out, sampling procedures may be very difficult and time consuming. Also, it may not be possible to get a total listing of some populations. Suppose a researcher wanted to interview 100 nurse administrators in the United States. If the 100 names were chosen through a simple random sampling procedure, it is quite likely the investigator would be faced with traveling to 100 different cities in the United States to conduct the interviews. This would be a very expensive and time-consuming activity. Another approach that might be used to obtain this sample of nurse administrators is cluster sampling.

In **cluster random sampling**, large groups, or clusters, become the sampling units. To obtain the sample of nurse administrators, the first clusters to be sampled would be acquired by drawing a simple random sample or stratified random sample of states in the United States. Then, cities would be chosen from these states. Next, hospitals from within those cities would be selected, and, finally, the nurse administrators from some of these hospitals would be interviewed. During each phase of sampling from the clusters, simple, stratified, or systematic random sampling may be used. Because the sample is selected from clusters in two or more separate stages, the approach is sometimes called multistage sampling.

Although cluster sampling may be necessary for large-scale survey studies, the likelihood of sampling error increases with each stage of sampling. A simple random sample is subject to a single sampling error, whereas a cluster sample is subject to as many sampling errors as there are stages in the sampling procedure. To compensate for the sampling error when cluster sampling is used, larger samples should be selected than would normally be chosen for a simple or stratified random sample. Table 11–1 lists the advantages and disadvantages of cluster sampling.

Cluster Random Sample

A study was conducted in Israel (Kagan, Ovadia & Kaneti, 2009) to examine the relationship between nurses' knowledge of blood-borne pathogens (BBPs) and their (a) professional behavior regarding handwashing, (b) compliance with standard precautions, and (c) avoidance of therapeutic contact with BBP-infected patients. Participants were sampled in clusters. From each hospital clinical division, clinical departments (clusters) were randomly selected. Questionnaires were then distributed to all individuals (240) within the clusters.

Systematic Random Sampling

Systematic random sampling involves selecting every *k*th element of the population, such as every fifth, eighth, or twenty-first element. The first step is to obtain a list of the total population (*N*). Then, the sample size (*n*) is determined. Next, the sampling interval width (*k*) is determined by *N/n*. For instance, if the researcher were seeking a sample of 50 from a population of 500, the sampling interval would be:

$$k = 500/50 = 10$$

Every tenth element of the population list would be selected for the sample. This method may be used to obtain any sample size from a given population.

This sampling method is the most controversial type of random sampling procedure. In fact, systematic sampling may be classified as either a probability or a nonprobability sampling method. Two criteria are necessary for a systematic sampling procedure to be classified as probability sampling: (a) the listing of the population (sampling frame) must be random with respect to the variable of interest, and (b) the first element or member of the sample must be selected randomly. If either of these criteria is not met, the sample becomes a nonprobability sample.

The first criterion for the inclusion of systematic sampling as a probability sampling method is the requirement that the listing of the elements of the population must be in random order. Suppose a researcher was choosing names from an alphabetized list. Certain ethnic groups have large numbers of surnames that begin with the same initial and are grouped together alphabetically. If systematic sampling is used, these ethnic groups may be underrepresented or overrepresented. As another example, the sample to be selected might be patients in hospital rooms. The decision might be made to sample every fifth hospital room. It might happen that every fifth room is a private room. Patients in private rooms may not respond in the same manner that patients in semiprivate rooms might respond.

The second criterion for considering systematic sampling as a type of probability sampling is that a random starting point must be chosen. The best way to obtain this starting point is through a table of random numbers. If the population size is 500 and a sample size of 50 is desired, a number between 1 and 500 is selected as the starting point. Suppose the first number randomly selected is 289. The sampling interval width ($k + 10$) is added to this number ($289 + 10 = 299$), and the next element selected would correspond to number 299. When 500 is reached, the researcher starts back over at the beginning of the list and continues, adding 10 to select each additional element of the sample. An alternate procedure, recommended in most texts, is to select the first element randomly from within the first sampling interval. If the sampling interval width was 10, a number between 1 and 10 would be selected as the random starting point. For example, suppose the number 4 is randomly chosen. The next element selected would correspond to number 14 ($4 + 10 = 14$). Although this latter procedure is technically correct, choosing a random starting point from across the total population of elements is appealing to me because every element has a chance to be chosen for the sample during the first selection step.

When careful attention is paid to obtaining an unbiased listing of the population elements, and the first element is randomly selected, systematic random sampling is similar to simple random sampling and much easier. Drawing 50 numbers from a table of random numbers is a much more laborious task than choosing 50 numbers through systematic sampling (see Table 11–1 for the advantages and disadvantages of systematic random sampling). A recent review of the published nursing research literature revealed few studies in which systematic random sampling was mentioned.

Systematic Random Sample

Systematic random sampling was used in a study of nurses who were members, in 2006, of the Australian College of Operating Room Nurses (ACORN) (Gillespie, Chaboyer, Wallis, & Grimbeek, 2007). From the accessible population of 2,860 members, 1,430 were selected by systematic random sampling. Every second member listed on the ACORN database was selected. The first element was chosen from a computer-generated list of members, and then every second member on the list was selected.

Nonprobability Sampling Methods

In **nonprobability sampling**, the sample elements are chosen from the population by nonrandom methods. Nonrandom methods of sampling are more likely to produce a biased sample than are random methods. The investigator cannot estimate the probability that each element of the population will be included in the sample. In fact, in nonprobability sampling, certain elements of the population may have no chance of being included in the sample. This restricts the generalizations that can be made about the study findings. Despite the limitations of nonprobability sampling, most nursing research studies involve this type of sampling procedure. True random samples are rare in nursing research.

The most frequent reasons for the use of nonprobability samples involve convenience and the desire to use available subjects. Samples may be chosen from available groups of subjects by several different methods, including convenience, quota, and purposive.

Convenience Sampling

Convenience sampling is also referred to as *accidental* or *incidental* and involves choosing readily available people or objects for a study. These elements may or may not be typical of the population. There is no accurate way to determine their representativeness. It is easy to see that this may be a very unreliable method of sampling. However, convenience sampling has probably been the most frequently used sampling method in nursing research. A recent review of the nursing research literature confirmed the continued use of convenience samples.

Convenience samples are chosen because of the savings in time and money. The researcher may choose a convenience sample from familiar people, as when a teacher uses students in her or his class, or from strangers, such as might be encountered when a nurse researcher conducts a survey among family members in an intensive care unit waiting room to determine their attitudes about visiting hours.

Convenience Sample

Walker, Pepa, and Gerard (2010) studied a convenience sample of 21 hospitalized inpatients and 34 outpatients to evaluate their health literacy levels. The inpatients were recruited from medical-surgical areas of the hospital. Outpatients were obtained from several settings, which included cardiac rehabilitation, preadmitting, and neuroscience clinics. Based on scores on the Test of Functional Health Literacy in Adults, 23% of the sample demonstrated marginal or inadequate functional health literacy. Literacy was significantly related to socioeconomic status and education.

Another method of obtaining a convenience sample is through **snowball sampling**, also called **network sampling**. This term is used to describe a method of sampling that involves the assistance of study subjects to help obtain other potential subjects. Suppose the researcher wanted to determine how to help people stop cigarette smoking. The researcher might know of someone who has been successful in refraining from cigarette smoking for 10 years. This person is contacted and asked if he or she knows others who have also been successful. This type of networking is particularly helpful in finding people who are reluctant to make their identity known, such as substance abusers.

Snowball Sample

Physical activity, stress, disease activity, and quality of life were studied in adults with Crohns disease (CD) (Crumbock, Loeb, & Fick, 2009). Snowball sampling was one method used to obtain the sample. The principal investigator of the study first contacted a small number of eligible persons who were known to have the disease. These participants were then asked to contact someone else who had CD.

Quota Sampling

Quota sampling is similar to stratified random sampling in that the first step involves dividing the population into homogeneous strata and selecting sample elements from each of these strata. The difference lies in the means of securing potential subjects from these strata. Stratified random sampling involves a random sampling method of obtaining sample members, whereas quota sampling obtains members through convenience samples.

The term *quota* arises from the researcher's establishment of a desired quota or proportion for some population variable of interest. The basis of stratification should be a variable of importance to the study. These variables frequently include subject attributes such as age, gender, and educational background. The number of elements chosen from each stratum is generally in proportion to the size of that stratum in the total population. For example, if the researcher wanted to determine whether more males or females receive yearly physical examinations, an equal proportion of males and females should be approached for the study. If convenience sampling is used, the two genders may not be equally represented in the sample. If a sample of 100 were desired, a quota of 50% males and 50% females would be set. Then, the first 50 males and first 50 females approached by the researcher would be asked to participate in the survey. Of course, because this would not be a probability sample, there is a risk that the sample would not be typical of all males and females. Examples of quota samples are difficult to find in recent studies published by nurses.

Quota Sample

Shuriquie, While, and Fitzpatrick (2008) obtained a quota sample to investigate Jordanian nurses' perceptions of their role in clinical practice. They surveyed nurses working in private, government, and army hospitals in Jordan. The researchers were able to obtain a minimum quota of 100 nurses working in each of these types of agencies.

Purposive Sampling

Purposive sampling involves handpicking of subjects. This method is also called **judgmental sampling**. Subjects are chosen that the researcher believes represent the accessible population, or an expert may be asked to select the subjects. This type of sampling is based on the assumption that the researcher or chosen expert has enough knowledge about the population of interest to select specific subjects for the study.

An investigator might want to determine some of the problems that are experienced by individuals with cancer who have a Port-a-Cath inserted for the administration of their chemotherapy. The investigator works in an oncology clinic and personally knows several clients who have been experiencing problems with their ports. These potential subjects are viewed as typical cases and asked to participate in the planned research study. It is evident that bias can enter into the selection of samples through purposive sampling procedures. Researchers may believe, however, that errors in judgment will tend to balance out; purposive samples are not uncommon in nursing research. Most qualitative studies use purposive samples.

Purposive Sample

A purposive sample of first-time fathers who were deployed to combat regions during the birth of their babies was studied by Schachman (2010). A phenomenological approach was used. The final sample consisted of 17 men who had returned recently from combat deployment in the Middle East. Interviews were conducted within 1 month of their return. Disruption of the "protector" and "provider" role were themes identified in the interviews. Online communication (e-mail, blogs, chat rooms) seemed to help these men provide protector and provider roles even though they were not physically present at the births of their babies.

TIME FRAME FOR STUDYING THE SAMPLE

The time frame for selecting and studying subjects in a research study is the criterion by which research studies are classified as longitudinal or cross-sectional. A **longitudinal study** follows subjects over a period of time in the future; a **cross-sectional study** examines subjects at one point in time. There is no agreed-upon time period for designating a study as longitudinal. Technically, if the researcher is interested in changes that occur over time, the research should be considered longitudinal, even if the time period is only 1 month or even 1 week.

A special type of longitudinal study is a cohort study. In a **cohort study**, the focus is on a subgroup of the population, frequently persons who are of a similar age group. As mentioned earlier in the book, I am a member of the Nurses' Health Study (NHS), a longitudinal cohort study conducted by researchers at Harvard Medical School. This study was begun in 1976. The population to be studied consisted of married, female RNs born between January 1, 1921, and December 31, 1946, and residing in 11 states with the largest number of RNs: New York, California, Pennsylvania, Ohio, Massachusetts, New Jersey, Michigan, Texas, Florida, Connecticut, and Maryland. The original sample for this study was composed of approximately 122,000 nurses. The study was designed to examine some of the health risks that pose a special threat to women. Included in these risks were cigarette smoking and the use of hair dyes and oral contraceptives. Nurses were chosen as the subjects for this study, according to Frank Speizer, the principal investigator, because the study called for "a sophisticated group of individuals who could report exposure and diseases more accurately than the general population" ("Massive Nurses' Health Study," 1983, p. 998). The study was later expanded to examine dietary patterns, stress factors, and the use of prescription drugs. In one of the study's more publicized aspects, 68,000 nurses sent their toenail clippings to be examined for dietary intakes of selenium (My children laughed when I sent my toenail clippings to Boston). The relationship between selenium intake and cancer was being examined.

The Nurses' Health Study was originally intended to last for only 4 years, but additional funding has been received down through the years, and the study has continued for approximately 35 years. A similar but younger cohort group of approximately 123,000 nurses began participating in the Nurses' Health Study II (NHS II) in 1989. One of the purposes of this study was to examine the long-term effects of contraceptive use. By 1989 most of us in the original study group no longer had to worry about contraceptives! A third arm of the Nurses' Health Study began in 1996 with approximately 11,000 children of the Nurses Health Study II participants. The main purpose of this study was to explore adolescent weight gain. Hundreds of articles have been published on the results of data gathered in all of these studies.

The Nurses' Health Study III (NHS III) was begun in 2008. For more details on these studies and the entire project, visit. http://NursesHealthStudy.org.

The data collection process in a cross-sectional study is quite different from that of a longitudinal study. Data are gathered on subjects at *one* specific point in time, but the data are collected from separate groups of people who represent different ages, time periods, or developmental states. Consider the previous example where the school nurse was interested in studying marijuana usage among high school students. She wants to know if changes in usage occur as students progress through high school. A longitudinal study might be conducted in which freshman students would be followed until graduation, and their marijuana usage compared over the 4 years of high school. Because of the time factor and cost involved in such a lengthy study, the nurse researcher might decide to gather all of the data at one time by sampling students in all four grades of high school and comparing the marijuana usage among these groups. Of course, the danger in this type of study is that an assumption must be made that the seniors will reply as the freshmen would have replied at the end of 4 years. This might be a risky assumption. A longitudinal study is a more accurate means of studying changes that occur over time. However, cross-sectional studies are conducted because they are less expensive and easier to conduct than longitudinal studies.

Cross-Sectional Study

A cross-section of 676 middle school students in Korea was studied to explore the relationship between Internet addiction and interpersonal problems (Seo, Kang, & Yom, 2009). Korean versions of the Internet Addiction Self-test Scale and Inventory of Interpersonal Problems were administered to participants aged 12 to 17 years. A statistically significant positive correlation ($r = .425$, $p = .000$) was found between Internet addiction and interpersonal problems.

SAMPLE SIZE

One of the most frequent questions posed to statisticians is "How large should my sample be?" Unfortunately, there is no simple answer. An important issue is whether the study will be of a quantitative or qualitative nature. Qualitative studies use much smaller samples than quantitative studies. Qualitative studies may use samples that are quite small, sometimes even smaller than 10. After patterns and themes have been extracted from the participants and no more new ideas are being uncovered, sampling ceases. Generally speaking, quantitative studies seek to obtain sample sizes large enough to talk about the population of interest.

There are no simple rules for determining the desired sample size for a quantitative study. Some factors to be considered are the homogeneity of the population, degree of precision desired by the researcher, and type of sampling procedure that will be used. If the population is very homogeneous, or alike, on all variables other than the one being measured, a small sample size may be sufficient. But if the researcher wants to be very precise in generalizing to the population based on sample data, a large sample may be necessary for the sample to represent the population accurately. Finally, when probability sampling methods are used, smaller samples are required than when nonprobability sampling techniques are employed.

According to Roscoe (1975), there are few instances in descriptive behavioral research when a sample size smaller than 30 or larger than 500 can be justified. A sample size of 100 ensures the benefits of the central limit theorem (see Chapter 15). Sample sizes as small as 30 are generally adequate to ensure that the sampling distribution of the mean will closely approximate the normal curve (Shott, 1990).

Large sample sizes may be needed in the following instances:

1. **Many uncontrolled variables are present.** The researcher thinks age may influence study results, but is not able to control for this variable.

2. **Small differences are expected in members of the population on the variable of interest.** Small, but important, differences between members of the population may not be uncovered when small samples are used.

3. **The population must be divided into subgroups.** Sample sizes must be increased to assure inclusion of members of each of the subgroups.

4. **Dropout rate among subjects is expected to be high.** This problem is especially likely to occur in longitudinal studies.

5. **Statistical tests are used that require minimum sample sizes.** Certain statistical tests require minimum numbers of responses in each cell of the data.

Although large samples are desirable, the law of diminishing returns applies. A sample of 100, or 10%, may be necessary to obtain the required precision desired for a population of 1,000. A 10% sample of a population of 1 million would require 100,000 elements. This would be a huge sample and would be unnecessary. In fact, samples of 5,000 or 6,000 are often sufficient to estimate the characteristics of the entire population of the United States. The next time you see a Gallup survey report, make a note of the number of participants who were included in the sample. A more important issue than the size of the sample is the representativeness of the sample. Election results can be predicted with very small percentages of votes counted because the polled voters have been thoroughly examined for representativeness in voting behavior. Does it make you angry when you see the media predict the winner of an election when only 25% of the votes are in?

It is always wise to set the sample size a little bit larger than what is actually desired (to allow for nonresponse or subject dropout). Also, an absolute minimum sample size should be declared at the beginning of a study. Should the study be conducted if only five people agree to participate? The researcher must make the decision about the minimum acceptable sample size before data collection begins.

Power analysis is a procedure that can be used to determine the needed sample size for a research study. Researchers want to ensure that they have enough sample elements to detect a difference or a correlation, if one actually exists between groups or within groups on some variable of interest. This procedure is very important in experimental studies. The power of a statistical test is its ability to detect statistical significance in a study, when it is present. When power is low, the likelihood of making a type II error is high (see Chapter 15). One factor that influences the power of a test is the sample size that was used in the study. In many studies, researchers erroneously conclude that no significant difference exists between the experimental and the control group when, in fact, a difference would have been detected if the sample had been larger.

Connelly (2008) asserted that a tradeoff exists between obtaining the desired sample size and the amount of time and resources available for a study. She also contended that it would be unethical to sample more people than is really needed, especially if the study is invasive.

Power Analysis

A study was conducted to compare undergraduate nursing students' knowledge acquisition in simulated clinical experiences compared to traditional clinical experiences (Schlairet & Pollock, 2010). There were 74 students in the sample, which was obtained over two semesters. Students acted as their own controls; they all received both traditional clinical and simulated clinical experiences. Before the study began, a power analysis was performed. The researchers determined that a sample size of 33 per group would be needed to obtain a medium effect size. Therefore, their sample size met the requirement. Results showed that the simulation experiences were as effective in knowledge acquisition as traditional clinical experiences.

Polit and Sherman (1990) studied 62 articles that were published in *Nursing Research* and *Research in Nursing and Health* during 1989. They concluded that a substantial number of published studies (and they presumed that even more unpublished studies) had insufficient power because of small sample sizes. However, a more recent review of the literature indicates an increasing number of researchers who discuss the use of power analysis to determine their sample size. Cohen, Jia, and Larson (2009) evaluated the use of power analysis in 152 studies published between September 2005 and August 2007 in five top nursing research journals. They concluded that power analysis was included in about one third (46 of 122) of the studies in which power analysis would have been appropriate.

A review of nursing literature in the past few years revealed many examples of studies in which power analysis was used: Albert et al., 2009; Ammouri, Neuberger, Nashwan, & Al-Haj, 2007; Hatfield, 2008; Hopkins-Chadwick & Ryan-Wenger, 2009; Kimball et al., 2010; Schlairet & Pollock, 2010; Valdovinos, Reddin, Bernard, Shafer, & Tanabe, 2009.

The researcher would be wise to perform a power analysis before conducting a study. If this analysis indicates that the needed sample size would be very difficult to obtain, the researcher might decide not to conduct the study. Nearly all external funding sources require that grant proposals present the results of the power analysis conducted to determine the optimum sample size for the proposed study. Although the procedure is not very difficult to perform, it is not discussed in this text. For more information, consult Cohen's (1988) book on power analysis.

Many nursing research studies are limited to small convenience samples. Generalizations to total populations, therefore, are usually difficult to make with any degree of confidence. The use of small sample sizes dictates the need for studies to be replicated. If several investigators find similar results when studying the same topic, generalizations to other populations are more appropriate.

SAMPLING ERROR AND SAMPLING BIAS

Although sampling error and sampling bias are sometimes discussed interchangeably, these two concepts should be considered separately. **Sampling error** may be defined as the difference between data obtained from a random sample and the data that would be obtained if an entire population were measured. Error may be contained in sample data even when the most careful random sampling procedure was used to obtain the sample. Sampling error is not under the researcher's control; it is caused by the chance variations that may occur when a sample is chosen to represent a population. Table 11–2 demonstrates how random samples vary from the true population values. The table contains pulse measurements on a population of 20 subjects. The mean pulse rate for the population is 71. The mean pulse rate for random sample 3 is also 71. The mean pulse rate for random sample 1 is considerably below the average for the population; the mean pulse rate for random sample 2 is well above the average.

Whereas sampling error occurs by chance, sampling bias is caused by the researcher. **Sampling bias** occurs when samples are not carefully selected. If names are written on slips of

TABLE 11–2 Sampling Error

Average pulse rates of a group of cardiac patients					
	66	80	59	70	71
	71	63	70	74	55
	70	65	67	92	83
	67	79	66	80	72 $\mu = 71$
Random Sample #1	66, 59, 70, 55, 66	$\bar{x} = 63$			
Random Sample #2	80, 92, 83, 79, 80	$\bar{x} = 83$			
Random Sample #3	71, 71, 70, 64, 67	$\bar{x} = 71$			

μ = population mean; $\bar{x}$ = sample mean. (See Chapter 14 for definitions of terms.)

paper and placed in a hat, each piece of paper would have to be the same size and thickness or bias could occur. Bias could also occur if the slips of paper stuck together in clumps. The literature is replete with examples of bias in sample selections. One of the most famous examples concerns the U.S. presidential election of 1936. *Literary Digest* magazine conducted a large poll among eligible voters to determine if people planned to vote for Alfred Landon, the Republican candidate, or Franklin Roosevelt, the Democratic candidate. The magazine predicted, on the basis of this poll, that Landon would win by a landslide margin. Roosevelt soundly defeated Landon! It was determined that biased sampling occurred as the result of selecting subjects from the telephone directory and through listings of automobile registrations. Depressed economic conditions were present in 1936, and members of the Republican Party were more likely than members of the Democratic Party to own telephones and automobiles.

All nonprobability sampling methods are subject to sampling bias. Also, random sampling procedures are subject to bias if some elements of the selected sample decide not to participate in the research study. If questionnaires were sent to a random sample of nurses to examine their knowledge of malpractice issues in nursing, it is possible that nurses who possessed considerable knowledge of malpractice issues would be more likely to return the questionnaire than nurses with little knowledge of this subject.

After the discussion about various types of sampling procedures, it must be pointed out that nursing research studies involve voluntary subjects, regardless of the type of sampling procedure employed. Even if a random sampling method is used to select potential study subjects, the ethics of research requires that subjects must voluntarily agree to participate in research studies. Not all selected subjects may agree to participate in a study. The nurse researcher must always keep in mind that data are based on voluntary responses. Unless all selected members of the sample actually participate in the research study, the potential for a biased sample is present.

Finally, a note of caution is presented about volunteers. **Volunteers** are subjects who approach the researcher asking to participate in the study. This type of sample is to be distinguished from a convenience sample, in which the researcher approaches the potential subjects and asks them to participate in a study. Volunteers may be greater risk takers than nonvolunteers. They also may be motivated to participate by monetary or other types of rewards.

Wewers and Ahijevych (1990) pointed out the differences between random samples and volunteer subjects. They studied the reactions of two groups of adult cigarette smokers to a smoking cessation campaign. One group was obtained through random telephone digit dialing; the other group was composed of volunteers who registered through the community lung association. The demographic characteristics, such as educational levels, were very different between the two groups. The volunteer group was found to be much more successful at attempting and maintaining cessation when compared to the randomly selected group. They confirmed that problems of generalizability exist when nonprobability samples are used in a study.

Step I
Random selection of sample from the population

Step II
Random assignment of subjects to groups

Step III
Random assignment of experimental treatments to groups

▶ FIGURE 11–1   Randomization steps in experimental research.

RANDOMIZATION PROCEDURES IN RESEARCH

Random sampling and random assignment are two areas that seem to cause a great deal of confusion among beginning researchers. These two terms involve quite different aspects of the research process, but both are considered a type of randomization procedure. *Random sampling* involves the selection of a sample from the population. *Random assignment* involves the unbiased placement of subjects to either the experimental or control groups in a study. Random assignment is a necessary condition of a true experimental design and was discussed under experimental studies in Chapter 9. It seems important to discuss this concept again because of the tendency to confuse the two types of randomization procedures. Figure 11–1 depicts the threefold randomization process for experimental studies that would represent the ideal study procedure. First, subjects are randomly selected from the population. Next, subjects are randomly assigned to groups. Finally, experimental treatments are randomly assigned to the groups.

CRITIQUING THE SAMPLING PROCEDURE

The critiquer of a research study should be concerned with the study population and sample. A research article or report may include a separate section on the population and sample, but this information is usually contained in the methods section. It is generally easy to find the information about the sample, but the population, from which the sample was selected, may not be discussed.

The reader of a research report would like to know the group to which the investigator wishes to generalize the study results (target population) and the group from which the sample was selected (accessible population). To help the reader determine if the sample represents the accessible population, the report should describe the accessible population. The characteristics of the members of this group should be presented, such as average age, gender, and educational level. The size of the accessible population should also be presented. If a study had 100 subjects, the reader of the report would like to know if these 100 subjects represent merely a fraction of the accessible population or a large portion of this group.

The specific type of probability or nonprobability sampling method should be presented. Although probability sampling is the ideal, many nursing research studies use nonprobability samples. The reader should try to determine how the sample was obtained. Were the subjects volunteers or were they approached and asked to participate in the study? The characteristics of the sample should be described.

The sample size is a very important area for critique. Many nursing studies have used small nonrandom samples. If a small sample size was used, did the researcher present the rationale for the sample size? Was power analysis used to determine the sample size? Were you able to determine if some of the subjects dropped out of the study? The researcher has an obligation to point out this fact to the reader. Frequently, the reader is made aware of subject dropout when examining the tables. For example, a sample size of n = 58 that is presented in a table may not agree with the sample size of 60 mentioned in the methods section. Two subjects have mysteriously disappeared! Box 11–1 presents guidelines for critiquing the sampling section of a research report.

Box 11–1. Guidelines for Critiquing the Sampling Procedure

1. Is the target population identified?
2. Is the accessible population identified?
3. Was a probability or nonprobability sampling method used?
4. Is the specific sampling method named?
5. Is the sampling method described?
6. Is the sampling method appropriate for the study?
7. Are the demographic characteristics of the sample presented?
8. Is the sample size adequate?
9. Is the sample representative of the population?
10. Are potential sampling biases identified?
11. Is subject dropout discussed?

SUMMARY

Populations are complete sets of people or objects that possess some common characteristic of interest to the researcher. The investigator wishes to generalize study findings to a target population, but generally is able to study only an accessible population. Studying entire populations is time consuming and expensive. Samples, or subsets of the population, are usually studied in nursing research. A single member of the population is called an **element**, and these elements are chosen from a **sampling frame**, or listing of the population elements.

Samples are chosen through two types of sampling procedures: probability and nonprobability. **Probability sampling**, or random sampling, involves random selection of a sample from a population. The four types of probability sampling methods are simple, stratified, cluster, and systematic. **Simple random sampling** assures that each element of the population has an equal and independent chance of being chosen. A **table of random numbers** may be used to obtain a random sample, which is usually computer-generated. **Stratified random sampling** involves dividing the population into subgroups, and then random samples are chosen from these groups. In **proportional stratified sampling**, samples are chosen from each stratum, and these samples are in proportion to the size of that stratum in the total population. When strata are unequal in size, **disproportional stratified sampling** may be used to assure adequate samples from each stratum. **Cluster random sampling** involves sampling from large groups called *clusters*. Individual members of clusters are selected in the final stage of the sampling process. Finally, in **systematic random sampling** every kth element of the population, such as every fifth element, is selected.

In **nonprobability sampling**, the sample elements are chosen by nonrandom methods. The types of nonprobability sampling methods are convenience, quota, and purposive. **Convenience sampling**, also called accidental or incidental, uses readily available people or objects. **Snowball sampling**, also called **network sampling**, is a type of convenience sampling in which subjects provide the names of other people they know who meet the criteria for the study. **Quota sampling** is similar to stratified random sampling, except that the desired number of elements for each stratum is selected through convenience sampling rather that random sampling. **Purposive sampling**, or **judgemental sampling** involves handpicking of subjects based on the researcher's consideration or that of an expert as to the subjects being typical of the desired sample.

Longitudinal studies gather data from the same subjects several times to determine change associated with the passage of time. In a **cohort study,** a subgroup of the population is studied, frequently people in a similar age group. **Cross-sectional studies** examine several different groups that are thought to represent different age groups, time periods, or developmental states. Data are gathered at one point in time.

Generally, large samples are more representative of the population than small samples. As a rule, a sample size of 30 should be considered the minimum size for each group that is studied. **Power analysis** is a procedure that can be used to determine the optimum sample size for a study, particularly an experimental study.

Sampling error is the difference between data obtained from samples and data that would be obtained if an entire population was studied. This error is related to chance and not under the researcher's control. **Sampling bias** occurs when samples are not carefully selected by researchers. **Volunteers** are subjects who approach the researcher asking to participate in a study.

Randomization procedures in research involve random sampling and random assignment. Random sampling concerns selection of a sample from a population. Random assignment involves the unbiased assignment of subjects into groups in experimental studies.

NURSING RESEARCH ON THE WEB

For additional online resources, research activities, and exercises, go to **www.mynursingkit.com.** Select Chapter 11 from the drop-down menu.

GET INVOLVED ACTIVITIES

1. Find a research article that indicates a probability sample was studied. Tell your peers how many studies you had to peruse before finding one that used a probability sampling method. Keep a checklist of the types of nonprobability sampling methods that were used.
2. When examining studies published in the literature, write down the size of the sample used in each study. Compare sample sizes of the studies you found with those found by your peers. Determine the smallest and largest sample sizes that were discussed in the research articles reviewed.
3. Compare the sample sizes used in quantitative and qualitative studies.
4. Divide into groups. Propose a study idea and identify the type of sampling technique that would be most appropriate.
5. Ask someone to bring a copy of Cohen's book on power analysis to class. Glance through the book and look at the tables that show desired sample sizes and how they are calculated.

SELF-TEST

Write T(True) or F(False) beside the following statements:

____ 1. The best means of obtaining an unbiased sample of subjects in a community is to select a random sample of names from the telephone directory.

____ 2. Nonprobability sampling means there is no probability that the subjects selected will constitute a biased sample.

____ 3. Researchers generally study samples rather than populations.

____ 4. A sampling frame is a listing of all elements of a population.

Identify the type of sampling method used in the following examples:

5. The clients in the hypertension clinics of two local hospitals are studied. _____

6. A total of 20 nursing service administrators are randomly selected from a random sample of 10 hospitals in the state. _____

7. Every fifth nurse is randomly selected from the mailing list of the American Nurses Association. _____

8. The first 30 men and first 30 women who are admitted to the hospital for abdominal surgery during the time of the research study are asked to participate. _____

9. To determine the frequency of the recording of nursing diagnoses by nurses, a sample of 100 charts is randomly selected from all of the patients' charts during the previous year. _____

10. To obtain mothers of children with cystic fibrosis, a researcher contacted one such mother who lived in her neighborhood and asked her if she knew any other mothers of children with cystic fibrosis. _____

REFERENCES

Abdrbo, A. A., Hudak, C. A., Anthony, M. K., & Douglas, S. L. (2009). Moderating and mediating roles of nurses' beliefs. *Western Journal of Nursing Research, 31*, 110–127. doi:10.1177/0193945908325078

Albert, N. M., Gillinov, A. M., Lytle, B. W., Feng, J., Cwynar, R., & Blackstone, E. H. (2009). A randomized trial of massage therapy after heart surgery. *Heart & Lung, 38*, 480–490.

Ammouri, A. A., Neuberger, G., Nashwan, A. J., & Al-Haj, A. M. (2007). Determinants of self-reported physical activity among Jordanian adults. *Journal of Nursing Scholarship, 39*, 342–348.

Cohen, J. (1988). *Statistical power analysis for the behavioral sciences* (2nd ed.). Hillsdale, NJ: Lawrence Erlbaum.

Cohn, E. G., Jia, H., & Larson, E. (2009). Evaluation of statistical approaches in quantitative nursing research. *Clinical Nursing Research, 18*, 223–241. doi:10.1177/1054773809336096

Connelly, L. M. (2008). Research considerations: Power analysis and effect size. *Medsurg Nursing, 17*, 41–42.

Crumbock, S. C., Loeb, S. J., & Fick, D. M. (2009). Physical activity, stress, disease activity, and quality of life in adults with Crohn disease. *Gastroenterology Nursing, 32*, 188–195.

Gillespie, B. M., Chaboyer, W., Wallis, M., & Grimbeek, P. (2007). Resilence in the operating room: Developing and testing of a resilience model. *Journal of Advanced Nursing, 59*, 427–438. doi:10.1111/j.1365-2648.2007.04340.x

Hatfield, L. A. (2008). Sucrose decreases infant biobehavioral pain response to immunizations: A randomized controlled trial. *Journal of Nursing Scholarship, 40*, 219–225.

Hopkins-Chadwick, D. L., & Ryan-Wenger, N. (2009). Stress in junior enlisted Air Force women with and without children. *Western Journal of Nursing Research, 31*, 409–427.

Kagan, I., Ovadia, K. L., & Kaneti, T. (2009). Perceived knowledge of blood-borne pathogens and avoidance of contact with infected patients. *Journal of Nursing Scholarship, 41*, 13–19. doi:10.1111/j.1547-5069.2009.01246x

Kimball, S., Buck, G., Goldstein, D., Largaespada, E., Logan, L., Stebbins, D., . . . Kalman-Yearout, K., 2010). Testing a teaching appointment and geragogy-based approach to medication knowledge at discharge. *Rehabilitation Nursing, 35*, 31–49.

Massive nurses' health study in seventh year, reports first findings on disease links in women. (1983). *American Journal of Nursing, 83*, 998–999.

Polit, D. F., & Sherman, R. E. (1990). Statistical power in nursing research. *Nursing Research, 39*, 365– 369.

Roscoe, J. (1975). *Fundamental research statistics for the behavioral sciences* (2nd ed.). New York: Holt, Rinehart & Winston.

Schachman, K. A. (2010). Online fathering. *Nursing Research, 59*, 11–17. doi: 10.1097/nnr.0b013e3181c3ba05

Schlairet, M. C., & Pollock, J. W. (2010). Equivalence testing of traditional and simulated clinical experiences: Undergraduate nursing students' knowledge acquisition. *Journal of Nursing Education, 49*, 43–47. doi:10.3928/01484834-20090918-08

Seo, M., Kang, H. S., & Yom, Y. (2009). Internet addiction and interpersonal problems in Korean adolescents. *CIN: Computers, Informatics, Nursing, 27*, 226–233.

Shott, S. (1990). *Statistics for health care professionals.* Philadelphia: W. B. Saunders.

Shuriquie, M., While, A., & Fitzpatrick, J. (2008). Nursing work in Jordan: An example of nursing work in the Middle East. *Journal of Clinical Nursing, 17*, 999–1010. doi: 10.111/j.1365-2702.2007.01973.x

Teng, C., Dai, Y., Shyu, Y., Wong, M., Chu, T., & Tsai, Y. (2009). Professional commitment, patient, safety, and patient-perceived care quality. *Journal of Nursing Scholarship, 41*, 301–309.

Valdovinos, N. C., Reddin, C., Bernard, C., Shafer, B., & Tanabe, P. (2009). The use of topical anesthesia during intravenous catheter insertion in adults: A comparison of pain scores using LMX-4 versus placebo. *Journal of Emergency Nursing, 35*, 299–304.

Walker, J., Pepa, C., & Gerard, P. S. (2010). Assessing the health literacy levels of patients using selected hospital services. *Clinical Nurse Specialist, 24*, 31–37.

Wewers, M. E., & Ahijevych, K. (1990). Differences in volunteer and randomly acquired samples. *Applied Nursing Research, 3*, 166–173.

Whitty, K. K., & Burnett, M. F. (2009). The importance of instruction on mass casualty incidents in baccalaureate nursing programs: Perceptions of nursing faculty. *Journal of Nursing Education, 48*, 291–295.

CHAPTER 12

Measurement and Data Collection

OUTLINE

OBJECTIVES

On completion of this chapter, you will be prepared to:

1. Demonstrate an understanding of the concept of measurement
2. Differentiate among the four levels of measurement
3. Determine the appropriate level of measurement for data in selected studies
4. Recall questions to be answered in the data-collection process
5. Identify data-collection methods
6. Discuss the selection of a data-collection instrument
7. List criteria for selection of a data-collection instrument
8. Compare and contrast three types of reliability
9. Compare and contrast four types of validity
10. Explain four sources of error that may occur in data collection
11. Critique the data-collection section of research reports

NEW TERMS DEFINED IN THIS CHAPTER

alternate forms reliability, pg 170

concurrent validity, pg 173

construct validity, pg 173

content validity, pg 172

criterion validity, pg 172

equivalence reliability, pg 170

face validity, pg 172

factor analysis, pg 174

internal consistency reliability, pg 171

interobserver reliability, pg 170

interrater reliability, pg 170

interval level of measurement, pg 165

known-groups procedure, pg 173

measurement, pg 164

nominal level of measurement, pg 164

ordinal level of measurement, pg 165

parallel forms reliability, pg 170

predictive validity, pg 173

ratio level of measurement, pg 165

reliability, pg 169

research instruments, pg 167

stability reliability, pg 169

validity, pg 171

Now the fun part of a research study beings! All of the preliminary phases of the study have been completed, and data collection is about to start. Many researchers get excited when they talk about the data-collection phase of their studies. This is the time when they get to interact with their study participants personally or through reading their responses on questionnaires. The real detective work begins!

In any study, the investigator must devise a way to examine or measure the concepts of interest. For example, anxiety could be measured in several ways, such as through galvanic skin response, pulse rates, or self-report questionnaires. Specific types of data-collection methods are discussed in Chapter 13.

MEASUREMENT PRINCIPLES

An understanding of measurement principles is crucial in the data-collection phase of a study. Research variables must be operationally defined. As you recall, operational definitions indicate how variables will be observed or measured.

Measurement is the process of assigning numbers to variables. Ways to assign these numbers include counting, ranking, and comparing objects or events. Human beings have been using some type of measurement system throughout history. Probably fingers and toes were the first method of counting and keeping track of numbers. Measurement, as used in research, implies the quantification of information. This means that numbers are assigned to the data. Some qualitative studies gather data in narrative form, and numbers are not associated with these data. These data, therefore, are not included in the concept of measurement as it is discussed in this book. If these qualitative data were summarized and placed into categories, they would then fit the criteria for measurement. In the classic sense, measurement implies that some kind of comparison is made between pieces of information. Numbers are the means of comparing this information.

LEVEL OF MEASUREMENT

The types of mathematical calculations that can be made with data depend on the level of measurement of the data. The terms *level of measurement* and *measurement scale* are frequently used interchangeably. Four levels of measurement or measurement scales have been identified: nominal, ordinal, interval, and ratio.

Using the **nominal level of measurement**, objects or events are "named" or categorized. The categories must be distinct from each other (mutually exclusive categories) and include all of the possible ways of categorizing the data (exhaustive categories). There may be only two categories or there may be many categories. Numbers are obtained for this type of data through counting the frequency or percentages of objects or events in each of the categories.

Examples of types of nominal data are gender, religious affiliation, marital status, and political party membership. The researcher could count the number of males and females in a study and report these as percentages or frequencies. No other mathematical operations could be performed with these data. You may have noticed that these types of variables are frequently assigned numbers on questionnaires, such as 0 for males and 1 for females. These numbers are only symbols used for data analysis purposes and have no quantitative meaning.

Some types of nominal data may appear to contain "real" numbers. Examples are Zip Codes and Social Security numbers. Actually, these numbers are symbols and can be placed only into categories. They should not be added or subtracted. The nominal level of measurement is considered the lowest level or least rigorous of the measurement levels.

Data that can be rank ordered as well as placed into categories are considered to be at the **ordinal level of measurement**. The exact differences between the ranks cannot be specified with this type of data. The numbers obtained from this measurement process indicate the order rather than the exact quantity of the variables. For example, anxiety levels of people in a therapy group might be categorized as mild, moderate, and severe. It would be appropriate to conclude that those individuals with severe anxiety are more anxious than those individuals with moderate anxiety. In turn, moderate anxiety sufferers in the group could be considered more anxious than group members with mild anxiety. You could not, however, determine the exact difference in anxiety levels of any individual within each of the categories. Frequency distributions and percentages are used with this type of data as well as some statistical tests that are discussed in Chapter 15.

Interval data consist of "real" numbers. **Interval level of measurement** concerns data that not only can be placed in categories and ranked, but also the distance between the ranks can be specified. The categories in interval data are the actual numbers on the scale (such as on a thermometer). If body temperature was being measured, a reading of 37°C might be one category, 37.2°C might be another category, and 37.4°C might constitute a third category. The researcher would be correct in saying that there is 0.2°C difference between the first and second category and between the second and third category. The researcher could even go one step further and find the average temperature reading.

Data collected at the ratio level of measurement are considered the "highest" or most precise level of data. **Ratio level of measurement** includes data that can be categorized and ranked; in addition, the distance between ranks can be specified, and a "true" or natural zero point can be identified. The zero point on the ratio scale means there is a total absence of the quantity being measured. The amount of money in your bank account could be considered ratio data because it is possible (and quite likely, at times!) to be zero.

If a researcher wanted to determine the number of pain medication requests made by patients, it would be possible for some patients to request no pain medications. This type of data would be considered ratio data.

There is a debate about classifying some data as interval or ratio. For example, should weight be considered as interval or ratio data? Most authors classify weight as ratio data. However, when measuring humans, can someone have *no* weight?

Although it may be great fun to debate about whether a certain piece of data should be classified as interval or ratio, it is really unimportant, for research purposes, to distinguish between these two levels of measurement. The same statistical tests may be used with both types of data. These two types are considered together in Chapter 14 and Chapter 15 when discussing analysis of data.

CONVERTING DATA TO A LOWER LEVEL OF MEASUREMENT

Data can always be converted from one level to a lower level of measurement, but not to a higher level. Interval and ratio data can be converted to ordinal or nominal data, and ordinal data can be converted to nominal data. For example, the number of requests by patients for pain medication could be converted to ordinal data. Requests could be categorized as follows: more than 10 requests per day, 5–10 requests per day, and 0–4 requests per day. This would be an instance of converting interval data to ordinal data. It would also be possible to change these data to nominal data by classifying the subjects into two groups: those with "no requests per day" and those with "1 or more requests per day." Rarely do researchers convert higher levels of data to lower levels, however, because precision is always lost.

DETERMINING THE APPROPRIATE LEVEL OF MEASUREMENT

Now that you are familiar with the levels of measurement, you may wonder how the determination is made of which level of measurement to use in a study. If the researcher is very concerned about the precision of the data, the interval or ratio level of measurement should be selected when possible. If ranked or categorized data will be sufficient to answer the research questions or test the research hypotheses, ordinal data may be used. Finally, if categories of data are all that is called for, nominal data will be appropriate.

If the researcher were trying to determine the differences in the number of complications experienced by patients with diabetes who have varying blood glucose levels, accuracy would be very important. The two categories of elevated and nonelevated blood glucose levels (nominal data) would not be precise enough for making comparisons among the patients. The operational definition of the variable will determine the level of data that will be gathered.

Some variables, by their very nature, can be measured at only one level. For example, gender can be measured at only a nominal level. A person is either a male or a female. The main considerations in determining the level of measurement for data are (a) the level of measurement appropriate for the type of data that are being sought, and (b) the degree of precision desired when it is possible to consider the data at more than one level of measurement.

DATA-COLLECTION PROCESS

There are five important questions to ask when the researcher is in the process of collecting data: Who? When? Where? What? How? Use the acronym WWWWH.

Who will collect the data? If the researcher is going to collect all of the data, this question is easy to answer. However, scientific investigations frequently involve a team of researchers. The decision will then need to be made about who will collect the data. Other people outside the research team may also be used in the data-collection phase; sometimes data collectors are paid for their services. Anytime more than one person is involved, assurances must be made that the data are being gathered in the same manner. Training will be needed for the data collectors, and checks should be made on the reliability of the collected data.

When will the data be collected? The determination will need to be made about the month, day, and sometimes even the hour, for data collection. Also, how long will data collection take? Frequently, the only way to answer this question is through a trial run of the procedure by the researcher. If questionnaires will be used, they should be pretested with people similar to the potential research participants, to determine the length of time for completion of the instrument. The decision may be made to revise the instrument if it seems to take too long for completion. Unfortunately, data collection usually takes longer than you envisioned!

Where will the data be collected? The setting for data collection must be carefully determined. Optimum conditions should be sought. Having subjects fill out questionnaires in the middle of the hallway while leaning up against a wall would definitely not provide the optimum setting. Sometimes it is difficult to decide on the setting. If questionnaires are being used, a researcher might ask respondents to complete the questionnaire while the researcher remains in the same immediate or general area. This procedure will help ensure return of the questionnaires. If, however, subjects happen to be tired or the room is too hot or too cold, the answers that are provided may not be valid. If respondents are allowed to complete the questionnaires at leisure, their answers may be more accurate. A disadvantage of using this procedure may be a reduction in the return rate of the questionnaires.

What data will be collected? This question calls for a decision to be made about the type of data being sought. For example, is the study designed to measure knowledge, attitudes, or behaviors? The type of data needed to answer the research questions or to test the research hypothesis should be the main consideration in data collection. If the researcher is concerned with the way crises affect people, the "what" of data collection becomes persons' behaviors or responses in crises.

How will the data be collected? Some type of research instrument will be needed to gather the data. This can vary from a self-report questionnaire to the most sophisticated of physiological instruments. Choosing a data-collection instrument is a major decision that should be made only after careful consideration of the possible alternatives. Chapter 13 contains a discussion of some of the types of instruments used in nursing research.

DATA-COLLECTION METHODS

The variable(s) of interest to the researcher must be measured in some fashion. This measurement is carried out through various data-collection methods. Data-collection methods are governed by several factors including (a) the research question(s) or hypothesis(es), (b) the design of the study, and (c) the amount of knowledge available about the variable of interest.

There are many alternatives to choose from when deciding on a data-collection method. Physiological measures, observation methods, self-report questionnaires, interviews, attitude scales, psychological tests, and other types of data-collection methods may be selected. Questionnaires are probably the most frequently reported method of data collection in published nursing studies.

Many studies use more than one data-collection method. In fact, nursing studies are increasingly reporting the use of more than one method of measuring the variable(s) of interest. When several types of data-collection methods produce similar results, greater confidence in the study findings will occur. Chapter 13 presents data-collection methods.

DATA-COLLECTION INSTRUMENTS

Research instruments, also called research tools, are the devices used to collect data. The instrument facilitates the observation and measurement of the variables of interest. The type of instrument used in a study is determined by the data-collection method(s) selected. If physiological data are sought, some type of physiological instrument will be needed. If observational data are needed to measure the variable of interest, some type of observational schedule or checklist will be called for. One area of the research over which the investigator has a great deal of control is in the choice of the data-collection instrument. Great care should be taken to select the most appropriate instrument(s).

Use of Existing Instruments

While conducting a review of the literature on the topic of interest, a researcher may discover that an instrument is already available to measure the research variable(s). The use of an already tested instrument helps connect the present study with the existing body of knowledge on the variables. Of course, the instrument selected must be appropriate to measure the study variable(s).

Many research instruments are available for nurse researchers. Some of the best sources are published compilations of instruments. These compilations are particularly useful because they contain discussions of the instruments, such as the reliability and validity of the tools. In some cases, the instrument is printed in its entirety in these sources. If not, information is provided about where a copy of the tool can be obtained.

The oldest and most well-known sources of research instruments are the *Mental Measurement Yearbooks* (MMYs). There are currently 18 volumes; the first was published in 1938, and the most recent one published in 2010. To be reviewed in the MMY, a test must be commercially available, be published in the English language, and be new, revised, or widely used since it last appeared in the MMY series.

A very useful source for nurse researchers is *Instruments for Clinical Health-Care Research* edited by Frank-Stromborg and Olsen (2004). Another well-used source of instruments for nursing research has been the four-volume series edited by Strickland and Waltz (1988a, 1988b, 1990a, 1990b). These volumes, titled *Measurement of Nursing Outcomes,* are devoted to measurement of client outcomes as well as nursing performance outcomes.

Many of the existing instruments are copyrighted. The copyright holder must be contacted to obtain permission to use such an instrument. Sometimes this permission is given without cost, and other times the researcher has to pay for permission to use the instrument or purchase copies of the tool. Instruments developed in research projects supported by public funding generally remain in the public domain. Investigators have free access to this type of instrument.

If an existing instrument will be used, it may be desirable to contact the developer of the instrument to obtain information on its use in past research. This information is usually provided freely. Tool developers are generally pleased when other researchers want to use their creations. Frequently, the only request that will be made is that a copy of the study results and the data, particularly data on the reliability and validity of the instrument, be forwarded to the person who developed the instrument.

Developing an Instrument

If no instrument can be discovered that is appropriate for a particular study, the researcher is faced with developing a new instrument. Also, it may be possible to revise an existing instrument. Caution must be exercised when this approach to instrument development is used. If any items are altered or deleted or new items added to an existing instrument, the reliability and validity of the tool might be altered. New reliability and validity testing will need to be conducted. Also, permission to revise the instrument will have to be obtained from the developer of the tool.

The development of a completely new instrument is a demanding task. Volumes of books have been written concerning tool development. You may consult some of these sources for further information on this subject.

Chapter 13 presents information on the development of questionnaires. Basic material on questionnaire development is included because nearly all nurses are faced with developing a questionnaire sometime during their nursing career, whether for use in research or for some other purpose.

Pilot Studies

One of the primary reasons a pilot study is conducted is to pretest a newly designed instrument. Whenever a new instrument is being used in a study, or a preexisting instrument is being used with people who have different characteristics from those for whom the instrument was originally developed, a pilot study should be conducted.

A pilot study is a small-scale trial run of the actual research project. A group of individuals similar to the proposed study subjects should be tested in conditions similar to those that will be used in the actual study. No set number of persons is needed for a pilot study. Factors such as time, cost, and availability of persons similar to the study subjects help determine the size of the pilot group.

In an article published in *Applied Nursing Research,* Jairath, Hogerney, and Parsons (2000) discussed the role of a pilot study and gave pointers on the process of conducting a pilot study. They wrote that the researcher may test a long and a short version of the data-collection instrument, try multiple instruments that are purported to measure the same factor or construct, or test various approaches for administering the tools or instruments.

CRITERIA FOR SELECTION OF A DATA-COLLECTION INSTRUMENT

Several criteria must be considered when deciding on a data-collection instrument; these include the practicality, reliability, and validity of the instrument.

Practicality of the Instrument

Before the researcher examines the reliability and validity of an instrument, questions should be asked about the practicality of the tool for the particular study being planned. The practicality of an instrument concerns its cost and appropriateness for the study population. How much will the instrument cost? How long will it take to administer the instrument? Will the population have the physical and mental stamina to complete the instrument? Are special motor skills or language abilities required of participants? Does the researcher require special training to administer or score the instrument? If so, is this training available? If a psychological instrument such as the Minnesota Multiphasic Personality Inventory (MMPI) will be used, is money available to purchase the instrument, and is someone available who is qualified to analyze the data? These are very important questions; the researcher must attend to the practicality of the instrument before considering the reliability and validity of the instrument.

Reliability of the Instrument

The researcher is always interested in collecting data that are reliable. The **reliability** of an instrument concerns its consistency and stability. If you are using a thermometer to measure body temperature, you would expect it to provide the same reading each time it was placed in a constant temperature water bath.

Regardless of the type of research, the reliability of the study instrument(s) is always of concern. Reliability needs to be determined whether the instrument is a mechanical device, a written questionnaire, or a human observer. The degree of reliability is usually determined by the use of correlational procedures. A correlation coefficient is determined between two sets of scores or between the ratings of two judges: The higher the correlation coefficient, the more reliable is the instrument or the judges.

Correlation coefficients can range between −1.00 and +1.00. Chapter 14 presents a more thorough explanation of correlation coefficients.

Correlation coefficients computed to test the reliability of an instrument are expected to be positive correlations. According to Polit and Beck (2008), it is risky to use an instrument with reliability lower than .70. These authors have cautioned researchers to check for reliability as a routine step in all studies that involve observational tools, self-report measures, or knowledge tests because of their susceptibility to measurement errors.

Correlation coefficients are frequently used to determine the reliability of an instrument. However, when observers or raters are used in a study, the percentage or rate of agreement may also be used to determine the reliability of their observations or ratings.

In general, the more items that an instrument contains, the more reliable it will be. The likelihood of coming closer to obtaining a true measurement increases as the sample of items to measure a variable increases. If a test becomes too long, however, subjects may get tired or bored.

Be cautious about the reliability of instruments. Reliability is not a property of the instrument that, once established, remains forever. Reliability must continually be assessed as the instrument is used with different subjects and under different environmental conditions. An instrument to measure patient autonomy might be highly reliable when administered to patients while in their hospital rooms, but very unreliable when administered to these same patients while lying on a stretcher outside the operating room waiting for surgery.

Researchers should choose the most appropriate type of reliability for their particular studies. Three different types of reliability are discussed here: stability, equivalence, and internal consistency.

Stability Reliability

The **stability reliability** of an instrument refers to its consistency over time. A physiological instrument, such as a thermometer, should be very stable and accurate. If a thermometer were to be used in a study, it would need to be checked for reliability before the study began and probably again during the study (test-retest reliability).

Questionnaires can also be checked for their stability. A questionnaire might be administered to a group of people, and, after a time, the instrument would again be administered to the same people. If subjects' responses were almost identical both times, the instrument would be determined to have high test-retest reliability. If the scores were perfectly correlated, the correlation coefficient (coefficient of stability) would be 1.00. The interval between the two testing periods may vary from a few days to several months or even longer. This period is a very important consideration when trying to determine the stability of an instrument. The period should be long enough for the subjects to forget their original answers on the questionnaire, but not long enough that real changes may have occurred in the subjects' responses.

Test-Retest Reliability

Test-retest reliability was one of the psychometric properties evaluated for the Health Quotient Questionnaire (Guo, Dixon, Whittemore, & He, 2010). This instrument combines Western and Eastern perspectives of holistic health. The questionnaire was completed twice by 27 individuals. Test-retest reliability from one testing to the second testing ranged from .72 to .82 for the five dimensions of the tool, which the researchers considered acceptable reliability.

If you were interested in developing a test to measure a personality trait, such as assertiveness, you might expect stability of responses. But because there has been a great deal of emphasis on assertiveness training in recent years, subjects might not score the same on an assertiveness test if the period between administrations is more than a few days. Many nursing studies are concerned with attitudes and behaviors that are not stable, and changes would be expected on two administrations of the same questionnaire. Stability over time (test-retest reliability), therefore, may not be the appropriate type of reliability to try to achieve for a research instrument.

Equivalence Reliability

Equivalence reliability concerns the degree to which two different forms of an instrument obtain the same results or two or more observers using a single instrument obtain the same results. **Alternate forms reliability** or **parallel forms reliability** are terms used when two forms of the same instrument are compared. **Interrater reliability** or **interobserver reliability** are terms applied to the comparisons of raters or observers using the same instrument. This type of reliability is determined by the degree to which two or more independent raters or observers are in agreement.

Interrater Reliability

A study was conducted to determine the interrater reliability of a tool used to grade online discussions made by students during a nursing research class (Lunney & Sammarco, 2009). These discussions concerned weekly reading assignments and applications of these readings to specific tasks. The correlations of two faculty raters' grades for 75 postings (5 weeks x 3 criteria x 5 students each week) was .837 ($p = .000$). Thus, the researchers concluded that interrater reliability for the tool was satisfactory.

When two forms of a test are used, both forms should contain the same number of items, have the same level of difficulty, and so forth. One form of the test is administered to a group of people; the other form is administered either at the same time or shortly thereafter to these same people. A correlation coefficient (coefficient of equivalence) is obtained between the two forms. The higher the correlation, the more confidence the researcher can have that the two forms of the test are gathering the same information. Whenever two forms of an instrument can be developed, this is the preferred means for assessing reliability. Researchers, however, may find it difficult to develop one form of an instrument, much less two forms!

Internal Consistency Reliability

Internal consistency reliability, or scale homogeneity, addresses the extent to which all items on an instrument measure the same variable. This type of reliability is appropriate only when the instrument is examining one concept or construct at a time. This type of reliability is concerned with the sample of items used to measure the variable of interest.

If an instrument is supposed to measure depression, all of the items on the instrument must consistently measure depression. If some items measure guilt, the instrument is not an internally consistent tool. This type of reliability is of concern to nurse researchers because of the emphasis on measuring concepts such as assertiveness, autonomy, and self-esteem.

Before computers, internal consistency was tedious to calculate. Today, it is a simple process, and accurate split-half procedures have been developed. A common type of internal consistency procedure used today is the coefficient alpha (α) or Cronbach's alpha, which provides an estimate of the reliability of all possible ways of dividing an instrument into two halves. Think about that a minute. How many possible combinations of two halves could be made from a 30-item questionnaire? A lot!

Internal Consistency Reliability

Internal consistency reliability was used to evaluate the psychometric properties of the Trust in Nurses Scale (Radwin, & Cabral, 2010). Coefficient alpha revealed an internal consistency reliability of .77, which the researchers considered acceptable reliability.

Validity of the Instrument

The **validity** of an instrument concerns its ability to gather the data that it is intended to gather. The content of the instrument is of prime importance in validity testing. If an instrument is expected to measure assertiveness, does it, in fact, measure assertiveness? It is not difficult to determine that validity is the most important characteristic of an instrument.

The greater the validity of an instrument, the more confidence you can have that the instrument will obtain data that will answer the research questions or test the research hypotheses. Just as the reliability of an instrument does not remain constant, neither does an instrument necessarily retain its level of validity when used with other subjects or in other environmental settings. An instrument might accurately measure assertiveness in a group of subjects from one cultural group. The same instrument might actually measure authoritarianism in another cultural group because assertiveness, to this group, means that a person is trying to act as an authority figure.

When attempting to establish the reliability of an instrument, all of the procedures are based on data obtained through using the instrument with a group of respondents. Conversely, some of the procedures for establishing the validity of an instrument are not based on the administration of the instrument to a group of respondents. Validity may be established through the use of a panel of experts or an examination of the existing literature on the topic. Statistical procedures, therefore, may not always be used in trying to establish validity as they are when trying to establish reliability. When statistical procedures are used in trying to establish validity, they generally are correlational procedures.

Four broad categories of validity are considered here: face, content, criterion, and construct. Face and content validity are concerned only with the instrument that is under consideration; criterion and construct validity are concerned with how well the instrument under consideration compares with other measures of the variable of interest.

Face Validity

An instrument is said to have **face validity** when a preliminary examination shows that it is measuring what it is supposed to measure. In other words, on the surface or the face of the instrument, it appears to be an adequate means of obtaining the data needed for the research project. The face validity of an instrument can be examined through the use of experts in the content area or through the use of individuals who have characteristics similar to those of the potential subjects. Because of the subjective nature of face validity, this type of validity is rarely used alone.

Face Validity

Feider and Mitchell (2009) sought to establish face validity of a survey on oral care practices for adult critically ill patients who are orally intubated. Input was sought from three lay individuals, who were not oral care subject matter experts. There was 100% agreement between these three individuals on the readability and clarity of the survey questions.

Content Validity

Content validity is concerned with the scope or range of items used to measure the variable. In other words, are the number and type of items adequate to measure the concept or construct of interest? Is there an adequate sampling of all the possible items that could be used to secure the desired data? There are several methods of evaluating the content validity of an instrument.

The first method is accomplished by comparing the content of the instrument with material available in the literature on the topic. A determination can then be made of the adequacy of the measurement tool in light of existing knowledge in the content area. For example, if a new instrument were being developed to measure the empathic levels of nurses in hospice settings, the researcher would need to be familiar with the literature on both empathy and the hospice setting.

A second way to examine the content validity of an instrument is through the use of a panel of experts, a group of people who have expertise in a given subject area. These experts are given copies of the instrument and the purpose and objectives of the study. They then evaluate the instrument, usually individually rather than in a group. Comparisons are made between these evaluations, and the researcher then determines if additions, deletions, or changes need to be made.

A third method is used when knowledge tests are being developed. The researcher develops a test blueprint designed around the objectives for the content being taught and the level of knowledge that is expected (e.g., retention, recall, and synthesis).

The actual degree of content validity is never established. An instrument is said to possess some degree of validity that can only be estimated.

Content Validity

Two experts were used to evaluate the content validity of The Knowledge, Attitudes, and Opinions Concerning Faith Community Nursing Survey (Thompson, 2010). One expert was a faith community nurse (FCN); the other was an educator in a basic faith community nursing educational program. They judged all items to be appropriate and clear.

Criterion Validity

Criterion validity is concerned with the extent to which an instrument corresponds to or is correlated with some criterion measure of the variable of interest. Criterion validity assesses the ability of an instrument to determine subjects' responses at the present time or predict subjects' responses in the future. These two types of criterion validity are called concurrent and predictive validity, respectively.

Concurrent validity compares an instrument's ability to obtain a measurement of subjects' behavior that is comparable to some other criterion of that behavior. Does the instrument under consideration correlate with another instrument that measures the same behavior or responses? For example, a researcher might want to develop a short instrument that would help evaluate the suicidal potential of people when they call in to a suicide crisis intervention center. A short, easily administered interview instrument would be of great help to the staff, but the researcher would want to be sure this instrument was a valid diagnostic instrument to assess suicide potential. Responses received on the short instrument could be compared with those received when using an already validated, but longer, suicide assessment tool. If both instruments seem to be obtaining the essential information necessary to make a decision about the suicide potential of a person, the new instrument might be considered to have criterion validity. The degree of validity would be determined through correlation of the results of the two tests administered to a number of people. The correlation coefficient must be at least .70 to consider that the two instruments are obtaining similar data.

Concurrent Validity

The Nursing Teamwork Survey (NTS) was designed to measure nursing teamwork in acute care hospital settings at the patient unit level (Kalisch, Lee, & Salas, 2010). The instrument was found to have good psychometric properties. Concurrent validity testing revealed a significant correlation between teamwork scores and an imbedded question related to overall satisfaction with teamwork ($r = .633$, $p < .001$).

The second type of criterion validity, **predictive validity**, is concerned with the ability of an instrument to predict behavior or responses of subjects in the future. If the predictive validity of an instrument is established, it can be used with confidence to discriminate between people, at the present time, in relation to their future behavior. This would be a very valuable quality for an instrument to possess. For example, a researcher might be interested in knowing if a suicidal potential assessment tool would be useful in predicting actual suicidal behavior in the future.

Construct Validity

Of all of the types of validity, construct validity is the most difficult to measure. **Construct validity** is concerned with the degree to which an instrument measures the construct it is supposed to measure. A construct is a concept or abstraction created or "constructed" by the researcher [see Chapter 7]. Construct validity involves the measurement of a variable that is not directly observable, but rather is an abstract concept derived from observable behavior. Construct validity is derived from the underlying theory that is used to describe or explain the construct.

Many of the variables measured in research are labeled constructs. Nursing is concerned with constructs such as anxiety, assertiveness, and androgyny.

One method to measure construct validity is called the **known-groups procedure**, in which the instrument under consideration is administered to two groups of people whose responses are expected to differ on the variable of interest. For example, if you were developing an instrument to measure depression, the theory used to explain depression would indicate the types of behavior that would be expected in depressed people. If the tool was administered to a group of supposedly depressed subjects and to a group of supposedly happy subjects, you would expect the two groups to score quite differently on the tool. If differences were not found, you might suspect that the instrument was not really measuring depression.

Construct Validity – Known Groups

A study was conducted by Tseng, Cleeland, Wang, and Lin (2008) with Taiwanese adolescents who were living with cancer. The researchers were evaluating the validity and reliability of the Taiwanese version of the M. D. Anderson Symptom Inventory (MDASI-T). One method of assessing the construct validity of the instrument was the "known-groups" technique. As predicted by the researchers, results demonstrated that the adolescents with low functional status had significantly higher MDASI-T scores (symptom severity) than did the adolescents with high functional status.

Another approach to construct validity is called **factor analysis**, a method used to identify clusters of related items on an instrument or scale. This type of procedure helps the researcher determine whether the tool is measuring only one construct or several constructs. Correlational procedures are used to determine if items cluster together.

Factor Analysis

Harrison (2009) developed and tested the Activity Effort Scale, which was designed for aging women who had contacted polio when they were young. The sample consisted of 500 women with a history of paralytic polio. Factor analysis of the 8-item scale indicated that the tool did, in fact, measure the frequency of effort that these women exerted beyond their levels of discomfort, pain, and fatigue.

Relationship Between Reliability and Validity

Reliability and validity are closely associated. Both of these qualities are considered when selecting a research instrument. Reliability is usually considered first because it is a necessary condition for validity. An instrument cannot be valid unless it is reliable. However, the reliability of an instrument tells nothing about the degree of validity. In fact, an instrument can be very reliable and have *low* validity.

Reliability was considered first in this chapter's discussion of reliability and validity. In actuality, validity is often considered first in the construction of an instrument. Face validity and content validity may be examined, and then some type of reliability is considered. Next, another type of validity may be considered. The process is not always the same. The type of desired validity and the type of reliability are decided, and then the procedures for establishing these criteria for the instrument are determined. A word of caution about using the term *established* in regard to reliability and validity of instruments: Strickland (1995), in an editorial in the *Journal of Nursing Measurement*, stated that reliability and validity cannot be established because there is always an error component in measurement. She wrote that it is more correct to use terms like "supported," "assessed," or "prior evidence has shown" (p. 91).

SOURCES OF ERROR IN DATA COLLECTION

Variations are usually expected in data that are collected from participants in a study. If the researcher did not expect to find some type of variation in the data, there would probably be no interest in conducting the study. Ideally, the variations or differences that are found are "real" rather than "artificial." Every researcher must recognize that some error component is likely to exist in the data that are obtained, especially when the data are being collected from human beings, and the degree of control that can be placed on the research situation is limited. The errors in data collection can arise from instrument inadequacies, instrument administration biases, environmental variations during the data-collection process, and temporary subject characteristics during the data-collection process.

Instrument inadequacies concern the items used to collect data and the instructions to subjects that are contained within the instrument, such as a questionnaire. Are the items appropriate to collect the data that are being sought? Do the items adequately cover the range of content? Will the order of the items influence subjects' responses? Are the items and the directions for completing items clear and unbiased?

Even when there are no errors in the research instrument, biases or errors may occur in the administration of the instrument. Is the instrument administered in the same fashion to all subjects? Are observers collecting data in the same manner?

Environmental conditions during data collection can also influence the data that are gathered. Is the location for data collection the same for all subjects? Are conditions such as temperature, noise levels, and lighting kept consistent for all subjects?

Finally, the characteristics of the subjects during data collection can be a source of error in research data. Are there any personal characteristics of the subjects, such as anxiety levels, hunger, or tiredness, influencing responses? This source of error may be called transitory personal factors.

PREPARING DATA FOR ANALYSIS

Once data have been gathered, this information must be prepared for analysis. If a computer will be used to analyze data, it is very important that the data are in a form that facilitates entry into the computer. Quantitative data, such as age and weight, may be entered directly into the computer. Qualitative data, such as information obtained from open-ended questions, will need to be transferred into data that the computer can understand if computer analysis will be used. It is important to have data ready for speedy entry. It is not the time to be shuffling pieces of paper searching for data. Data coding should be considered, and decisions about missing data made before data entry begins.

USE OF A STATISTICAL CONSULTANT

Many nurse researchers now have personal computers and statistical software packages and are able to do much of their data analysis on their own. However, the use of a statistical consultant is still needed in many research projects. Most research projects require several hours of consultation time. More time will be required if the statistician is asked to do programming or to perform complicated statistical analyses. If a grant is being written, statistical consultation costs should be included in the budget.

Some researchers visit a statistician after their data are collected to find out what "to do" with their data. This is not the proper way to use the statistician's talents. The time to seek help is in the early planning stages of a study. Shott (1990) has cautioned researchers to seek statistical consultation early in the project to prevent the entire project from "sinking." She wrote that it is too late after the study is completed to find that the data-collection form is a mess and the sample size is much too small.

CRITIQUING DATA-COLLECTION PROCEDURES

It is important for the reader of a research report to determine if the measurement and collection of data has been conducted appropriately. This may be a very difficult task because the reader will not get to see the instruments. Even when questionnaires are used, they are rarely contained in the research article or report. However, there are some guidelines that may be used and some questions that may be asked (Box 12–1) when critiquing the data-collection section of a research report.

The reader first tries to find a section in the research report where the measurement and collection of data are reported. The information sought concerns who collected the data, when the data were collected, where the data were collected, what data were collected, and how the data were collected.

A determination is made of the level of measurement that would be appropriate to test the research hypothesis(es) or answer the research question(s). For example, if compliance with diabetic

---

Box 12–1. Guidelines for Critiquing the Data-Collection Procedures

1. Did the research report provide information on who collected the data, when the data were collected, where the data were collected, what data were collected, and how the data were collected?
2. Was the appropriate level of measurement used to measure the research variables?
3. Was there a section in the research report where the data-collection instruments were described?
4. Was the description of the instruments thorough?
5. Had the instrument(s) been used previously?
6. Had the instrument(s) been tested for reliability?
7. If so, what type of reliability was assessed, and was there sufficient evidence to indicate that the instrument(s) was(were) reliable?
8. Had the instrument(s) been tested for validity?
9. If so, what type of validity was assessed, and was there sufficient evidence to indicate that the instrument(s) was(were) valid?
10. Was a pilot study conducted using the instruments?

---

regimen was the dependent variable, has the researcher used a physiological measure of compliance or has the patient been asked to self-report compliance?

The research instruments should be described clearly and thoroughly. Information should be provided about the reliability and validity of the instruments. The types and degree of reliability and validity should be reported.

Finally, the results of the pilot study should be reported. If a pilot study was not conducted, the rationale for failure to do so should be discussed.

SUMMARY

Measurement is the process of assigning numbers to variables. The four levels of measurement are nominal, ordinal, interval, and ratio. **Nominal level of measurement** produces data that are "named" or categorized. **Ordinal level of measurement** categorizes and ranks the data. The distance between the ranks can be specified with **interval level of measurement**. In addition to these characteristics, **ratio level of measurement** specifies a true zero point.

Five important questions need to be answered concerning the data-collection process: Who will collect the data? When will the data be collected? Where will the data be collected? What data will be collected? How will the data be collected?

There are many alternatives to choose from when selecting a data-collection method. These methods include physiological measures, observational methods, questionnaires, interviews, attitude scales, and psychological tests. The devices used to collect data are called the **research instruments** or tools. The researcher may use an existing instrument or develop a new instrument.

A pilot study should be conducted whenever a new instrument is being developed or when a preexisting instrument is being used with people who have different characteristics from those for whom the instrument was originally developed.

Factors to be considered when choosing a data-collection instrument are the practicality, reliability, and validity of the instrument. The practicality of an instrument concerns its cost and appropriateness for the population. The **reliability** of an instrument determines its consistency and stability. **Validity** concerns the ability of the instrument to gather the data that it is intended to gather.

Types of reliability are stability, equivalence, and internal consistency. The **stability reliability** of an instrument refers to its consistency over time and is usually determined by test-retest procedures. **Equivalence reliability** concerns the degree to which two forms of an instrument obtain the same results or two or more observers obtain the same results when using a single instrument. **Alternate forms reliability** or **parallel forms reliability** are terms used when two forms of the same instrument are compared. **Interrater reliability** or **interobserver reliability** is the degree of agreement on ratings or observations made by independent judges. **Internal consistency reliability** addresses the extent to which all items on an instrument measure the same variable.

Types of validity are face, content, criterion, and construct. **Face validity** measures the degree to which an instrument appears, on the surface, to measure the variable of interest. **Content validity** is concerned with the scope or range of items used to measure the variable. **Criterion validity** considers the degree to which an instrument correlates with some criterion measure on the variable of interest. Two types of criterion validity are concurrent and predictive. **Concurrent validity** compares data obtained through the use of a new instrument with data gathered through the use of an existing instrument that measures the same variable. **Predictive validity** examines the ability of an instrument to predict behavior of subjects in the future. Finally, **construct validity** concerns the measurement of a variable that is not directly observable, but rather a construct or abstract concept derived from observable behavior. Two types of construct validity are the **known-groups procedure** and **factor analysis**.

Reliability and validity are closely associated. Reliability is a necessary condition for validity. An instrument, however, can be reliable and not valid.

Errors in the data-collection process can arise from (a) instrument inadequacies, (b) instrument administration biases, (c) environmental variations during the data-collection process, and (d) temporary subject characteristics during the data-collection process.

The researcher must prepare data for analysis. In many studies, nurse researchers use statistical consultants early in the project as well as in the data-analysis phase.

NURSING RESEARCH ON THE WEB

For additional online resources, research activities, and exercises, go to **www.mynursingkit.com.** Select Chapter 12 from the drop-down menu.

GET INVOLVED ACTIVITIES

1. Contact a nurse researcher that you know and ask this person to share with you information about the reliability and validity of an instrument used in her or his research.
2. Examine five research articles in nursing journals. Determine the types of reliability and validity that are discussed in each article. Keep a tally of the different types that you find and the statistics that are presented (such as the reliability coefficients). Bring these to your group for discussion. Make a list on a blackboard or poster board of each type of reliability and validity that has been discovered and the number of times each one was mentioned in the literature.
3. Based on the preceding information, determine the most common types of reliability and validity being used by nurse researchers.
4. Determine the number of research instruments that are mentioned in these articles that have been shown to have a reliability of at least .70.
5. Identify the number of times that a research article does not discuss or even present reliability data on an instrument that has been used in the research study being discussed.
6. Divide into groups. Discuss an instrument that you might develop for a particular study. Decide the types of reliability and validity that you think would be most appropriate for your instrument.

SELF-TEST

Examine the following statements. Determine the type of reliability or validity that is indicated in each statement.

1. The Assertiveness Inventory was administered to a group of subjects at two different times, with 1 week between the administrations. The correlation between the scores on the two administrations was .85. _____

2. The items look like they will obtain the data needed to measure assertiveness. _____

3. The difference between the subjects' scores on assertiveness and submissiveness was highly significant. _____

4. The correlation between nurses' empathy levels 1 year and 10 years after graduation was .75. _____

5. The correlation between subjects' scores on Form A and Form B of the Assertiveness Inventory was .60. _____

Examine the following statements concerning reliability and validity and determine if each statement is true (T) or false (F).

_____ 6. The internal consistency of the Assertiveness Inventory is .90. That means that this instrument is a valid measure of assertiveness.

_____ 7. By increasing the number of items on the Assertiveness Inventory from 20 to 30, the reliability of the instrument will probably increase.

_____ 8. An instrument can be reliable without being valid.

_____ 9. If the test-retest reliability of the Assertiveness Inventory was determined to be .35, the validity of the instrument would be in serious doubt.

_____ 10. Reliability is the *most* important factor to take into account when considering an instrument for use in research.

REFERENCES

Feider, L. L., & Mitchell, P. (2009). Validity and Reliability of an oral care practice survey for the orally intubated adult critically ill patient. *Nursing Research, 58,* 374–377.

Frank-Stromborg, M., & Olsen, S. (Eds.). (2004). *Instruments for clinical health-care research* (3rd ed.). Boston: Jones Bartlett.

Guo, J., Dixon, J. K., Whittemore, R., & He, G.-P. (2010). Psychometric testing of the Health Quotient questionnaire: A measure of self-reported holistic health. *Journal of Advanced Nursing, 66,* 653–663. doi: 10.1111/j.1365-2648.2009.05205.x

Harrison, T (2009). Development of the activity effort scale for women aging with paralytic polio. *Journal of Neuroscience Nursing, 41,* 168–176.

Jairath, N., Hogerney, M., & Parsons, C. (2000). The role of the pilot study: A case illustration from cardiac nursing research. *Applied Nursing Research, 13,* 92–96.

Kalisch, B. J., Lee, H., & Salas, E. (2010). The development and testing of the nursing teamwork survey. *Nursing Research, 59,* 42–50.

Lunney, M., & Sammarco, A. (2009). Scoring rubric for grading students' participation in online discussions. *CIN: Computers, Informatics, Nursing, 27,* 26–31.

Polit, D., & Beck, C. T. (2008). *Nursing research: Principles and methods* (8th ed.). Philadelphia: Lippincott Williams & Wilkins.

Radwin, L. E., & Cabral, H. J. (2010). Trust in Nurses Scale: Construct validity and internal reliability evaluation. *Journal of Advanced Nursing, 66,* 683–689. doi: 10.1111/j.1365-2648.2009.05168.x

Shott, S. (1990). *Statistics for health professionals.* Philadelphia: W. B. Saunders.

Strickland, O. L. (1995). Can reliability and validity be "established?" *Journal of Nursing Measurement, 3,* 91–92.

Strickland, O. L., & Waltz, C. F. (Eds.). (1988a). *Measurement of nursing outcomes: Vol. 1. Measuring client outcomes.* New York: Springer.

Strickland, O. L., & Waltz, C. F. (Eds.). (1988b). *Measurement of nursing outcomes: Vol. 2. Measuring nursing performance: Practice, education, and research.* New York: Springer.

Strickland, O. L., & Waltz, C. F. (Eds.). (1990a). *Measurement of nursing outcomes: Vol. 3. Measuring clinical skills and professional development in education and practice.* New York: Springer.

Strickland, O. L., & Waltz, C. F. (Eds.). (1990b). *Measurement of nursing outcomes: Vol. 4. Measuring client self-care and coping skills.* New York: Springer.

Thompson, P. (2010). Clergy knowledge and attitudes concerning faith community nursing: Toward a three-dimensional scale. *Public Health Nursing, 27,* 71–78. doi: 10.1111/j.1525-1446.2009.00828.x

Tseng, T., Cleeland, C. S., Wang, X. S., & Lin. C. (2008). Assessing cancer symptoms in adolescents with cancer using the Taiwanese version of the M. D. Anderson Symptom Inventory. *Cancer Nursing, 31,* E9–E12.

CHAPTER 13

Data-Collection Methods

OUTLINE

OBJECTIVES

On completion of this chapter, you will be prepared to:

1. Recognize the importance of questionnaires as a data-collection method
2. Enumerate the general characteristics of questionnaires

3. Construct items for a questionnaire
4. List the advantages and disadvantages of questionnaires as a data-collection method
5. Acknowledge the importance of interviews as a data-collection method
6. Recognize the necessity for training of interviewers before data collection
7. Differentiate among the three different levels of structure that can be used in interviews
8. List guidelines to be used in the three phases of an interview
9. Recognize the influence of the interviewer on the subjects' responses
10. List the advantages and disadvantages of interviews as a data-collection method
11. Recognize the importance of observation as a data-collection method
12. Determine the need for physiological and psychological data-collection methods
13. Compare and contrast the various types of data-collection methods
14. Critique the data-collection methods used in research studies reported in the literature

NEW TERMS DEFINED IN THIS CHAPTER

ambiguous questions, pg 183

attitude scales, pg 193

attribute variables, pg 183

closed-ended questions, pg 183

collectively exhaustive categories, pg 183

contingency questions, pg 184

Delphi technique, pg 196

demographic questions, pg 183

demographic variables, pg 183

double-barreled questions, pg 183

event sampling, pg 191

filler questions, pg 185

interview, pg 187

interview schedule, pg 188

Likert scale, pg 193

mutually exclusive categories, pg 183

nonparticipant observer (covert), pg 191

nonparticipant observer (overt), pg 191

observation research, pg 190

open-ended questions, pg 184

participant observer (covert), pg 192

participant observer (overt), pg 192

personality inventories, pg 195

physiological measures, pg 192

preexisting data, pg 197

probes, pg 187

projective technique, pg 195

Q sort, pg 196

questionnaire, pg 181

semantic differential, pg 194

semistructured interviews, pg 188

structured interviews, pg 188

structured observations, pg 191

telephone interviews, pg 188

time sampling, pg 191

unstructured interviews, pg 187

unstructured observations, pg 191

visual analogue scale, pg 197

"**W**ould you mind filling out this short questionnaire?" You have probably received such a request. Surveys or polls in which questionnaires are used are a common occurrence in our society. You may have walked in the opposite direction at the mall when you saw someone taking a poll.

Questionnaires are one of the most common data-collection methods used by nurse researchers. Other data-collection methods include interviews, observational methods, and various physiological and psychological measures.

Try not to be confused by the wide variety of data-collection methods. Once you have had experience in critiquing and helping plan research studies, you will be able to select the most appropriate data-collection methods more easily. As you read about the various methods presented in this chapter, try to envision a research project that might call for each type of data-collection method discussed.

QUESTIONNAIRES

A **questionnaire** is a paper-and-pencil self-report instrument. It contains questions that respondents are asked to answer in writing.

Many people mistakenly believe that developing a good questionnaire is a fairly easy task. Oppenheim (1966) wrote, "The world is full of well-meaning people who believe that anyone who can write plain English and has a modicum of common sense can produce a good questionnaire" (p. vii). This is definitely not true. Many questionnaires have been used only one time because they were poorly constructed and did not obtain the type of data for which they were designed. Many literature resources are available for use in the construction of questionnaires. Also, help can be sought from experts in the area of questionnaire construction.

Questionnaires may be used to measure knowledge levels, opinions, attitudes, beliefs, ideas, feelings, and perceptions, as well as to gather factual information about respondents. Of course, the validity of the data obtained through this method is governed by the respondents' willingness or ability to provide accurate information. Nevertheless, questionnaires are extremely important in nursing research and may be the only method of obtaining data on certain human responses. More information is presented on questionnaires than on the other methods of data collection because each one of you will probably be involved in the construction of a questionnaire at some time during your career.

Overall Appearance of Questionnaire

The old saying that "first impressions are lasting impressions" may hold true as potential research participants scan a study questionnaire. Remember, a spell-check software program cannot differentiate between words like "hear" and "here" and "seam" and "seem." Researchers must always proof their questionnaires.

There are many methods of duplicating questionnaires, but it is important to use a high-quality printing process and paper. Questionnaires should be neat in appearance, grammatically correct, and error free. The spacing of questions is important. A questionnaire that has a cluttered or crowded appearance may be difficult and confusing for the subject to complete. Adequate margins and spacing of the questions are needed. It may be better to add another page to the questionnaire rather than crowding too many questions on one page. Keep in mind, however, that if the questionnaire seems too long, potential respondents may become discouraged and discard the questionnaire or fail to answer all of the questions.

Language and Reading Level of Questions

A questionnaire should be written in the respondents' preferred language (e.g., English, Spanish) and appropriate for the knowledge and reading level of the least educated respondents.

A survey of adult's literacy levels was conducted in 2003 by the National Center for Education Statistics. This survey included a component on health literacy. Health literacy was reported at four levels: Below Basic, Basic, Intermediate, and Proficient. The majority (53%) of respondents had "Intermediate" health literacy, 22% had "Basic" health literacy, 14% had "Below Basic" health literacy, with only 11% being "Proficient" in health literacy. Adults with "Below Basic" or "Basic" health literacy were less likely than adults with higher health literacy to obtain health information from written sources, such as newspapers, magazines, books, brochures, or the Internet. They were more likely to obtain health information from radio and television. (For more information go to http://nces.ed.gov/pubsearch/pubsinfo.asp?pubid=2006483)

Walker, Pepa, and Gerard (2010) assessed the health literacy levels of 55 patients in an urban and a suburban hospital. Using the Test of Functional Health Literacy in Adults, they found that 23% of participants had marginal or inadequate functional health literacy. Significant relationships were found between health literacy and socioeconomic status ($p = <.001$) and education ($p = <.001$). Assessed reading levels for 30% of the participants were below the completed grade levels that they had reported.

The readability of 35 pieces of patient education materials used for low-income populations was evaluated by Wilson (2009). Using three different reading-level formulas, materials were determined to be written at a 7th to 9th grade level, which Wilson concluded, is too high for the average adult.

Many formulas are available that determine the reading level of various printed material, including the Flesch Reading Ease, Fog, Flesch-Kincaid Grade Level, and SMOG (Simple Measure of Gobbledygook). The Flesch Reading Ease formula examines the average length of sentences and number of syllables per word. It provides a number from 0 to 100, with a higher score indicating an easier reading level. The Fog formula is similar to the Flesch Reading Ease formula in that it examines sentence and syllable lengths. A score of 5 is assigned to material that is considered readable; a score of 20 is assigned to material that is very difficult. The Flesch-Kincaid Grade Level formula provides a U.S. school grade level. For example, a score of 8.2 means that an average student in the eighth grade would understand the material. SMOG is a readability formula that estimates the years of education needed to understand a written passage and looks at the number of multisyllable words.

If you would like to find out the reading level of a small passage you have written, go to an Internet browser, such as Google. Type in "readability calculation." Click on a link to one of the readability formulas listed. Also, some computer software programs provide readability scores. For example, Microsoft Word provides Flesch Reading Ease scores and Flesch-Kincaid Grade Level scores. After you have checked your document for spelling and grammar in Microsoft Word, you can ask for readability scores.

The readability level of the first paragraph in this chapter was assessed, and the Flesch Reading Score was reported to be 73 (the higher the score, the easier is the passage to read). The Flesch-Kincaid Grade Level score was 6th grade. You are probably thinking, "Yes, that paragraph was simple, but check out some of the other paragraphs in this book!"

The Flesch-Kincaid Grade Level score was calculated for the Self-Management of Type I Diabetes (SMOD-A) developed for use with adolescents with type I diabetes (Schilling et al., 2009). Microsoft Word revealed a 5.9 grade level for the tool.

Freda (2005) studied the readability of American Academy of Pediatrics patient education brochures. The mean readability for all 74 brochures was grade 7.94 using the Flesch-Kincaid formula and grade 10.1 using the SMOG formula. Using an eighth-grade reading level criterion for acceptability, the researcher determined that more than half of the brochures were written at an unacceptable level.

Length of Questionnaire and Questions

The length of a questionnaire may influence respondents' willingness to participate in a study. Although research results are inconclusive on the length of a questionnaire most likely to be returned, generally speaking, short questionnaires are more likely to be returned than long ones. It would probably be advisable to limit the required completion time to 10 minutes or less, which means the questionnaire should probably not be longer than two or three pages.

Questions should be kept as short as possible. Keep in mind that the purpose of the questions is to seek data and not to test the respondents' reading ability and tenacity. A desirable length for a question is less than 20 words. A question may need to be divided into two questions if the length becomes excessive or the question asks the respondent to consider more than one idea at a time.

Wording of Questions

The most difficult aspect of questionnaire construction is the actual wording of individual questions. Here are some general guidelines:

1. State Questions in an Affirmative Rather Than a Negative Manner

   Negative words, such as *never*, can be overlooked, and the respondent will answer the exact opposite of an intended response. Students often complain about the use of negative wording in questions. You are now going to have revealed to you a well-kept secret of teachers.

Questions are written this way because it is much easier to write *one* incorrect answer and *three* correct answers for a question than it is to write *three* plausible incorrect responses and *one* correct response.

2. Avoid Ambiguous Questions

   Ambiguous questions contain words that have more than one meaning or can be interpreted differently by various people. Examples of such words are *many, usually, few, often, large, several,* and *generally.*

3. Avoid Double Negative Questions

   It is difficult for respondents to reply to a question like this: "Don't you disagree with the idea that . . ."

4. Questions Should Contain Neutral Wording

   Any question that implies the type of answer to be given may result in biased responses. Consider the following question: "Do you believe that smoking is a disgusting habit?" The desired answer is quite obvious. Even if you think that smoking is a disgusting habit, you would not want to bias the answers of respondents. Examples of a neutrally worded question, a subtly biased question, and a completely biased question follow:
   A. What is your opinion about cigarette smoking?
   B. Would you say that you are against cigarette smoking?
   C. You do not believe that people should smoke cigarettes, do you?

5. Avoid Double-Barreled Questions

   Double-barreled questions ask two questions in one. An example of such a question might be, "Do you plan to pursue a master's degree in nursing and seek an administrative position upon graduation?" When a question contains "and," it is quite likely that two questions are being asked rather than one.

Types of Questions

There are many ways to categorize questions. This section examines these categories of questions: demographic, close-ended, open-ended, contingency, and filler questions. These types of questions are not mutually exclusive. For example, a demographic question could be written as an open-ended or a closed-ended question.

Demographic Questions

Demographic questions gather data on the characteristics of the sample. These characteristics, sometimes called **demographic variables** or **attribute variables**, include such factors as age, educational background, and religious affiliation. Nearly every questionnaire seeks some kind of demographic data. These data are used to describe the study sample. Also, these data may be statistically analyzed to examine relationships between respondents' characteristics and other variables of interest in the study.

Closed-Ended Questions

The most structured questions are **closed-ended questions**, those in which the respondents are asked to choose from given alternatives. There may be only two alternatives, as in a true-or-false question, or many, as in a checklist type of question where respondents are asked to check all items that apply to them. Other types of closed-ended questions include multiple-choice questions and matching questions.

When closed-ended items are used on a questionnaire, the response categories must be collectively exhaustive and mutually exclusive. **Collectively exhaustive categories** means that all possible answers are provided, and **mutually exclusive categories** means that there is no overlap between categories. The following example demonstrates categories that are collectively exhaustive and mutually exclusive.

How many apples do you eat each week?

_____ A. None
_____ B. 1–2
_____ C. 3–4
_____ D. More than 4

The following question *violates* the rule concerning collectively exhaustive categories:

Please check your highest level of education:

_____ A. Elementary
_____ B. High school
_____ C. College

How would subjects respond who had not completed elementary school? Other categories are needed to cover all possible answers that respondents might provide. Sometimes researchers find a quick solution to this problem by adding an "other" category. A blank is provided beside the word *other* for respondents' answers.

The researcher also must provide answers that are mutually exclusive. A respondent should be able to check only one response from among a set of alternatives. The following is a sample question that *violates* this rule:

Please check the length of time that you have dieted:

_____ A. 1–4 weeks
_____ B. 4–8 weeks
_____ C. 8–12 weeks
_____ D. More than 12 weeks

Did you notice the overlap between the categories? A respondent's answer to the preceding question may well depend on the amount of weight loss. If a woman has been on a diet for 4 weeks and is feeling guilty because she has lost only 2 pounds, the 1- to 4-weeks category might be checked, rather than the 4- to 8-weeks category.

Open-Ended Questions

The researcher asks respondents to complete questions in their own words in **open-ended questions**. Essay and fill-in-the-blank are types of open-ended questions. Open-ended questions may be used in combination with closed-ended questions. After the closed-ended item is presented, a space may be provided for respondents to answer in their own words.

Contingency Questions

Questionnaire items that are relevant for some respondents and not for others are called **contingency questions**. The determination of whether respondents should answer certain questions is dependent, or contingent, on their answers to other questions. For example, a researcher might want to determine if a client has been satisfied with the type of nursing care received during previous hospitalizations. If the client has not been hospitalized previously, an answer could not be provided to this particular question.

1. Have you ever been hospitalized before?
_____ Yes $\longrightarrow$ How would you rate the care you received during
your *last* hospitalization?
_____ Poor _____ Fair _____ Good

_____ No
2. . . .

The arrow indicates that respondents who answer "Yes" also should answer the question on the right. Respondents who answer "No" will continue downward on the questionnaire.

Filler Questions

Occasionally, the researcher wishes to decrease the emphasis on the specific purpose of the study to avoid the tendency for respondents to provide answers they believe the researcher is seeking. **Filler questions** are items in which the researcher has no direct interest but are included on a questionnaire to reduce the emphasis on the specific purpose of other questions. For example, if the main purpose of a study was to gain information concerning patients' perceptions of the nursing care they had received, the researcher might include other questions about the food they had been served, visiting hours, and so forth. Patients might answer more honestly if a few questions about the nursing care they had received were scattered in among a lot of other questions.

Placement of Questions

All questions about a certain topic should be grouped together. Also, demographic questions, which ask for factual information about the respondents, should be grouped together. There is much discussion about the order or placement of questions in certain areas of the questionnaire, such as at the beginning or at the end. Demographic questions are frequently placed at the beginning of a questionnaire because these types of questions are easy to answer and may encourage the respondent to continue with the questionnaire. However, the researcher may choose to place the demographic questions at the end of the questionnaire in the belief that some demographic questions, such as those asking for income or age, may be threatening to the respondents.

Cover Letter

A cover letter should accompany all mailed questionnaires and is helpful anytime a questionnaire is administered. The letter should be brief and contain the following information:

1. Identification of the researcher and any sponsoring agency or person
2. Purpose of the research
3. How participant was selected
4. Reason the respondent should answer the questionnaire
5. Length of time to complete the questionnaire
6. How data will be used or made public
7. Deadline for return of questionnaire
8. An offer to inform respondent of results of the study
9. Contact phone number, mailing address, or e-mail address
10. Personal signature of the researcher

The cover letter is extremely important and may be the single most important factor in motivating respondents to complete questionnaires. Consider what approach or what information would impress you the most and make you want to complete the questionnaire.

Completion Instructions

Information on how to complete the questionnaire must be clear and concise. If all questions are to be answered using the same type of format, a general set of instructions may be written at the top of the questionnaire. Frequently, however, several different types of questions are included on the instrument, and instructions need to precede each type of question. It is very helpful to provide the respondent with an example of the appropriate way to respond to a particular type of question.

Distribution of Questionnaires

There are many methods of distributing questionnaires. They may be given to potential respondents in a one-to-one contact, such as might occur when the nurse researcher distributes instruments to hospitalized patients. Researchers may hand out questionnaires to students in a classroom or distribute questionnaires to members of an organization as they enter a meeting room. Questionnaires also may be placed in a container in a given location where potential respondents can take one if they so desire. One of the most frequently used methods of distributing questionnaires is through a mailing system, such as a hospital interdepartmental mailing system or the U.S. Postal Service.

According to Curtis and Redmond (2009), the postal questionnaire is becoming less frequent because we live in an electronic age. The Internet has opened up a valuable new method for distributing questionnaires and collecting data. Some of you may be familiar with SurveyMonkey (http://surveymonkey.com), an online software program designed for the creation of questionnaires. It is very inexpensive and easy to use. Hart, Brennan, Sym, and Larson (2009) used SurveyMonkey to examine return rates of questionnaires sent out to program directors of nurse practitioner (NP) programs in the U.S. These researchers pointed out the advantages of using electronic survey methods. Northam, Yarbrough, Haas, and Duke (2010) also used SurveyMonkey to query nursing journal editors concerning their publication policies, including their reasons for rejection of manuscripts. Just today (March 8, 2010), an e-mail was received from the American Nurses Association, which asked for my participation in a membership survey. SurveyMonkey was used to obtain responses.

Baernholdt and Clarke (2006) published an article titled "Internet Research in an International Context." They described the benefits of electronic surveys, including the fact that this medium may offer a more efficient way to reach respondents across international borders. Of course, they also pointed out issues that have to be addressed, such as language barriers and security of responses.

Factors Influencing Response Rates

One serious disadvantage of questionnaires is the frequent low return rate. If you were to mail a survey to a random sample of people listed in a phone book, you would probably not receive a return rate greater than 20%. Factors that positively influence response rates include the following:

1. Mailing at a time other than holiday seasons or popular vacation times
2. Hand-addressed outer envelopes
3. Personal signature of the researcher on the cover letter
4. Information in the cover letter that motivates respondents
5. Neatness and clarity of the instrument
6. Ease of completion of the instrument
7. Time to complete the instrument does not exceed 10 to 15 minutes
8. Guarantee of anonymity
9. Inclusion of a preaddressed, stamped envelope
10. An incentive, such as a small cash payment or an instant coffee sample to drink while completing the questionnaire

A study was conducted to determine influences on health behaviors in rural, low-income people (Kaiser, Brown, & Baumann, 2010). Data were collected through face-to-face interviews, which lasted approximately 40 minutes. Participants were given $5.00 at the end of the interview.

Questionnaires were distributed to nursing staff members' mailboxes in a study designed to test the psychometric properties of the Nursing Teamwork Survey (Kalisch, Lee, & Salas, 2010). A candy bar, as a token of appreciation, was included in each 9 x 11 envelope that contained a questionnaire.

Advantages of Questionnaires

1. Questionnaires are a quick and generally inexpensive means of obtaining data from a large number of respondents.
2. Testing for reliability and validity is easier than for many other research instruments.
3. The administration of questionnaires is less time consuming than interviews or observation research.
4. Data can be obtained from respondents in widespread geographical areas.
5. Respondents can remain anonymous.
6. If anonymity is assured, respondents are more likely to provide honest answers.

Disadvantages of Questionnaires

1. Mailing of questionnaires may be costly.
2. Response rate may be low.
3. Respondents may provide socially acceptable answers.
4. Respondents may fail to answer some of the items.
5. There is no opportunity to clarify items that may be misunderstood by respondents.
6. Respondents must be literate.
7. Respondents must have no physical disability that would deter them from completing a questionnaire.
8. Respondents may not be representative of the population.

INTERVIEWS

The phone rings and you answer it. A voice on the other end of the line says, "Hello, I'm conducting a research study on _____. It will take only 5 to 10 minutes of your time, and the information you provide will be very important to the results of this study." Have you ever received such a call? If so, did you provide information or did you hang up the phone? If you have received such a call or have participated in a study in which interviews were conducted, you are already familiar with some of the material on interviews.

An **interview** is a method of data collection in which an interviewer obtains responses from a subject in a face-to-face encounter, through a telephone call, or, today, through an Internet connection. Interviews are used to obtain factual data about people, as well as to measure their opinions, attitudes, and beliefs about certain topics. Information is provided here about how to conduct interviews because it is possible that you will be a data collector sometime even if you never serve as a principal investigator.

Types of Interviews

Interviews can be very unstructured or very structured. Most interviews, however, range between the two ends of the continuum. For simplification in discussion, interviews are categorized here as unstructured, structured, and semistructured.

In **unstructured interviews**, the interviewer is given a great deal of freedom to direct the course of the interview. Unstructured interviews are conducted more like a normal conversation, and topics are pursued at the discretion of the interviewer. Unstructured interviews are particularly appropriate for exploratory or qualitative research studies where the researcher does not possess enough knowledge about the topic to develop questions in advance of data collection. The interviewer may start the interview with a broad opening statement like, "Tell me what it was like for you after your husband had his heart attack." Depending on how the spouse responds to this opening question, further questions are formulated. **Probes** are additional prompting questions that encourage the respondent to elaborate on the topic being discussed. When accurate comparisons between subjects are not a critical issue, unstructured interviews produce more in-depth information on subjects' beliefs and attitudes than can be obtained through any other data-gathering procedure.

Structured interviews involve asking the same questions, in the same order, and in the same manner of all respondents in a study. Structured interviews are most appropriate when straightforward factual information is desired. The interviewer uses an interview schedule that has been planned in detail because one of the main purposes of this type of interview is to produce data that can be compared across respondents. Interviewers must try to remain very objective during the interview and avoid unnecessary interactions with respondents.

Most interviews fall somewhere in between the structured and the unstructured types of interviews. In **semistructured interviews**, interviewers are generally required to ask a certain number of specific questions, but additional probes are allowed or even encouraged. Both closed-ended and open-ended questions are included in a semistructured interview. In this type of interview, data are gathered that can be compared across all respondents in the study. In addition, individualized data may be gathered that will provide depth and richness to the findings.

Interview Instruments

Data obtained in interviews are usually recorded on an instrument referred to as an interview schedule. The **interview schedule** contains a set of questions to be asked by the interviewer and space to record the respondents' answers.

Respondents' answers can be entered directly on the interview schedule or recorded on a separate coding sheet, such as one that can be tallied by the use of a computer or grading machine. Data obtained from an interview also can be recorded on audiotapes or videotapes. Some researchers believe the written recording of responses jeopardizes rapport and reduces the amount of eye contact that can be established between the interviewer and the interviewee. Also, through tape-recording devices, the total interview process can be captured, and the interviewer is free to observe the respondents' behavior. However, respondents may be reluctant to give permission to be taped. Written permission is required, and the permission form should indicate how the information will be used and how confidentiality will be maintained.

Telephone interviews involve the collection of data from subjects through the use of phone calls, rather than in face-to-face meetings. This data-collection method is a quick and inexpensive means of conducting interviews. Another advantage of telephone interviews is that the respondents' anonymity can be protected. However, several disadvantages are associated with telephone interviews. Many people have unlisted numbers. Some people have caller IDs installed on their phones; they may not answer the phone if they do not recognize the caller's phone number. Many people use cell phones, and their phone numbers cannot be obtained. Another disadvantage of phone interviews is that the interviewer cannot observe nonverbal responses of participants.

Interview Questions

The difficulty in developing good items for a questionnaire has been discussed. You might think that questions for an interview would be much simpler to construct because the interviewer will be present to explain any unclear items. This may be true to some extent, especially for unstructured interviews. Even items for an unstructured interview, however, must be given thoughtful consideration. Once the data are collected, it is too late to add, subtract, or alter questions.

Items must be clear, unambiguous, and short. When questions are long or complex, it may be difficult to ask them orally. If items cannot be simplified, it may be advantageous to print these questions on cards and have subjects read them before they respond. Of course, this procedure would require that subjects could read.

There are two basic categories of questions: open-ended and closed-ended. Both types of questions were described in the section on questionnaires.

Interviewer Training

The investigator of a study in which interviews will be conducted has the responsibility to provide training for all interviewers who will collect data during the study. The training must be quite rigorous. The research investigator should continue to work closely with the interviewers throughout the study.

During the training session(s), the researcher should provide interviewers with a description of the study and its purpose. General procedures are discussed, and the interview schedule is reviewed in detail. The purpose of each question is pointed out, and the meanings of all words are clarified. The process of recording information must be explicitly communicated. Special attention should be given to the use of probes, and any variations that will be allowed in the interview process should be discussed.

Interviewer training should be carried out in groups, so that all interviewers receive the same instructions. Role-playing of interviews helps the interviewer gain some appreciation of what the actual interviews will be like. Each interviewer should role-play both the interviewer's part and the respondent's part. By acting as a respondent, the interviewer gains a greater insight into the experience of potential study participants.

Timing and Setting for Interviews

Choosing the most appropriate time for conducting an interview can present a real challenge. If home interviews are conducted, the interviewer should try to determine when respondents would be at home. In past years, interviewers found many women at home during the daytime. This is not true today, as women have increased in the workforce.

If hospitalized patients are to be interviewed, the nurse researcher should become familiar with hospital routines and procedures to determine the most convenient times for interviews. Routines to be considered are patient care activities, visiting hours, and physicians' rounds.

Regardless of the setting, the interviewer should attempt to seek as much privacy as possible for the interview. The respondent and interviewer should be alone, and interruptions should be avoided. The television or radio should be turned off.

Interviewer Guidelines

Although each interview is unique, some guidelines are presented here that can be followed in most circumstances. The guidelines will be presented in three phases: before the interview, during the interview, and after the interview.

Before the interview is conducted, the interviewer should introduce herself or himself to the potential participants. The purpose of the study should be explained. Potential participants should be told how they were chosen and how the information will be used. Each person should be told how long the interview will last.

Once the person has agreed to the interview, the interviewer should ensure a comfortable interview atmosphere. Participants should be seated in a comfortable position or lying down, as in some hospital interviews. Unnecessary noises must be controlled as much as possible. The interviewer should use language that is clearly understood and should talk in a conversational tone. Participants should be informed that there are no right or wrong answers. No pressure should be applied for answers. Sensitive questions should be left until the end of the interview, when rapport may be more fully established.

After the interview has concluded, participants should be asked if they have any questions. Further explanations of the study may be made at this time. Common courtesy dictates that people be thanked for their participation in the study. In some studies, compensation may be provided. Anytime compensation is provided, the possibility of biased data must be considered. Finally, the interviewer should indicate how study participants may obtain the results of the study.

Influence of Interviewers on Respondents

In face-to-face interviews, the interviewer may have a great deal of influence on the outcome. In non-experimental research, this phenomenon is referred to as the Rosenthal effect (See Chapter 9). In experimental studies, it is referred to as the experimenter effect. Studies have shown that certain characteristics of the interviewer, such as ethnic background, age, gender, manner of speaking, and clothing, influence the answers provided by respondents. In telephone interviews, the interviewer's verbal mannerisms, such as tone of voice and dialect, may be a positive or a negative factor in soliciting cooperation from respondents.

First impressions are very important in face-to-face interviews. If an appointment has been made for the interview, punctuality should be maintained. Interviewers should be neat in appearance, courteous, friendly, and relaxed. Flashy jewelry should be avoided as well as any item that would identify the interviewer with some social group or organization. It is desirable for interviewers to possess similar demographic characteristics and dressing styles as the respondents.

Advantages of Interviews

1. Responses can be obtained from a wide range of individuals.
2. The response rate is high.
3. Most of the data obtained are usable.
4. In-depth responses can be obtained.
5. Nonverbal behavior and verbal mannerisms can be observed.

Disadvantages of Interviews

1. Training programs are needed for interviewers.
2. Interviews are time consuming and expensive.
3. Arrangements for interviews may be difficult to make.
4. Respondents may provide socially acceptable responses.
5. Respondents may be anxious because answers are being recorded.
6. Respondents may be influenced by the interviewers' characteristics.
7. Interviewers may misinterpret nonverbal behavior.

OBSERVATION METHODS

Although observations can be made through all of the senses, generally speaking, **observation research** is concerned with gathering data through visual observation. Nurses are well qualified to conduct observation research because they observe clients in health care settings every day. The researcher must decide what behaviors will be observed, who will observe the behaviors, what observational procedure will be used, and what type of relationship will exist between the observer and the subjects.

Determining Behaviors to Be Observed

The research question or study hypothesis should determine the behaviors that will be observed. Psychomotor skills can be evaluated, such as the ability of clients with diabetes to perform insulin injections. Personal habits, such as smoking and eating behaviors, might be of interest. Nonverbal communication patterns, such as body posture or facial expressions, are frequently observed. The types of observations that are of interest to nurse researchers are quite numerous.

Research Observers

If the researcher decides to use other people to collect or help collect data, training sessions are necessary. It is generally preferable to have more than one observer so that estimates of the reliability of the data can be made. Human error is quite likely to occur in visual observations. Interrater reliability is the degree to which two or more raters or observers assign the same rating or score to an observation.

Observation Procedures

The researcher must determine how and when observations will be made. The degree of structure of the observations and the period for gathering data must be considered.

Structured and Unstructured Observations

Observations may range from very structured to very unstructured observations. Most observations lie somewhere in between these two ends of the continuum. **Structured observations** are carried out when the researcher has prior knowledge about the phenomenon of interest. The data-collection tool is usually some kind of checklist. The expected behaviors of interest have been placed on the checklist. The observer needs to indicate only the frequency of occurrence of these behaviors. In **unstructured observations**, the researcher attempts to describe events or behaviors as they occur, with no preconceived ideas of what will be seen. This requires a high degree of concentration and attention by the observer. Frequently, a combination of structured and unstructured observations is used in research. The observation guide or instrument is designed with some preconceived categories identified, but the observer is also instructed to record any additional behaviors that may occur. This combination of structured and unstructured observations provides the quantitative and qualitative types of data that have become important to nurse researchers.

Event Sampling and Time Sampling

Observation research may be classified as either event sampling or time sampling. **Event sampling** involves observation of an entire event. **Time sampling** involves observations of events or behaviors during certain specified times. If a researcher were interested in determining the ability of nursing students to perform catheterization procedures correctly, event sampling probably would be most appropriate because the entire procedure would need to be observed. If the area of interest was territorial behaviors of families in intensive care unit waiting rooms, it might be more appropriate to conduct time-sampling observations. Some initial trial observation periods probably would be useful to help determine when observations should be made during the 24-hour day. Also, the researcher might select random times to observe family members.

Relationship Between Observer and Subjects

There are four ways to categorize observation research according to the relationship between the observer and the subjects: (a) nonparticipant observer (overt), (b) nonparticipant observer (covert), (c) participant observer (overt), and (d) participant observer (covert).

As a **nonparticipant observer (overt)**, the observer openly identifies that she or he is conducting research and provides subjects with information about the types of data that will be collected. This type of observer might wear a laboratory coat, carry a clipboard and pen, and be clearly identified as a researcher.

The **nonparticipant observer (covert)** is one who does not, before the beginning of data collection, identify herself or himself to the subjects who are being observed. Generally, this type of research is not ethical. Except for instances of public behavior, observation research should be conducted only when permission has been obtained from those who will be the subjects of the study or with the consent of appropriate persons, such as family members when children are being observed. Public behavior research might involve observations of the number of people who have their seat belts fastened while driving on the highway. This type of observation would be ethical.

Nurse researchers must not abuse their privilege as nurses by covertly observing the behaviors of clients. Researchers may contend that concealed observations are necessary because subjects will alter their behavior if they know they are being observed. People may initially change their behavior, but if an adjustment period is allowed, they will generally respond as they normally would.

Such devices as hidden cameras and one-way mirrors may be used as long as subjects are fully informed about them. Therapy groups are frequently observed, with the members' permission, by observers in an adjoining room that contains a one-way mirror.

In some research studies, the observer becomes involved in interactions with the participants. This interaction may be overt or covert. The **participant observer (overt)** becomes involved with participants openly and with the full awareness of those people who will be observed. Margaret Mead conducted many of her famous anthropological field research studies in this manner. She lived with the people, such as the Samoans, and observed their behaviors in their day-to-day living. The participant observer (overt) role is used frequently in qualitative research.

In contrast, as a **participant observer (covert)**, the observer interacts with the participants and observes their behavior without their knowledge. This type of observer might be disparagingly called a "plant" or "spy" by people who find out the real purpose of the researcher's behavior. There are very few situations in which this type of observation is ethical.

The Role of the Nurse Versus the Researcher

Nurse researchers frequently have difficulty in maintaining the role of researcher in observation studies. For example, consider the situation where a nurse researcher is sitting in a patient's room observing his or her behavior after some treatment procedure. Will the nurse researcher sit silently and continue with the planned observations if the patient seems to be in pain, if the room seems to be too warm, or if the bottle of intravenous fluid is almost empty? It is hoped not! The client's welfare should always take precedence over the gathering of research data. If the researcher, however, varies from the guidelines for the data-collection procedure, the accuracy of the data may be in question.

Sterling and Peterson (2005) wrote that it is challenging to be both a nurse and researcher. They discussed their family systems study in which parents accepted the nurses as researchers, but viewed the researchers *first* as nurses. The researchers were asked advice about schools, the children's health status, and the health care delivery system.

PHYSIOLOGICAL MEASURES

Physiological measures involve the collection of physical data from subjects. These types of measures are generally more objective and accurate than many of the other data-collection methods. It is much more difficult for subjects to provide biased data on physiological measures, intentionally or unintentionally, than on self-report measures.

One of the greatest advantages of physiological measures is their precision and accuracy. One of the greatest disadvantages is that special expertise may be necessary to use some of these devices. Another disadvantage is that the presence of certain data-collection instruments may adversely influence the subjects. For example, the process of applying the equipment to measure a person's blood pressure may, in fact, cause the blood pressure readings to be elevated.

In the past, only a small percentage of nursing studies have examined physiological variables. A review of the nursing research literature uncovered many studies in which psychosocial variables were the *only* variables studied.

Although the inclusion of physiological variables is still not very common in nursing research studies, some studies do report physiological data in their findings. In a study of physiological correlates of HIV- related fatigue (Barroso, Pence, Salahuddin, Harmon, & Leserman, 2008), blood was drawn to measure several physiological variables, including hepatic function, thyroid function, HIV viral load, gonadal function, and serum cortisol. Facial expression, crying duration, heart rate, and oxygen saturation were the physiological variables examined in a study of oral sucrose given to reduce procedural pain in newborn infants (Harrison, Loughnan, Manias, Gordon, & Johnston, 2009). The incidences of aspiration and pneumonia were compared between mechanically ventilated patients on tube feedings who received usual care and those who received a three-pronged intervention to reduce aspiration (Metheny, Davis-Jackson, & Stewart, 2010).

Increasing numbers of published studies are reporting data that have been collected from both physiological measures and self-report measures. The use of multiple data-collection instruments provides a more valid measure of a variable than when only one of these types of instruments is employed.

ATTITUDE SCALES

Attitude scales are self-report data-collection instruments that ask respondents to report their attitudes or feelings on a continuum. Attitude scales are composed of a number of related items, and respondents are given a score after the item responses are totaled. Respondents' attitudes may be compared by examining the scores that are obtained for each person or each group. The most commonly used attitude scales are the Likert scale and the semantic differential scale.

Likert Scales

The **Likert scale** was named after its developer, Rensis Likert. These scales usually contain five or seven responses for each item, ranging from strongly agree to strongly disagree. Figure 13–1 provides an example of a Likert scale.

Some researchers prefer to eliminate the "uncertain" category and force respondents into some form of agreement or disagreement with the items. When the "uncertain" option is eliminated, however, respondents may be forced to select answers that are really not their choice.

An approximately equal number of positively and negatively worded items should be included on a Likert instrument. Respondents are then required to read each question carefully. They will not be able to rapidly complete an instrument by checking *one* category of responses all the way through the instrument.

Nursing Diagnosis Questionnaire

Please read the following items and indicate your agreement or disagreement by checking the appropriate category.

SD = Strongly disagree
 D = Disagree
 U = Uncertain
 A = Agree
SA = Strongly agree

	SD	D	U	A	SA
1. Nursing diagnoses should be written on all nursing care plans.	_____	_____	_____	_____	_____
2. The use of nursing diagnoses enables nurses to be autonomous health care professionals.	_____	_____	_____	_____	_____
3. The medical diagnosis is more important in determining clients' health care needs than is the nursing diagnosis.	_____	_____	_____	_____	_____
4. Nursing care should be based on the nursing diagnosis.	_____	_____	_____	_____	_____
5. Nurses waste valuable time in trying to formulate nursing diagnoses.	_____	_____	_____	_____	_____
6. The term *nursing* diagnosis is a popular phrase that will soon become forgotten.	_____	_____	_____	_____	_____

▶ FIGURE 13–1   Example of a Likert scale

If five responses are used, scores on each item generally range from 1 to 5. A score of 1 is usually given to "strongly disagree," 2 to "disagree," 3 to "uncertain," 4 to "agree," and, finally, 5 to "strongly agree." Negatively worded items are reverse scored: "Strongly disagree" responses to negative items would receive a score of 5, rather than 1. If 20 items were included on an instrument, the total score could vary from 20 to 100.

Although data from a Likert scale are generally at the ordinal level of measurement, some statistical texts indicate that arithmetic operations may be performed with this type of data and, therefore, the more powerful parametric statistical tests may be used in analyzing the data (see Chapter 15). An article in *Nursing Research* (Wang, Yu, Wang, & Huang, 1999) discussed the pros and cons of treating ordinal data as interval data.

Likert Scale

A 7-point Likert scale was used by Sutton and Raines (2010) to measure health-related quality of life following a surgical weight loss intervention. The scale measures eight dimensions of health: physical functioning, role physical, bodily pain, general health, vitality, social functioning, role emotional, and mental health.

Semantic Differential Scales

Although not as commonly used as the Likert scale, the semantic differential is a useful attitude scale for nurse researchers. The **semantic differential** asks subjects to indicate their position or attitude about some concept along a continuum between two adjectives or phrases that are presented in relation to the concept being measured. The technique was developed by Osgood, Suci, and Tannenbaum (1957) to measure the psychological meaning of concepts. They used the term *semantic differential* to indicate that the difference in subjects' attitudes could be compared by examining their responses in "semantic space" or attitudinal space.

Study participants usually are asked to describe or evaluate a particular situation or experience. This technique also may be used to evaluate a setting, a person, a group, or an educational course. The positions along the continuum or scale are assigned numerical values. The number of positions on the continuum varies from five to nine, with seven being used commonly. Scores are derived much the same way as in the Likert procedure. Figure 13–2 presents an example of a semantic differential scale.

Evaluation of Clinical Instructor

Each item below concerns characteristics of instructors. Words are presented in pairs and represent opposite characteristics. Please place a (✓) above the line on the scale at the place which you believe comes the closest to describing your evaluation of the instructor.

Example:
Kind _____ ✓ _____ _____ _____ _____ _____ Unkind

1. Friendly _____ _____ _____ _____ _____ _____ Unfriendly
2. Sensitive _____ _____ _____ _____ _____ _____ Insensitive
3. Praises _____ _____ _____ _____ _____ _____ Criticizes
4. Caring _____ _____ _____ _____ _____ _____ Uncaring
5. Flexible _____ _____ _____ _____ _____ _____ Inflexible
6. Helpful _____ _____ _____ _____ _____ _____ Unhelpful

▶ FIGURE 13–2   Example of a semantic differential scale

The semantic differential scale is generally easier for subjects to complete than a Likert scale. Subjects, however, may not understand the adjectives that are used on a semantic differential scale or become bored with the format of the items and select the middle scale position throughout the entire instrument.

Semantic Differential

Nursing students in their first and fourth years of a baccalaureate program were measured on their knowledge and attitudes toward older adults following the introduction of a context-based (CBL) curriculum or a traditional, lecture-based curriculum (Williams, Anderson, & Day, 2007). The participants' attitudes toward aging were measured using the Aging Semantic Differential, which consisted of 32 pairs of bipolar adjectives describing attributes or characteristics thought to be equally applicable to all ages.

PSYCHOLOGICAL TESTS

Researchers have devised many methods to assess the personality characteristics of people. Personality inventories and projective techniques are two of these methods.

Personality Inventories

Personality inventories are self-report measures used to assess the differences in personality traits, needs, or values of people. These inventories seek information about a person by asking questions or requesting responses to statements that are presented. Scores are then derived for each person for the trait being measured. Many of the personality inventories have preprinted scoring guides that allow comparisons between subjects and also allow comparisons with a "norm" or "average" group. Because these devices are self-reports, they are accurate to the extent that subjects respond honestly to the items.

Some of the more commonly used personality inventories are the Minnesota Multiphasic Personality Inventory (MMPI), Edwards Personal Preference Schedule (EPPS), and Sixteen Personality Factor Questionnaire (16 PF). The MMPI contains 550 affirmative statements that require an answer of True, False, or Cannot Say. This test is composed of 10 subdivisions, including areas such as depression, paranoia, and hysteria. The MMPI has been used with people considered normal and those with psychological problems. The EPPS contains 15 scales that measure concepts such as autonomy and dominance. The 16 PF measures personality dimensions such as reserved versus outgoing, practical versus imaginative, and relaxed versus tense.

Projective Technique

One of the criticisms of self-report psychological measures is that they may elicit socially acceptable answers or answers desired by the researcher rather than the true feelings or attitudes of the subjects. A data-collection method believed to be more accurate in gathering psychological data is the projective method. In a **projective technique**, a respondent is presented with stimuli designed to be ambiguous or to have no definite meaning. Then, the person is asked to describe the stimuli or to tell what the stimuli appear to represent. The responses reflect the internal feelings of the subjects that are projected onto the external stimuli.

Probably the most famous of all the projective measures is the Rorschach Inkblot Test. Respondents are presented with cards that show designs, which are actually inkblots rather than true pictures or drawings. One person might interpret a card to be two figures dancing; another might describe the same scene as two people fighting. Of course, only specialists should interpret this type of data.

Another commonly used projective test is the Thematic Apperception Test (TAT). The TAT consists of a set of pictures, and individuals are asked to tell a story relating what they think is happening in the pictures. Projective tests are particularly useful with small children because of their limited vocabularies. Children may be given dolls and asked to arrange the dolls in a particular setting that is provided by the researcher. Children also may be given finger paint, crayons, or clay to use in telling a story.

Projective Techniques

A study of 7- to12-year-old Korean and Korean American children used a projective technique to describe their emotional reactions to illness and hospitalization (Park, Foster & Cheng, 2009). The children were presented with vignettes about being sick, going to the doctor, and being hospitalized. When responding to the vignettes, the children expressed stressful emotions through words that indicated being scared, worried, nervous, frightened, and afraid.

Q SORT

The **Q sort**, also called Q methodology, is a means of obtaining data in which subjects sort statements into categories according to their attitudes toward, or rating of, the statements. Q sorts may be used to "identify attitudes, perceptions, feelings, and values as well as explore life experiences such as stress, self-esteem, body image, and satisfaction" (Akhtar-Danesh, Baumann, & Cordingley, 2008, p. 759). Participants receive cards or pieces of paper with a number of words or statements written on them. The number of items the participants are to place into each category or pile is predetermined by the researcher. This forced-choice arrangement usually calls for piles to be distributed in the form of a bell-shaped curve. If 100 items were being used, the distribution might look like this:

$$1 \quad 4 \quad 11 \quad 21 \quad 26 \quad 21 \quad 11 \quad 4 \quad 1$$

The respondents are asked to arrange the items from left to right in front of them according to their attitude toward or rating of the items. The first pile should contain the item about which the person has the most positive attitude or strongest belief about its importance to the topic of interest; the last pile on the right should contain the item about which the person has the most negative attitude or weakest belief about the item's importance. The other piles will contain items of varying intensity of attitudes or beliefs. This type of data-collection procedure may present a difficult task for respondents. Therefore, clear instructions must be provided.

Q Sort

Dziopa and Ahern (2009) were interested in the different ways in which mental health nurses develop therapeutic relationships with their patients. A total of 140 attributes were identified as important to the formation of a relationship. Through a Q sort, these attributes led to the identification of three clusters of mental health nurses: "Equal Partner," "Senior Partner," and "Protective Partner."

DELPHI TECHNIQUE

The term **Delphi technique** is used to describe a data-collection technique that employs several rounds of questions to seek a consensus on a particular topic from a group of experts. The technique received its name from the famous Greek oracle at Delphi. As you may remember, the ancient Greeks sought answers to important questions from the deities. The purpose of this data-collection method is to obtain group consensus from the panel of experts without bringing this group together in a face-to-face meeting. This type of procedure is appropriate to examine the opinions, beliefs, or future predictions of knowledgeable people on some special topic of interest.

A classic Delphi study was conducted by Lindeman (1975). The purpose of this study was to determine priorities for future clinical nursing research. Of the 433 leaders in nursing originally contacted, 341 experts responded to all four rounds of questionnaires. The results indicated that the most important priority for clinical nursing research was the development of valid and reliable indicators of quality nursing care. Other important areas were identified as (1) effective ways to decrease the psychological stress experienced by patients, (2) means of enhancing the quality of life for the aged, and (3) interventions to manage pain.

Delphi

A Delphi study was conducted to identify and gain consensus benchmarks for effective primary care-based nursing services for adults with depression (McIlrath, Keeney, McKenna, & McLaughlin, 2010). Three rounds of a survey tool were completed by 67 multi-professional experts in the United Kingdom. Consensus was achieved on 73 benchmarks: 45 were related to structures, 18 to processes, and 10 to outcomes.

VISUAL ANALOGUE SCALE

The **visual analogue scale** (VAS) presents subjects with a straight line drawn on a piece of paper. The line is anchored on each end by words or short phrases that represent the extremes of some phenomenon, such as pain. Subjects are asked to make a mark on the line at the point that corresponds to their experience of the phenomenon. Frequently, the line is 100 mm in length, which simulates a 0 to 100 rating scale. From their review of the literature, Huang, Wilkie, and Berry (1996) concluded that the VAS is a "simple, reliable, reproducible, valid, and sensitive tool" (p. 370).

Note: If you are trying to photocopy a VAS for use in a study, the length of the line may change slightly (lengthen) during the photocopying process and you will not end up with a 100-mm line. The VAS line may be drawn either horizontally or vertically on the paper. Some authors have suggested that the vertical scale is easier for subjects to use (Flaherty, 1996). It appears to be universally recognized that the bottom of a vertical scale is low, and the top of a vertical scale is high. On the other hand, not all cultural groups view the far left on a horizontal scale as indicating a low score and the far right as indicating a high score.

The VAS is being used with increasing frequency in nursing research studies. It has been found to be particularly useful with patients who are experiencing discomfort, such as nausea, pain, fatigue, or shortness of breath.

Visual Analogue Scale

A comparison of patient satisfaction with nurse practitioner and physician services was conducted using a visual analog scale (Guzik, Menzel, Fitzpatrick, & McNulty, 2009). The results showed no significant difference in overall patient satisfaction with the services provided by these two groups of health care providers.

PREEXISTING DATA

Nurse researchers have available a wealth of data that may be used for research. As a data-collection method, **preexisting data** involves the use of existing information that may not have been collected for research purposes. Sources of existing data include records from agencies and organizations such as hospitals and the U.S. government.

Many large databases are available that are valuable to nurse researchers. Secondary analysis of these data sets can be the focus of an investigator's entire research program (Lacey & Hughes, 2007). Large data sets are available from federal and state agencies and associations for a small fee, or even for free. These large data sets offer researchers the opportunity to test new hypotheses or answer research questions.

The Agency for Healthcare Research and Quality (AHRQ) is the health services arm of the U.S. Department of Health and Human Services (HHS). It is the nation's leading federal agency for research on health quality, costs, outcomes, and patient safety. This agency sponsors the Healthcare Cost & Utilization Project (HCUP). HCUP has put together databases of patient-level information, which have been gathered from state organizations, hospital associations, private data organizations, and the Federal government. For more information visit http://ahrq.gov/.

There are many local sources of data for nurse researchers. These include local public health departments, churches, and professional organizations. Personal documents, such as diaries and letters, may be examined, as well as almanacs and professional journals.

Diaries

Twenty heart failure (HF) patients took part in a tailored, one-on-one educational intervention (White, Howie-Esquivel, & Caldwell, 2010). After the intervention, diaries were used to measure adherence to daily weight monitoring. Diary data were collected for 3 months. Of the 16 participants who returned diaries for analysis, the mean adherence score for weight monitoring was 79.4%. The researchers concluded that diaries offer the opportunity for patients to engage in self-care practices.

CRITIQUING DATA-COLLECTION METHODS

In Chapter 12, some general critiquing guidelines were presented concerning the data-collection process reported in a research report. The specific data-collection methods used also need to be critiqued. Box 13–1 presents some general guidelines for critiquing data-collection methods and some specific questions to ask about questionnaires and interviews.

If a questionnaire was used in a study, sufficient information should be provided to enable the reader to determine if the tool was appropriate for use in the study. The manner in which the questionnaire was developed, the reliability and validity of the instrument, the number of questions, how the instrument was scored, and the range of possible scores should be presented.

When an interview has been used, the reader needs information about how long the interviews took, who conducted the interviews, and how the interviewers were trained.

Observation research requires that the reader be able to determine how observations were made, who made the observations, and how data were recorded. Were subjects aware that they were being observed?

If physiological instruments were used, the accuracy of these data-collection measures needs to be addressed. Does it appear that the researcher had the expertise to use these instruments?

The researcher may have used a psychological data-collection method, such as an attitude scale or a personality test. The reader will need to determine the appropriateness of these instruments and the qualifications of the researcher to use them.

The reader may not be familiar with data-collection methods such as the Delphi technique or Q sort that are mentioned in research articles. It would be advisable to consult research textbooks to learn more about the data-collection methods cited in research reports.

Box 13–1. Guidelines for Critiquing Data-Collection Methods

General Criteria

1. Were the data-collection methods described thoroughly?
2. Were the data-collection methods appropriate to test the research hypotheses or answer the research questions?
3. Was a self-report or psychological method used when a physiological method might have gathered more valid data?
4. How many methods were used to collect data? If only one method was used, would the study have benefited from more than one method?

Questionnaires

1. Was information provided on the number of questions, the length of the questionnaire, and how long it would take to complete the questionnaire?
2. Was the response rate provided for the return of the questionnaires?
3. Were sampling biases discussed?
4. Was anonymity or confidentiality assured?

Interviews

1. Was information provided on how long the interview would take?
2. Was information provided about training for the interviewers?
3. Was confidentiality assured?

Other Methods

1. Was the specific method identified (e.g., semantic differential)?
2. Was the rationale for use of the method presented?
3. Was the instrument described in detail?
4. Was the scoring method clearly discussed?

SUMMARY

A **questionnaire** is a paper-and-pencil self-report instrument. Factors to consider in constructing questionnaires are overall appearance, language and reading level, length of questionnaire and questions, wording of questions, types of questions, and placement of questions.

Ambiguous questions contain words that have more than one meaning. **Double-barreled questions** ask two questions in one. **Demographic questions** concern subject characteristics. These subject characteristics are called **demographic**

variables or **attribute variables**. **Closed-ended questions** are very structured, and respondents are asked to choose from given alternatives. The term **collectively exhaustive categories** indicates that a category is provided for every possible answer. **Mutually exclusive categories** are categories that are uniquely distinct; no overlap occurs between categories. **Open-ended questions** enable respondents to answer questions in their own words. **Contingency questions** are items that are relevant for some respondents and not for others. **Filler questions** are items in which the researcher has no direct interest but are included on a questionnaire to reduce the emphasis on the specific purpose of other questions.

A cover letter should accompany all mailed questionnaires. Questionnaires may be distributed in a one-to-one contact, through group administration, through a mailing system, or through the Internet. Response rates of questionnaires are frequently low. There are many advantages and disadvantages in using questionnaires as a method of data collection.

An **interview** is a data-collection method in which an interviewer obtains responses from a subject in a face-to-face meeting or from **telephone interviews**. Data are recorded on an **interview schedule** or may be tape recorded. **Unstructured interviews** contain open-ended questions and are appropriate for exploratory studies in which the researcher possesses little knowledge of the study topic. **Probes** are additional prompting questions that encourage the respondent to elaborate on a certain topic. **Structured interviews** are made up of closed-ended questions and are generally used to obtain straightforward factual information. **Semistructured interviews** contain both open-ended and closed-ended questions. The majority of interviews are of the semistructured type.

Observation research gathers data through visual observations. In **structured observations**, the expected behaviors are predetermined, and the frequency of occurrence is noted during data collection. In **unstructured observations**, the researcher describes events or behaviors as they occur, with no preconceived ideas of what will be seen. **Event sampling** involves observation of an entire event, whereas **time sampling** involves observation of events or behaviors during certain specified times.

As a **nonparticipant observer (overt)**, the observer openly identifies that research is being conducted. The **nonparticipant observer (covert)** does not identify herself or himself as a researcher. This type of observation is quite likely to be unethical. The **participant observer (overt)** becomes involved with participants openly and with the full awareness of those who will be observed in their natural settings. In contrast, the **participant observer (covert)** interacts with individuals and observes their behavior without their knowledge. Again, this type of observation may be unethical.

Physiological measures involve the collection of physical data from study participants. These measures are generally quite accurate.

Attitude scales ask respondents to report their attitudes or feelings on a continuum. The scales are composed of a number of related items, and respondents are given a score after the item responses are totaled. The **Likert scale** and the **semantic differential** are two commonly used attitude scales.

Personality inventories are self-report measures that seek information about someone's personality traits, needs, or values by requesting responses to statements that are presented.

In a **projective technique**, individuals are presented with stimuli designed to be ambiguous. Responses reflect internal feelings of the subjects that are projected on the external stimuli.

When a **Q sort** is used, participants are asked to sort statements into categories according to their attitudes toward, or rating of, the statements. The statements are written on cards or pieces of paper, and the participants are asked to arrange the items in piles according to the intensity of their attitudes or beliefs about the items.

A **Delphi technique** uses several rounds of questionnaires to seek consensus on a particular topic from a group of experts. This procedure is appropriate for examining the opinions, beliefs, or future predictions of knowledgeable people on a topic of interest.

The **visual analogue scale** (VAS) presents subjects with a straight line drawn on a piece of paper. Respondents are asked to make a mark on the line at the point that corresponds to their experience of pain, for example. The line may be drawn either horizontally or vertically.

Preexisting data are data from records of agencies or organizations such as hospitals, the U.S. government, and public health departments. Large data sets are available to nurse researchers for secondary analysis. Also, diaries, letters, almanacs, and professional journals may be examined.

NURSING RESEARCH ON THE WEB

For additional online resources, research activities, and exercises, go to **www.mynursingkit.com.** Select Chapter 13 from the drop-down menu.

GET INVOLVED ACTIVITIES

1. Read through research articles until you find at least three that have used some data-collection method other than a questionnaire. List these different data-collection methods.

2. Divide into groups. Design a question to obtain marital status and one to obtain educational level. You will find that both of these variables present a challenge when trying to choose categories that are mutually exclusive and collectively exhaustive.

3. Divide into pairs. One person will role-play an interviewer and the other person will role-play the respondent. The interviewer will ask the respondent to provide information on what she or he ate during the last week. Switch roles. The interviewer will ask the respondent to describe the last movie that he or she saw. This exercise ideally will help you experience some of the feelings that accompany these two roles in research.

4. Locate an abstract picture or draw an abstract picture. Ask five classmates or colleagues, out of earshot of each other, to tell what the picture means to them. Compare their responses to gain a better understanding of the projective technique.

5. From a bowl with slips of paper naming each of the data-collection methods listed in this chapter, draw one method and develop an idea for a study in which this method would be used.

SELF-TEST

Examine the following question and determine if any errors exist in the construction of the question:

1. What is your age category?
   _____ 6–20
   _____ 20–25
   _____ 25–30
   _____ 30 and older

2. What is your highest educational level?
   _____ completed grade school
   _____ eighth grade to twelfth grade
   _____ high school graduate
   _____ college graduate

Circle the letter before the *best* answer.

3. Which of the following is an *advantage* of an interview method of data collection versus a questionnaire?
   A. Data are less expensive to obtain.
   B. The collected data tend to be more complete.
   C. Data collectors do not need to be trained.
   D. Data may be collected more easily from a widespread geographical area.

4. A researcher wants to determine future priorities for research in psychiatric nursing. The participants will be clinical specialists in psychiatric nursing. Which of the following data-collection methods would probably be used?
   A. projective technique
   B. observation method
   C. delphi technique
   D. semantic differential

5. Which of the following data-collection methods is *most* likely to prevent participants from providing socially acceptable responses to questions?
   A. attitude scale
   B. projective technique
   C. self-report questionnaire
   D. interview

Choose the letter of the data-collection method that matches the method described in statements 6 to 10.
   A. Semantic differential
   B. Projective technique
   C. Q sort
   D. Likert scale
   E. Delphi

_____ 6. Presents statements to which respondents indicate level of agreement or disagreement along a continuum.

_____ 7. Contains sets of bipolar adjectives; asks respondents to select a point on a scale between two adjectives.

_____ 8. Participants are asked to place statements into categories according to their attitudes toward or rating of the statements.

_____ 9. Subjects are asked to look at pictures and tell what meaning the pictures have for them.

_____ 10. Leaders in critical care nursing are asked to identify research priorities for critical care nursing in the next 5 years.

REFERENCES

Akhtar-Danesh, M., Baumann, A., & Cordingley, L. (2008). Q-methodology in nursing research. *Western Journal of Nursing Research, 30*, 759–773. doi: 10.1177/0193945907312979

Baernholdt, M., & Clarke, S. P. (2006). Internet research in an international context. *Applied Nursing Research, 19*, 48–50.

Barroso, J., Pence, B. W., Salahuddin, N., Harmon, J. L., & Leserman, J. (2008). Physiological correlates of HIV-related fatigue. *Clinical Nursing Research, 17*, 5–9. doi: 10.1177/1054773807311382

Curtis, E. A., & Redmond, R. A. (2009). Survey postal questionnaire: Optimizing response and dealing with non-response. *Nurse Researcher, 16*, 76–87.

Dziopa, & Ahern, K. (2009). Three different ways mental health nurses develop quality therapeutic relationships. *Issues in Mental Health Nursing, 30*, 14–22.

Flaherty, S. A. (1996). Pain measurement tools for clinical practice and research. *Journal of the American Association of Nurse Anesthetists, 64*, 39.

Freda, M. C. (2005). The readability of American Academy of Pediatrics patient education brochures. *Journal of Pediatric Healthcare, 19*, 151–156.

Guzik, A., Menzel, N. N., Fitzpatrick, J., & McNulty, R. (2009). Patient satisfaction with nurse practitioner and physician services in the occupational health setting. *AAOHN Journal, 57*, 191–197.

Harrison, D., Loughnan, P., Manias, E., Gordon, I., & Johnston, L. (2009). Repeated doses of sucrose in infants continue to reduce procedural pain during prolonged hospitalizations. *Nursing Research, 58*, 427–434.

Hart, A. M., Brennan, C. W., Sym, D., & Larson, E. (2009). The impact of personalized prenotification on response rates to an electronic survey. *Western Journal of Nursing Research, 31*, 17–23.

Huang, H., Wilkie, D. J., & Berry, D. L. (1996). Use of a computerized digitizer to score and enter visual analogue scale data. *Nursing Research, 45*, 370–372.

Kaiser, B. L., Brown, R. L., & Baumann, L. C. (2010). Perceived influences on physical activity and diet in low-income adults from two rural counties. *Nursing Research, 59*, 67–75.

Kalisch, B. J., Lee, H., & Salas, E. (2010). The development and testing of the nursing teamwork survey. *Nursing Research, 59*, 42–50.

Lacey, S., & Hughes, R. G. (2007). Is power everything? What can we learn from large data sets. *Applied Nursing Research, 20*, 50–53. doi: 10.1016/j.apnr.2006.10.007

Lindeman, C. (1975). Delphi survey of priorities in clinical nursing research. *Nursing Research, 24*, 434–441.

McIlrath, C., Keeney, S., McKenna, H., & McLaughlin, D. (2010). Benchmarks for effective primary case-based nursing services for adults with depression: A Delphi study. *Journal of Advanced Nursing, 66*, 269–281.

Metheny, N. A., Davis-Jackson, J., & Stewart, B. J. (2010). Effectiveness of an aspiration risk-reduction protocol. *Nursing Research, 59*, 18–25.

Northam, S., Yarbrough, S., Haas, B., & Duke, G. (2010). Journal editor survey information to help authors publish. *Nurse Educator, 35*, 29–36.

Oppenheim, A. (1966). *Questionnaire design and attitude measurement.* New York: Basic Books.

Osgood, C., Suci, G., & Tannenbaum, P. (1957). *The measurement of meaning.* Urbana: University of Illinois Press.

Park, J., Foster, R., & Cheng, S. (2009). Language used by Korean and Korean American children to describe emotional reactions to illness and hospitalization. *Journal of Transcultural Nursing, 20*, 176–186.

Schilling, L. S., Dixon, J. K., Knafl, K. A., Lynn, M. R., Murphy, K., Dumser, S., & Grey, M. (2009). A new self-report measure of self-management of type I diabetes for adolescents. *Nursing Research, 58*, 228–236.

Sterling, Y. M., & Peterson, J. W. (2005). Lessons learned from a longitudinal qualitative family systems study. *Applied Nursing Research, 18*, 44–49.

Sutton, D., & Raines, D. A. (2010). Health-related quality of life following a surgical weight loss intervention. *Applied Nursing Research, 23*, 52–56.

Walker, J., Pepa, C., & Gerard, P. S. (2010). Assessing the health literacy levels of patients using selected hospital services. *Clinical Nurse Specialist, 24*, 31–37.

Wang, S., Yu, M., Wang, C., & Huang, C. (1999). Bridging the gap between the pros and cons in treating ordinal scales as interval scales from an analysis point of view. *Nursing Research, 48*, 226–229.

White, M. M., Howie-Esquivel, J., Caldwell, M. A. (2010). Improving heart failure symptom recognition: A diary analysis. *The Journal of Cardiovascular Nursing, 25*, 7–12.

Williams, B., Anderson, M. C., & Day, R. (2007). Undergraduate nursing students' knowledge of and attitudes toward aging: Comparison of context-based learning and a traditional program. *Journal of Nursing Education, 46*, 115–120.

Wilson, M. (2009). Readability and patient education materials used for low-income populations. *Clinical Nurse Specialist, 33*, 33–39.

Descriptive Statistics

OUTLINE

OBJECTIVES

On completion of this chapter, you will be prepared to:

1. Recognize statistical symbols for population parameters and sample statistics
2. Identify the two broad classifications of statistics
3. Discuss four major groups of descriptive statistics
4. Compare categories within each of the four major groups of descriptive statistics
5. Determine appropriate descriptive statistics to use in presenting selected data
6. Construct graphs to present selected descriptive statistics
7. Critique descriptive statistics presented in research reports

NEW TERMS DEFINED IN THIS CHAPTER

I'm sure that statistics is your favorite subject. Right? You have just been waiting to read this chapter and the next one on statistics. However, if you are one of those people who try to avoid anything involving mathematics, rest assured that only minimal math skills are necessary to understand the material here. According to Norwood (2000), all that is needed is basic arithmetic and logical thinking skills. Does that make you feel better? Rather than understanding each of the various statistical tests, it is much more important that you are familiar with both the type of data you have collected or someone else has collected and the types of statistical tests that might be appropriate for these data. Also, you really do not need to know how to calculate statistics. In this age of computers, it is quite unlikely you will ever have to hand compute any statistics.

The word *statistics* is derived from the Latin word for "state." In the mid-18th century, the term was used in a political context to describe the resources of states and kingdoms. The term is used much more broadly today, and statistics are used by many disciplines. Statistics, as a singular noun, is a branch of knowledge used to summarize and present numerical data. As a plural noun, statistics are numerical characteristics of samples. According to Polit and Beck (2008), statistical procedures allow the researcher to " organize, interpret, and communicate numeric information" (p. 556).

This chapter and the next one present a review of statistical concepts. If you need more information, many statistics textbooks are available. One that may be of particular interest to you is *Statistics for the Terrified* by G. Kranzler, Moursand, and J. Kranzler (2006) (see Amazon.com for more information). Some free statistical textbooks can now be found online. As of July 2010, here are the Web addresses of three of these books:

http://onlinestatbook.com/
http://davidmlane.com/hyperstat/
http://statsoft.com/textbook/esc1/

STATISTICAL SYMBOLS

When discussing numerical characteristics of populations, the word **parameters** is used. When discussing numerical characteristics of samples, the term **statistics** is used. An easy way to recall this information is to remember that population and parameter both begin with a *p*, and sample and statistics both begin with an *s*. You, therefore, have population *parameters* and sample *statistics*. Different symbols are used to depict parameters and statistics.

Greek letters such as mu (µ) are used to designate population parameters; English letters such as s and SD are used to indicate sample statistics. When you encounter these symbols in descriptions of research studies and in tables that accompany studies, you will be able quickly to determine which type of data is being reported.

	Population Symbols	**Sample Symbols**
Mean	μ	$\overline{X}$
Standard deviation	σ	s, SD
Variance	σ^2	s^2, SD^2

In many research articles, words are used instead of symbols. A recent review of the literature revealed that words and letters rather than symbols are used frequently to depict both population parameters and sample statistics. For example, in reviewing some recent research articles, the word "mean" or "average" and the letter "M" were found more frequently than the $\overline{X}$ to depict the mean.

CLASSIFICATIONS OF STATISTICS

There are two broad classifications of statistics—descriptive and inferential. **Descriptive statistics**, very simply defined, are those statistics that organize and summarize numerical data gathered from samples. **Inferential statistics** are concerned with populations and use sample data to make an "inference" about a population. Inferential statistics help the researcher determine if the difference found between two groups, such as an experimental and a control group, is a real difference or only a chance difference that occurred because an unrepresentative sample was chosen from the population. Any time that sample data are used to estimate the characteristics of a population, there is a chance the estimate will be inaccurate. Inferential statistics are used to determine the likelihood that the sample chosen for a study is actually representative of the population.

DESCRIPTIVE STATISTICS

Descriptive statistics allow the researcher to examine the characteristics, behaviors, and experiences of study participants (Polit, 1996). There are many different ways to categorize descriptive statistics. In this book, they are divided into four classifications: (a) measures to condense data, (b) measures of central tendency, (c) measures of variability, and (d) measures of relationships.

Measures to Condense Data

When the researcher is faced with analyzing a large amount of data, some method is needed to condense the data into a more understandable form. **Measures to condense data** are statistics used to summarize and condense data. Some of the various ways to condense or summarize the data include frequency distributions, graphic presentations, and percentages.

Frequency Distributions

One of the simplest ways to present data is through frequency distributions. Frequencies are obtained by counting the occurrence of values or scores represented in the data. Frequency distributions are appropriate for reporting all level of data (nominal, ordinal, interval, and ratio). In a **frequency distribution**, all values or scores are listed, and the number of times each one appears is recorded. Values may be listed from highest to lowest or from lowest to highest.

TABLE 14–1 Frequency Distribution of Respiration Rates

Respiration	Rate Tallies	Frequency
14	///	3
15	//	2
16	₩	5
17	////	4
18	///	3
19	//	2
20	/	1
		20

It is helpful to use the familiar slash method of recording frequencies: Four vertical lines are listed for the first four occurrences of a score, and a slash line is used to indicate the fifth occurrence (₩). This procedure is repeated until all scores are recorded.

Frequency distributions present useful summaries of data. For example, the reader will get a much clearer picture of students' scores on a test or the pulse rates of a group of patients.

If the range of scores in a frequency distribution is small, say less than 20, each score may be listed individually, as in Table 14–1. When the range of scores is large, it may be helpful to group the scores before counting frequencies, as is seen in Table 14–2.

Groups of scores in a frequency distribution are called **class intervals**. These intervals are arbitrarily chosen to depict the data in the most meaningful way. Class intervals may be in units of 3, 5, 10, and so forth. The intervals must be exhaustive (include all possible values) and mutually exclusive (no overlapping of categories). Of course, when data are grouped, some information is lost. Consider the following examples:

EXAMPLE A

Score	Frequency
20	3
21	5
22	6
	14

EXAMPLE B

Score	Frequency
20–22	14

TABLE 14–2 Frequency Distribution of Pulse Rates

Pulse Rate	Tallies	Frequency
56–60	//	2
61–65	//	2
66–70	₩	5
71–75	₩ //	7
76–80	₩ ///	8
81–85	₩ ₩	10
86–90	₩ //	7
91–95	₩	5
96–100	////	4
		50

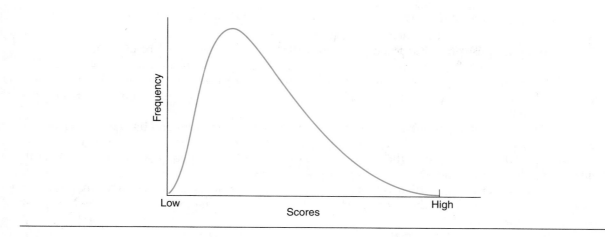

▶ FIGURE 14–1   Positively skewed distribution

In example A, you can determine exactly how many people received a score of 20, 21, or 22. In example B, you are able to determine only that 14 people scored between 20 and 22. This loss of information is the price that is paid when data are summarized into groups or classes.

Frequency distributions may be described according to their shape. Distribution shapes may be characterized as either symmetrical or nonsymmetrical. **Symmetrical distributions** are those in which both halves of the distribution are the same. If the left half of the distribution were folded over the right half, the two halves would match. **Nonsymmetrical distributions**, also called **skewed**, are those in which the distribution has an off-center peak. If the tail of the distribution points to the right (Figure 14–1), the distribution is said to be **positively skewed**; if the tail points to the left (Figure 14–2), the distribution is said to be **negatively skewed**. An example of a variable that tends to be positively skewed is personal income. A lot of people have small or middle incomes, and a few people have large incomes. An example of a negatively skewed distribution would be the age of people who have chronic illnesses. A few young and middle-age men and women have chronic illnesses, but many more elderly people have chronic conditions.

A theoretical frequency distribution of particular importance in statistics is the normal distribution. The **normal distribution** is a symmetrical distribution that has one central peak or set of values in the middle of the distribution. The **normal curve** is a bell-shaped curve that graphically presents a

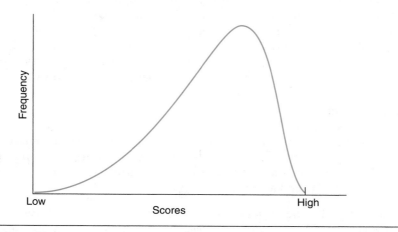

▶ FIGURE 14–2   Negatively skewed distribution

normal distribution (See Figure 14-3). The normal curve is sometimes called the Gaussian curve because Carl Gauss developed the concept of the normal distribution.

As with all graphic presentations of frequency distributions, the values of the distribution are placed on the horizontal axis, and the frequencies of the values are placed on the vertical axis. The one difference in this type of graph compared with a histogram or frequency polygon is that the vertical axis is usually not displayed. The actual frequency of the values is therefore not depicted on the graph of a normal curve.

Normal is a mathematical rather than a medical or psychological term and used in the sense that a normal distribution is frequently found in many happenings in nature. Such variables as height and weight are normally distributed in the population. For example, most people are of average height. There are a few very short and a few very tall people, but most people are within a few inches of each other in height. For a frequency distribution to approximate the normal curve, a fairly large number of values are needed. However, the normal curve is closely approximated with sample sizes of at least 30 (Roscoe, 1975; Shott, 1990).

The characteristics of the normal curve include the following:

1. It is bell shaped, with a symmetrical distribution, and the maximum height is the mean.
2. The mean, median, and mode are the same value.
3. Most of the values cluster around the mean.
4. A few values occur on both extreme ends of the distribution curve.
5. The point where the curve begins to grow faster horizontally than vertically is called an *inflection point* and lies at 1 SD (standard deviation) above and 1 SD below the mean.
6. The tails of the curve never touch the base because the distribution is theoretical rather than empirical.

In the normal curve, 50% of the values lie on the left half of the distribution, and 50% lie on the right half. Other percentages can be determined by assessing the distances of various values from the mean. For example, 34.13% of the area under the curve lies between the mean and +1 SD from the mean. Because the distribution is symmetrical, 34.13% of the area under the curve lies between the mean and –1 SD from the mean. Therefore, 68.26% of the distribution lies within ±1 SD from the mean, 95.44% of the distribution lies within ±2 SD from the mean, and 99.72% lies within ±3 SD of the mean. Although theoretically the curve never touches the base, nearly 100% of the values lie between –3 SD and +3 SD. Only 0.14% of the values lie above +3 SD and 0.14 % below –3 SD. Figure 14–3 depicts the areas under the normal curve.

The percentages under the normal curve may be thought of as probabilities. These probabilities are usually stated in decimal form. For example, 34.13% of the area under the normal curve lies between the mean and +1 SD. When this percentage is converted to a decimal, it becomes .3413. The probability that a value in a normal distribution lies between the mean and +1 SD is .3413. The probability that a value lies above +1 SD is .1587 (.5000 – .3413 = .1587). An understanding of probabilities is very important when considering inferential statistics and is discussed further in Chapter 15.

Graphic Presentations

Data may be presented in a graphic form that makes the frequency distribution of the data readily apparent. Graphic presentations also have a visual appeal that may cause the reader to analyze the data more closely than would be the case if a written description of the data were presented. Various graphic displays are appropriate according to the level of measurement of the variable to be presented. A graphic display is called a "figure."

Bar Graph   A **bar graph** is a figure used to represent a frequency distribution of nominal data and some types of ordinal data. The bar graph is especially useful when the categories of the variables are qualitative rather than numerical. As you can see in Figure 14–3, the lengths of the bars represent the

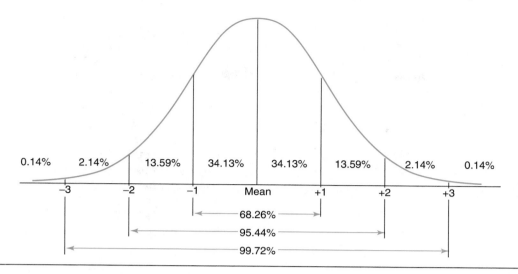

▶ FIGURE 14–3 Normal curve

frequency of occurrence of the category. Bar graphs may be drawn with the bars extending in a horizontal direction (as in Figure 14–4) or with the bars extending in a vertical direction. To show that the data being represented are separate categories, the bars do not touch each other. Data are presented on only one variable in a bar graph. In Figure 14–4, the variable is "reasons for missed clinic appointments." Each of the reasons given by the respondents represents a separate category of the variable being measured.

Histogram   A **histogram** is a graph that uses bars to represent the frequency distribution of a variable measured at the ordinal, interval, or ratio level (Figure 14–5). Data are presented on only one variable in a histogram. The bars in a histogram are of equal width and touch each other to indicate that data are being presented on a continuum. The width of the bar represents the size of the class interval. The height of the bar represents the frequency of occurrence of each class interval. To construct a histogram, two axes are drawn: a vertical axis and a horizontal axis. The vertical axis is called the *ordinate*, and the horizontal axis the *abscissa*. Beginning at 0, the ordinate axis is marked off in equal intervals up to the highest possible frequency of the category being measured. The abscissa

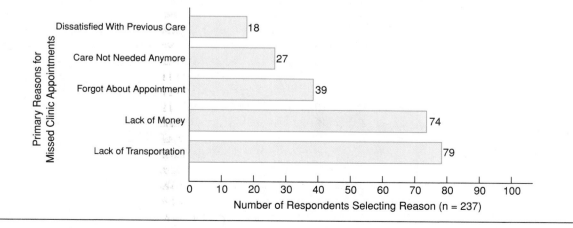

▶ FIGURE 14–4   Bar graph of reasons for missed clinic appointments

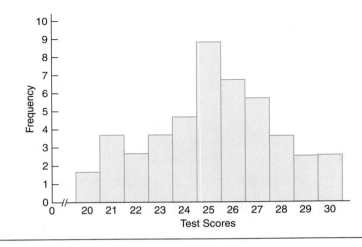

▶ FIGURE 14–5   Histogram of test scores

is marked off with the class intervals or categories of the variable. For good graphic proportions, the vertical axis is generally drawn about two-thirds the length of the horizontal axis.

Frequency Polygon   A **frequency polygon** is a graph that uses dots connected with straight lines to represent the frequency distribution of ordinal, interval, or ratio data (Figure 14–6). A dot is placed above the midpoint of each class interval; these dots are then connected. Although not strictly correct, it is customary to bring the distribution down to the horizontal axis by adding a 0 frequency at each end of the distribution.

As is the case with histograms, the class intervals of the variable are represented on the horizontal axis of the frequency polygon, and the frequencies of the class intervals are represented on the vertical axis. The height of each dot indicates the frequency of a particular class interval.

Percentages
A **percentage** is a statistic that represents the proportion of a subgroup to a total group, expressed as a percentage ranging from 0 to 100. A percentage is the number of parts per 100 that a certain portion of the whole represents. The size of the total group on which a percentage is based should be reasonably

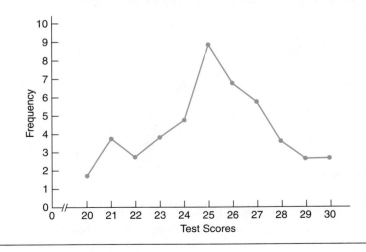

▶ FIGURE 14–6   Frequency polygon of test scores

large for the percentage to be a useful or valid statistic. The minimum number for the computation of percentages should be at least 20. This number assures that each element in a group represents only 5% of the total group. To illustrate the need for fairly large numbers of scores or values when computing percentages, consider the following example. A friend comes up to you and says, "I just heard that they conducted a survey, and 60% of the students interviewed said they thought another year should be added to our educational program." If you were a student in the program, your first instinct might be to go find the traitors and give them a piece of your mind. First, however, it would be wise to ask how many students were interviewed. If told that only five students were interviewed, you would probably not consider the sample to be very representative of the student population and would probably not worry about the survey's results.

Measures of Central Tendency

In many cases, the condensing of data will not be of as much interest or importance as the average value of a distribution. **Measures of central tendency** are statistics that describe the average, typical, or most common value for a group of data. *Central* refers to the middle or average value; *tendency* refers to the general trend of the numbers to cluster in a certain way. A measure of central tendency summarizes a frequency distribution by the use of a single number.

Nurse researchers are frequently interested in this type of question: "What is the average level of anxiety of nursing students prior to an exam between those who practiced progressive relaxation before the exam compared with those who did not practice progressive relaxation?" Of course, the frequency distribution of the anxiety scores would be of interest, but the average anxiety level would provide a much more exact indication of any difference that might exist in the anxiety levels of the two groups.

Although average is frequently used to indicate the arithmetic mean, there are also two other measures of central tendency: the mode and the median. The level of measurement of the data determines which measure of central tendency should be used in presenting the average value of a set of data.

Mode

The **mode**, sometimes abbreviated as Mo, is the category or value that occurs most often in a set of data under consideration. It may be thought of as the most representative category or value in the group. The mode is determined by visually analyzing and counting data.

The mode is the only measure of central tendency appropriate for nominal data. When the data are only categories rather than actual numbers, as is the case with nominal data, the category with the greatest frequency is called the **modal class**. For example, if a sample was composed of 50 nurses, 40 occupational therapists, 35 dental technicians, and 30 physical therapists, the modal class would be nurses.

The mode may also be reported for ordinal, interval, or ratio data. In the following distribution of scores, the mode is 13 because it appears twice and the other six numbers only appear once:

$$16 \quad 15 \quad 13 \quad 13 \quad 12 \quad 9 \quad 6 \quad 4$$

If the distribution of the values is symmetrical in a frequency distribution, the mode is the same value as the median and the mean. A set of data with one value that occurs most frequently is called **unimodal**. If two values have the same high frequency, the distribution is called **bimodal**. If more than two values have the same high frequency, the distribution is said to be **multimodal**. Although the mode is an interesting statistic, it is rarely reported in the literature because it is only a crude estimate of the average value of the data.

Median

The **median**, sometimes abbreviated as Md or Mdn, is the middle score or value in a group of data. With interval and ratio data, the median divides the frequency distribution of the data in half. If the number of scores or values is uneven, the median is the middle value. If the number of scores is even, the median is the midpoint between these two middle values and is found by averaging these two values. Consider the following examples:

Uneven Numbers of Scores		Even Number of Scores	
16 15 13 13 }	50% of values	16 15 13 13 }	50% of values
12	Median	(12.5)	Median
9 6 4 3 }	50% of values	12 9 6 4 }	50% of values

The median is appropriate for ordinal, interval, and ratio data. When ordinal data are analyzed, the average category can be identified. For example, if anxiety levels were classified as mild, moderate, severe, and panic, the average category might be moderate. When percentiles are being calculated, the median is the 50th percentile. If grouped data from a frequency distribution are being used, a formula is needed to compute the median. One of the most valuable qualities of the median is that it is not influenced by extreme values. The median is frequently used in reporting average income because extremely high or low incomes do not affect the median, as would be the case if the mean were calculated.

Mean

The **mean**, sometimes abbreviated as M or presented as $\overline{X}$, is the average sum of a set of values found by adding all values and dividing by the total number of values. This measure of central tendency is also called the *arithmetic mean*. Whereas the mode and median indicate the position of certain values in a distribution, the mean considers all of the values as a whole.

The mean is appropriate for interval and ratio data. It is considered the most stable measure of central tendency for these levels of data if the distribution is normal. If the distribution is not normal and extreme values are present, the mean will not present an accurate picture of the distribution. As mentioned under the discussion of the median, if average income were reported as the mean, a few extremely wealthy people could make the rest of us appear rich.

The symbol for a sample mean is $\overline{X}$, and the symbol for the population mean is μ. The mean is figured in the following manner:

$$\overline{X} = \frac{\Sigma X}{N}$$

where X = score; Σ = a summation sign, indicating that all scores are added; and N = total number of scores.

$$
\begin{array}{r}
16 \\
15 \\
13 \\
13 \\
12 \\
9 \\
6 \\
\underline{4} \\
\Sigma X = 88
\end{array}
$$

$$\overline{X} = \frac{\Sigma X}{N} = \frac{88}{8} = 11$$

Measures of Variability

Measures of variability describe how spread out the values are in a distribution of values. Although measures of central tendency are very important, sometimes it may be of more interest to know how spread out the values are in a distribution. Consider the following pulse rates:

Group A	Group B
80	100
79	90
78	80
78	70
75	50
$\Sigma X = 390$	$\Sigma X = 390$
X = 78	X = 78

As you can see, the mean of both groups of pulse rates is the same. However, pulse rates of people in Group A are homogeneous, or alike, whereas pulse rates of people in Group B are heterogeneous, or dissimilar. This information would be very important because the arithmetic mean is not very appropriate to use in describing Group B or to use in comparing the two groups of pulse rates. The most common measures of variability are range, percentile, standard deviation, variance, and z-scores.

Range

The distance between the highest and lowest value in a group of values or scores is called the **range**. The range is the simplest measure of variability. It is presented as a single number. Frequently, the word *range* is used incorrectly to indicate the lowest and highest values. For example, you might hear this statement: "The scores ranged from 40 to 60." Although this type of statement is fairly common, technically the range for these scores is 20 (60 – 40 = 20). The range is a measure that can be used to gain a quick picture of the dispersion of the data. It has limited usefulness because one extreme score can change the range drastically.

To correct for the influence of extreme scores or values, the interquartile range (IQR) may be reported. The **interquartile range** contains the middle half of the values in a frequency distribution

$$IQR = Q_3 - Q_1$$

where Q_3 = the point below which three-fourths of the distribution lies, and Q_1 = the point below which one-fourth of the distribution lies. The **semiquartile range** (SQR) is found by dividing the interquartile range in half: SQR = IQR/2.

Percentile

A **percentile** is a datum point below which lies a certain percentage of the values in a frequency distribution. If you score at the 80th percentile on a test, it means that 80% of the other students received lower scores. You might also say that 20% of the other students scored higher (it depends on whether you are an optimist or a pessimist!).

The median of a frequency distribution lies at the 50th percentile. Percentile is a common statistic used to allow people to compare their performance with that of others. Raw scores, or untreated data, are transformed into percentile ranks. For an explanation of how to compute percentiles, consult a statistics book.

Percentiles are used a great deal in the assessment of infants and children. Imagine that you read a child's chart and find out that, for his age group, he is at the 95th percentile in height and the 15th percentile in weight. What would you expect the physical appearance of this child to be like in height and weight? Tall and skinny, right?

An anxiety test used frequently in nursing research is the State-Trait Anxiety Inventory by Spielberger (1983). Spielberger views state anxiety as a current feeling of emotional and physical uneasiness, whereas trait anxiety refers to a person's anxiety proneness and is considered a relatively stable personality trait. The test booklet that accompanies this anxiety test provides information about the test and furnishes percentile ranks for groups on which the test was normed. The lowest possible score is 20 and the highest possible score is 80 on the two scales that measure state and trait anxiety. You might think that an average anxiety score would be 50, which is halfway between 20 and 80. Not so! A raw score of 50 on the state anxiety scale is at the 82nd percentile when compared with a group of female college students who were used in establishing norms for the test. A score of 66 is at the 99th percentile.

Standard Deviation

The standard deviation is the most widely used measure of variability when interval or ratio data are obtained. This statistic describes how values vary about the mean of the distribution. The word *standard* is used to mean average. The **standard deviation**, abbreviated SD or s, is a measurement that indicates the average deviation or variation of all the values in a set of values from the mean value of those data. Like the arithmetic mean, the standard deviation takes into consideration all the values in a distribution. The actual definition of the standard deviation is a little bit difficult to understand. Mathematically, the standard deviation is equal to the square root of the sum of the squared deviations about the mean divided by the total number of values. Were you able to follow that statement?

You may wonder when you would ever use the SD in nursing. I am sure that all of you are familiar with critical pathways. They are useful in planning care for a group of patients with the same condition and who have a predictable course of recovery. If, for example, the SD for length of stay (LOS) for a group of patients with a certain serious condition is 5.2 days, it might be very difficult to develop a critical pathway. It appears there may be too much variability in recovery time for one plan of care to be suitable for all patients with this condition.

Variance

The **variance** is a measure that is used in several inferential statistical tests. Mathematically, the variance is equal to the sum of the squared deviations about the mean divided by the total number of values. Got that? The variance is discussed infrequently because it is not in the same unit of measurement as the variable being examined, as is the case with the standard deviation.

Z Scores

A **z score** is a standard score that indicates how many SDs from the mean a particular value lies. A z score is called a standard score because it is interpreted in relation to SD units above or below the mean. This is the formula for calculating z scores:

$$z = \frac{X - \overline{X}}{s}$$

where z = z score, X = score or value, $\overline{X}$ = mean of scores or values, and s = standard deviation.

The z score is a very useful statistic for interpreting a particular value in relation to the other values in a distribution. Also, z scores allow you to compare the performance of someone on nonequivalent tests. If a score is 1 SD above the mean, it has a z score of 1. Consider the following example. You received a raw score of 92 on a test with 110 questions. The mean raw score was 98, and the SD was 3. How well did you score on the test compared with others who took the examination?

$$\frac{92 - 98}{3} = \frac{-6}{3} = -2.0$$

You did not do too well! Your z score is –2.0. This means that only 2.28% of the group scored lower than you did. Review Figure 14–3 again, and you will see that 2.14% of the values lie between –2 SD and –3 SD, and .14% of the values lie beyond –3 SD. Thus, 2.28% of the values lie beyond –2 SD (2.14 + .14 = 2.28). Tables are available in statistical texts if you wish to determine the percentage of a distribution above and below any given z score.

Measures of Relationships

So far, the material in this chapter has been concerned with the analysis of data on one variable at a time. The frequency distributions that were discussed might be referred to as univariate frequency distributions. In nursing research, however, we are frequently concerned with more than one variable. **Measures of relationships** concern the correlations between variables. As you recall, a correlation concerns the extent to which values of one variable (X) are related to values of a second variable (Y). You might want to determine if there is a correlation between the amount of time spent with a patient and the number of requests for pain medication made by that patient. A record might be made of the total time nurses spent in a patient's room during a given time period of the day and the number of requests for pain medication made by the patient during that same time period. These data would be gathered on a group of patients. You would want to know if these two values seemed to vary together. When the time spent with the patient increased, did the number of requests for pain medications increase or decrease? There are several ways to examine a relationship such as this. Correlation coefficients, scatter plots, and contingency tables, along with various types of correlational procedures, are discussed here.

Correlation Coefficients

Correlations are computed through pairing the value of each subject on one variable (X) with the value on another variable (Y). As you will recall from the discussion of correlational studies in Chapter 9, the magnitude and direction of the relationship between these two variables is presented through a measurement called a correlation coefficient. The correlation coefficient can vary between –1.00 and +1.00. These two numbers represent the extremes of a perfect relationship. A correlation coefficient of –1.00 indicates a perfect negative relationship, whereas +1.00 indicates a perfect positive relationship, and 0 indicates the absence of any relationship. Correlation coefficients are frequently symbolized by the letter r.

An r = +.80 indicates that as the value of one variable (X) increases, the value of the other variable (Y) tends to increase. It also means that as the value of one variable decreases, the value of the other variable tends to decrease. In other words, a positive relationship means that the values of the two variables tend to increase or decrease together. Although a plus sign has been included to show a positive relationship (+.80), the sign is usually not included and the assumption is made that the relationship is positive if no sign is present (.80). An r = −.80 denotes a negative (inverse) relationship and indicates that as the value one variable increases, the value of the other variable tends to decrease.

A positive relationship might be found between anxiety levels and pulse rates. As anxiety levels go up, pulse rates go up. A negative relationship might be found between anxiety levels and test scores. As anxiety levels go up, test scores go down.

Whereas the sign of the correlation coefficient shows the direction or nature of the relationship (positive or negative), the size of the correlation coefficient indicates the magnitude or strength of the relationship. An r = .80 denotes a stronger relationship than an r = .60. Also, an r = −.50 indicates a stronger relationship than an r = −.40. Remember, the sign only indicates the direction of the relationship.

Generally, correlation coefficients are calculated on measurements obtained from each subject on two variables. Correlation coefficients, however, may be calculated on the measurements of one variable that are obtained from two groups of matched subjects, such as fathers and sons. A researcher might want to determine if there is a relationship between the height of fathers and their sons. Also, as discussed in Chapter 12, correlation coefficients can be used to measure reliability. For example, the reliability of an instrument can be determined by examining subjects' scores at Time 1 versus scores at Time 2. This is called test-retest reliability.

Caution must be exercised in interpreting correlations. It cannot be emphasized too much that correlation does not equate with causation. If a strong positive relationship is found between anxiety levels and pulse rates, you should not conclude that the anxiety levels *caused* the pulse rates to go up. It is possible that the pulse rates increased and then the anxiety levels increased or that some other variable caused the pulse rates to rise and also increased anxiety.

You may wonder how to determine if a correlation is weak or strong. Does $r = .30$ indicate a mild or a moderate relationship? There are no set criteria to evaluate the actual strength of a correlation coefficient. The nature of the variables being studied will help determine the strength of the relationship. According to Polit (1996), correlations between psychosocial variables rarely exceed .50. Roscoe (1975) wrote, "a correlation of .70 between scholastic aptitude in the first grade and grade point average in college would be phenomenal" (p. 101). He cautioned, however, that a correlation of .70 between two tests that were supposedly equivalent would be too low.

The coefficient of determination is a statistic that should be calculated after the computation of a correlation coefficient. The **coefficient of determination** is obtained by squaring the correlation coefficient (r^2) and is interpreted as the percentage of variance shared by the two variables. The coefficient of determination for an $r = .50$ would be .25 ($.50 \times .50 = .25$), which would then be multiplied by 100 and read as 25%.

Suppose that a correlation of .60 were obtained between anxiety scores and pulse rates. The coefficient of determination would be .36, which would mean that these two variables share a common variance or overlap of 36%. If you knew a person's anxiety score, you would have 36% of the information needed to predict that person's pulse rate. Because the coefficient of determination is reversible, you would have 36% of the information needed to predict that person's anxiety level if you knew his or her pulse rate. Of course, you would still be lacking 64% of the knowledge needed to predict one of these variables based on knowledge of the other variable! Table 14–3 displays the percentage of variance explained by different correlation coefficients. An $r = .708$ is necessary before 50% of the variance is explained. Perhaps researchers will begin to report this statistic more often because it gives a much clearer picture of the value of a correlation coefficient than the tests of significance of correlation coefficients, which are discussed in Chapter 15. It is possible for a very low correlation coefficient, such as .20 or even lower, to be statistically significant when a large sample size is used. Only 4% of the shared variance of two variables is explained by a correlation coefficient of .20. If the coefficient of determination is not presented in a research article in which correlation coefficients are presented, you can quickly do the calculation yourself.

TABLE 14–3 Percentage of Variance Explained by Correlations

Correlation Coefficient (r)	Coefficient of Determination (r^2)	Percentage of Variance Explained
.950	.9025	90
.850	.7225	72
.750	.5625	56
.708	.5013	50
.650	.4225	42
.550	.3025	30
.450	.2025	20
.350	.1225	12
.250	.0625	6
.150	.0225	2

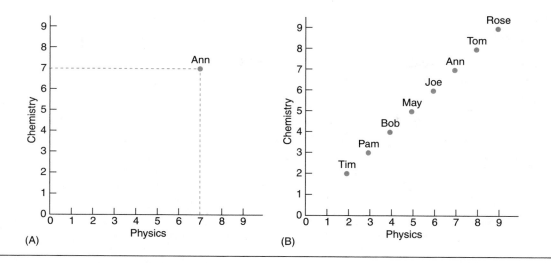

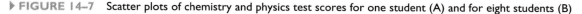

▶ FIGURE 14–7   Scatter plots of chemistry and physics test scores for one student (A) and for eight students (B)

Scatter Plots

A **scatter plot**, also called a **scatter diagram** or a **scattergram**, is a graphic presentation of the relationship between two variables. The graph contains variables on an X axis and a Y axis. The X variable is plotted on the horizontal axis; the Y variable is plotted on the vertical axis. The scatter plot is a visual device that can be used to eyeball a correlation between two variables. The magnitude of the relationship as well as the direction of the relationship can be determined.

Pairs of scores are plotted on a graph by the placement of dots to indicate where each pair of Xs and Ys intersects. For a positive correlation, the lowest score or value for each variable is placed at the lower left corner of the graph. Values increase as they go up the vertical axis and as they go toward the right on the horizontal axis. If the dots seem to be distributed from the upper left corner down toward the lower right corner, a negative correlation is said to exist.

Examine Figure 14–7. This graph depicts chemistry and physics examination scores. One student's score is plotted on the graph (Figure 14–7A). As can be seen, the student, Ann, scored a 7 on both tests. If each student receives the same score on both tests (5 and 5, 6 and 6), a perfect positive correlation is said to exist, and the dots would all fall on a straight line drawn from the lower left corner of the graph to the upper right corner. Figure 14–7B shows the placement of the dots for 8 students' scores (note the name of the person who scored the highest!).

Generally you will not find a perfect correlation as seen in Figure 14–7B. Figure 14–8 depicts varying degrees of correlations. The closer the dots are to a straight line, the higher is the correlation. When the dots are scattered all over the graph, it indicates that no relationship exists between the two variables.

Contingency Tables

If data are nominal or categorical, relationships cannot be depicted on a scatter plot. No actual scores are available for nominal data; rather the frequencies of the occurrences of the categories are presented. A **contingency table**, also called a cross-tabulation table, is a visual means of displaying the relationship between sets of nominal data. For example, the researcher might wish to determine if a relationship exists between gender and exercise behavior. Table 14–4 depicts the data that were gathered on 50 male and 50 female subjects.

The data from Table 14–4 seem to indicate that more men than women participate in regular exercise programs. The chi-square statistic (see Chapter 15) can be calculated to determine if there is a significant relationship between these variables. If a significant relationship is found, the researcher

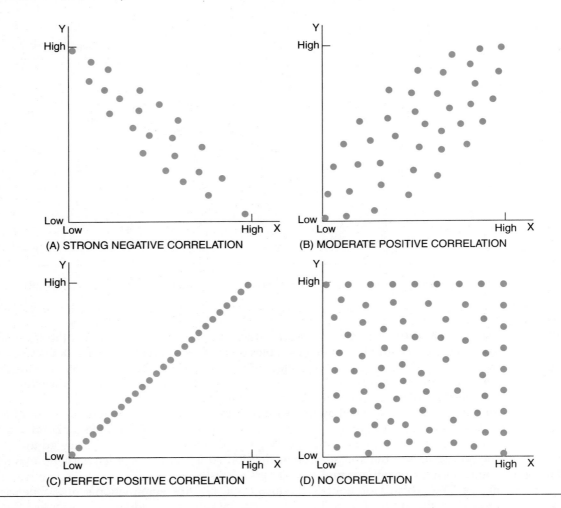

▶ FIGURE 14–8   Scatter plots of correlations

cannot conclude that gender "causes" one to participate in an exercise program. The reason for the existence of the relationship would still remain unknown.

Table 14–4 is called a 2 × 2 table because there are two variables and each variable has two categories. If exercise had been divided into three categories, such as never exercises, exercises occasionally, and exercises frequently, the table would have been called a 2 × 3 table.

TABLE 14–4 Example of Contingency Table

	Exercise Regularly	Do Not Exercise Regularly	Total
Males	35	15	50
Females	10	40	50
Total	45	55	100

Types of Correlational Procedures

There are many different correlational procedures. The most common correlational procedure used in nursing research when both sets of data are at the interval or ratio level is the Pearson product-moment correlation (Pearson r), symbolized by the letter r.

Pearson r

The Pearson r test was used by Edrington et al. (2010) in their study of the relationships among pain characteristics, mood disturbances, and acculturation in 50 Chinese American patients with cancer. Significant negative correlations were found between level of acculturation and least pain scores ($r = -.404$) and between level of acculturation and worst pain scores ($r = -.332$). Significant negative correlations were also found between level of acculturation and walking ability ($r = -.309$), ability to do work ($r = -.4$), and sleep ($r = -.323$).

The Spearman rho is the correlational procedure commonly used with ordinal data. It is symbolized by r_s, r_{rho}, or rho. Although this correlational procedure is used less frequently than the Pearson r because it is not as powerful (see Chapter 15 for an explanation of the power of a statistical test), many published research studies present the Spearman rho because at least some of the data were gathered at the ordinal level.

Spearman Rho

Roos, Kärner, and Hallert (2009) examined the relationship between gastrointestinal (GI) symptoms and psychological well-being in Scandinavian adults who were on a gluten-free diet because of celiac disease. Data were not normally distributed; therefore, the Spearman rho correlation coefficient was used. A negative relationship ($-.65$, p $<$ .05) was found between GI symptoms and psychological well-being.

Finally, several correlational procedures are appropriate for nominal data: contingency coefficient, phi coefficient, and Cramer's V. These correlations depend on the chi square (χ^2). Chapter 15 explains the calculation of χ^2.

Sometimes researchers gather two levels of data in a correlational study. For example, a researcher might study the correlation between anxiety levels and pulse rates. Anxiety levels might be measured at the ordinal level (panic anxiety, high anxiety, moderate anxiety, and mild anxiety), whereas pulse rates are measured at the interval level (numerical pulse rates). The researcher would be forced to use the Spearman rho rather than the Pearson r. In other words, the researcher must select the correlational statistic that is appropriate for the lowest level of data. If a correlation were being examined on two sets of data that were gathered at the ordinal and nominal levels of measurement, a statistical procedure would be used that is appropriate for nominal data, which is the lower of these two levels of measurement.

In this chapter, correlations were discussed as a type of descriptive statistics. In Chapter 15, correlations are taken a step further and discussed under inferential statistics.

INTRAOCULAR METHOD OF DATA ANALYSIS

The researcher should always use the so-called intraocular method when analyzing data. This is a humorous term used to indicate that you should eyeball your data. Many mistakes could be avoided in data analysis if the researcher's eyes and common sense were used. For example, imagine that the following group of scores were obtained: 78, 79, 80, 76, and 74. When the average is calculated, it is found to be 68. The intraocular method should tell the researcher that a mistake has been made in calculation. After glancing at the data, an estimate should be made of the results of data analysis. This procedure provides a checks-and-balances system that frequently pays off in the detection of an error in calculations or an error in the data entry process.

CRITIQUING DESCRIPTIVE STATISTICS IN RESEARCH REPORTS

It is often difficult for the beginning reader of research reports to critique the statistical content of these reports. The reader may not have taken a basic statistics course. Even if such a course was completed, the content may have been forgotten or misunderstood. Therefore, many consumers of research examine the study statistics with "fear and trembling."

It is desirable to have some background in statistics before reading research reports. However, the background knowledge needed to critique most reports is not extensive. Knowledge of a few statistical concepts goes a long way toward helping the reader understand data analysis presented in research articles and other types of research reports. Box 14–1 lists some guidelines for critiquing descriptive statistics.

The first task is to identify the various descriptive statistics that were used to analyze data. Nearly every research study uses descriptive statistics to present the demographic characteristics of the sample. For example, the ages, educational levels, and incomes of the subjects may be presented through descriptive statistics. If the mean was used to present the average income, the reader should try to determine if the median would have been a more appropriate measure of central tendency. This would be true if some of the subjects reported extremely high or low incomes.

The level of measurement of each variable should be determined, if possible, and then a decision made about the appropriateness of the descriptive statistics reported. Was gender treated as a nominal variable or reported as an interval variable? It makes no sense to see gender reported as an average of 1.2. This might occur if the researcher had assigned a value of 1 to women and 2 to men and did not relay this information to the statistician who analyzed the data. The best way to determine the level of measurement for variables is to search for the researcher's operational definitions. These are frequently found in the discussion of the instruments used in the study.

Were the descriptive data presented both in the text of the report and in tables and graphs? If so, do the data agree? If the data were not presented in tables or graphs, would the use of these methods of reporting data have made the material more easily understood?

Descriptive statistics should be presented in a manner that can be understood by the average practicing nurse. If this is not done, the results of the study will not be considered for implementation in practice.

Box 14-1 Guidelines for Critiquing Descriptive Statistics

1. What types of descriptive statistics are included in the research report?
2. Were the descriptive statistics appropriate for the level of measurement of the variable(s)?
3. Were measures of central tendency and variability both presented?
4. Do the descriptive statistics clearly present the demographic characteristics of the subjects?
5. Are the descriptive statistics clearly presented in the text? In tables and graphs?
6. Do the descriptive statistics presented in the text agree with those presented in the tables?

SUMMARY

Statistics is a branch of knowledge used to summarize and present numerical data. Numerical characteristics of populations are called **parameters**; numerical characteristics of samples are called **statistics**.

Statistics can be classified as descriptive and inferential. **Descriptive statistics** are those that organize and summarize numerical data from populations or samples. **Inferential statistics** are concerned with populations and use sample data to make an inference about a population. Types of descriptive statistics are (a) measures to condense data, (b) measures of central tendency, (c) measures of variability, and (d) measures of relationships.

Measures to condense data are statistics that summarize and condense data. Included in this category are frequency distributions, graphic presentations, and percentages. **Frequency distributions** are used with all levels of data. Groups of scores in a frequency distribution are called **class intervals**.

Distribution shapes can be classified as symmetrical or nonsymmetrical. **Symmetrical distributions** are those in which both halves of the distribution are the same. **Nonsymmetrical distributions,** also called **skewed** distributions, are those in which the distribution has an off-center peak. The tail of the distribution points to the right in a **positively skewed** distribution and to the left in a **negatively skewed** distribution. The **normal distribution** is a symmetrical distribution that has one central peak or set of values in the center of the distribution. The **normal curve** is a bell-shaped curve that graphically presents a normal distribution. The distribution is symmetrical, with 50% of the values contained on the left half of the curve and 50% on the right half. Approximately 68% of the distribution of a normal curve lies within ±1 SD of the mean. Approximately 95% of the distribution lies within ±2 SD of the mean, and about 99% lies within ±3 SD of the mean.

Graphic presentations include bar graphs, histograms, and frequency polygons. A **bar graph** is used to depict nominal data and some types of ordinal data. A **histogram** and a **frequency polygon** are used to display ordinal, interval, and ratio data.

A **percentage** is a statistic that represents the proportion of a subgroup to a total group, expressed as a percentage ranging from 0 to 100.

Measures of central tendency are used to describe the average value of a set of values. The **mode** is the category or value that occurs most often in a set of data. **Modal class** is the category of nominal data with the greatest frequency. A frequency distribution that contains one value that occurs more frequently than any other is called **unimodal**. If two values have the same high frequency, the distribution is **bimodal**. If more than two values have the same high frequency, the distribution is **multimodal**.

The **median** is the middle score or value in a group of data, and the **mean** is the average sum of a set of values.

Measures of variability describe how spread out the values are in a distribution of values. Measures of variability are range, percentile, standard deviation, variance, and z score. The **range** is the distance between the highest and lowest value in a group of values. The **interquartile range** contains the middle half of the values in a frequency distribution. The **semiquartile range** is found by dividing the interquartile range in half. A **percentile** is a data point below which lies a certain percentage of the values in a frequency distribution. The **standard deviation** is a measure that indicates the average deviation or variability of all the values from the mean of a set of values. The standard deviation is the most widely used measure of variability when interval or ratio data are described. The **variance** is the standard deviation squared. A **z score** is a standard score that indicates how many SDs from the mean a particular value lies.

Measures of relationships are concerned with the correlation between variables. Correlation coefficients, scatter plots, and contingency tables are means of presenting correlations.

The magnitude and direction of a relationship between two variables is presented through a correlation coefficient that varies between –1.00

and $+1.00$. The **coefficient of determination** is a statistic obtained through squaring a correlation coefficient. This statistic is interpreted as the percentage of variance shared by two variables.

A **scatter plot**, also called a **scatter diagram** or a **scattergram**, is a graphic presentation of the relationship between two variables. Pairs of scores are plotted on a graph by the placement of dots to indicate where each pair of Xs and Ys intersects.

A **contingency table** is a means of displaying the relationship between two sets of nominal data. No actual scores are presented; rather, the table includes the frequencies of occurrence of the categories.

The most common correlation procedures used in nursing research are the Pearson product-moment correlation (Pearson r) and the Spearman's rho. The Pearson r is used with interval and ratio data, and Spearman's rho is used with ordinal data. Three common correlational procedures used with nominal data are the contingency coefficient, phi, and Cramer's V.

NURSING RESEARCH ON THE WEB

For additional online resources, research activities, and exercises, go to **www.mynursingkit. com.** Select Chapter 14 from the drop-down menu.

GET INVOLVED ACTIVITIES

1. Write down all of the different kinds of descriptive statistics found in this chapter. Also, list the various types of figures discussed. Take these two lists and examine the first five research articles that you locate in nursing journals. Place a check mark on your list beside each type of descriptive statistic mentioned in the articles. Also, place a check mark beside each type of figure that you observe in these articles.
2. Bring your list to class and compare it with the lists compiled by your classmates or colleagues. Determine the most common descriptive statistic that is reported in nursing research articles. Determine the most common type of figure displayed in these research articles.
3. Divide into two debate groups. Select a variable and debate whether it is more appropriate to use the mean or the median when reporting the data on this variable. Examples of variables that might be selected are height, weight, or age of clients in a particular clinic population. Each side should present specific circumstances that would indicate the need for either the mean or the median to be used.
4. Have an open discussion with your classmates or colleagues concerning your feelings about statistics. Compile a list of the most common reasons that nurses and nursing students tend to avoid statistics.
5. Identify an incident in which statistics were used on a nursing unit where you worked or where you had clinical experiences.

SELF-TEST

Circle the letter before the *best* answer.

1. Which type of statistics is used to examine the characteristics of samples?
   A. descriptive statistics
   B. inferential statistics
   C. parametric statistics
   D. normative statistics

2. What is the mode of the following group of vision test results? 20/20; 20/30; 20/40; 20/30; 20/50; 20/40; 20/100; 20/30
   A. 20/20
   B. 20/30
   C. 20/40
   D. 20/50
   E. 20/100

3. Which of the following measures of central tendency would be appropriate to describe the average pulse rates of a group of hospitalized patients?
   A. mode
   B. median
   C. mean

4. The standard deviation is a measure of
   A. skewness.
   B. correlation.
   C. central tendency.
   D. variability.

5. What does it mean if a person's score is 2.5 standard deviations above the mean on a test?
   A. All of the scores on the test are high.
   B. The person has an unusually high score compared with others who took the test.
   C. An error has been made in recording the score.
   D. The score is 25% higher than the mean.

6. As a nurse researcher conducting a research study with a group of children, you discover that the average weight of the subjects is at the 90th percentile for their age. Which of the following statements would be correct?
   A. The subjects are not eating enough.
   B. The subjects are 90% *above* the average weight for their age.
   C. The subjects are 90% *below* the average weight for their age.
   D. The subjects are well above the average weight for their age.

7. Which of the following statements is true?
   A. The most reliable and accurate measure of central tendency is the mode.
   B. The standard deviation indicates how spread out the scores are in a distribution.
   C. The type of graph that shows the relationship between two variables is a histogram.
   D. The range of a group of scores is figured by adding the highest and lowest numbers.

8. Correlation is a procedure used to determine if
   A. X comes before Y.
   B. X causes Y.
   C. X and Y are different.
   D. X and Y vary together.

9. A nurse researcher examines the correlation between anxiety levels and pain. She calculates a correlation coefficient of 1.29. The size of this correlation indicates
   A. a strong positive relationship.
   B. a significant correlation.
   C. an error in calculation.
   D. no relationship between the two variables.

10. Which of the following correlation coefficients would indicate the strongest relationship between anxiety and the ability to concentrate?
   A. $r = .30$
   B. $r = -.30$
   C. $r = -.50$
   D. $r = -.60$
   E. $r = -1.30$

REFERENCES

Edrington, J., Sun, A., Wong, C., Dodd, M., Padilla, G., Paul, S. & Miaskowski, C. (2010). A pilot study of relationships among pain characteristics, mood disturbances, and acculturation in a community sample of Chinese American patients with cancer. *Oncology Nursing Forum, 37*, 172–182. doi: 10.1188/10.onf.172–181.

Norwood, S. L. (2000). *Research strategies for advanced practice nurses.* Upper Saddle River, NJ: Prentice Hall Health.

Polit, D. F. (1996). *Data analysis & statistics for nursing research.* Stamford, CT: Appleton & Lange.

Polit, D. F., & Beck, C. T. (2008). *Nursing research: Principles and methods* (8th ed.). Philadelphia: Lippincott Williams & Wilkins.

Roos, S., Kärner, A., & Hallert, C. (2009). Gastrointestinal symptoms and well-being of adults living on a gluten-free diet. *Gastroenterology Nursing, 32*, 196–201.

Roscoe, J. (1975). *Fundamental research statistics for the behavioral sciences* (2nd ed.). New York: Holt, Rinehart & Winston.

Shott, S. (1990). *Statistics for health care professionals.* Philadelphia: W. B. Saunders.

Spielberger, C. (1983). *Manual for the state-trait anxiety inventory.* Palo Alto, CA: Consulting Psychologists Press.

CHAPTER 15

Inferential Statistics

OUTLINE

OBJECTIVES

On completion of this chapter, you will be prepared to:

1. Recall the two purposes of inferential statistics
2. Discuss the sampling distribution of the mean
3. Define terms used in inferential statistics
4. Distinguish between a one-tailed and a two-tailed test
5. Describe type I and type II errors
6. Differentiate between parametric and nonparametric statistical tests
7. Discuss the power of a statistical test
8. List criteria for selecting a statistical test
9. Identify statistical tests commonly reported in nursing studies
10. Critique the inferential statistics section of research reports

NEW TERMS DEFINED IN THIS CHAPTER

analysis of covariance (ANCOVA), pg 240

analysis of variance (ANOVA), pg 236

canonical correlation, pg 240

central limit theorem, pg 226

chi-square test, pg 237

confidence interval, pg 227

critical region, pg 233

critical value, pg 233

degrees of freedom, pg 233

dependent t test, pg 235

effect size, pg 240

independent t test, pg 235

level of significance, pg 231

meta-analysis, pg 240

metasynthesis, pg 241

multiple regression, pg 239

multivariate analysis of variance (MANOVA), pg 240

nonparametric tests, pg 234

one-tailed test of significance, pg 232

parametric tests, pg 234

power of a statistical test, pg 234

region of rejection, pg 233

sampling distribution, pg 227

standard error of the mean, pg 227

t test, pg 235

two-tailed test of significance, pg 232

type I error, pg 233

type II error, pg 233

Here we are! We have arrived at your favorite chapter—inferential statistics! I wish I could insert a smiley face right here.

The material in this chapter is not really difficult to understand, but if you have not been exposed to this type of material before or did not absorb the content during a statistics class, you may think it is tough. If so, take it as a challenge to understand the material. I hope your efforts will gain for you a greater appreciation of the value of statistics in making decisions about data obtained in research studies. You may also be able to use your knowledge of statistics in many areas of nursing.

Chapter 14 discussed descriptive statistics. These types of statistics are used to present the characteristics of samples or populations. This chapter discusses inferential statistics, which use sample data to make decisions or inferences about a population. The population is the group of interest when inferential statistics are used, even though data are obtained from samples.

Inferential statistics are based on the laws of probability. The word *chance* is used in discussing probability. Other terms that are sometimes used interchangeably in the literature are *sampling error* and *random error*. All inferential statistical tests are based on the assumption that chance (sampling error, random error) is the only explanation for relationships that are found in research studies. For example, if one group of respondents scores higher than another group on a test, the assumption is made that the difference is related to chance. Reread that sentence several times. The concept of chance is used throughout this chapter. A researcher wants to demonstrate that chance is *not* the reason for the relationships found in research.

The larger the difference found between groups, the lower the probability is that the difference occurred by chance. In other words, the groups really are different on the variable being measured. The same can be said of tests that examine the significance of correlations: The larger the correlation between variables measured on members of the sample, the greater the likelihood is that the variables are, in fact, correlated in the population.

Inferential statistics are based on the assumption that the sample was randomly selected. Recall from Chapter 11 that when a random sample is selected, each member of the population has an equal chance of being selected. At this point, you may be wondering how inferential statistics can be useful because random samples are generally not obtained. Some of the reasons for using nonprobability samples involve time, money, and ethical issues. Spatz and Johnston (1984) presented the rationale for the use of inferential statistics with nonrandom samples. "Usually, the results based on samples that are unsystematic (but not random) are true for other samples from the same population" (p. 162). Shott (1990) stated that it is appropriate to make a statistical inference from a nonrandom sample to the population, as long the researcher does not deliberately select a biased sample. Polit (1996) agreed that inferential statistics may be used with nonrandom samples, but cautioned the researcher to be conservative in interpreting study findings.

The use of a nonrandom sample greatly reduces the ability to generalize study results. You can now be able to better understand the need for replication studies in nursing. Agreement among the findings of several similar studies conducted with nonrandom samples allows conclusions to be derived from the data that are similar to the conclusions that could be made if one large random sample had been used.

PURPOSES OF INFERENTIAL STATISTICS

The two broad purposes of inferential statistics are to estimate population parameters from sample data and to test hypotheses. The second purpose has been of more interest to nurse researchers because hypotheses are often tested in nursing research studies. However, estimating population parameters, which involve determining confidence intervals, is also an important purpose of inferential statistics.

A distinguishing point between the two purposes concerns the time of data collection. The estimation of population parameters is considered after the data are collected, whereas the testing of hypotheses is considered before data collection. Hypotheses are formulated before the data collection begins. Of course, the decision to support or not support the hypothesis is made after the data are analyzed.

Estimating Population Parameters

To estimate population parameters from sample data, an understanding of sampling error and sampling distribution is necessary. Whenever a sample is chosen to represent a population, there is some likelihood that the sample will not accurately reflect the population. Even when a true random sample is chosen, the sample may not be an average or representative sample. Sampling error occurs when the sample does not accurately reflect the population. Reexamine the example in Table 11–3. The table contains pulse measurements on a population of 20 subjects. The mean pulse rate for the population is 71. One sample of 5 subjects drawn from the population is shown to have an average pulse rate of 71. Another sample of 5 subjects has an average pulse rate of 63, and still another sample has an average pulse rate of 83. These last two samples demonstrate what sampling error means. The pulse rates of these two samples of subjects do not accurately reflect the average pulse rate of the population.

An interesting phenomenon may be observed about sampling error. The majority of the samples chosen from a population will accurately reflect the population. In the previous example, if an infinite number of separate samples were chosen from the population, the majority of the mean pulse rates of these samples would be close to the population average pulse rate of 71. Most of the samples would have average rates such as 69, 70, 71, 72, and 73. A few samples would have average rates that were quite different from the population mean, like the previously mentioned 63 and 83. The phenomenon in which sample values tend to be normally distributed around the population value is known as the **central limit theorem**.

Whenever a large number of sample values are arranged in a frequency distribution, those values will be normally distributed even if the original population of values was *not* normally distributed. This may be hard to believe, but it has been demonstrated to be true, if the sample size is fairly large. The sampling distribution of the mean approximates the normal curve when samples contain 100 or more observations or values. Sample sizes as small as 30 are generally adequate to ensure that the sampling distribution of the mean will closely approximate the normal curve (Shott, 1990).

A theoretical frequency distribution, based on an infinite number of samples, is called a **sampling distribution**. This distribution is said to be theoretical because you never actually draw an infinite number of samples from a population. Instead, decisions are made based on one sample. The concept of sampling distributions, however, is used over and over in inferential statistics. The researcher works with one sample, but inferential statistics are based on the idea of what would occur if the researcher had actually drawn an infinite number of samples from *one* population. You may want to reread that sentence again. The reason the concept of sampling distributions is difficult for some people to understand is that it deals with "what ifs" rather than actual data. Sampling distributions are based on mathematical formulas and logic. You will never have to calculate or plot out sampling distributions. Statisticians figured out these theoretical distributions years ago (thank goodness!).

Every inferential statistical test uses the concept of sampling distributions, and each test has its own particular set of sampling distributions that are referred to when analyzing the data obtained in a study. The sampling distribution of the mean is a sampling distribution used quite often in inferential statistical tests.

Sampling Distribution of the Mean

As discussed in Chapter 14, when scores or values are normally distributed, approximately 68% of the values lie between ±1 SD, and approximately 95% lie between ±2 SD. To be exact, 95% of the values in a normal distribution lie between ±1.96 SD from the mean. That figure of 1.96 will become more important as you read on in this discussion about the use of inferential statistics to estimate population parameters, but it will be even more important during the discussion of hypothesis testing.

Let us turn now to the theoretical sampling distribution of the mean. The standard deviation of any sampling distribution is called the standard error (rather than the standard deviation). The standard deviation of the sampling distribution of the mean is called the **standard error of the mean** ($s_{\bar{x}}$). The term *error* indicates that when a theoretical sampling distribution of the mean is used to estimate a population mean, some error is likely to occur in this estimate. The smaller the standard error of the mean, the more confidence you can have that the mean from a sample is an accurate reflection of the population mean. How can you tell how much error is likely to exist in your estimate of the population mean based on only one sample? A simple formula allows you to calculate the $s_{\bar{x}}$.

$$s_{\bar{x}} = \frac{SD}{\sqrt{n}}$$

where SD = standard deviation of sample and n = sample size.

Suppose 25 subjects have taken a test. Their average raw score is 70. The standard deviation is 10. Plug these data into the formula for $s_{\bar{x}}$.

$$s_{\bar{x}} = \frac{10}{\sqrt{25}} = \frac{10}{5} = 2$$

The standard error of the mean ($s_{\bar{x}}$) is 2. You can now determine there is approximately a 68% likelihood that the population mean lies between 68 and 72 (70 ± 2). Also, there is about a 95% likelihood that the population mean lies between 66 and 74 (70 ± 4).

Confidence Intervals

Although the value of a sample mean may be chosen as the value that is most likely to be the actual population mean, most researchers are not very comfortable with this choice. As you recall, any one sample chosen from a population may or may not be an accurate representation of the population. Researchers establish a range of values within which the population parameter is thought to occur. A **confidence interval** (CI) is a range of values that, with a specified degree of probability, is thought to contain the population value. Confidence intervals contain a lower and an upper limit. The researcher asserts with some degree of confidence that the population parameter lies within those boundaries.

Suppose a nurse researcher named Joan wishes to determine how knowledgeable the nurses in her state are about legal responsibilities in their practice. A test is located (or she develops one) that measures knowledge of legal issues in nursing practice. Joan is able to obtain the mailing list for all the 10,000 registered nurses in her state. When she examines her financial situation, the cost of mailing a questionnaire to all of the nurses does not fit in her budget. She decides to select a random sample of 100 nurses from the list. Let us assume that all 100 of the nurses return the questionnaire (which is highly unlikely). Data analysis shows the mean score of this group to be 31 (of a possible 35 points), with a standard deviation of 3. The mean score is rather encouraging. Joan decides that the nurses in her state are fairly knowledgeable about legal issues. Excitedly, she reports the results to a friend. The friend says, "How can you be so confident about your results? There were only 100 nurses in the sample. I don't think you would find an average score of 31 if you tested all of the nurses in the state." Feeling somewhat deflated, Joan decides to determine how much confidence to place in the results. This is done by estimating the knowledge level of the total population of nurses in the state based on the test scores of a sample of 100 nurses. She decides that she wants to be 95% confident about her estimation when she goes back to talk to her friend again. First she determines the standard error of the mean ($s_{\bar{x}}$).

$$s_{\bar{x}} = \frac{3}{\sqrt{100}} = \frac{3}{10} = 0.3$$

Next, she inserts 0.3 into the formula for obtaining the 95% confidence interval (LL = lower limit, UL = upper limit).

$$LL = \bar{X} - 1.96\,(s_{\bar{x}})$$
$$UL = \bar{X} + 1.96\,(s_{\bar{x}})$$
$$LL = 31 - 1.96\,(0.3)$$
$$31 - 0.588 =$$
$$30.412$$
$$UL = 31 + 1.96\,(0.3) =$$
$$31 + 0.588 =$$
$$31.588$$

Joan then determines the 95% confidence interval to have a lower boundary of 30.41 and an upper boundary of 31.59. She was right after all! Her estimation of the knowledge of legal issues in nursing practice among the total population of nurses in her state indicates that their knowledge levels would be quite close to the mean of her sample of 100 nurses. She can be 95% confident that if she had selected another sample of 100 nurses from the mailing list, the mean score would be between 30.41 and 31.59. Another way to state this is that she is 95% confident the interval of 30.41 to 31.59 contains the population mean. If she wanted to be 99% confident of her estimate, she would replace 1.96 in the formula with the figure 2.58.

$$LL = 31 - 2.58\,(0.3) =$$
$$31 - 0.774 =$$
$$30.226$$
$$UL = 31 + 2.58\,(0.3) =$$
$$31 + 0.774 =$$
$$31.774$$

Joan is now 99% confident that the mean of the population lies between 30.23 and 31.77. With this statistical ammunition she can again approach her friend and see if she is any more successful in convincing this friend that nurses in her state are fairly knowledgeable about legal issues in nursing practice.

Imagine that you were asked to be a subject in a weight loss study. The researcher tells you that you will lose significantly ($p < .05$) more weight on this new diet than you did on the one you had previously tried. Wouldn't you also want to know how *much* weight you would lose? If the researcher said, "I am 95% sure that you will lose between 10 pounds and 15 pounds in 6 weeks," she would be giving you a confidence interval.

For some reason, confidence intervals have not been reported very often in nursing studies. Generally, only significance levels are reported for hypothesis-testing studies. Many medical studies report both of these statistics. Nurse researchers should become aware of the value of reporting confidence intervals in their research reports. Rothstein and Tonges (2000) contended that confidence interval analysis is a "useful approach to quantify the effect of an intervention and predict the results that can be expected from implementation" (p. 69). According to Melynk and Fineout-Overholt (2005), confidence intervals are the best indicators of the effectiveness of a treatment.

A review of research journals pointed out that some nurse researchers are beginning to report confidence intervals. Tarnow and King (2004) reported on intradermal injections given with the bevel up versus the bevel down. They found that the bevel-up injections took 4.64 seconds less time than bevel-down injections, with a 95% confidence interval of 1.42 to 7.85 seconds. Can you tell from this confidence interval that the amount of time (in seconds) that it took for the injection varied quite a bit? Kolanowski, Litaker, and Buettner (2005) reported a 95% confidence interval in their study of the efficacy of theory-based activities for behavioral symptoms of dementia. A confidence interval (95%) was also reported by Fincher, Ward, Dawkins, Magee, and Wilson (2009) in their study of patients with Parkinson disease. They found visualization through videophone sessions to be more effective than telephone sessions in counseling these patients about their medications and self-management activities. In another study (Marshall, Cowell, Campbell, & McNaughton, 2010), cancer screening rates were compared between women with diabetes and those without diabetes. Again, a 95% confidence interval was reported in this study. Women with diabetes were less likely to receive cervical screening when compared to women in the general population.

Testing Hypotheses

As previously mentioned, the testing of hypotheses is very important to nurse researchers. Steps in testing hypotheses include the following:

1. State the study hypothesis (generally, a directional research hypothesis).
2. Choose the appropriate statistical test.
3. Decide on the level of significance (alpha level).
4. Decide if a one-tailed or two-tailed test will be used.
5. Calculate the test statistic, using the research data.
6. Compare the calculated value to the critical value for that particular statistical test.
7. Reject or fail to reject the null hypothesis.
8. Determine support or lack of support for the research hypothesis.

The Study Hypothesis

A researcher should take great pains in formulating the hypothesis(es) for a study. The hypothesis should be based on the theoretical/conceptual framework of the study; therefore, the hypothesis should generally be a directional research hypothesis that predicts the results of the study.

Although the research hypothesis is of primary interest to an investigator, this hypothesis is never tested statistically. The null hypothesis (H_0) is the one subjected to statistical analysis. The null hypothesis states that no difference exists between the populations from which the samples were chosen or no correlation exists between variables in the population. Because this is not what the researcher expects to find, why is the null hypothesis necessary? Statistical tests are set up to test the null hypothesis. Remember, all inferential statistical tests are based on the assumption that no difference or relationship (correlation) exists. If small differences or low correlations are found, chance is considered to be the reason, and the null hypothesis is not rejected. If the results of the analysis show that the difference or correlation is too large to be the result of chance, the null hypothesis is rejected. Of course, rejection of the null hypothesis provides support for the research hypothesis. Researchers are never able to say that they "proved" their research hypotheses. It is possible for them to say, however, with a specified degree of certainty, how likely it is that the null hypothesis is false.

The null hypothesis is frequently depicted using the following symbols:

$$H_0 : \mu_A = \mu_B$$

The symbols are those used for population parameters. Remember that statistical inference uses data from samples to draw conclusions about populations. The null hypothesis in the preceding formula indicates that there is no difference in the two populations from which the samples were drawn. Even if the two samples were drawn from the same population, for statistical purposes the samples are assumed to have come from two separate populations concerning the variable of interest. For example, suppose a group of patients were divided into two treatment groups by a random assignment procedure. The null hypothesis assumes that these two groups have been selected from one hypothetical population. Although this idea is somewhat difficult to understand or to visualize, the concept is used in all of the inferential statistical tests that examine differences between groups. If the null hypothesis is rejected, the statistical decision is made that the two samples came from two hypothetical populations that were different on the variable being measured. If the null hypothesis is not rejected, the statistical decision is made that the two samples came from the same hypothetical population in respect to the variable being studied.

The correct words to use when discussing the results of testing the null hypothesis are *reject* or *fail to reject*. *Retain* is also an acceptable word to use when the null hypothesis is not rejected. Although you will also see the word *accept* used in the literature, technically you never accept the null hypothesis. As Elzey (1974) has remarked, "We can only 'not reject' the hypothesis that there is no difference. We are not justified in concluding that there is no difference" (pp. 36–37).

When discussing the research hypothesis, it is correct to say that the hypothesis was "supported" or "not supported." You do not "reject" the research hypothesis because it was never actually tested. These points may seem minor and overly fussy, but if you learn to use the correct terminology in the beginning of your research career, you will not have to change bad habits later on.

Choosing a Statistical Test

Being able to choose an appropriate statistical test to use in analyzing your data and knowing the rationale for this choice are more important than being able to calculate the statistic. Currently, nearly all of the actual numerical calculations are done by computer. Although it is important to be familiar with the theoretical principles behind formulas used in the various tests, there is no need to memorize these formulas. When students take a statistics course, frequently they are so concerned with being able to perform mathematical calculations that they lose sight of the purposes of the various statistical tests and of how the choice of a particular test is made.

Basically, there are two types of inferential procedures: those that search for differences in sets of data and those that search for correlations between sets of data. Are you trying to determine if there is a significant difference between groups (i.e., between the experimental and control groups) or do you want to know if there is a significant correlation between variables within one group (levels of pain reported and number of requests for pain medication by open heart surgery patients)?

The choice of a statistical test is based primarily on the hypothesis for the study or the research question(s). The hypothesis will indicate, for example, that the pain level of one group of subjects is going to be measured before and after some specific nursing intervention to relieve pain. The study design based on this hypothesis (one group, pretest and posttest) tells you that you will have two sets of dependent data. The data are considered dependent or related because the same subjects are measured both times. If the level of measurement of the dependent variable (pain) is interval or ratio, the most appropriate statistical test is a paired *t* test. The *t* test will be discussed later in this chapter.

Here are some of the questions that need to be answered when choosing the appropriate inferential procedure:

1. Are you comparing groups or sets of scores? Are you correlating variables?
2. What is the level of measurement of the variables (nominal, ordinal, or interval/ratio)?
3. How large are the groups (sample size)?
4. How many groups or sets of scores are being compared?
5. Are the observations or scores dependent or independent?
6. How many observations are available for each group?

Level of Significance

After analyzing data from a study, the decision must be made whether to reject or fail to reject the null hypothesis. The researcher wants to know how likely it is that a wrong decision has been made when two groups are said to be different or when an independent variable is said to cause the change in the dependent variable. To make this decision, the researcher must decide how certain or how accurate the decision must be. In other words, how willing is the researcher to be wrong when declaring that one group really is different from the other group on the variable being measured? The **level of significance** can be defined as the probability of rejecting a null hypothesis when it is true, and it should not be rejected. The difference or relationship that is found is caused only by chance or sampling error, and the researcher has mistakenly said that the difference is related to the treatment variable.

The level of significance, represented by the Greek letter alpha (α), is an extremely important concept in inferential statistics. No matter what statistical test is used, a decision must be made about whether or not the specified level of significance was reached and, therefore, whether or not to reject the null hypothesis.

The letter *p* and the symbol α are used to symbolize the probability level that is set. The most common level of significance that is found in nursing studies is $p = .05$ (notice that no leading zero (0) is needed before the decimal point). Traditionally, scientists have set this value as a cutoff point for testing the null hypothesis. A significance level of .05 means that the researcher is willing to risk being wrong 5% of the time, or 5 times out of 100, when rejecting the null hypothesis. If the decision needs to be much more accurate, such as deciding if a drug is effective or not, the level of significance might be set at .01 or even at .001. With a .01 level of significance, the researcher stands the risk of being wrong 1 time out of 100 when rejecting the null hypothesis. At the .001 level of significance, the risk of error is 1 time out of 1,000.

An argument is occasionally made for setting a less stringent level of significance, such as .10. In research where no great harm would come from rejecting a true null hypothesis, a .10 level of significance might be acceptable. Again, nursing has accepted the .05 level as the standard in most studies. Note that the researcher must decide how accurate the decision needs to be concerning the hypothesis.

It is important not to confuse level of significance with clinical significance or clinical importance. Although findings that are statistically significant are more likely to be clinically significant than findings that are not statistically significant, the two do not always go hand in hand. Findings that are statistically significant may not be clinically significant. The reverse situation is also possible.

One-Tailed and Two-Tailed Tests

A research hypothesis may be stated in the directional form (the degree of difference or type of correlation is predicted) or the nondirectional form (a difference or correlation is predicted, but the degree of difference or type of correlation is not indicated). Directional research hypotheses should be based on a sound conceptual or theoretical framework. In other words, the rationale for the prediction

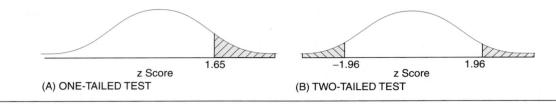

▶ **FIGURE 15–1**   Significant values for one-tailed and two-tailed tests at $\alpha = .05$

contained in a directional research hypothesis should be quite clear. Information on hypotheses was presented in Chapter 8.

If the researcher has stated a directional research hypothesis, it is appropriate to use a one-tailed test of significance. When a **one-tailed test of significance** is selected, differences or correlations are sought in only one tail of the theoretical sampling distribution (either the right or the left tail). The word *tail* is used to indicate the values on each end of the distribution. A **two-tailed test of significance** is used to determine significant values in both ends of the sampling distribution. The nondirectional research hypothesis, therefore, calls for a two-tailed statistical test.

The type of research hypothesis that is chosen will determine the significance level needed to reject the null hypothesis. It is much easier to reject the null hypothesis when a one-tailed test rather than a two-tailed test is used. The entire area of rejection of the null hypothesis is in one tail, rather than being split between the two tails, as would be necessary if a two-tailed test were used. If a two-tailed test is used, and the .05 level of significance has been chosen, the .05 must be divided into .025 in each tail of the distribution. For a one-tailed test, the region of rejection is all in one end of the distribution, and the entire .05 is sought in one tail. A z score of 1.65 is significant at the .05 level for a one-tailed test. A z-score of 1.96 is necessary for significance at the .05 level for a two-tailed test. Figure 15–1 shows the area of significant values for a one-tailed and a two-tailed test when the probability level is set at .05.

To illustrate the use of a one-tailed test, consider the following example. The framework for a study indicates that play is an effective means of introducing children to unfamiliar environments or unfamiliar equipment. This is the hypothesis for the study: "Four-year-old children who have played with physical examination equipment, including a stethoscope and a tongue blade, before a physical examination are more cooperative during the examination than children who have had no such previous play experience." This hypothesis would allow the researcher to expect higher cooperation scores for the experimental group who had had experience with physical examination equipment than for the control group. The entire .05 probability level will be sought in the right tail or the positive end of the distribution. Suppose that the mean cooperation score of the experimental group was higher than the mean score of the control group. If a z score of 1.65 or higher was obtained for the difference between the means of the experimental and control groups, the researcher would conclude that the children in the experimental group were significantly more cooperative than the children in the control group.

Nursing research that is based on a conceptual or theoretical framework allows the prediction of the results. One-tailed tests, therefore, are appropriate for studies based on a sound study framework.

Calculating the Test Statistic

Although this step in hypothesis testing may seem like the most difficult, these days you rarely have to do any hand calculations. Numerous statistical software programs are available. Of course, a nurse researcher may want to take advantage of a statistician.

Comparing Calculated Value and Critical Value

Critical values may be determined by consulting tables found in the back of statistics textbooks. However, today computer printouts generally provide critical values with which to compare the statistical results. A **critical value** is a scientific cutoff point. It denotes the value in a theoretical distribution at which all obtained sample values that are equal to or beyond that point in the distribution are said to be statistically significant. Critical values are found in the tails of a distribution. All values beyond the critical value are said to lie in the **critical region** or **region of rejection.** The critical value is determined by the level of significance chosen and the degrees of freedom. If the computed value of a statistic is less than the critical value, the null hypothesis is not rejected; if the computed value is equal to or greater than the critical value, the null hypothesis is rejected.

The interpretation of a statistical test depends on the degrees of freedom (df). **Degrees of freedom** concerns the number of values that are free to vary. Although the degrees of freedom indicate the number of values that can vary, the concern is really focused on the number of values that are *not* free to vary. Procedures to calculate the degrees of freedom for a particular statistical test are usually included in the description of that test. Degrees of freedom are generally denoted by the letters df and a number (e.g., df = 2). The concept of degrees of freedom is somewhat complex. A simplified example may help you gain a basic understanding of this concept. Suppose you were told to pick a number between 1 and 10. You would have 10 degrees of freedom because you could pick any of 10 numbers. Now imagine you are told to pick three numbers that add up to 10. After you have picked the first two numbers, the third number is not free to vary. For example, if you chose the numbers 3 and 5, the third number must be 2 to arrive at a sum of 10. You were, thus, allowed 2 degrees of freedom in this calculation.

Support for the Study Hypothesis

If a directional research hypothesis has been formulated for a study, support for this hypothesis is based on whether or not the null hypothesis is rejected. In nearly every study, the goal of the researcher is to reject the null hypothesis. Occasionally, the null hypothesis is actually a statement of the researcher's expectation. For example, in a study to determine if an inexpensive educational program was as effective as an expensive program, the researcher's prediction or expectation might be that there would be no difference in the effectiveness of these two programs. Again, as previously mentioned, the researcher generally hopes to be able to reject the null hypothesis.

After examining the obtained p value, if it is less than the level of significance that was set for the study (generally, $p = .05$), the researcher rejects the null hypothesis. Conversely, if the p value is greater than the set level of significance, the researcher must fail to reject the null hypothesis. Therefore, a researcher would reject the null hypothesis if the obtained value was .03 and would fail to reject the null hypothesis if the obtained value was .30, for example.

TYPE I AND TYPE II ERRORS

Four possible decisions may be made concerning the null hypothesis. Two of the decisions are correct ones. If the null hypothesis is actually false and you reject it, you have made a correct decision. If the null hypothesis is actually true and you fail to reject it (retain the null), you have made a correct decision. However, two mistakes can be made: type I and type II errors. If the null hypothesis is actually true and you reject it, you have made a **type I error**. If the null hypothesis is actually false and you fail to reject it, you have made a **type II error**.

Figure 15–2 depicts these four decisions. Because sample data are used to make a decision about a population, you never know for sure if you have made the correct decision.

As the probability of a type I error increases, the probability of a type II error decreases and vice versa. The level of significance (α) set for a study determines the probability of a type I, or alpha, error. For example, if the level of significance for a study is set at .05, the probability of a type I error is .05 or 5%. The probability of a type II, or beta, error (β) can be controlled by using power analysis (see Chapter 11).

Type I errors in research findings usually result in unnecessary changes being instituted, whereas type II errors result in failure to institute needed changes. Both of these errors may be serious. In general, however, researchers are more concerned with a type I error than a type II error. A

ACTUAL SITUATION IN POPULATION
Null Hypothesis

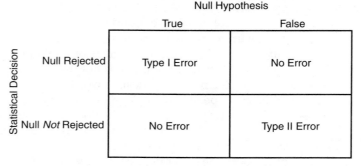

	True	False
Null Rejected	Type I Error	No Error
Null *Not* Rejected	No Error	Type II Error

(Statistical Decision)

▶ FIGURE 15–2   Type I and type II errors in hypothesis testing

type I error seems to be more embarrassing to the researcher because something, such as an intervention, is said to work when it actually does not work. For example, a significant difference might be said to exist between the reactions to an intervention by the experimental group compared to the control group when, in fact, the difference was related to chance.

PARAMETRIC AND NONPARAMETRIC STATISTICAL TESTS

Inferential statistical tests may be classified as parametric and nonparametric. As the term implies, **parametric tests** are concerned with population parameters, and these tests make assumptions about the population from which a sample was drawn. **Nonparametric tests** are less stringent in the requirements for their use and do not make assumptions about the population from which a sample is selected. The assumptions of parametric statistical tests include the following: (a) the level of measurement of the data is interval or ratio, (b) data are taken from populations that are normally distributed on the variable being measured, and (c) data are taken from populations that have equal variances on the variable being measured.

Because nonparametric tests make no assumptions about the distribution of the population, they are often called distribution-free statistics. Nonparametric statistical tests may be used with nominal and ordinal data, and when sample sizes are small.

A growing body of research suggests that violations of the assumptions of parametric tests do not adversely affect statistical decisions. The parametric tests are quite *robust*, which means that these tests are still reliable even if one of the assumptions of the test has been violated. Some researchers, therefore, routinely use parametric tests if data meet the requirement of being at the interval or ratio level of measurement.

Because it appears that nonparametric tests have fewer restrictions, you may ask why these types of tests are not used when analyzing all data. The answer lies in the power of the tests. If the assumptions of parametric tests are met, these types of statistical tests are more powerful than nonparametric tests. However, if the assumptions are violated, it is possible that a nonparametric test might be more powerful.

POWER OF A STATISTICAL TEST

The **power of a statistical test** is defined as the ability of the test to reject a null hypothesis when it is false. In other words, the more powerful a test, the more likely it will detect a significant difference between groups or a significant correlation between variables in one group. The power of a statistical test depends on the sample size and the level of significance that is chosen. The larger the sample chosen, the more power the statistical test will have. The higher the level of significance that is selected (.05 rather than .01, for example), the more power the statistical test will have. Also, a test will be more powerful if a one-tailed test rather than a two-tailed test is used.

STATISTICAL TESTS USED IN NURSING RESEARCH

Three of the most common statistical tests used in nursing research are the *t* test, analysis of variance, and chi-square, and are discussed next.

t Test

The **t test** is a parametric test that examines the difference between the mean values of some variable in two groups. It is one of the most popular statistical tests. The *t* test is appropriate for samples of nearly any size, but is particularly useful with small sample sizes (fewer than 30). Because the test compares means, interval or ratio data are required. Also, because the *t* test is a parametric test, the sample data are assumed to have been selected from populations that are normally distributed and have equal variances on the variable being measured.

Another name for the *t* test is the Student *t* test. This name was derived from the pseudonym used by the originator of the test, William Gosset. Gosset worked for a brewery in Dublin, Ireland. To maintain brewing secrets, a company policy prohibited publications by employees. Gosset chose to publish his mathematical formulas secretly under the pseudonym of Student.

The *t* test uses a *t* distribution. Actually, there is a set of *t* distributions, one for each different degree of freedom. As the number of degrees of freedom decreases, the shape of the distribution flattens from that of the normal curve. The more the number of degrees of freedom increases, the more the distribution shape resembles the normal curve.

There are two forms of the *t* test. One form is used with independent samples, and the other is used with dependent samples. An independent sample is one in which there is no association or connection between the scores of the groups that are being observed (e.g., an experimental group and a control group are compared). The test for independent samples is called an **independent t test** or *independent samples t test* or *unrelated samples t test*.

Independent *t* Test

An independent *t* test was used to analyze data from a study concerning the effectiveness of an aspiration risk-reducing protocol (Metheny, Davis-Jackson, & Stewart, 2010). The incidence of aspiration was compared between the usual care group (n = 329) and the Aspiration Risk-Reduction Protocol (ARRP) group (n = 145). One aspect of the protocol involved higher elevation of the head of the bed for patients in the ARRP group. Aspiration was significantly lower in the ARRP group patients than the usual care group patients, as determined by a lower mean percentage of pepsin-positive tracheal secretions (p = <.001). The incidence of at least one aspiration was half as likely in the ARRP group as in the usual care group.

The **dependent t test,** also called *paired t test* or *correlated samples t test,* is used when scores or values are associated or have some connection. For example, anxiety scores of mothers and daughters might be compared. If each mother is matched with her daughter on some variable such as age or weight, the sets of values are dependent data. Dependent data are also obtained when the same subjects are measured before and after they receive an experimental treatment.

Dependent *t* Test

Staff nurses at two participating hospitals (n = 58) participated in an online, computer-based learning module of arterial blood gas (ABG) interpretation (Schneiderman, Corbridge, & Zerwic, 2009). Nurses' post-test scores were compared to their pre-test scores. A paired *t*-test (dependent *t* test) demonstrated increased knowledge (p < .001) after completion of the online learning module.

Separate formulas are used to calculate the independent t test and the dependent t test. These can be found in statistics textbooks. The t value obtained is compared with the critical value associated with the t distribution appropriate for the data (based on the degrees of freedom). If the t value that is obtained is greater than the critical value, the null hypothesis is rejected, and the mean scores or values for the groups are considered to be significantly different.

Analysis of Variance

The t test is a very useful technique to determine the significance of the difference between two means. However, many studies compare more than two groups. For example, a researcher might want to compare the effectiveness of four different methods of teaching clients how to give insulin injections (four levels of the independent variable). The dependent variable might be the number of correct insulin injections that patients are able to perform in a given time period. If four groups were being compared, six separate t tests would have to be computed. Suppose Groups A, B, C, and D were being compared. The following pairs would result: A and B, A and C, A and D, B and C, B and D, and C and D (for a total of six comparisons).

Whenever the researcher wishes to compare the difference(s) among more than two means, the appropriate statistical test is the **analysis of variance** (ANOVA; pronounced un-nóv-uh). ANOVA enables the researcher to analyze the difference between several means at one time.

ANOVA is a parametric statistical test and, therefore, is based on the assumption that data are interval or ratio level and the data have been selected from populations that are normally distributed and have equal variances on the variable being measured.

ANOVA uses the F distribution, named after Sir Ronald Fisher. As is true with the t distribution, there is more than one F distribution. Each F distribution is based on the degrees of freedom. There are several different types of ANOVA procedures: one-way ANOVA, two-way ANOVA, and repeated measures ANOVA. The one-way ANOVA is discussed here.

As the name of the statistic indicates, analysis of variance examines the variance in data obtained. Two types of variation are examined: variation between the means of the groups and variation of individual scores within each of the groups. These two types of variation are called "mean square between" groups and "mean square within" groups. These terms are symbolized by MS_B and MS_W.

You may wonder why the difference between the means of the groups does not provide enough information to make a decision about the difference between the groups. It has been determined that the variability of the scores or values in the population affects the mean. By examining only the differences among the means of the samples, the researcher might falsely conclude that a true difference exists between the populations represented by the sample data when, in actuality, this seeming difference occurred because there is a great deal of variability within the samples. To avoid rejecting a true null hypothesis, the ANOVA examines two types of variability: the variability between the groups and the variability within each of the groups. The means of each of the groups are compared to the grand mean of all of the groups combined. Then each value within a group is compared to the mean value for that particular group. These two estimates of population variation are then compared by dividing the "between" estimate by the "within" estimate. An F ratio is obtained. This F ratio is symbolized by:

$$F = \frac{MS_B}{MS_W} \quad \begin{array}{l} \text{(Between group variance)} \\ \text{(Within group variance)} \end{array}$$

If the null hypothesis is true, these two measures of variability should be very similar, and the result of the division will be a value less than 1. If the null hypothesis is false, a value greater than 1 will be found. The larger the F value, the greater is the variation or difference between the groups as compared to the variation within the groups. The significance of the F value or F ratio is determined by consulting an F table in a statistics textbook to ascertain the critical value for F. If a computer program is used to analyze the data (which is nearly always the case today), the computer printout will usually provide the obtained value and the critical value.

If the difference or variation between the groups is significantly greater than the difference within the groups, the null hypothesis is rejected. In contrast, if the between-groups variation is not significantly greater than the within-groups variation, the null hypothesis is not rejected.

If the F value is significant, the researcher knows there is a significant difference between the means of at least two of the groups. The F statistic, however, does not tell exactly where the difference occurs. Other statistical procedures are necessary. You might think that the appropriate statistic to calculate would be t tests between all of the various pairs of groups. This technique will result in an increased likelihood of a type I error. The more comparisons that are made, the more likely it is that one of the comparisons will be significant, by chance. For example, if 20 t tests were run and the level of significance was set at .05, the researcher could expect to find statistical significance in at least one of these tests even if there was no true difference between the means of any of the groups that were being compared. Several multiple comparison tests may be used that decrease the probability of making a type I error, including the Duncan, Newman-Keuls Tukey B, and Scheffé tests.

Analysis of Variance (ANOVA)

Internet addiction among Korean adolescents was studied by Seo, Kang, and Yom (2009). Adolescents were classified as general users (547 or 80.9%), potential risk users (108 or 16%), and high-risk users (21 or 3.1%). ANOVA revealed significant differences among the three groups on all subscales of interpersonal problems ($F = 34.57$; $p = .000$). Duncan post hoc follow-up tests revealed that the high-risk group adolescents were much more likely to have interpersonal problems than adolescents in the other two groups.

Chi-Square

Statistical tests that were previously discussed, the t test and ANOVA, are appropriate for interval data. The **chi-square test** is a nonparametric inferential technique appropriate for comparing sets of data that are in the form of frequencies or percentages (nominal data). The chi-square statistic (χ^2) is probably the most commonly used statistic with nominal data.

Using the chi-square technique, the researcher compares the frequencies that are obtained or observed in categories with the frequencies that would be expected to occur if the null hypothesis is true. Observed frequencies are compared to expected frequencies. If the observed frequencies are quite different from the expected frequencies at a specified level of significance (such as .05), the null hypothesis is rejected.

The chi-square distribution is the theoretical sampling distribution used when the chi-square statistic is calculated. Actually, there is a set of chi-square distributions. The shape of each of these distributions is governed by the degrees of freedom. To consult a chi-square table, you need to know the degrees of freedom, just as you do when examining a t-distribution table or an F-distribution table.

Although the chi-square distribution may be used for several purposes, probably the most common use is with the *chi-square test for independence,* also called the *chi-square test for contingency tables.* Chapter 14 described contingency tables as those tables used to illustrate data that are presented in frequencies. The chi-square test for contingency tables is used to analyze the data that are displayed in contingency tables. The observed and expected frequencies in each cell of the table are compared.

Examine the data in Table 15–1. The research problem of the study was to determine whether psychiatric nurses are more or less likely to smoke than medical-surgical nurses. The sample has 100 psychiatric nurses and 100 medical-surgical nurses. The data show that half of the total sample, or 100 subjects, are smokers, and 100 subjects are nonsmokers. The data also show that 60 psychiatric nurses smoke, and 40 psychiatric nurses do not smoke. The figures are reversed for the medical-surgical nurses. The number 50 displayed in the upper-right corner of each cell in the table is the number of smokers and nonsmokers that would be expected in each group if these two variables were not related.

TABLE 15–1 Smoking Behavior of Psychiatric and Medical-Surgical Nurses

	Smokers		Nonsmokers		Total
		50		50	
Psychiatric nurses	60		40		100
		50		50	
Medical-surgical nurses	40		60		100
Total	100		100		200

The chi-square distribution will be used to determine if the observed values might have occurred by chance. If many samples, each containing 100 psychiatric nurses and 100 medical-surgical nurses, were chosen from the population, how many times would this size difference between groups occur by chance? To make this decision, the obtained value is compared to the critical value. In this case the obtained value for χ^2 is 8.00, and the critical value is 3.84. The null hypothesis, therefore, would be rejected, and the researcher would conclude that this large a difference would occur by chance less than 5 times out of 100. Therefore, the conclusion is made that there is a significant difference in the smoking behavior of the two groups. Psychiatric nurses are more likely to smoke than medical-surgical nurses.

Because the chi-square test that was used is called the chi-square test of independence, another way to state the results is that smoking behavior *depends* on the type of nurse (psychiatric versus medical-surgical) you are. The null hypothesis says that smoking behavior and type of nurse are independent, or not related, and, therefore, there will be no difference between the observed frequencies and the expected frequencies in the cells of the table. Rejection of the null hypothesis indicates that these two variables are dependent or related. Smoking behavior and type of nurse (psychiatric versus medical-surgical) are related.

Chi-Square Test

A survey was sent to 236 program directors or other designated individuals from nurse practitioner (NP) programs (Hart, Brennan, Sym, & Larson, 2009). Response rates were compared between individuals who were sent a prenotification by e-mail or phone (242 or 76%) about the upcoming survey and those who received no notice (76 or 24%). The response rate of the 76% who were notified prior to being sent the survey was 49% versus 45% for the 24% who did not receive the prenotification. This 4% difference was not found to be significant (χ^2, $p > .1$)

As you can see, the p value of $>.10$ indicates that the chi-square statistic was not significant. The 4% difference could have occurred by chance. The null hypothesis of no difference between the response rates of the two groups of program directors could *not* be rejected.

TESTING THE SIGNIFICANCE OF CORRELATION COEFFICIENTS

Chapter 14 discussed correlation coefficients as descriptive statistics. A correlation coefficient presents the degree to which the values of one variable (X) are related to the values of another variable (Y). The closer the correlation coefficient is to $+1.00$ or -1.00, the greater is the relationship between these two variables. Although the size of the correlation coefficient gives some indication of the degree to which two variables are related, an inferential statistical procedure is necessary to determine if this correlation coefficient is the result of chance (sampling error) or whether there is a true relationship between these variables in the population.

In testing the significance of a correlation coefficient, the researcher wants to determine if the obtained r, based on sample data, came from a population of pairs of values for which the actual correlation is 0. The null hypothesis states that there is 0 correlation between these two variables in the population. If the correlation coefficient that is obtained from the sample data is too high to have come from a population in which the correlation is actually 0, the null hypothesis is rejected, and the conclusion is made that the two variables are correlated at a level that is significantly higher than 0.

If a correlation of .80 is obtained between two variables, the variables are quite probably actually related. However, if a correlation coefficient such as .15 or .20 is obtained, this value possibly occurred as a result of sampling error or chance.

To determine if a correlation coefficient is significant, a t test can be calculated or a table of significant values consulted. The degrees of freedom for the Pearson product-moment correlation are equal to the number of subjects minus 2 (n − 2). When the sample contains a large number of subjects, the size of the correlation coefficient may be quite small and still be significant. For example, with 20 degrees of freedom (22 subjects), an $r = .42$ is significant at the .05 level. If the degrees of freedom are increased to 80 (82 subjects), a correlation of $r = .22$ is significant at the .05 level. When interpreting the significance of correlation coefficients, it is important to examine the sample size. Comparisons can be found in tables in the backs of statistics books or determined by examining a computer printout of the data.

As mentioned in Chapter 14, rather than using an inferential procedure to determine the statistical significance of a correlation coefficient, a more accurate interpretation of a correlation coefficient is obtained by squaring the coefficient (r^2), thereby determining the percentage of variance shared by the two variables. The r^2 for the first example, $r = .42$, would be .18 ($.42 \times .42 = .1764$). This means that these two variables share a common variance or overlap of 18%. If you knew the value of one variable, you would possess 18% of the knowledge you needed to be able to predict the value of the other variable. A correlation coefficient of .42 may not sound very significant to you now even though it might have been determined to be statistically significant. Remember, when a correlation coefficient is determined to be statistically significant, it only means that it is significantly different from 0. It does not take a very large correlation for it to be larger than 0! It is hoped that this information will help you understand why some small correlations that are reported in research articles are said to be statistically significant. Occasionally, you will see correlation coefficients as small as .15 or even .09 reported in the literature, and they will be starred (*) as being significant at the .05 level or even doubled starred (**) for the .01 level. Don't let these stars (******) fool you. Look at the actual size of the correlation coefficient.

ADVANCED STATISTICAL TESTS

Many advanced statistical tests are available for the researcher who wishes to study more than two variables in one study. One frequently used inferential procedure is multiple regression. **Multiple regression** is the procedure used when the researcher wishes to determine the influence of more than one independent variable on the dependent variable. For example, a researcher might want to determine what factors would most accurately predict a woman's decision to perform breast self-examination. A number of factors might be examined, such as history of breast cancer in the family, fear of cancer, and type of teaching received concerning the performance of breast self-examination.

Multiple Regression

A study by Chard (2010) examined how perioperative nurses define, attribute the cause of, and react to intraoperative nursing errors. One aspect of the study used multiple regression to determine variables that predict defensive changes in practice: (a) accepting responsibility, (b) distancing, (c) seeking social support, (d) escape/avoidance, (e) planful problem solving, and (f) self-control. Accepting responsibility and using self-control were the most significant predictors of defensive changes in practice in regard to nursing errors.

Another frequently used test is the **analysis of covariance (ANCOVA)** . ANCOVA is a powerful statistical test used when the researcher wishes to control statistically for some variable that may have an influence on the dependent variable. This test can also be used to make two groups statistically equal on some variable for which they are quite different before the experimental treatment is administered. For example, suppose a researcher wishes to determine if the anxiety levels of open-heart surgery patients will be lower postoperatively in the group that receives explicit pictorial information about postoperative procedures compared to the group that receives only verbal information. It is self-evident that the anxiety levels of patients preoperatively will influence their postoperative anxiety levels, regardless of the intervention that they receive. Therefore, the researcher needs to measure the preoperative anxiety levels of both groups. Even if subjects are randomly assigned to the experimental and control groups, the average anxiety levels of one group, just by chance, might be higher than the other group. ANCOVA enables the researcher to make the two groups statistically similar. You might consider it like a golf game where an average player is given a handicap to allow him or her to have a chance of winning against a great player. Improvement is the criterion.

Analysis of Covariance (ANCOVA)

Harrington and Walker (2009) used analysis of covariance (ANCOVA) when studying the effects of computer-based fire safety training on caregivers' fire knowledge, attitudes, and practices in small residential care facilities in Maryland. ANCOVA was used to compare the posttest scores of the treatment and control groups while controlling for any differences between the two groups on their pretest scores. The treatment group outperformed the control group on the knowledge subtest [$F(1,57) = 56.82$, $p = .001$].

Two other advanced statistical tests that you may read about in research reports are canonical correlation and multivariate analysis of variance. **Canonical correlation** examines the correlation between two or more independent variables and two or more dependent variables. **Multivariate analysis of variance (MANOVA)** examines the difference between the mean scores of two or more groups on two or more dependent variables that are examined at the same time.

Researchers may examine the results of several research studies simultaneously, using statistical measures. **Meta-analysis** is a technique that combines the results of several quantitative studies that have been conducted on the same topic. The results of a large number of different studies are combined and statistically analyzed as if only one study had been conducted with one large group of subjects. An effect size is presented for a treatment or intervention. The **effect size** indicates how useful a treatment or intervention was in several studies as indicated by the difference between data from control groups and experimental groups. The effect size may be reported as small, medium, or large, or the actual effect size may be reported (such as .23, .44, etc). Anderson (2003) wrote that meta-analysis is a "rigorous statistical procedure that synthesizes results from multiple primary research studies on a common clinical problem or issue" (p. 1). She called for researchers to provide all of the needed information in their research articles that would allow their studies to be included in a meta-analysis. For example, the exact p value should be reported (rather than just reporting that the results were significant or not significant). In an editorial in the *Western Journal of Nursing Research*, Conn (2009) reported that the literature contains many small studies with insufficient statistical power because of small sample sizes. She asserted that meta-analysis provides a means of examining patterns across many small related studies.

Meta-Analysis

Quality-of-life (QOL) outcomes following physical activity interventions were examined in a meta-analysis conducted by Conn, Hafdahl, and Brown (2009). They synthesized the results of 66 reports that contained a total of 7,291 subjects who had chronic illnesses. Both published and unpublished primary research studies were examined. This meta-analysis study revealed an overall modest improvement in QOL outcomes for the study subjects compared to the control subjects (effect size $= .11$).

A fairly new "meta" term is appearing in the literature. **Metasynthesis** is a technique used in summarizing reports of qualitative research studies—it combines the results of several qualitative studies that cover the same topic. Beck (2009) called for qualitative researchers to synthesize their findings in order to promote qualitative research as a reliable source of evidence for evidence-based practice.

Metasynthesis

A metasynthesis was conducted by Duggleby et al. (2010) to describe the hope experience of family caregivers of persons with a chronic illness. Fourteen studies were examined, all of which revealed the importance of hope. Themes derived from the data were: (a) transitional refocusing from a difficult present to a positive future, (b) dynamic possibilities within uncertainty, (c) pathways of hope, and (d) hope outcomes.

CRITIQUING INFERENTIAL STATISTICS IN RESEARCH REPORTS

As mentioned in Chapter 14, readers are quite often intimidated by the statistics of a research report. The inferential statistics are even more intimidating than the descriptive statistics to many consumers of research. Although a thorough background in statistics is necessary to understand each and every statistical test discussed in research reports, a minimal understanding of inferential statistics is sufficient for the reader to understand the majority of the study results. Many of the same inferential statistics (e.g., t tests, ANOVA) are reported in a large number of research articles. Box 15–1 presents some guidelines for critiquing inferential statistics.

Box 15-1 Guidelines for Critiquing Inferential Statistics

1. Are inferential statistics presented in the research report?
2. If inferential statistics are presented, is enough information presented for the reader to determine whether or not the appropriate tests were used?
3. Is the reader provided with the calculated value of the inferential statistic, the degrees of freedom, and the level of significance that was obtained?
4. Were parametric or nonparametric tests used when the other type would have been more appropriate?
5. Are the chosen tests appropriate considering the level of measurement of the variables, the number of groups that were tested, the size of the sample, and so on?
6. Are inferential statistics presented for each hypothesis that was stated in the study?
7. Are the results of inferential tests clearly and thoroughly discussed?
8. Are the results presented both in the text and in the tables?

First, the reader searches the report for any inferential statistics used in data analysis. Every time you see a p value listed, you know an inferential statistical test was used. Then a determination must be made if there is enough information to make a decision about the appropriateness of each test that was used. For example, the research report should include the level of measurement of the variables, number of groups that were tested, and sample size.

The reader should be provided with the value of the statistical test that was obtained, the degrees of freedom, and the significance level reached when each hypothesis was tested. The actual p value should be listed, not just that the p value was significant or not significant. The reader should be able to determine if each of the researcher's hypotheses was or was not supported. Therefore, every research report should clearly present the results of hypothesis testing. These results should be presented both in the text of the report and in tables.

SUMMARY

The two broad purposes of inferential statistics are to estimate population parameters from sample data and to test hypotheses. The second purpose has been of more interest to nurse researchers.

When a sample is chosen to represent a population, there is some likelihood that the sample will not accurately reflect the population. The phenomenon in which sample values tend to be normally distributed around the population value is known as the **central limit theorem**. A frequency distribution based on an infinite number of samples is called a **sampling distribution**. Theoretical sampling distributions are used to estimate population characteristics. The standard deviation of the sampling distribution of the mean is called the **standard error of the mean** ($s_{\bar{x}}$).

A **confidence interval** is a range of values that, with a specified degree of probability, is thought to contain the population value. The researcher might establish a 95% confidence interval or a 99% confidence interval, for example.

Steps in hypothesis testing include (a) stating the study hypothesis, (b) choosing an appropriate statistical test, (c) deciding on the level of significance, (d) deciding if a one-tailed or a two-tailed test will be used, (e) calculating the test statistic, (f) comparing the calculated value to the critical value, (g) rejecting or failing to reject the null hypothesis, and (h) determining support or lack of support for the research hypothesis.

Although the study hypothesis (generally a directional research hypothesis) is of primary interest to an investigator, the null hypothesis (H_0) is the one subjected to statistical analysis.

Some of the questions that need to be answered when choosing a statistical procedure include the following: Are you comparing groups? Are you correlating variables? What is the level of measurement of the variables? How large are the groups? How many groups are being compared? Are the observations dependent or independent? How many observations are available on each group?

The **level of significance**, also called alpha (α), is defined as the probability of rejecting a null hypothesis when it is true. The most common level of significance used is .05. This means that the researcher is willing to risk being wrong 5% of the time or 5 times out of 100 when rejecting the null hypothesis. More stringent levels of significance are .01 and .001.

If the researcher has stated a directional research hypothesis, it is appropriate to use a one-tailed test of significance. If a **one-tailed test of significance** is employed, values will be sought in only one tail of the theoretical sampling distribution. A **two-tailed test of significance** is used to determine significant values in both ends of the sampling distribution.

A **critical value** is a cutoff point that denotes the place in a theoretical distribution at which all obtained values from a sample that are equal to or beyond that point are said to be statistically significant. Values beyond the critical value are said to lie in the **critical region** or **region of rejection.** If the computed value of a statistic is equal to or greater than the critical value, the null hypothesis is rejected.

The interpretation of a statistical test depends on the degrees of freedom (df). **Degrees of freedom** concern the number of values that are free to vary.

If the null hypothesis is actually true and it is rejected, a **type I error** is made. If the null hypothesis is actually false and is not rejected, a **type II error** is made. The level of significance set for the study determines the probability of a type I error. Power analysis will help prevent a type II error.

Inferential statistical tests can be classified as parametric and nonparametric. **Parametric tests** require interval or ratio data and assume that the sample data have been taken from populations that are normally distributed and have equal variances. **Nonparametric tests** can be used with nominal and ordinal data and make no assumptions about the distribution of the population. Nonparametric tests are sometimes called distribution-free statistics.

The **power of a statistical test** is the ability of the test to reject a null hypothesis when it is false. The power of a test depends on the sample size and the level of significance chosen.

The **t test** is a parametric test that examines the difference between the means of two groups. The *t* test uses the *t* distribution. One form of the test is used with independent samples and is called the **independent t test** or *independent samples t test* or *unrelated t test*. The **dependent t test,** also called *paired t test* or *correlated samples t test*, is used when scores or values are associated.

Analysis of variance (ANOVA) is used to compare the difference among more than two means. The ANOVA is a parametric test that uses the *F* distribution.

The **chi-square test** is a nonparametric inferential technique that is appropriate for comparing sets of data that are in the form of frequencies or percentages. The frequencies that are obtained or observed are compared to the expected frequencies. The chi-square distribution is the theoretical sampling distribution used when the chi-square (χ^2) statistic is calculated.

An inferential procedure is necessary to determine if a correlation coefficient is statistically significant. The researcher may determine the significance of a correlation coefficient using a *t* test or by consulting a table of significant values.

Advanced statistical tests include **multiple regression, analysis of covariance** (ANCOVA), **canonical correlation,** and **multivariate analysis of variance** (MANOVA). **Meta-analysis** combines the results of several similar studies that gathered quantitative or numerical data. An **effect size** indicates how useful a treatment or intervention was in several studies as indicated by the difference between data from the control and experimental groups. **Metasynthesis** combines the results of several similar studies that involve qualitative inquiries.

NURSING RESEARCH ON THE WEB

For additional online resources, research activities, and exercises, go to **www.mynursingkit.com.** Select Chapter 15 from the drop-down menu.

GET INVOLVED ACTIVITIES

1. Write down all of the different kinds of inferential statistics found in this chapter and any others that you may recall from any statistics course you have taken. Leave space on this list for adding other inferential tests you may locate that are not on your list. Take this sheet of paper to the library or to your computer. Examine three nursing research articles that were published in the 1980s, three nursing research articles that were published in the 1990s, and three recent nursing research articles. Place a check mark on your list beside each type of inferential statistic mentioned in the articles. Write in any other tests mentioned that you do not have on your list. Additionally, write down as many levels of significance (*p* values) as you find.

2. Bring your list and compare it with the lists compiled by your classmates or colleagues. Determine the most common inferential statistic that is reported in nursing research articles. Make a tally of the number of times each type of inferential statistic was mentioned in the nursing research literature.

3. Make a comparison among the articles published in the 1980s, the 1990s, and those published in recent years. Have the numbers and types of tests changed in recent years?

4. Compare the probability values (p values) that you located in the literature. Were most of them significant ($< .05$)? How many articles published results that were not significant?

5. Divide into groups. Propose an idea for a study and determine the type of descriptive statistic(s) that your group would use to report data on subjects and the type of inferential statistics you would use to report the results of hypothesis testing or to present the answers to research questions.

SELF-TEST

Circle the letter before the *best* answer.

1. Statistical significance means that the study findings
   A. are important to the nursing profession.
   B. apply to a large target population.
   C. are not likely to be the result of sampling error.
   D. have proven the study hypothesis.

2. If study findings are statistically significant, this implies that the
   A. null hypothesis should be rejected.
   B. research hypothesis should be rejected.
   C. null hypothesis should not be rejected.
   D. research hypothesis should not be rejected.

3. Parametric statistical tests would be appropriate for which of the following types of data?
   A. pulse rates
   B. religious affiliation
   C. blood type
   D. patients' identification numbers

4. Which of the following is true concerning nonparametric statistical tests?
   A. should never be used with interval/ratio data
   B. estimate population parameters
   C. are generally used with large samples
   D. none of the above

5. A research hypothesis states that "Male appendectomy patients ask for more pain medication on the first postoperative day than female appendectomy patients." When the data are analyzed, the mean number of re-

quests for pain medication is 3.5 for males and 2.3 for females. The p value is calculated to be .04. What decision should be made about the findings of this study?
   A. Male appendectomy patients asked for significantly more pain medication on the first postoperative day than did female appendectomy patients.
   B. Female appendectomy patients needed less pain medication on the first postoperative day than did male appendectomy patients.
   C. There was no statistically significant difference in male and female patients' requests for pain medication on the first postoperative day after an appendectomy.
   D. No determination can be made about the difference in male and female appendectomy patients' requests for pain medication on the first postoperative day.

A researcher is trying to determine if the type of educational preparation is associated with the level of professional commitment. The mean scores on the *Commitment to the Nursing Profession* instrument are obtained for 30 diploma school graduates, 30 associate degree graduates, and 30 baccalaureate graduates. The probability level associated with the obtained F value is .03. (Questions 6 through 10 pertain to this situation.)

6. What is the level of measurement of the dependent variable?
   A. nominal
   B. ordinal
   C. interval/ratio

7. How many sets of scores are being compared?
   A. one
   B. two
   C. three
   D. four

8. The scores on the dependent variable are
   A. dependent.
   B. independent.

9. What inferential statistic was calculated?
   A. dependent t test
   B. analysis of variance
   C. independent t test
   D. chi-square test

10. Which of the following decisions concerning scores on the *Commitment to the Nursing Profession* instrument is correct, based on the probability level of .03 that was obtained when the data were analyzed?

A. No significant difference was found among diploma, associate degree, and baccalaureate graduates' scores.
B. A significant difference was found among diploma, associate degree, and baccalaureate graduates' scores.
C. No decision can be made as to whether a significant difference was found among diploma, associate degree, and baccalaureate graduates' scores.

11. A computer printout reveals $t = -2.5$; df = 40; $p = .03$. The researcher would
   A. reject the null hypothesis.
   B. fail to reject the null hypothesis.
   C. conclude that an error in calculation had been made.
   D. none of the above.

REFERENCES

Anderson, E. H. (2003). Facilitating meta-analysis in nursing [guest editorial]. *Nursing Research, 52*, 1.

Beck, C. T. (2009). Metasynthesis: A goldmine for evidence-based practice. *AORN Journal, 90*, 701–702; 705–710.

Chard, R. (2010). How perioperative nurses define, attribute causes of, and react to intraoperative nursing errors. *AORN Journal, 91*, 132–145.

Conn, V. S. (2009). Celebrity endorsement of meta-analysis? (editorial). *Western Journal of Nursing Research, 31*, 435–436. doi: 10:1177/0193945909332292

Conn, V. S., Hafdahl, A. R., & Brown, L. M. (2009). Meta-analysis of quality-of-life outcomes from physical activity interventions. *Nursing Research, 58*, 175–183.

Duggleby, W., Holtslander, L., Kylma, J., Duncan, V., Hammond, C., & Williams, A. (2010). Metasynthesis of the hope experience of family caregivers of persons with chronic illness. *Qualitative Health Research, 20*, 148–158.doi: 10.1177/1049732309358329

Elzey, F. (1974). *A first reader in statistics* (2nd ed.). Monterey, CA: Brooks/Cole.

Fincher, L., Ward, C., Dawkins, V., Magee, V., & Wilson, P. (2009). Using telehealth to educate Parkinson's disease patients about complicated medication regimens. *Journal of Gerontological Nursing, 35*, 16–24.

Harrington, S. S., & Walker, B. L. (2009). The effects of computer-based fire safety training on the knowledge, attitudes, and practices of caregivers. *The Journal of Continuing Education in Nursing, 40*, 79–86.

Hart, A. M., Brennan, C. W., Sym, D., & Larson, E. (2009). The impact of personalized prenotification on response rates to an electronic survey. *Western Journal of Nursing Research, 31*, 17–23.

Kolanowski, A. M., Litaker, M., & Buettner, L. (2005). Efficacy of theory-based activities for behavioral symptoms of dementia. *Nursing Research, 54*, 219–228.

Marshall, J. G., Cowell, J. M., Campbell, E. S., & McNaughton, D. B. (2010). Regional variations in cancer screening rates found in women with diabetes. *Nursing Research, 59*, 34–41.

Melynk, B. M., & Fineout-Overholt, E. (2005). Rapid critical appraisal of randomized controlled trials (RCTs): An essential skill for evidence-based practice (EBP). *Pediatric Nursing, 31*, 50–52.

Metheny, N. A., Davis-Jackson, J., & Stewart, B. J. (2010). Effectiveness of an aspiration risk-reduction protocol. *Nursing Research, 59*, 18–25.

Polit, D. F. (1996). *Data analysis & statistics for nursing research.* Stamford, CT: Appleton & Lange.

Rothstein, H., & Tonges, M. C. (2000). Beyond the significance test in administrative research and policy decisions. *Journal of Nursing Scholarship, 32*, 65–70.

Schneiderman, J., Corbridge, S., & Zerwic, J. J. (2009). Demonstrating the effectiveness of an online, computer-based learning module for arterial blood gas analysis. *Clinical Nurse Specialist, 33*, 151–155.

Seo, M., Kang, H. S., & Yom, Y. (2009). Internet addiction and interpersonal problems in Korean adolescents. *CIN: Computers, Informatics, Nursing, 27*, 226–233. doi: 10.1097/NCN.0b013e3181a91b3f

Shott, S. (1990). *Statistics for health care professionals.* Philadelphia: W. B. Saunders.

Spatz, C., & Johnston, J. (1984). *Basis statistics: Tales of distribution* (3rd ed.). Monterey, CA: Brooks/Cole.

Tarnow, K., & King, N. (2004). Intradermal injections: Traditional bevel up versus bevel down. *Applied Nursing Research, 17*, 275–282.

CHAPTER 16

Presentation and Discussion of Study Findings

OUTLINE

OBJECTIVES

On completion of this chapter, you will be prepared to:

1. Describe the methods used to present research findings
2. Discuss the findings of research studies
3. Relate study findings to study hypotheses
4. Distinguish between statistical and clinical significance
5. Identify the conclusions of research studies
6. Determine the implications of research studies
7. Discuss the recommendations of research studies
8. Critique the findings, conclusions, implications, and recommendations of published research studies

NEW TERMS DEFINED IN THIS CHAPTER

W e have reached the final steps in the research process. However, these final steps are very important. You might say, "The best has been saved for last." The findings, discussion of findings, conclusions, implications, and recommendations help pull together all of the pieces of a research study. They indicate not only what has been learned from this particular study, but also point out what needs to be done in the future related to this area of research.

The presentation of these final sections of a study may be placed under various headings in the research report. In theses and dissertations, you will probably find each of these sections under a separate heading. In research journal articles, there is a great deal of variation. All of these elements of a report may be found under a section titled "Discussion of Findings" or there may be a section on "Findings" and another section for "Discussion." Many qualitative study reports contain a section titled "Discussion." Some articles may have a section titled "Results and Conclusions." Regardless of the division of the material under various headings, each research report should contain the elements mentioned: findings, discussion of findings, conclusions, implications, and recommendations. Each area is discussed individually here.

FINDINGS OF THE STUDY

The findings of a quantitative study are the results presented in the form of empirical data or facts. Have you ever seen reruns of the old TV show *Dragnet?* Sergeant Friday would say, "Just the facts, ma'am, just the facts." This holds true for the findings of a research study. This is not the place for the researcher to express opinions or reactions to the data.

Findings are written in the past tense, of course, because data are being reported that have already been gathered and analyzed before the writing of the report. A note of caution: *Data are plural.* The word *data* frequently is used incorrectly as a singular noun rather than a plural noun. *Datum*, the singular noun, is rarely used because the information that is gathered nearly always involves more than one piece of information.

The findings come from the analysis of the data obtained in the study. Descriptive statistics are always used to describe the sample and to present the findings. Inferential statistics are always used to present the findings in studies in which hypotheses were tested.

PRESENTATION OF FINDINGS

Most research reports present the findings in both a narrative form and in tables. There is some disagreement about the function of the table in relation to the narrative presentation. Some people want to see all of the results in both places. Other individuals contend that results presented in tables should not be reported in their entirety in the text; only highlights or important items from the table should be presented in the narrative. According to the publication manual of the American Psychological Association (2010), if the text discusses every item in the table, the table is unnecessary.

Narrative Presentation of Findings

The findings of a study should be clearly and concisely presented in the text. In qualitative studies, narrative presentations predominate. These narrations generally contain direct quotes from participants. The researcher may then present a summary of the findings by discussing patterns and themes found in the data. Do the themes appear to capture the meaning found in the participants' own words?

In quantitative studies where hypotheses are tested, the narrative presentation should present data that support or fail to support each study hypothesis. Certain information should always be included in the text when discussing the study hypothesis(es). The statistical test that was used, the test results, degrees of freedom, and the probability value should be listed. Here are two common methods of reporting the same information:

$$t\,(30) = 2.75; \quad p = .01$$
$$t = 2.75; \quad df = 30; \quad p = .01$$

In the past, the probability value was frequently reported with a "less than" symbol in front of it ($p = < .05$) to indicate that the actual probability level was less than the given figure. Today, with the use of computers, the exact probability value should be reported. The computer printout will usually provide the probability value to four or more decimal places. The probability value is then listed in a research report as two decimal places. So, if the probability level was .0212, it probably would be reported as .02 and not as $< .05$, as was common in years past.

In qualitative research studies, hypotheses are not tested. Therefore, inferential statistics are not included in these reports.

Tables

Tables are a means of organizing data so they may be more easily understood and interpreted. The discussion of the table should be as clear as possible in the text. Some of the responsibility, however, for understanding the table is left with the reader. If a table is being used to present the results of hypothesis testing, the results should be placed in the table or a footnote added that provides the test results, degrees of freedom, and probability level. This information would be presented in the format described under the narrative type of presentation. For example, the following might be found under a table:

$$\chi^2 = 13.39; \quad df = 5; \quad p = .02$$

Here are some general guidelines concerning tables:

1. Tables should appear as soon as possible in the report after they have been referred to in the text.
2. Information presented in tables should also be discussed in the narrative of the report.
3. Titles should be clear, concise, and contain the variables that are presented in the data. The name of the statistical test should not be used. For example, the following would be an inappropriate title: *T Test for Difference in Anxiety Levels of Cardiac Patients*. An appropriate title might be: *Guided Relaxation and Anxiety Levels of Cardiac Patients*.
4. All data entries should be rounded to the same number of decimal places (one or two decimal places is common).
5. The decimal points, if present, should be lined up under each other in the data columns.
6. If data are not available for a section of the table, a dash (—) should be entered, rather than leaving a blank space, to make it clear that no data have accidentally been left off the table.

Some tables contain rows, some contain columns, and some contain both rows and columns. The vertical entries in a table are referred to as **columns,** and the horizontal entries are called **rows**. **Cells** are the boxes that are formed where rows and columns intersect.

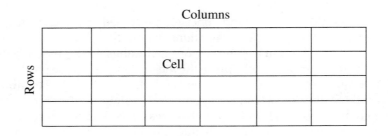

Figures

The word *figure* is the term used to indicate any type of visual presentation other than a table. Figures include graphs, diagrams, line drawings, and photographs. Figures may help enliven a narrative presentation and should be considered as a valuable means of displaying research results. These methods are particularly useful in presenting demographic data about subjects. See Chapter 14 for examples of various types of figures.

DISCUSSION OF FINDINGS

The discussion of the findings is a much more subjective section of a research report than the presentation of the findings. The discussion section of a study report allows the researcher to make interpretations of the findings. The findings are interpreted in light of the theoretical framework and within the context of the literature review. No literature sources should be cited in the discussion of the findings section that were not referred to in the review of the literature section of the report. When new literature sources are cited, it appears as if the investigator went back to the library or the Internet after the data were collected to search for a source or sources that would be in agreement with the study findings.

In the discussion of the findings, the researcher discusses aspects of the results that are in agreement and those that are not in agreement with previous research and theoretical explanations. The researcher also reports study limitations. As mentioned in Chapter 3, study limitations are uncontrolled variables that may affect study results and "limit" the generalizability of the findings.

Limitations

Landis, Parker, and Dunbar (2009) studied the associations among sleep, hunger, satiety, food cravings, and caloric intake in adolescents. One unexpected finding was that increased daytime sleep was associated with a greater total food-cravings score, which the researchers contended could lead to obesity. Some of the study limitations mentioned were (a) nonrandom sampling procedure, (b) self-report sleep data, and (c) use of a single 24-hour diet recall.

Although study limitations should be discussed, this is not the time to focus on every fault of the study. A beginning researcher frequently lists all of the weaknesses and problems of the study and appears to ask the reader to disregard the findings of the present study when they are not in agreement with the theoretical framework or past research results. Experienced investigators are able to interpret findings within the context of the strengths and the weaknesses of their studies.

DISCUSSION OF STUDY HYPOTHESES

Nurses need to have a basic understanding of hypothesis testing prior to reading an article that contains a hypothesis. Ren (2009) published an informative article in the *Journal of Emergency Nursing* about the importance of understanding statistical hypothesis testing. She pointed out that hypothesis testing does not directly answer a research question but enables the researcher to draw conclusions or make decisions about a population based on data from a sample.

The most important aspect of the findings in studies where hypotheses have been formulated is the presentation of inferential statistics used to test the hypotheses. As discussed in Chapter 15, the null hypothesis is subjected to statistical analysis, and the results allow the researcher to reject or fail to reject the null hypothesis. If the null hypothesis is rejected, support is provided for the research hypothesis. Remember, the research hypothesis predicts study results based on the theoretical framework or on previous research studies.

The results of hypothesis testing fall into one of three categories: (a) the null hypothesis is not rejected; (b) the null hypothesis is rejected, and the research hypothesis is supported; and (c) the null hypothesis is rejected, and the results are in the opposite direction from the prediction of the research hypothesis.

When the study results are congruent with the study prediction found in the research hypothesis, the researcher is overjoyed, and the task of describing the results of the study is relatively easy. The explanation for the findings will have already been discussed in the section on the theoretical framework or in the review of the literature section where previous research results were presented. Although the researcher should never say that the results "proved" the study hypothesis, the findings of a study provide empirical support for the hypothesis, and the investigator asserts with a degree of certainty (probability level) that the results were not related to chance. When significant results are found, the researcher will feel like celebrating and may begin to think about publishing the results.

When the null hypothesis is not rejected, the researcher may become discouraged and start trying to determine "what went wrong." Beginning researchers are particularly prone to start picking apart their studies when the null hypothesis is not rejected. They discuss the small sample size and the inadequate instrument and all the other limitations that can be identified. It is not uncommon for a graduate student who is writing a thesis to become upset after discovering nonsignificant study results. Researchers must be objective when considering negative results (those not in agreement with the prediction). Negative results may be as important as positive results. They just are not as exciting for the researcher.

Some researchers think the only studies that are published are those in which the findings are in agreement with the study predictions. Many of the published research studies *do* report positive findings. In fact, you will find that most of the study results you examine report positive findings. However, a recent review of the research journals revealed that studies are being published in which nonsignificant results were found. As previously mentioned, negative results may be as important as positive results.

Although the discovery of nonsignificant results is disheartening, the discovery of results that are in the opposite direction of the study prediction is even more disappointing and puzzling. These types of results do not support the study's theoretical framework. These results may also be incongruent with previous research results. For an investigator faced with this dilemma, the best thing that can be done is to try to make some sense out of the findings and give some tentative explanations for the results. Recommendations may then be made for further research based on these explanations.

STATISTICAL AND CLINICAL SIGNIFICANCE

It is very important to distinguish between statistical and clinical significance. Statistical significance means that the null hypothesis has been rejected and that the differences found between groups on the variable of interest, or the correlations found between two variables, are not likely to be a chance occurrence. The differences or correlations are probably real. These real differences or correlations, however, may not be clinically important. Clinical significance means that the findings can be useful in the clinical setting with patients. The researcher's greatest desire is that study findings are *both* statistically and clinically significant.

Statistical and Clinical Significance

A study examined pain scores following the application of a topical anesthetic cream (LMX-4) or placebo (hand cream) to the hands of a sample of healthy adult volunteers who received IV catherization (Valdovinos, Reddin, Bernard, Shafer, & Tanabe, 2009). The mean pain score for the LMX-4 hand was 3.2 on a 0–10-cm visual analog scale; the placebo hand score was 4.67. The mean paired difference of −1.37 cm in pain scores was determined to be both statistically significant ($t = -3.17, p = .003.$) and clinically significant.

The significance of a correlation coefficient depends on the sample size. As the sample size increases, the smaller the correlation needs to be to reach significance. For example, with a sample size of 15, a correlation coefficient of .48 is needed to be statistically significant at the .05 level. With a sample of 100 subjects, a correlation of .19 is statistically significant at the .05 level. Remember, a statistically significant correlation means only that you are reasonably sure the actual correlation between these two variables in the population from which the sample was obtained is greater than 0. It doesn't take a very large correlation to be greater than 0!

Sometimes the difference between the scores of two groups (experimental and control) on the dependent variable are so large that the statistical and clinical significance are quite apparent. However, there are instances where no statistical significance is found, but the researcher believes the findings have some clinical significance. Sometime the researcher will find an intervention to have no significant effect for the experimental group, as a whole, but will find the intervention to be effective for a certain subgroup within the experimental group.

CONCLUSIONS

The study conclusions are the researcher's attempt to show what knowledge has been gained by the study and are also an attempt to generalize the findings. In writing conclusions, the researcher returns to the study problem, purpose, hypothesis, and theoretical framework. Was the study problem addressed adequately? The research purpose met? The research hypothesis supported? The theoretical framework supported? The researcher should leave no doubt in the reader's mind about what the study has demonstrated in these areas. Conversely, it is probably wise to be somewhat conservative in drawing conclusions from the findings.

In formulating conclusions, the researcher must consider the sample size and the population from which the sample was drawn. An example of a study conclusion that was generalized beyond the findings of the study is found in Jones's (1981) report published in *Nursing Research*. Self-reported theft behavior among 33 nurses in one hospital in the Northeast was examined. These nurses were asked if they ever took anything home from the hospital (supplies, etc.). Based on their responses, the investigator reported that theft behavior was fairly prevalent among this group of nurses. One of the researchers' conclusions was, "These figures suggest that employee theft among nursing personnel is widespread and needs to be reduced" (p. 35). Do you agree that this is an example of overgeneralization? A sample size of 33 nurses in one hospital does not warrant the use of the word *widespread*. Although this study is 30 years old, it has been included in each edition of this textbook because the conclusion is so awful!

Whereas the findings of a study are concrete and tied into the specific data of the study, the conclusions are more abstract and are presented in more general terms. Conclusions are *not* just a restatement of the findings. It is somewhat common to find a conclusion in a student's initial research report that states, "There is a significant relationship between anxiety and test scores among nursing students." This is a finding and not a conclusion. The conclusions should go beyond the findings. For example, a study finding might be, "There is a significant increase in the exercise performance of a group of senior citizens who have used mental practice to increase their exercise performance." A conclusion based on this finding would be, "Mental practice appears to be an effective means of increasing exercise performance in the elderly." You may think that these two statements are quite similar, but examine them more closely and you will see that the conclusion goes beyond the finding. The finding addresses the difference in exercise performance of one group of people from the pretest to the posttest. A conclusion is an attempt to generalize the result to other senior citizens and to other points in time. The word *appear* may worry you. You have been taught in nursing to avoid words that could have subjective meanings. You would never chart "It appears that the patient is bleeding." That statement probably makes you cringe! However, the word *appears* is an acceptable term for a study conclusion. Conclusions are tentative. We never "prove" our findings when we conduct research with human beings, which is usually the case in nursing research. We can say only "mental practice appears to increase exercise performance in the elderly."

The purpose of scientific quantitative research, as you may recall, is to be able to generalize results to the broad population, not just to the study sample. In some types of research, such as phenomenological studies, nurses may be more interested in the responses of individuals than in those of groups. However, in the traditional scientific method the interest is in populations rather than in samples or in individuals. The generalization of findings, therefore, is of great interest to quantitative study investigators.

Generalizations are risky business, however. The study design and sampling procedures must always be considered. If the senior citizens in the previous example had consisted of 10 volunteers who said before the study that they enjoyed exercising, there would be no basis for making the conclusion that mental practice was the reason for the increase in exercise performance. There would be too many threats to the validity of the study because of the design used and the sampling technique. You would have no way of knowing if the group changed because of the treatment or other factors, such as the Hawthorne effect. Because the subjects were volunteers who said that they enjoyed exercising, they may have been more motivated to increase their exercise performance.

IMPLICATIONS

Both quantitative and qualitative researchers should present the implications of their studies. This section of the research report gives the researcher an opportunity to be creative. Imagine that you have the power to change the way certain courses are taught in your curriculum or certain procedures are carried out in the hospital where you work. Based on the findings and conclusions of your study, what changes would you suggest?

The implications of a study contain the "shoulds" or what needs to happen next. "Nurse educators should . . ." or "it would be appropriate for nurse clinicians to . . ." are the types of statements found in the implications section of a research report. Based on the study, what changes, if any, should be considered?

A study implication might be that no change is needed, or that more research is called for to further verify the study results, or that changes need to be made based on the study conclusions. Although it is possible that no change is deemed necessary and that nurses should continue with their current practices, it is more common to see implications that call for more research in the subject area or for certain changes to be made based on the conclusions of the study.

For every conclusion of a study, there should be at least one implication. Implications can be addressed to any or all of the following: clinicians, educators, researchers, administrators, or theorists.

Consider this conclusion: "Guided relaxation is an effective means of controlling anxiety in patients about to undergo a proctoscopic examination." An implication of this conclusion might be "Nurses might want to consider using guided relaxation techniques with patients about to undergo proctoscopic examinations." Another implication might be that nurse educators teach nursing students about the usefulness of guided relaxation techniques in their nursing practice. Although these implications may seem to be quite simple and derived from common sense, the implications of a study may be very challenging to write at times.

RECOMMENDATIONS

It has often been said that every research study raises more questions than it answers. The last section of every research report should contain recommendations for further research. Both quantitative and qualitative researchers should make recommendations for future research, based on their studies. This section may propose replication of the study or a new study, in which the present study limitations are considered. The researcher might also suggest some logical extension of the present study.

Replication of the Research Study

Replication of a study involves carrying out a study similar to one that has previously been done. Only minor changes are made from the previous study, such as using a different type of sample or setting. Partial replication studies are probably more common than exact replications. If an instrument is changed or a new tool is added, it is probably more accurate to call this type of study a partial replication study.

Nurses have appeared to be reluctant to replicate the studies of other investigators. Beck (1994) decried the small number of replication studies. She contended that the lack of replication studies has seriously hampered the implementation of research findings. Beck admonished nurses who consider replication studies as "simple, dull, and repetitive" (p. 193). She asserted that this type of research takes "considerable imagination and skill" (p. 191). An excerpt from a replication study is provided in Chapter 5. Fah, Morgan, Kalman (2003) have made a strong call for replication studies.

As a result of nurses' reluctance to replicate studies, many isolated pieces of nursing research exist. Researchers must become convinced of the value of replication. The body of nursing knowledge needs to be based on research findings. Hypotheses must be tested over and over on different samples and in different settings to build confidence in research results.

Replication studies are very appropriate for beginning researchers. This type of research is an excellent means of gaining research experience. Experienced researchers must also be willing to conduct replications to verify or repudiate previous research results. Unfortunately, few replication studies are found in the nursing literature.

Consideration of Study Limitations in Future Research

When recommending future research studies, the limitations of the present study should be considered. Some of the most common recommendations that are made concerning limitations are (a) alteration in the sample (different age group or educational level of the subjects), (b) alteration in the instrument (either a change in an existing instrument or use of another instrument), (c) control of variables (taking only a certain age group in the sample or selecting a random sample instead of using a convenience sample), and (d) change in methodology (providing 6 weeks of the experimental treatment instead of 4 weeks or using structured observations to collect data from respondents rather than using self-report measures).

Extensions of the Research Study

Recommendations concerning extension of the research study should answer the question, "What comes next?" After completing a study, the investigator should be in a good position to determine the next step that needs to be taken to examine the subject area under consideration. It is important to distinguish extensions of the study from the common recommendations often found in research studies. These common recommendations suggest a larger sample, or a different setting, or more reliability studies on the instrument. Although the limitations of a study need to be discussed, this is not the most important function of the recommendations section. In this section of the report, the researcher has the opportunity to make suggestions for future research based on the findings of this particular study, the findings of previous research, and the current state of the theoretical framework used in the study. This is a great challenge.

Recommendations for Future Research

A study was conducted to examine the experience of research coordinators (RCs) concerning scientific misconduct (Habermann, Broome, Pryor, & Ziner, 2010). Registered nurses made up 64% of the sample, which was obtained from RCs who belonged to the Association of Clinical Research Professionals. RCs reported research misconduct in 70% of the cases where they had identified misconduct. The authors of this study recommended that future research be conducted to determine why many RCs do not report misconduct. The researchers also suggested examining the research integrity of entire research teams, as well as that of individual RCs.

ETHICAL ISSUES IN PRESENTING RESEARCH FINDINGS

The researcher has the responsibility to ensure that no subjects can be identified. The names of subjects should never be reported. Generally, in quantitative studies, only group data are presented. In qualitative studies, narratives by individual participants are common. Therefore, protecting subjects from being identified in a qualitative report is very important.

If data are collected in an agency, the name of this agency should never be mentioned, unless permission has been obtained. The agency should be described in very general terms such as "a large public teaching hospital in the northeastern United States."

CRITIQUING THE PRESENTATION OF STUDY FINDINGS

When presenting the findings of a study, the investigator must be very objective. None of the investigator's personal opinions should be included. However, in discussing the study results, the researcher has an opportunity to interject some subjective interpretation of the data. For example, the researcher might mention some environmental factor that was thought to affect the study results. In one study, a group of subjects were trying to improve the time needed to complete a run around a track. Subjects had been taught the use of guided imagery to help them run faster. During the time the subjects were running the track, a dust storm came up. The researcher proposed that this might have been the reason for the nonsignificant study findings.

The discussion section of a research report should discuss the findings of each hypothesis that was tested or each research question that was answered. The findings should be interpreted in light of the study framework and previous literature on the topic. If the study hypotheses was not supported, the researcher should present an argument about why these findings may have occurred. If these findings were thought to be related to the limitations of the study, the researcher should acknowledge these limitations and make suggestions for how these problems could be corrected in future studies. The study conclusions should be presented; implications for nursing practice, nursing education, and nursing research should be indicated; and recommendations for replication or extension of the study should be suggested. Box 16–1 presents some guidelines for critiquing the presentation and discussion of study findings.

Box 16-1 Guidelines for Critiquing the Presentation of Study Findings

1. Is the information concerning the study findings presented clearly and concisely?
2. Are the findings presented objectively?
3. In qualitative studies, are the participants' subjective narrations clear and do the themes derived from these narratives capture the meaning of the data?
4. In quantitative studies, is each study hypothesis or research question addressed separately?
5. Are the findings described in relation to the study framework?
6. Are the findings compared to those of other studies discussed in the literature review section of the report?
7. Does the investigator discuss the limitations that may have influenced the findings of the study?
8. Is clinical significance discussed, and is statistical significance discussed in a quantitative study where inferential statistics are presented?
9. Are study conclusions clearly stated?
10. In quantitative study reports, are generalizations made that are based on the data and take into consideration the sample size and sampling method, or does it appear the investigator has overgeneralized the findings of the study?
11. Are implications suggested for nursing practice, nursing education, and/or nursing research?
12. Are recommendations made for future research studies? If so, do these recommendations take into consideration the limitations of the present study?

SUMMARY

Each research report should contain the findings, discussion of findings, conclusions, implications, and recommendations for future research. These elements of a research report may be found under various types of headings.

The findings of a study are the presentation of the results in the form of empirical data. Methods of presenting findings include narrative presentations, tables, and figures.

The findings of a study should be clearly and concisely presented in the narrative text of the study report. The results of hypothesis testing should contain the statistical test used, the test results, the degrees of freedom, and the obtained probability level.

Tables are a means of organizing data to make study findings more easily understood and interpreted. Tables should never appear in a report unless they have been discussed in the text and should appear as soon as possible after they have been referred to. The vertical entries in a table are the **columns**; the horizontal entries are called **rows**. **Cells** are the boxes formed where rows and columns intersect.

The word *figure* is the term used to indicate any visual presentation of data, other than a table. Figures include graphs, diagrams, line drawings, and photographs.

The discussion of findings is a more subjective section of a research report than the presentation of findings. The researcher interprets the findings in light of the theoretical framework and in the context of the literature review. The researcher also discusses any problems that may have occurred while conducting the study.

An important aspect of the findings of a study is the discussion of the hypothesis testing results. Results fall into one of three categories: (a) the null hypothesis is not rejected, and, therefore, the research hypothesis is not supported; (b) the null hypothesis is rejected, and the research hypothesis is supported; and (c) the null hypothesis is rejected, and the results are in the opposite direction from the prediction of the research hypothesis.

It is important to distinguish between statistical and clinical significance. Statistical significance means that the null hypothesis has been rejected and the study findings are probably not related to chance. Clinical significance means that the findings may be useful in the clinical setting.

The study conclusions are the researcher's attempt to generalize the findings. Conclusions are based on the findings and take into consideration the study problem, purpose, hypothesis, and theoretical framework. The population, sample, and sampling method must also be considered when trying to generalize study results.

The implications of a study contain the "shoulds" that result from the study. Appropriate changes are recommended that should be carried out by nurses in any of the following roles: clinician, educator, researcher, administrator, and theorist.

Recommendations for further research should be contained in each research report. This section of the report should propose replication of the study or a new study in which the present study limitations are considered. The researcher might also suggest some extensions to the present study.

When presenting research results, the rights of subjects must be protected. Names of subjects should never be reported, and, generally, only group data are presented.

NURSING RESEARCH ON THE WEB

For additional online resources, research activities, and exercises, go to **www.mynursingkit.com.** Select Chapter 16 from the drop-down menu.

GET INVOLVED ACTIVITIES

1. Find study conclusions in three published research articles. Peruse the final section(s) of research articles (these sections are usually labeled "Discussion of Findings," "Discussion and Conclusions," or some similar heading). Search for the sentence(s) in which the researcher attempts to generalize the results of the study. What word(s) indicated to you that the conclusion(s) had been located? When meeting with your classmates or colleagues after this exercise, share with them any difficulty you had in finding conclusions in the research articles you reviewed.

2. In these same research articles you have reviewed, determine if the researcher presented any implications. If implications were found, did they appear to be aimed at clinicians, educators, administrators, researchers, or theorists?

3. Visit your library and locate the section that contains theses and dissertations written by nurses. Read some of the recommendations sections of these research reports. Write

down two recommendations that are most appealing to you for future studies. Bring these suggestions to your group of colleagues. Determine, by vote, the single most worthwhile recommendation for a nursing study.

4. Locate a replication study in the nursing research literature. How long did it take you to find such a study? Did the original researcher conduct the replication? Was the study an exact replication or a partial replication? How long after the original study was the replication done? Did the researcher obtain similar results to those found in the original study?

5. Discuss the need for replication studies among your classmates or colleagues who are meeting together. Make suggestions for areas of research for which replication studies seem to be the most critical in nursing's attempt to develop a body of knowledge for the profession.

6. Examine some of the recommendations of several published studies. Decide on a study recommendation that is most appealing to your group.

SELF-TEST

Circle the letter before the *best* answer.

1. The conclusions of a study are based on the
   A. findings of the study.
   B. review of the literature.
   C. implications of the study.
   D. recommendations for future research.

2. Which of the following statements is true concerning statistical and clinical significance?
   A. Statistical significance is necessary for clinical significance.
   B. Findings may be both statistically and clinically nonsignificant.
   C. If findings are said to be clinically significant, they must also be statistically significant.
   D. Findings must be either statistically significant or clinically significant.

3. Guidelines for the use of tables in research studies include which of the following?
   A. A table should appear in a research report after the narrative discussion of the table.

B. If data are missing, a blank space should appear in the table to indicate missing data.
   C. Titles should include the name of the statistical test used to analyze the data.
   D. Information presented in a table does not need to be discussed in the research report narrative.

4. Consider the following conclusion: "There is a positive relationship between children's anxiety levels and their failure to cooperate with physical examinations." Determine an appropriate implication derived from this conclusion.
   A. Nurses must discover why high anxiety levels cause children to be uncooperative during physical examinations.
   B. Nurses should try to assess the anxiety levels of children before physical examinations.
   C. Physical examinations should be conducted infrequently with small children.
   D. A parent should be instructed to remain in the room with the child during a physical examination.

5. The recommendations of a study might contain which of the following?
   A. a discussion of the study findings
   B. suggestions for extension of the study
   C. comparisons of results with previous research findings
   D. a means of implementing the study findings

Write true (T) or false (F) beside the following statements:

____ 6. The names of subjects are listed in a research report unless the subjects specifically ask not to be identified.

____ 7. The implications of a study are based on the recommendations of the study.

____ 8. The most important recommendations of a research report are those that suggest a larger sample size or a different type of sample.

____ 9. Study generalizations should take into consideration the sampling method used in the study.

____ 10. Study conclusions are based on the implications of the study.

____ 11. Recommendations for future research are usually not made if the results of the present study are significant.

____ 12. The researcher should present at least one implication for each study conclusion.

REFERENCES

American Psychological Association. (2010). *Publication manual of the American Psychological Association* (6th ed.). Washington, DC: Author.

Beck, C. T. (1994). Replication strategies for nursing research. *Image: Journal of Nursing Scholarship, 26,* 191–194.

Fahs, P. S., Morgan, L. L., & Kalman, M. (2003). A call for replication. *Journal of Nursing Scholarship, 35,* 67–71.

Habermann, B., Broome, M., Pryor, E. R., & Ziner, K. W. (2010). Research coordinators' experiences with scientific misconduct and research integrity. *Nursing Research, 59,* 51–57.

Jones, J. (1981). Attitudinal correlates of employee theft of drugs and hospital supplies among nursing personnel. *Nursing Research, 30,* 349–351.

Landis, A. M., Parker, K. P., & Dunbar, S. B. (2009). Sleep, hunger, satiety, food cravings, and caloric intake in adolescents. *Journal of Nursing Scholarship, 41,* 115–123.

Ren, D. (2009). Understanding statistical hypothesis testing. *Journal of Emergency Nursing, 35,* 57–59.

Valdovinos, N. C., Reddin, C., Bernard, C., Shafer, B., & Tanabe, P. (2009). The use of topical anesthesia during intravenous catheter insertion in adults: A comparison of pain scores using LMX-4 versus placebo. *Journal of Emergency Nursing, 35,* 299–304.

CHAPTER 17

Communication and Utilization of Nursing Research

OUTLINE

Communication of Nursing Research Findings
- Preparing a Research Report
- Presenting Research Results at Professional Conferences
  - Presenting a Research Paper
  - Presenting a Research Poster
- Publishing a Journal Article
  - Preparing the Article
  - Selecting a Journal
  - Choosing Between Refereed and Nonrefereed Journals
  - Sending Query Letters
  - Reasons for Manuscript Rejection
- Preparing Research Reports for Funding Agencies
- Preparing Theses and Dissertations
Utilization of Nursing Research Findings
- Barriers to Nursing Research Utilization
  - Nurses' Lack of Knowledge of Research Findings

- Nurses' Negative Attitudes Toward Research
- Inadequate Dissemination of Research Findings
- Lack of Institutional Support for Research
- Findings Are Not Ready for Use in Practice
- Bridging the Gap Between Research and Practice
  - WCHEN Project
  - CURN Project
  - Rogers's Innovation-Diffusion Model
  - Stetler Model of Research Utilization
  - Iowa Model of Evidence-Based Practice
  - Research Utilization Studies
Summary
Nursing Research on the Web
Get Involved Activities
Self-Test

OBJECTIVES

On completion of this chapter, you will be prepared to:
1. Discuss the preparation of a research report
2. Describe two means of presenting research results at professional meetings
3. Explore the steps in publishing a journal article
4. Recognize the responsibility for preparing a research report for an agency that has provided funds for a study
5. Discuss theses and dissertations as means of presenting research results
6. Recognize the barriers to nursing research utilization
7. Discuss measures that have been taken to facilitate nursing research utilization
8. List the five stages in Rogers's innovation-diffusion model

9. Recall the five phases of Stetler's model for research utilization

10. Identify the steps in the Iowa model of evidence-based practice

11. Discuss a research utilization study conducted in the past 5 years

NEW TERMS DEFINED IN THIS CHAPTER

blind review, pg 266

call for abstracts, pg 261

galley proofs, pg 263

impact factor, pg 265

nonrefereed journal, pg 265

open review, pg 266

peer review, pg 265

query letter, pg 266

refereed journal, pg 265

research report, pg 260

Your research project is completed, and you have been asked to present your study results at a national research conference. Does this sound like delusions of grandeur? Maybe so, but it is hoped that some day you will present the results of a study you have conducted. Once a researcher has completed a study, plans should be made to communicate or disseminate the results. In fact, these plans should be made before the beginning of the project. A research project is really not completed unless the findings have been communicated to others. Patricia Grady, director of the National Institute of Nursing Research, referred to the old saying that "research not published is research not done" (Grady, 2000, p. 54).

Although the communication of research findings is frequently considered to be the last formal step in the research process, it is only the beginning of the most important phase of research—the utilization of research findings. Therefore, in the last edition of the book, utilization of research findings was added as the final step of the research process. Nurse researchers need to exert as much effort in implementing research findings as they do in conducting research in the first place. This chapter discusses various means of communicating nursing research findings and promoting their utilization.

COMMUNICATION OF NURSING RESEARCH FINDINGS

Researchers can communicate the results of their studies in two major ways: They can talk about them or write about them.

A nurse researcher might begin by presenting study results to peers. Next, this researcher might attend a research conference at which study results are discussed in an oral presentation or in a poster session. As a next step, study results might be published in a journal article. If funding has been received for a research project, the researcher probably will be required to submit a written report of the study to the funding agency. Finally, many nurses are pursuing advanced degrees and will present their research results associated with their theses and dissertations.

Although researchers have the prime responsibility of communicating the findings of their studies, other nurses and nursing organizations also bear the responsibility of seeing that research findings are distributed inside the nursing profession, to other health care professionals, and even to the general public.

Preparing a Research Report

A **research report** is a written or oral summary of a study. No research project is complete until the final report has been written. Even when a verbal presentation is planned, the research report should be written out in its entirety.

Writing is not easy. Hegyvary (2005) has contended that effective writing is not an innate skill. She said that this skill, like any skill, must be continually polished. Of course, that takes time.

Effective writing is the result of planning and organization before writing begins. Good writing should be clear, accurate, and concise. Technical or scientific writing is not meant to be humorous or entertaining, but it also should not be dull. The results of a study should be presented in an interesting and informative manner.

The research report should be presented in the order of the research process, beginning with the problem of the study and ending with conclusions, implications, and recommendations for future studies. The major part of the research report is written in the past tense because the study has already occurred. Hypotheses and conclusions are written in the present tense, and the implications and recommendations are directed toward the future.

Presenting Research Results at Professional Conferences

Many nurse researchers give first consideration to nursing journals as a publication medium for their research results. However, the time delay for publication of a report in a journal may be 2 years or longer. This process has been speeded up in recent years, because journal editors now allow manuscripts to be submitted online. However, presentations of research findings at local, regional, and national conferences provide more rapid distribution of study results. Nurses should present their research results at nursing conferences as well as at interdisciplinary conferences.

The two ways to disseminate research results at professional conferences are oral presentations and poster presentations. Traditionally, oral presentations have been used most frequently, but in the last 15 to 20 years, poster presentations have increased in popularity.

Nurses have many opportunities to present their study results at research conferences and seminars. Nursing organizations such as the American Nurses Association and Sigma Theta Tau sponsor research seminars. Many nursing schools and regional nursing associations sponsor research conferences. Some organizations make special provisions for presentations by students.

Potential participants are contacted through a **call for abstracts**, which request summary of a study that the researcher wishes to present at a conference. These requests are published in professional journals and distributed to educational institutions, health care agencies, and potential participants whose names have been obtained through the mailing lists of professional organizations. Notices of research conferences are generally distributed 6 to 12 months before the event.

Each conference or seminar will provide special guidelines for presenters and deadlines for submission of abstracts. The required length of the abstract varies from 50 to 1,000 words, but many have a 200- to 300-word limit. Abstracts should contain the purpose, research question(s) or hypothesis(es), design, methodology, major findings, and conclusions. If the research is still in progress, the last two items are not required. Abstracts will be evaluated, and participants will be notified about the selection decisions.

Generally, those individuals selected to be presenters at conferences receive no pay and are required to cover their own travel expenses. Sometimes the conference registration fee is waived or reduced for participants. A commitment to nursing research is a prime motivator for participants. Of course, personal recognition is also a reward.

Presenting a Research Paper

The oral presentation of a research report is usually referred to as a paper presentation. The word *paper* is used because the report of the study has been written out on paper and is referred to or read by the investigator during the presentation. Guidelines for paper presentations are found in the literature (e.g., Billings & Kowalski, 2009; Ulrich, 2007).

If the principal investigator is unable to attend the conference, a co-investigator or another person familiar with the study presents the paper. A written report of the study will be necessary if the proceedings of the conference are to be published.

Presenting research results at a conference has advantages over publishing the findings in a journal article. First, the investigator has the opportunity to present findings that are recent. Because of the time lag in publishing, research presented in journals may be outdated when it is printed. Second, the researcher will have the opportunity to interact with those people who are interested in the study and will be able to locate other researchers who are studying the same or similar phenomena.

Although many presentations are read directly from the research paper, more interest is created when an outline is used and the presenter communicates with the audience informally. The use of audiovisual aids, such as slides and PowerPoint displays, greatly enhances a presentation. Audiences generally appreciate written handouts in the form of abstracts or summaries of the study.

A presenter is usually allotted 15 to 30 minutes. At some conferences, additional time is allocated for questions. At other conferences, the presenter may have to allow time for questions if questions are desired. Even when no time remains for questions, presenters are usually willing to respond to questions during break times or after the conferences.

The format of the oral presentation is similar to that of a journal article or other written presentation of the study, in that the steps of the research process are usually presented in chronological order. The main difference lies in the condensation of the material to fit the time constraints of the conference. Some presenters prefer to attract the attention of the audience by reporting the findings first, proceeding with the other parts of the study, and then returning to discuss the findings in more detail later in the presentation. The review of the literature is usually not discussed in detail; only pertinent studies are mentioned.

Generally, conference organizers distribute evaluation sheets so the audience can rate each presenter. The presenter should try to read the evaluations with an open mind. Although 99 of 100 comments may be favorable, the presenter probably will react most strongly to that one unfavorable comment. One colleague was devastated when reading a comment given to her after a presentation. The comment read, "You forgot to take the price tag off your dress sleeve." She was able to laugh about it later but was thoroughly embarrassed at the time.

Presenting a Research Poster

A popular way to present research results is through poster presentations. This visual method of presentation may be seen by a large number of people in a short time period. Because of time constraints, a research conference participant can attend only a few oral presentations in a 1- or 2-day research conference. However, it is possible to view a fairly large number of posters in just an hour or two. At a poster session, the presenters usually remain with their posters and interact with the viewers. In fact, Hand (2010) asserted that a poster should be a springboard for discussion.

Occasionally, educational institutions and clinical agencies hold research conferences in which the only method of presentation is through posters. If posters are placed in a hallway in a clinical setting, patients, their visitors, and the nursing staff can view the materials at their leisure.

The size of the posters varies according to different research conference requirements. Many conferences are held in hotels, and the size of the assigned rooms may dictate the number and size of the posters. If a poster is displayed on a table, some type of support is needed to make the poster stand erect. Commercial products may be purchased or a support can be built out of materials such as plastic foam blocks or wooden wall moldings. When posters must be transported long distances, such as by airplane, care should be taken that the poster does not get dirty or bent.

Careful consideration should be given to the construction of posters. Technical help may be sought from a graphic artist, or researchers may design and construct their own posters. The poster should not appear as if it had been thrown together at the last minute or constructed by a group of young cub scouts. The initial view of the poster is important. Attractive color combinations should be used. Some examples that have been found to be eye catching are black on tan, white on blue, and white on black. Size, thickness, and color of the poster board may be determined after visiting an art store.

Posters should contain the research question(s), hypothesis(es), a description of the sample, the methods, the findings, and major conclusions. Diagrams, graphs, and tables are effective means of presenting certain aspects of the study, such as the findings.

It is better not to place too much material on a poster. A cluttered poster distracts the viewers or, worse yet, causes them to pass by the poster because they think it will take too long to decipher the meaning of all of the material. Berg (2005) has called for the material to be arranged and rearranged until the poster is appealing to the eye.

The major titles on the poster should be in large letters, at least 1 inch high. Viewers need to be able to see these letters from about 3 feet away. Typed material should be prepared with large letters. Computer software programs have this capability. Letters also can be prepared freehand, with the use of a stencil or vinyl adhesive letters.

Many sources in the nursing literature discuss the process of constructing a poster: Berg, 2005; Briggs, 2009; DeSisto, 2008; Hand, 2010; Moore, Augspurger, King, & Proffitt, 2001.

Research poster sessions are an excellent way for beginning researchers to present their research findings. This type of presentation does not seem as scary as the idea of standing up in front of an audience and discussing a study orally. Also, make it a point to attend poster sessions. These sessions are an excellent source of research information, particularly for beginning researchers.

Publishing a Journal Article

The growth of the nursing profession depends on the ability of its members to build and share a body of knowledge. According to Northam, Yarbrough, Haas, and Duke (2010), nurses "have an obligation to the profession and to society to share their knowledge and experience through publishing" (p. 36). Nursing research is the method of building knowledge, and publications are the major outlet for sharing this knowledge.

The preparation of an article for a journal is a service to the profession as well as a means of obtaining recognition for the author(s). Nurse authors usually do not receive any compensation. Some journals provide an author with several complimentary copies of the journal issue in which the article appears. Other journals send reprints of the article to the author.

The process of manuscript submission has been speeded up, as mentioned before. Many journals allow submission either by e-mail attachments or directly to a Web site. *Nursing Research* has requested that authors submit their manuscripts to a Web-based editorial manager system (http://www.editorialmanager.com/nres/).

Galley proofs show how the article will appear in typeset form. When the author receives the galleys (about 2 months before the publication date), these pages must be proofread for errors.

The length of time from submission of a manuscript to the decision about acceptance varies. In the study by Northam et al. (2010), this time period varied from 4 months to more than 20 months. When an author receives an acceptance letter from a journal, an approximate date or month of publication is usually included. The time period from acceptance to publication is called "lag time." The nurse editors in Freda and Kearney's (2005) survey reported a mean lag time of 6 months for the 90 journals they surveyed, with a range of 1 to 18 months. In January 2009, *The Journal of Nursing Education* reported a 17–24 month backlog in manuscripts awaiting publication. The editors indicated the desire to reduce the backlog to 6–9 months (Tanner & Bellack, 2009).

One of the reasons for the lag time is because many manuscripts have to be revised. Patricia Yoder-Wise, Editor-in-Chief of *The Journal of Continuing Education in Nursing*, discussed manuscript resubmission in a March 2009 editorial (Yoder-Wise, 2009). She reported that requests for manuscript resubmission approximate 75%.

The *Journal of Nursing Education* is trying to speed up the availability of articles to readers by a feature called "Online Advanced Release." These articles have been peer-reviewed and accepted for publication and are posted online a few weeks or even a month before they can be found in the print publications. They appear before final proofing has been done. Online versions will disappear once the final version is available in print (http://journalofnursingeducation.com/advanced.asp). Other journals, including *Advances in Nursing Science* and *Research in Gerontological Nursing*, have this same feature. Anyone can access the abstracts that accompany these articles, but a subscription to the journal is necessary to read the entire article.

The acceptance rate for manuscripts is quite varied. *The Journal of Nursing Education* reported an acceptance rate of 20% for 2009 compared to 42% in 2005 (Bellack, 2010). The journal received 279 manuscripts in 2005 and 473 in 2009. Authors may want to become familiar with the acceptance rates of the journals of interest before they submit their manuscripts.

The number of nursing journals continues to grow. The survey by Northam et al. (2010) revealed 230 English-language nursing journals. *Nurse Author & Editor*, accessed March 7, 2010 (www.nurseauthor.com/), provides direct links to more than 250 editors of nursing journals. In addition to journals published in the United States, this Web site contains links to journals in countries such as Australia, Brazil, Canada, England, Japan, Netherlands, New Zealand, Scotland, and South Africa. Of course, the number of journals published in foreign countries is very small compared to the number of journals available in the United States.

The results of several surveys of nursing journal editors have been published since 1990. These include: Swanson, McCloskey, & Bodensteiner (1991); McConnell (1995); McConnell (2000); Freda and Kearney (2005); and Northam et al. (2010).

The survey by Swanson et al. (1991) examined journals published in the United States. The next two surveys focused on English-language journals that were published outside the United States. The survey by Freda and Kearney (2005) examined the roles and practices of nurse editors of 71 journals published in the United States and 19 journals published in other countries. These included journals published in England, Australia, Canada, and South Africa. Finally, Northam et al. (2010) obtained information from editors of 63 English-language journals, most of which are located in the United States.

Preparing the Article

Because of space constraints, journal articles provide somewhat brief coverage of research reports. The length of journal articles varies a great deal, but most editors prefer manuscripts of 10 to 15 typed pages. The sections of the article and the format vary according to the journal. Most articles contain these parts: introduction, review of literature, methods, findings, and discussion. It is important for the researcher to examine the target journal carefully for style and format.

Selecting a Journal

Selecting an appropriate journal for an article is an important decision. With each passing year, more nursing and allied health journals are coming into existence. Before 1978, *Nursing Research* was the only journal devoted to the publication of nursing research studies. Since that time, more research-focused journals have become available: *Applied Nursing Research, Biological Research for Nursing, Clinical Nursing Research, Research and Theory for Nursing Practice, Research in Gerontological Nursing, Research in Nursing and Health, Western Journal of Nursing Research*, and *Worldviews on Evidence-Based Nursing*. Additionally, journals such as *Advances in Nursing Science* and the *Journal of Nursing Scholarship* devote a large percentage of space to coverage of research studies. Many other journals, including journals that focus on clinical issues, contain research reports.

The *Journal of Undergraduate Nursing Scholarship* (http://juns.nursing.arizona.edu/) is an online publication sponsored by the University of Arizona. This journal provides an opportunity for students in baccalaureate nursing programs to publish original research reports and papers on current issues in health care and the nursing profession.

Research Study by Baccalaureate Nursing Students

Fortune et al. (2009) compared blood pressure (BP) measurements in the forearm and upper arm of a sample of 100 healthy young adults. They hypothesized that BP readings would be significantly higher in the forearm than in the upper arm. Their hypothesis was supported. Readings were approximately 6 mmHg higher in the forearm than in the upper arm. Significant differences were found in systolic readings ($p = < .0001$) and diastolic readings ($p = < .0001$).

The choice of a journal may be made before or after a manuscript is prepared. If the manuscript is written first, the author then seeks a journal that is appropriate for the proposed article. Another option is to determine the journal most appropriate for the content of the article and then prepare the manuscript according to the guidelines of that particular journal and the needs of that journal's readers.

A journal may be selected based on its impact factor. The **impact factor** (IF) is a number used to evaluate the influence of a particular journal. The higher the impact factor number, the more influence the journal is thought to have on the scientific community. Impact factors are listed in the *Journal Citation Reports* published by Thomson Reuters. You may be able to gain access to the entire database through your library. In Northam et al.'s 2010 survey of nursing journal editors, 50 of the 63 editors did not report an impact factor, and several indicated their journal had not been rated.

The rating is based on how frequently the articles in a particular journal are cited. The 2-year impact factor is calculated by dividing the number of citations in a given year by the number of articles published in that journal during the previous 2 years. For example, to determine a specific journal's impact factor for 2011, first a search is made of the number of citations from 2009 and 2010 journal issues found in the 2011 literature. Then, the number of articles that were actually published in those 2009 and 2010 issues is recorded. For example, if 100 articles were published in the 2009 and 2010 issues, and 75 citations of these articles appeared in the 2011 literature, the impact would be 0.75 ($75/100 = .75$). The impact factor would actually be reported in early 2012 after all of the 2011 literature had been examined. The Web site for *Nursing Research* listed an impact factor of 1.538, whereas the *Journal of Professional Nursing* listed an impact factor of 0.667 (both accessed March 11, 2010 from their Web sites). The 1.58 impact factor indicates that articles published 1 or 2 years ago in *Nursing Research* have been cited, on average, 1.58 times. The *Journal of the American Medical Association's* impact factor was reported to be 28.899 on November 10, 2010 (http://freemedicaljournals.com/).

The nurse author should not forget magazines designed for the general public. Although the format would need to be simple and the content presented in easily understood terms, nurses will reach a wide section of health care consumers by publishing study results in appropriate lay magazines.

Choosing Between Refereed and Nonrefereed Journals

The author must make the choice to publish in a refereed or nonrefereed journal. Generally speaking, a **refereed journal** is one in which subject experts, chosen by the journal's editorial staff, evaluate manuscripts. A **nonrefereed journal** uses editorial staff members or consultants to review manuscripts. The issue of publication in refereed versus nonrefereed journals seems to be almost a moot issue. In Freda and Kearney's 2005 report of the policies of 90 journals, all of the nurse editors indicated that peer review was in place at their journals. In both refereed and nonrefereed journals, the journal editor makes the final decision about the publication of an article.

Panels of expert colleagues evaluate each manuscript submitted to refereed journals. In Freda and Kearney's (2005) survey of nurse editors, the median size of the review panels for their journals was 40, with a range of 7 to 1,500. These nurse editors indicated several ways of providing recognition for their reviewers. Nurse editors of most journals (91%) reported that reviewers' names were listed each year. Some journals provided free journal subscriptions (25%); only six (7%) of the journals provided an honorarium to reviewers.

The review of manuscripts by professional colleagues who are content or methodological experts is called **peer review**. According to Smeltzer (2005), peer review is the gold standard of scientific publishing. Oman (2009) wrote in an editorial in the *Journal of Emergency Nursing* that peer reviewers are "necessary partners with authors and editors in the effort to publish innovative, creative, and valid contributions to nursing science" (p. 278). This process allows journal editors to obtain objective opinions about a manuscript from experts in the field. Peer review is usually an unpaid contribution to the nursing profession by some of its accomplished members. Journals usually list their reviewers for the past year in their December issue or in next year's January issue. The January 2010 issue of *Heart & Lung* listed 196 reviewers for 2009.

In a **blind review**, the reviewers are not aware of the author's identity before the manuscript is evaluated. This process is very important to a writer with a limited publication record. An unknown writer would have an equal chance with a well-known author. Blinded peer review was reported by 98% of the journals in Freda and Kearney's (2005) survey of nurse editors.

Some journals are beginning to introduce an open review process. In an editorial in *Nursing Research,* Molly Dougherty (2005), the editor, reported that the journal took the first step toward open peer review. In an **open review**, the reviewer signs his or her reviews. Some of these reviews for *Nursing Research* articles are posted at http://nursing-research-editor.com/authors/open.php. These posted reviews enable the reader to examine the original manuscript and see the reviewers' comments. A posted open review for *Nursing Research* (Manuscript 59) is for the article titled "Regional Variations in Cancer Screening Rates Found in Women With Diabetes." It was published in the January/February 2010 issue (accessed online March 11, 2010).

Applied Nursing Research uses a unique approach to manuscript review. Each manuscript submitted to this journal is sent to two teams of reviewers. Each team consists of a clinician and a researcher (who is generally in an academic setting). These individuals have expertise in the content area or the research methods presented in the manuscript. Each team member individually writes a review of the manuscript, and then the two reviewers write a joint review.

Sending Query Letters

Before submitting an article to a journal, it may be wise for the author to first determine the journal's interest in the manuscript. A **query letter** contains an outline of a manuscript and important information about the manuscript that is sent to an editor to determine interest in publication. The letter should be addressed to the editor by name. It is never wise to address a query letter to "The Editor of . . ." or to "Dear Sir or Madam." Many journals allow query letters to be submitted via e-mail.

The advantage of a query letter is that the writer does not waste time submitting a manuscript to a journal where such an article is already in line for publication (Moos, 2010) or for which the content of the proposed manuscript is not appropriate for the targeted journal. In the survey conducted by Northam et al. (2010), 24 editors (38%) rated query letters as somewhat important, and 10 (16%) rated them as very important. Query letters may be sent to several journals simultaneously. However, a manuscript should be sent to only *one* journal at a time. Most journals require a signed statement that the manuscript is not being considered by any other journal.

Reasons for Manuscript Rejection

Swanson et al.'s (1991) survey revealed that the highest-ranked reason for rejection of manuscripts by editors of nursing journals was that the manuscript was poorly written. A poorly written manuscript continued to be the highest-ranked reason for rejection reported in McConnell's (2000) survey of English-language journals published outside the United States. It appears that nurse authors must work on their writing skills, because a poorly written manuscript was, again, the most common reason for rejection of manuscripts (35.8%), according to a survey of 63 nursing journal editors published in the January/February 2010 issue of *Nurse Educator* (Northam et al., 2010).

Other reasons reported by Northam et al. (2010) were that the topic was not relevant to the focus of the journal (32.8%), or the manuscript had methodology problems (16.4%). Additionally, seven editors indicated that manuscripts were "too short and superficial."

If an article is rejected outright, the reasons for the rejection will be indicated. Rejection of an article does not necessarily mean that it is not a good article. There is a lot of competition for the limited space in the nursing and allied health journals. Editors do not want to discourage authors. In fact, the editor of the journal who rejects a manuscript may make suggestions for submission to another journal.

Preparing Research Reports for Funding Agencies

Research projects cost money, and researchers frequently seek funding sources. Many organizations provide funds for nursing research. Some public organizations that might be approached for support are the National Institute of Nursing Research, National Institute of Mental Health, Veterans Administration, and the U.S. Public Health Service.

Although public sources have provided most of the funding for nursing research, nurses are increasingly seeking funds from private foundations. Some of these private foundations are AARP, Robert Wood Johnson, John Hartford, Kellogg, Alcoa, and Lilly. Voluntary health organizations such as the American Cancer Society and the American Heart Association have supported nursing research. Businesses and corporations such as Apple Computer Corporation and Del Monte Foods have provided funds for nurse researchers. Charitable organizations, including churches and sororities, as well as individual philanthropists, may be approached for funding. Intramural funding is available in many universities and health care agencies. Finally, various groups within the nursing profession, such as Sigma Theta Tau and the American Nurses Foundation (ANF), make funds available for research. Since 1955, the ANF has provided over $4 million dollars to more than 950 beginning and experienced nurse researchers (http://anfonline.org/).

If funding is received for a study, the researcher is nearly always expected to provide a final report at the completion of the project. This report may be a brief summary or a lengthy report.

Preparing Theses and Dissertations

Theses and dissertations are an important means of communication for research studies conducted to fulfill educational requirements. Because these documents serve a dual purpose of communicating research findings and providing educators with evidence of the students' ability to perform scholarly work, theses and dissertations are usually lengthy documents that may contain 100 pages or more, divided into several chapters. Dissertations contain more in-depth investigations than theses and provide new knowledge for the profession. Theses are usually concerned with testing existing theory, whereas dissertations focus on refining existing theories or generating new theories.

UTILIZATION OF NURSING RESEARCH FINDINGS

How often do you use research findings in your nursing practice? You probably use research more often than you think. Do you irrigate Foley catheters every 8 hours? Did I hear you answer "No"? Well, I did when I was a nursing student and a young nurse. You ask, "Why"? We thought we were preventing urinary tract infections. Research has shown just the opposite to be true.

Now that you are near the end of this textbook, recall the first goal for conducting nursing research listed in Chapter 1: to promote evidence-based nursing practice. Therefore, for nursing research to be useful to the profession, study findings must be implemented in nursing practice.

The use of research findings in nursing practice is called research utilization. It means going beyond the somewhat artificial research setting to the real world of nursing. In the past, many actions of nurses have been based on tradition or authority. This is no longer acceptable in this day of evidence-based practice. Nurses should be able to justify the decisions they make and the care they give.

Many nursing leaders have indicated the high priority that should be placed on the utilization of research findings in nursing practice. However, they have pointed out the continued gap between nursing research and nursing practice (Chau, Lopez, & Thompson, 2008; Fink, Thompson, & Bonnes, 2005; Hutchinson & Johnston, 2004; Kajermo et al., 2008; McCleary & Brown, 2003; Paramonczyk, 2005; Winch, Henderson, & Creedy, 2005; Yava et al., 2009).

Barriers to Nursing Research Utilization

More than 30 articles have been published that list barriers to the utilization of research findings by nurses in the United States and around the world (e.g., Funk, Champagne, Tornquist, & Wiese, 1995; Chau, Lopez, & Thompson, 2008; Funk, Champagne, Wiese, & Tornquist, 1991a, 1991b; Hutchinson & Johnston, 2004; Kajermo, Nordström, Krusebrant, & Björvell, 1998; Kajermo et al., 2008; McCleary & Brown, 2003; Paramonczyk, 2005; Pravikoff, Tanner, & Pierce, 2005; Retsas, 2000; Schoonover, 2009; Yava et al., 2009).

There are many barriers to the utilization of nursing research findings in nursing practice. Five of the most common barriers are: (a) nurses' lack of knowledge of nursing research, (b) nurses' negative attitudes toward research, (c) inadequate means of disseminating nursing research findings, (d) lack of institutional support for research, and (e) study findings that are not ready for use in nursing practice. The following sections discuss these topics.

Nurses' Lack of Knowledge of Research Findings

A great deal of evidence indicates that nurses are unaware of many research findings. Funk et al. (1991b) sent a survey concerning barriers to research utilization to 5,000 nurses selected from the ANA membership roster. Returns were received from 1,989 individuals (40%). The third most important barrier was that the nurse is unaware of research findings. In 1995 these same authors published the findings from the sample of nurse administrators who responded to their 1991 survey. Nurses' lack of awareness of research was listed by 77.2% of the administrator respondents as the greatest barrier to research utilization. Among Australian nurses in a study by Hutchinson and Johnston (2004), 66.2% of them listed lack of awareness of research as a barrier. In Paramonczyk's (2005) study of Canadian nurses, lack of awareness of research findings was listed as the second highest barrier. Schoonover (2009) studied nurses practicing in a community hospital in the state of Washington and found that lack of awareness of research was also a barrier to research utilization.

Some research indicates that nurses may have knowledge about research but are reluctant to change their traditional practices. The American Academy of Pediatrics (AAP) has recommended exclusive use of the supine sleep position for young infants. Research has consistently shown that this position is most likely to prevent sudden infant death syndrome (SIDS). In a study of nursery staff (Stastny, Ichinose, Thayer, Olson, & Keens, 2004), 72% of the nurses indicated awareness of the recommendations of the AAP, but only 30% reported most often placing infants to sleep in the supine position. Additionally, 65.3% of the sample reported that they had not advised new mothers to use only the supine sleep position for their infants. This study needs to be replicated. Hopefully, the results would be different today.

Nurses' Negative Attitudes Toward Research

Champion and Leach (1989) found that nurses' attitudes toward research were positively related to research utilization ($r = .55$). Nurses with positive attitudes were more likely to use research findings. Attitude was more strongly correlated with research utilization than the other two variables that were considered: institutional support and availability of research findings.

In Funk et al.'s (1991b) study, approximately 35% of the respondents did not see the value of research for practice. Approximately 31% of Australian nurses in a study by Retsas (2000) did not recognize the value of research findings.

There is some hopeful news about nurses' attitudes toward research. Fink et al. (2005) received survey responses from 215 nurses who worked in a large university-affiliated magnet hospital. Their attitudes toward research were much more positive than nurses in previous studies. Of course, you must take into consideration that these nurses worked in a magnet hospital where the research climate was more supportive than would be found in many other hospitals.

Inadequate Dissemination of Research Findings

Inadequate dissemination of nursing research findings involves two areas. First, most nursing research studies are never published or presented at research meetings or workshops. Second, published or presented studies are often not written or verbally presented at a level at which the practicing nurse can understand the findings.

Many references are found in the literature that attest to practicing nurses' unhappiness with the dissemination of nursing research findings (Gennaro, 1996; Hutchinson & Johnston, 2004; Kajermo et al., 1998; Retsas, 2000). Swedish nurses in Kajermo et al.'s (1998) study ranked the lack of availability of research findings as the greatest barrier to the use of these findings. Fifty-one percent of

Australian nurses in Hutchinson and Johnston's (2004) study reported that research reports are not readily available.

Practicing nurses complain about their inability to understand articles in the research journals. The language is technical, and the articles are often lengthy. Research reports are frequently written for researchers rather than clinicians. In Funk et al.'s (1991b) study, respondents suggested that research be reported in the journals that are read most frequently by clinicians and that these reports be more readable and contain clinical implications. Nurse researchers tend to present their research findings in very formal research meetings and in research publications. Researchers in academic settings are sometimes rewarded (e.g., promotions, salary raises, tenure) more for publications in prestigious research journals than for publications in practice journals.

Nurses need to make an effort to publish in the popular clinical journals. This does not mean that nurse researchers should not prepare publications for the scholarly journals, but they also have an obligation to disseminate the findings in a manner understandable to the nurse in practice; this usually means publishing findings in practice journals. Brooten et al. (1999) asserted, "The lay public in general is woefully uninformed of the research conducted by nurses" (p. 133). It appears that we have made very little progress in communicating the results of nursing research to nurses, much less to the general public! Kennedy (2004) and Ulrich (2005) have asserted that nurse researchers must let other nurses and the general public know about their research results. As Ulrich said, nurses must get better about "tooting our own horns."

Lack of Institutional Support for Research

Nurses frequently perceive that there is little institutional support for nursing research. Lack of institutional support has been identified as a barrier to research utilization in all of the published studies.

In Funk et al.'s (1991b) study of approximately 2,000 nurses in the United States, the two greatest barriers to research utilization were the nurses' report that they did not have "enough authority to change patient care procedures" and "insufficient time on the job to implement new ideas." Nurse administrators ranked "insufficient time on the job to implement new ideas" as the second highest barrier to research (Funk et al., 1995). One of the most frequent suggestions concerned increasing administrative support and encouragement. Funk et al., proposed that nursing staff must believe the environment is conducive for the use of research findings before they will believe that they have the authority to change their practice based on research results.

McCleary and Brown (2003) surveyed 176 pediatric nurses in two teaching hospitals in Ontario, Canada. They listed lack of time to read research as the most frequent barrier to research utilization.

Nurses in Fink et al.'s (2005) study of RNs employed at a large university-affiliated magnet hospital in the United States indicated "difficulty in changing practice" as their most problematic barrier. Many respondents indicated that they felt powerless to change practice based on research. They listed lack of support and lack of mentoring as top barriers to the use of research in practice.

Pravikoff et al. (2005) surveyed 760 nurses who worked in clinical settings across the United States. Fifty-seven percent of the respondents reported that their facility did not have a medical or health sciences library. Three percent of the nurses said that their facility's library was available only to physicians.

In a study of 833 nurses in Sweden, Kajermo et al. (2008) found that a barrier to research utilization was lack of support from immediate superiors. Unclear and unrealistic workplace goals was another barrier. The researchers called for head nurses and nurse managers to create strategies that would support nurses' professional development and foster the implementation of research findings in clinical practice.

Chinese nurses also reported the organization to be the greatest barriers to research utilization (Chau, Lopez, & Thompson, 2008). These included lack of: time, authority to change practice, and cooperation from physicians.

Nurses in Turkey (n = 631) reported that organizational management support was very important in their ability to utilize research findings (Yava et al., 2009). Lack of time (54%) and insufficient facilities (52.8%) were reported by nurses in this study.

Findings Are Not Ready for Use in Practice

In an editorial in *Nursing Research,* Downs (1981) asserted, "Research is not something that can be brewed over night and ingested the next morning" (p. 322). She warned against the "premature consumption" of research findings. She stated that this practice might be "hazardous to someone's health" (p. 322).

Blegen (2005), in an editorial in *Nursing Research*, asserted that no research exists on which to develop protocols for many nursing practice problems. She further asserted that some nursing practice problems have a few studies on the topic, but some of these studies contain serious threats to validity, which makes use of their findings questionable. Duffy (2004), in contrast, contended that since the mid-1980s, qualified nurse researchers have completed, presented, and published many studies. She asserted that an available knowledge base is waiting to be used in the development of evidence-based practice.

No study findings should be implemented if the study has not been replicated in several clinical settings, with similar results being found. Polit (1996) called for replication studies because nurse researchers use nonrandom samples so frequently. Fahs, Morgan, and Kalman (2003) published an entire article in the *Journal of Nursing Scholarship* that called for replication studies. These authors asserted that replication of research is essential to the "building and continued development of the scientific basis of any discipline" (p. 67). Polit and Beck (2008) have contended that a strong evidence-based practice requires replication studies. Burns and Grove (2009) called for a commitment from journal editors to publish these types of studies. Results of replication studies are still scarce in the nursing literature.

Bridging the Gap Between Research and Practice

In the past few years, the nursing literature has shifted some of the emphasis from research utilization (RU) to evidence-based practice (EBP). Although these terms sometimes are used interchangeably, distinctions can be made between these two concepts.

Burns and Grove (2009) have described RU as "the process of synthesizing, disseminating, and using research-generated knowledge to make an impact on or a change in the existing practices in society" (p. 720). EBP is viewed as broader in scope than RU. Burns and Grove asserted that EBP is the "conscientious integration of best research evidence with clinical expertise and patient values and needs in the delivery of quality, cost-effective health care" (p. 699). EBU encompasses evidence based on both scientific findings and on expert clinical opinion and patient and family preferences. EBU is discussed in Chapter 18.

Many nursing research utilization projects have been described in the literature, beginning in the 1970s. Two widely known projects that have fostered research utilization are the Western Council on Higher Education for Nursing (WCHEN) Regional Program for Nursing Research Development project conducted in the early 1970s and the Conduct and Utilization of Research in Nursing (CURN) project conducted later that same decade. Both projects received funding from the Division of Nursing. Three models of research utilization are also discussed: Rogers's innovation-diffusion model, Stetler's model of research utilization, and the Iowa model for evidence-based practice.

WCHEN Project

In the research utilization aspect of the WCHEN project, nurses from various settings attended 3-day workshops in which they were taught how to use the change process to bring about research utilization. The nurses came in pairs from the same geographic location but worked in different settings. For example, a school nurse and a community health nurse who came from a rural community developed together a plan to provide nursing interventions for elementary school students who had high rates of absenteeism (Elliott, 1977). Although the WCHEN project was considered successful, one major problem encountered was the lack of reliable nursing studies that were appropriate for implementation in nursing practice.

CURN Project

The most well-known nursing research utilization project is the CURN project, a 5-year project sponsored by the Michigan Nurses Association. The two major goals of this project were to stimulate the conduct of research in clinical settings and to increase the use of research findings in the daily practice of nurses. As a result of this project, nursing innovations (protocols) were developed for nine practice problems. The titles of the nine published volumes are:

- *Mutual Goal Setting in Patient Care*
- *Closed Urinary Drainage Systems*
- *Distress Reduction Through Sensory Preparation*
- *Pain*
- *Intravenous Cannula Change*
- *Preventing Decubitus Ulcers*
- *Preoperative Sensory Preparation to Promote Recovery*
- *Reducing Diarrhea in Tube-Fed Patients*
- *Structured Preoperative Teaching*

Rogers's Innovation-Diffusion Model

Rogers's (1995) innovation-diffusion model contains five stages: knowledge, persuasion, decision, implementation, and confirmation.

In the knowledge stage, the nurse becomes aware of a research-based nursing intervention. This knowledge can be obtained through such sources as conferences, journal articles, and from talks with colleagues.

In the persuasion stage, the nurse forms a positive or negative attitude toward the intervention. This attitude can be based on the intervention's advantage, compatibility, complexity, trialability, and observability.

After an attitude is formed, the decision stage is reached. In this stage, the nurse decides whether or not to adopt the new intervention. The decision should be based on the research evidence that has been gathered.

The implementation phase is reached when the nurse actually puts into practice the intervention or uses the knowledge indirectly, such as by discussing the findings with colleagues or citing the findings at a conference or in one of his or her own publications. An intervention may be introduced exactly as it was described in research studies or there might be some adaptation for the particular health care setting where the intervention is being introduced.

Finally, in the confirmation stage, the intervention is evaluated for its effectiveness. The decision is then made whether or not to continue using the intervention.

Stetler Model of Research Utilization

The Stetler model of research utilization was first described in 1976. Stetler and Marram (1976) wrote a classic article about the steps to be taken before the nurse decides research findings are applicable for nursing practice. They listed three phases of critical thinking: validation, comparative evaluation, and decision making. Stetler's (2001) revised model has five phases: preparation, validation, comparative evaluation and decision making, translation/application, and evaluation. The validation phase is called "research utilization critique" (Stetler, 1994, p. 20), and during this phase the decision is made to accept or reject a particular study. The revisions to the Stetler model are discussed in the November/December issue of *Nursing Outlook* (Stetler, 2001).

Validation concerns the overall examination of the strengths and weaknesses of a study. The consumer must question every step of the research process that was carried out. A traditional research critique is done. If a biased sample was used, operational definitions were not provided, or invalid statistical procedures were used, the findings would be questionable for application in practice. If the study design and procedures were determined to be valid, nurse consumers should also search for findings and conclusions that might be valid in their clinical settings.

If the nurse determines that the study is valid, then a comparative evaluation should be done. What variables would affect the decision to change practice based on research findings? Would it be possible to implement the findings in the nurse's practice? The nurse would want to know how similar the research setting was to her or his own setting and how similar the study sample was to patients/clients with whom the nurse works. Finally, in doing a comparative evaluation, the nurse must determine the feasibility of implementing the findings based on the constraints of the particular practice setting. Are there any legal or ethical risks to the involved clients, nurses, or institution? Are the resources available (time, money, equipment)?

Once the nurse has examined the feasibility, the decision about application is made. The nurse may decide against application or make a cognitive or direct application of the findings. Cognitive application means that the nurse is not yet ready to apply the findings in practice but will use the information to enhance her or his knowledge base and may consider moving to a direct application in the future. Direct application of research findings means that the nurse chooses to test out the findings in practice.

Iowa Model of Evidence-Based Practice

The Iowa model (Titler et al., 2001) has several steps. First, a problem is identified that is based on either problem-focused or knowledge-focused triggers. Problem-focused triggers might come from risk management data or identified clinical problems. Knowledge-focused triggers might come from new research literature or national standards and guidelines.

The decision is then made as to whether the problem is a priority for the organization. Are the necessary resources available? Will organizational or unit goals be met by the proposed change in practice?

Next, a team is assembled to develop, implement, and evaluate the project. An existing research committee might be able to take charge of the project. However, all "stakeholders" must be involved.

The literature is then searched. This is a very important step. Existing systematic reviews are an excellent source of information.

After the literature is searched, the critiquing process begins. How consistent are the findings and the quality of the studies? How relevant are the findings to the clinical setting? What is the ratio of benefits to risks of carrying out the project?

Only after all of these steps are completed is the evidence-based project ready for implementation. Of course, evaluation of the project must follow.

Research Utilization Studies

Many research utilization studies and projects have been discussed in recent literature. One project is presented here:

Research Utilization Study

The Iowa Model of Evidence-Based Practice to Promote Quality Care was used in a collaborative project of a clinical nurse specialist (CNS), health science librarian, and a nurse (Krom, Batten, & Bautista, 2010). Their aim was to heighten staff nurses' awareness of the evidence-based practice (EBP) process. They developed an EBP educational program for staff nurses. The CNS was considered an expert advisor for knowledge transformation because of clinical expertise, advanced educational preparation, and exposure to graduate-level research. The librarian was deemed capable of meeting the nurses' information needs. A staff nurse was considered the appropriate person to ask clinical questions and to find and critique relevant literature. The collaborators concluded that the project had increased staff nurse exposure to, and knowledge of, EBP principles and techniques.

SUMMARY

A **research report** is a written or spoken communication of the findings of a study. The report should be presented in the order of the research process. Research reports may be presented as oral presentations, poster presentations, journal articles, written reports for funding agencies, and in theses and dissertations.

Research conferences are sponsored by many nursing organizations. Participants are contacted through a **call for abstracts**, which is a request for summaries of research studies that researchers wish to present.

An oral presentation of a research report at a conference is referred to as a *paper presentation.* The researcher may also present research results in the form of a poster.

Research is generally published in journal articles. **Refereed journals** use subject experts to review manuscripts. **Nonrefereed journals** use editorial staff members or consultants to review manuscripts. **Impact factor** is a journal rating based on the number of article citations from that journal in a given year compared to the actual number of articles published in that journal in the past, usually a 2-year period.

During the **peer review** process, professional colleagues who have content and methodological expertise in the study area review the manuscript. Journals frequently use a **blind review** process in which no authors' names are included on the manuscripts. In an **open review**, reviewers sign their names to their reviews.

Before submitting an article, a letter of inquiry, called a **query letter**, should be sent to determine the editor's interest in reviewing a certain manuscript. A manuscript, however, must never be sent to more than one journal at a time.

About 2 months before an article is published, the author will receive the galleys. **Galley proofs** contain the article, as it will appear in typeset form.

If funding is received for a study, the researcher is usually expected to provide a final report at the completion of the project. This report may be either a brief summary or a lengthy report.

Theses and dissertations are a means of communicating results of research studies that are conducted in conjunction with educational requirements. These documents are generally quite long and divided into several chapters.

Five common barriers to utilization of nursing research findings are (a) nurses' lack of knowledge of research findings, (b) nurses' negative attitudes toward nursing research, (c) inadequate means of disseminating nursing research findings, (d) lack of institutional support, and (e) study findings that are not ready for use in nursing practice.

Two widely known nursing research utilization projects are the Western Council on Higher Education for Nursing (WCHEN) Regional Program for Nursing Research Development project conducted in the early 1970s and the Conduct and Utilization of Research in Nursing (CURN) project conducted in the late 1970s. Three models that have been very influential in the utilization of research findings in nursing are Rogers's innovation-diffusion model, Stetler's model for research utilization, and the Iowa model for evidence-based practice.

NURSING RESEARCH ON THE WEB

For additional online resources, research activities, and exercises, go to **www.mynursingkit. com.** Select Chapter 17 from the drop-down menu.

GET INVOLVED ACTIVITIES

1. Determine an area in which you would like to conduct research in the future. Choose a funding source that you might approach to gain support for your project.

2. Discuss with your colleagues various methods that might be used to ensure that nurses at each of the hospitals where you work or have clinical experience are aware of the importance of research findings (consider the principles of change theory when determining approaches to use).

3. Locate a nursing study that you believe has very important findings but needs to be replicated before the findings are implemented in nursing practice.

4. Identify a nursing study finding that you think is ready for implementation at your work or clinical site but for which you believe there would be resistance.

5. Identify two nursing practice actions that are based on research. Indicate how you are *sure* that these practice actions are based on research.

6. Discuss some of the existing journals that publish nursing research findings. Determine which journal is most likely to be read by you and your colleagues.

SELF-TEST

Circle the letter before the *best* answer.

1. What communication medium is most likely to reach the largest percentage of nurses?
   A. dissertation
   B. journal article
   C. conference oral presentation
   D. poster

2. The communication medium for research findings that is probably most appropriate for a beginning researcher is a
   A. journal article.
   B. oral presentation at a conference.
   C. research paper.
   D. poster presentation.

3. Which of the following is true concerning journal articles?
   A. Revisions are generally not needed in manuscripts that are submitted to journals.
   B. Many journals prefer that a query letter be sent before a manuscript is submitted.
   C. There is a general agreement among nursing journals about the format for research articles.
   D. Journals do not accept manuscripts from beginning researchers.

4. Support for nursing research has been furnished primarily by
   A. public sources.
   B. private foundations.
   C. businesses.
   D. individual philanthropists.

5. Which of the following statements is true?
   A. Most nurses have adequate knowledge of nursing research findings.
   B. Many nursing research findings are never published.
   C. Inadequate research skills of nurses is the most frequently cited reason for lack of utilization of research findings.
   D. Most nursing research findings are ready for use in practice.

Write true (T) or false (F) beside the following statements:

_____ 6. If a study has been replicated at least once, there is no need for further research in that same area of study.

_____ 7. The Conduct and Utilization of Research in Nursing (CURN) is one of the most well-known nursing research utilization projects.

_____ 8. Replication studies are the most common type of nursing research studies.

_____ 9. Surveys of nurses have found that most nurses have positive attitudes toward the utilization of research findings.

_____ 10. Most nursing research journals pay authors an honorarium.

REFERENCES

Bellack, J. P. (2010). Get ready, get set, write. *Journal of Nursing Education, 49*, 63–64.

Berg, J. A. (2005). Creating a professional poster presentation: Focus on nurse practitioners [Editorial]. *Journal of the American Academy of Nurse Practitioners, 17*, 245–248.

Billings, D. M., & Kowalski, K. (2009). Strategies for making oral presentations about clinical issues: Part II. At professional conferences. *The Journal of Continuing Education in Nursing, 40,* 198–199.

Blegen, M A. (2005). Research thrust changing? At risk [editorial]. *Nursing Research, 54,* 1.

Briggs, D. J. (2009). A practical guide to designing a poster for presentation. *Nursing Standard, 23* (34), 35–39.

Brooten, D., Youngblut, J. M., Roberts, B. L., Montgomery, K., Standing, T., Hemstrom, M., . . . & Polis, N. (1999). Disseminating our breakthrough: Enacting a strategic framework. *Nursing Outlook, 47,* 133–137.

Burns, N., & Grove, S. K. (2009). *The practice of nursing research: Appraisal, synthesis, and generation of evidence* (6th ed.). St. Louis, MO: Saunders Elsevier.

Champion, V. L., & Leach, A. (1989). Variables related to research utilization in nursing: An empirical investigation. *Journal of Advanced Nursing, 14,* 705–710.

Chau, J. P., Lopez, V., & Thompson, D. R. (2008). A survey of Hong Kong nurses' perceptions of barriers to and facilitators of research utilization. *Research in Nursing & Health, 31,* 640–649.

DeSisto, M. (2008). Creating powerful poster presentations. *NASN Newsletter, 23,* 27–28.

Dougherty, M. C. (2005). Open peer review [Editorial]. *Nursing Research, 53,* 213.

Downs, F. (1981). Soap [Editorial]. *Nursing Research, 30,* 322.

Duffy, M. E. (2004). Resources for building a research utilization program. *Clinical Nurse Specialist, 18,* 279–281.

Elliott, J. E. (1977). Research programs and projects of WCHEN. *Nursing Research, 26,* 277–280.

Fahs, P. S., Morgan, L. L., & Kalman, M. (2003). A call for replication. *Journal of Nursing Scholarship, 35,* 67–71.

Fink, R., Thompson, C. J., & Bonnes, D. (2005). Overcoming barriers and promoting the use of research in practice. *Journal of Nursing Administration, 35,* 121–129.

Fortune, M., Jeselnik, K., Johnson, S., Zhao, J., Wiley, L., Smith, A. . . . Crigger, N. J. (2009). A comparison of forearm and upper arm blood pressure measurements in a sample of healthy young adults. *Journal of Undergraduate Nursing Scholarship, 11*(1). Retrieved from http://juns.nursing.arizona.edu/articles/Fall%202009/contents11.htm

Freda, M. C., & Kearney, M. (2005). An international survey of nurse editors' roles and practices. *Journal of Nursing Scholarship, 37,* 87–94.

Funk, S. G., Champagne, M. T., Tornquist, E. M., & Wiese, R. A. (1995). Administrators' views on barriers to research utilization. *Applied Nursing Research, 8,* 44–49.

Funk, S. G., Champagne, M. T., Wiese, R. A., & Tornquist, E. M. (1991a). Barriers: The Barriers to Research Utilization Scale. *Applied Nursing Research, 4,* 39–45.

Funk, S. G., Champagne, M. T., Wiese, R. A., & Tornquist, E. M. (1991b). Barriers to using research findings in practice: The clinician's perspective. *Applied Nursing Research, 4,* 90–95.

Gennaro, S. (1996). Research utilization: An overview. *Journal of Gynecological and Neonatal Nursing, 23,* 313–319.

Grady, P. A. (2000). News from NINR. *Nursing Outlook, 48,* 54.

Hand, H. (2010). Reflections on preparing a poster for an RCN conference. *Nurse Researcher, 17,* 52–59.

Hegyvary, S. T. (2005). Writing that matters [Editorial]. *Journal of Nursing Scholarship, 37,* 193.

Hutchinson, A. M., & Johnston, L. (2004). Bridging the divide: A survey of nurses' opinions regarding barriers to, and facilitators of, research utilization in the practice setting. *Journal of Clinical Nursing, 13,* 304–315.

Kajermo, K. N., Nordström, G., Krusebrant, Å., Björvell, H. (1998). Barriers to and facilitators of research utilization as perceived by a group of registered nurses in Sweden. *Journal of Advanced Nursing, 27,* 798–807.

Kajermo, K. N., Undén, J., Gardulf, A., Eriksson, L. E., Orton, M.-L., Arnetz, B. B., & Norsdtröm, G. H. (2008). Predictors of nurses' perceptions of barriers to research utilization. *Journal of Nursing Management, 16,* 305–314. doi: 10.1111/j.1365-2834.2007.00770x

Krom, Z. R., Batten, J., & Bautista, C. (2010). A unique collaborative nursing evidence-based practice initiative using the Iowa Model. *Clinical Nurse Specialist, 24,* 54–59.

Kennedy, M. S. (2004). Not your grandma's nursing research [Editorial]. *American Journal of Nursing, 104,* 11.

McCleary, L., & Brown, G. T. (2003). Barriers to paediatric nurses' research utilization. *Journal of Advanced Nursing, 43,* 364–372.

McConnell, E. A. (1995). Journal and publishing characteristics for 42 nursing publications outside the United States. *Image: Journal of Nursing Scholarship, 27,* 225–229.

McConnell, E. A. (2000). Nursing publications outside the United States. *Journal of Nursing Scholarship, 32,* 87–92.

Moore, L. W., Augspurger, P., King, M. O., & Proffitt, C. (2001). Insights on the poster preparation and presentation process. *Applied Nursing Research, 14,* 100–104.

Moos, D. (2010). Writing for publication: An interview with the editors. *Journal of Perianesthesia Nursing, 25,* 46–49. doi:10.1016/j.jopan.2009.11.004

Northam, S., Yarbrough, S., Haas, B., & Duke, G. (2010). Journal editor survey information to help authors publish. *Nurse Educator, 35,* 29–36.

Oman, K. (2009). Peer review: The art of supporting colleagues and advancing our profession. [Editorial] *Journal of Emergency Nursing, 35,* 278. doi: 10.1016/j.jen.2009.05.011

Paramonczyk, A. (2005). Barriers to implementing research in clinical practice. *The Canadian Nurse, 101,* 12–15.

Polit, D. F. (1996). *Data analysis & statistics for nursing research.* Stamford, CT: Appleton & Lange.

Polit, D. F., & Beck., C. T. (2008). *Nursing research: Principles and methods* (8th ed.). Philadelphia: Lippincott Williams & Wilkins.

Pravikoff, D. S., Tanner, A. B., & Pierce, S. T. (2005). Readiness of U.S. nurses for evidence-based practice. *American Journal of Nursing, 105*(9), 40–52.

Retsas, A. (2000). Barriers to using research evidence in nursing practice. *Journal of Advanced Nursing, 31,* 599–606.

Rogers, E. M. (1995). *Diffusion of innovations* (4th ed.). New York: Free Press.

Schoonover, H. (2009). Barriers to research utilization among registered nurses practicing in a community hospital. *Journal for Nurses in Staff Development, 25,* 199–212.

Smeltzer, S. C. (2005). Is that information safe for patient care? *Nursing, 35,* 54–55.

Stastny, P. F., Ichinose, T. Y., Thayer, S. D., Olson, R. J., & Keens, T. G. (2004). Infant sleep positioning by nursery staff and mothers in newborn hospital nurseries. *Nursing Research, 53,* 122–129.

Stetler, C. B. (1994). Refinement of the Stetler-Marram model for application of research findings to practice. *Nursing Outlook, 42,* 15–25.

Stetler, C. B. (2001). Updating the Stetler model of research utilization to facilitate evidence-based practice. *Nursing Outlook, 49,* 272–279.

Stetler, C. B., & Marram, G. (1976). Evaluating research findings for applicability in practice. *Nursing Outlook, 24,* 559–563.

Swanson, E. A., McCloskey, J. C., & Bodensteiner, A. (1991). Publishing opportunities for nurses: A comparison of 92 U.S. journals. *Image: Journal of Nursing Scholarship, 23,* 33–38.

Tanner, C. A., & Bellack, J. P. (2009). The new wave of nursing education scholarship [Editorial]. *Journal of Nursing Education, 48,* 3–4.

Titler, M. G., Kleiber, C., Steelman, V., Rakel, B. A., Budreau, G., Everett, L. Q., . . . Goode, C. (2001). The Iowa model of evidence-based practice to promote quality care. *Critical Care Nursing Clinics of North America, 13,* 497–509.

Ulrich, B. (2005, August 15). Intersecting worlds: Nursing and NASA. *NurseWeek*—South Central Edition, p. 3.

Ulrich, B. (2007). Professional communications: Publications and presentations. *Nephrology Nursing Journal, 34,* 503–508.

Winch, S., Henderson, A., & Creedy, D. (2005). Read, think, do!: A method for fitting research evidence into practice. *Journal of Advanced Nursing, 50,* 20–26.

Yava, A., Tosun, N., Çiçek, H., Yavan, T., Terakye, G., & Hatipoglu, S. (2009). Nurses' perceptions of the barriers to and the facilitators of research utilization in Turkey. *Applied Nursing Research, 22,* 166–175.

Yoder-Wise, P. S. (2009). Manuscript resubmissions: The dialog of changes [Editorial]. *The Journal of Continuing Education in Nursing, 40,* 99–100.

CHAPTER 18

Evidence-Based Nursing Practice

OUTLINE

OBJECTIVES

On completion of this chapter, you will be prepared to:

1. Discuss the history of evidence-based practice in the field of medicine
2. Discuss the importance of the Cochrane Collaboration and the Cochrane Nursing Care Field to evidence-based practice
3. Recognize the contribution of the Agency for Health Care Research and Quality to evidence-based practice
4. Differentiate between research utilization and evidence-based nursing practice
5. Rank-order sources of evidence according to the hierarchy proposed by Stetler and colleagues
6. Identify some of the nonresearch sources of evidence that are being proposed for making health care decisions
7. Recall the names of at least two evidence-based nursing practice centers
8. Project possible future developments in the field of evidence-based nursing practice
9. Write clinical questions using the PICOT format

NEW TERMS DEFINED IN THIS CHAPTER

Have you heard the term "evidence-based practice"? If your answer is, "No," then you must be living on another planet! If your answer is, "Yes," you may also reply that you are tired of hearing the term. However, this term is vital for the future of nursing care.

Everyone is talking about "evidence-based practice," "best practice," "evidence-based nursing," and "evidence-based nursing practice." You have probably heard the old adage "In God we trust; all others bring data." Nursing's goal of evidence-based practice must be based on data, especially data gained from nursing research. Putting evidence into practice is a "challenging yet necessary component of healthcare delivery" (Titler & Moore, 2010, p. S2).

In May 2010 a search of the term "evidence-based nursing practice" in Google, a general Internet search engine, came up with 25,800,000 results! Of course, many of these were duplicates, and other hits were only closely related. ProQuest Nursing & Allied Health Source revealed 1,543 documents, mostly articles, on evidence-based nursing practice (EBNP).

Why are we currently so concerned with the use of evidence in nursing practice? Have we not always searched for the best evidence when seeking answers to clinical questions? Unfortunately, we have not. In an editorial published in the *Journal of Nursing Scholarship*, Hegyvary (2006) asserted that the emphasis on evidence-based practice was long overdue to replace traditions and rituals that lack documentation of their effectiveness.

HISTORY OF EVIDENCE-BASED PRACTICE

The term *evidence-based practice* originated in the field of medicine. Most people credit the beginning of the movement toward evidence-based practice to Archie Cochrane (1909–1988), a British medical researcher and epidemiologist. In 1972 Cochrane published a book titled *Effectiveness and Efficiency: Random Reflections on Health Services.* His book pointed out the lack of solid evidence about the effects of health care. Cochrane suggested that because health care resources would always be limited, these resources should be used to provide the most effective health care. He emphasized the importance of using evidence from randomized controlled trials (RCTs), also called randomized clinical trials. This type of study is considered the gold standard or strongest evidence that can be used as a basis for practice decisions.

When Cochrane's book was published in 1972, the medical profession did not seem ready for Cochrane's ideas about the need to examine the effectiveness of medical interventions. Physicians may not have wanted to hear that their care might not be effective. It took another 20 years before the evidence-based practice movement really began to flourish.

In 1996 Sackett et al. wrote an editorial, "Evidence Based Medicine: What It Is and What It Isn't," that was published in the *British Medical Journal.* They defined evidence-based medicine as "the conscientious, explicit, and judicious use of current best evidence in making decisions about the care of individual patients" (p. 71). This editorial caught the attention of the medical profession, and the idea of evidence-based medicine began to be accepted by many physicians.

You will encounter many terms in the literature that relate to the use of evidence in the practice decisions of health care professionals:

Evidence-based medicine (EBM)

Evidence-based practice (EBP)

Evidence-based care (EBC)

Evidence-based health care (EBHC)

Evidence-based nursing (EBN)

Evidence-based nursing practice (EBNP)

Although the idea of evidence-based practice has been in existence since the 1970s, it seems to have become very important in all areas of health care in this short period of time. All health care professionals have an obligation to become familiar with the term and all related terms. Nurses have always wanted what is best for their patients/clients. This goal can best be accomplished through evidence-based nursing practice.

THE COCHRANE COLLABORATION

The Cochrane Collaboration is an international nonprofit organization that supports evidence-based practice. There are over 27,000 contributors from more than 100 countries. The Cochran Collaboration was established in 1993 and named after Archie Cochrane, the medical researcher and epidemiologist mentioned previously.

The Cochrane Collaboration prepares systematic reviews of health care interventions, known as *Cochrane Reviews*. A **systematic review**, also called integrative review, is a rigorous scientific approach that combines results from a group of original research studies and looks at the studies as a whole. A systematic review can summarize many studies at once, while focusing on a single area of interest. There has been a growing interest in systematic reviews.

There are 52 Cochrane Review Groups. Each group focuses on a specific topic area, such as breast cancer, drugs and alcohol, multiple sclerosis, and sexually transmitted diseases. These review groups provide authors with methodological and editorial support to prepare *Cochrane Reviews*. They also manage the editorial process, which includes peer review. Funding is provided by a variety of sources, including government, universities, hospital trusts, charities, and personal donations. Information can be obtained from the Cochrane organization's Web site (http://cochrane.org/).

The Cochrane Library

The Cochrane Library is the medium used to publish the work of the Cochrane Collaboration. It consists of six databases that contain evidence to promote decision-making in health care. These six databases are: (a) *Cochrane Database of Systematic Reviews (CDSR)*, (b) Cochrane Central Register of Controlled Trials, (c) Cochrane Methodology Register, (d) Database of Abstracts of Reviews of Effects, (e) Health Technology Assessment Database, and (f) NHS Economic Evaluation Database. A seventh database provides information about the groups in the Cochrane Collaboration.

Cochrane Reviews are published online monthly (from 2010), with quarterly DVDs. Abstracts of *Cochrane Reviews* are available free on the Internet to everyone. These summaries are provided in easily understandable terms.

Cochrane Database of Systematic Reviews

The main output of the Cochrane Collaboration, the *Cochrane Reviews*, is found in The *Cochrane Database of Systematic Reviews*, which is published electronically as part of *The Cochrane Library*. More than 4,000 reviews were available in May 2010. These reviews are updated regularly as new information is located. Also, more than 2,000 protocols for *Cochrane Reviews* are available. These protocols describe the research methods and objectives for reviews that are in progress.

Cochrane Reviews are based on the best available information about health care interventions. These reviews provide evidence for and against the effectiveness and appropriateness of treatments, which include medications, surgery, and educational programs. The following three reviews are examples that might be of interest to nurses: (a) Nursing Interventions for Smoking Cessation, (b) Psychosocial and Psychological Interventions for Preventing Postpartum Depression, and (c) Regular Self-Examination or Clinical Examination for Early Detection of Breast Cancer.

The results of the review on breast self-examination were rather surprising. Two large studies, involving 388,535 women from Russia and Shanghai, revealed no statistically significant difference in breast cancer mortality between women who performed breast self-examination and those who did not. Another section of the review examined a large trial in which clinical breast examination and breast self-examination were combined as an intervention. This part of the review was discontinued because of poor compliance with follow up. No conclusions were drawn from this part of the study.

Cochrane Centers

Cochrane Centers are located through the world, including locations in Australia, Brazil, Canada, China, Denmark, France, Germany, Italy, Netherlands, South Africa, Spain, the United Kingdom, and the United States. All Cochrane Centers share the responsibility for helping coordinate and support the Cochrane Collaboration. Each center is unique and reflects the interests of the individuals associated with that particular center. Some of the common responsibilities of all of the Cochrane Centers include helping people to find out about the Cochrane Collaboration and its reviews, providing training for people who will do reviews, fostering collaboration among people with similar research interests, and organizing workshops, seminars, and colloquia to support the Cochrane Collaboration.

COCHRANE NURSING CARE FIELD

The Cochrane Collaboration established a nursing entity in March 2009, titled the Cochrane Nursing Care Network (CNCN). It became one of the 16 fields and networks within the Cochrane Collaboration. In April 2010 the name of the nursing field was officially changed to the Cochrane Nursing Care Field (CNCF). Also, all other existing Cochrane Networks are now officially called fields. The CNCF is coordinated from Adelaide, South Australia.

The CNCF's mission is to improve health outcomes through (a) increasing the use of *The Cochrane Library* by nurses and others; (b) engaging nurses and others involved in delivering, leading, or researching nursing care with the Cochrane Collaboration; and (c) supporting the Cochrane Collaboration and its role in providing an evidence base for nursing care (http://cncf.cochrane.org). The CNCF's January 2010 newsletter listed nearly 1,000 members. Membership is open to consumers of nursing care, nurses, formal and informal caregivers, other health care professionals, researchers, and others involved in the delivery of nursing care.

The CNCF will be developing a number of resources such as nursing care Cochrane Review Summaries, nursing care-relevant podcasts, CNCF news, and on-line and face-to-face involvement of its members in preparing summaries and other materials. Volunteers are needed to help with all of these projects and are asked to register their interests at the Web site.

AGENCY FOR HEALTHCARE RESEARCH AND QUALITY

The Agency for Healthcare Research and Quality (AHRQ) is the health services research branch of the U.S. Department of Health and Human Services (HHS). The AHRQ serves as a major source of funding and technical assistance for health services research and training. The 2009 budget was $372 million.

The agency works with public and private organizations to build a knowledge base for health care. According to the AHRQ Web site (http://ahrq.gov), the main goal of research is "measurable improvements in heath care in America, gauged in terms of improved quality of life and patient outcomes, lives saved, and value gained for what we spend." Nurses are very involved in the AHRQ, and many nursing studies have been funded by the organization.

AHRQ-Funded Nursing Study

Predictors of RN's intention to continue working were studied by Brewer, Kovner, Greene, and Cheng (2009). A randomly selected sample was sought from 40 urban geographic regions in 29 U.S. states. Responses were received from 1,907 female RNs under age 65. Nurses who are satisfied in their current position and whose organization supports them are more likely to stay in their jobs. Desire to quit work is positively related to higher levels of education, working in a smaller metropolitan area, ease of finding another job, and work-family conflict.

Evidence-Based Practice Centers

In 1997 the Agency for Health Care Policy and Research, now known as the Agency for Healthcare Research and Quality (AHRQ), began its initiative to promote evidence-based practice. Twelve evidence-based practice centers (EPCs) were established. Today, there are 14 EPCs. Contracts were awarded to institutions in the United States and Canada. The EPCs develop evidence reports and technology assessments on topics related to clinical, social science/behavioral science, economic, and other health care organization and delivery issues. Topics for consideration are nominated by such groups as professional societies, insurers, employers, and patient groups. The AHRQ Web site offers resources for both professionals and health care consumers. The goal is to improve the quality, effectiveness, and appropriateness of health care delivery in the United States.

In May 2010, 14 EPCs were funded by the AHRQ. Eleven of these centers are located in the United States, and three are located in Canada:

Blue Cross and Blue Shield Association in Chicago, Illinois

Duke University, Durham, North Carolina

ECRI, Plymouth Meeting, Pennsylvania

Johns Hopkins University, Baltimore, Maryland

McMaster University, Hamilton, Ontario, Canada

Minnesota Evidence-Based Practice Center, Minneapolis, Minnesota

Oregon Evidence-Based Practice Center, Portland, Oregon

RTI International, University of North Carolina at Chapel Hill, North Carolina

Southern California Evidence-Based Practice Center/Rand Corporation, Santa Monica, California

Tufts Medical Center, Boston, Massachusetts

University of Alberta, Edmonton, Alberta, Canada

University of Connecticut, Hartford, Connecticut

University of Ottawa, Ottawa, Canada

Vanderbilt University, Nashville, Tennessee

U.S. Preventive Services Task Force

The U.S. Preventive Services Task Force (USPSTF) has been in existence since 1984. It has been sponsored by the Agency for Healthcare Research and Quality (http://ahrq.gov/clinic/uspstfix.htm) since 1998. It is the leading independent panel of private-sector experts in the area of primary care and preventive services.

The USPSTF is supported by the 14 EPCs previously mentioned. The EPCs conduct systematic reviews on clinical preventative services, and the results of their reviews are used in making sets of recommendations for use in primary care settings. The USPSTF then reviews the evidence and determines the benefits and harms for each preventive service.

The Task Force grades its recommendations as follows: (A) Recommends the service; there is high certainty that the net benefit is substantial; (B) Recommends the service; there is high certainty that the net benefit is moderate or there is moderate certainty that the net benefit is moderate to substantial; (C) Recommends the service; there is at least moderate certainty that the net benefit is small; (D) Recommends against the service; there is moderate or high certainty that the service has no net benefit or that the harms outweigh the benefits; (I) The current evidence is insufficient to assess the balance of benefits and harms of the service.

At least once every 5 years, the decision is made to either update a recommendation or inactivate a topic. Topics may be inactivated when they are no longer relevant to clinical practice.

The USPSTF celebrated its 25th anniversary in 2009, with the publication of *The Guide to Clinical Preventive Services 2009*. *The Guide to Clinical Preventive Services 2010–2011* is now available at http://ahrq.gov/clinic/pocketgd.htm. It covers recommendations from 2002 through March 2010.

National Guideline Clearinghouse

The National Guideline Clearinghouse (NGC) is a database of evidence-based clinical practice guidelines and related documents. The NGC is sponsored by the AHRQ, U.S. Department of Health and Human Services (http://guideline.gov/). In May 2010 the NGC contained 2,392 summaries of guidelines, with 409 guidelines in progress.

Every nurse should be knowledgeable about the practice guidelines that are specific for her or his area of practice. Many nurses have been involved in developing practice guidelines. In 1992 Nancy Bergstrom, a nurse expert in the field of pressure ulcers, was the chairperson of the committee that formulated the guidelines *Pressure Ulcers in Adults: Prediction and Prevention*. The Family Nurse Practitioner Program at the University of Texas School of Nursing developed guidelines in 2002 for the diagnosis and treatment of pediculosis capitis (head lice) in children and adults. An updated version of the guidelines was published in 2008. The Registered Nurses' Association of Ontario (RNAC) developed guidelines in 2004 for promoting asthma control in children. The guidelines were updated in 2008 to include two additions: nurses should advocate against exposure to tobacco smoke and refer youth or parents/caregivers to tobacco cessation programs, if indicated.

EVIDENCE-BASED NURSING PRACTICE

You may have wondered how evidence-based nursing practice and research utilization differ. *Research utilization* is a more narrow term than evidence-based nursing practice. Research utilization involves the use of results from specific research studies that concentrated on one clinical problem. Knowledge is accumulated over time and works its way into practice. As mentioned in Chapter 17, we no longer routinely irrigate urinary drainage systems or clamp and disconnect the tubing when the patient ambulates. Research has demonstrated that interrupting the closed system increases the likelihood of a urinary tract infection. This is an example of research utilization. This research was supported by the CURN project, a federally funded demonstration project, which was discussed in Chapter 17.

Evidence-based nursing practice is broader in scope. Whereas nursing research utilization begins with existing research that needs to be implemented in practice, evidence-based nursing practice seeks a solution to a clinical problem for which there is no apparent solution.

To show the importance of evidence-based nursing practice, journals and books are being devoted to this topic. Two journals that focus on evidence-based nursing practice are *Evidence-Based Nursing* and *Worldviews on Evidence-Based Nursing*. Several books are also available. One of the more recent books, *Evaluating Research for Evidence-Based Nursing Practice*, was written by Fawcett and Garity (2008).

ASKING CLINICAL QUESTIONS

Evidence-based nursing practice requires that nurses write clinical questions. Chapter 5 discusses problem statements and research questions. This section focuses on writing a question for a specific clinical problem.

The acronym PICOT is a commonly used format for writing clinical questions. Developed by Fineout-Overholt and Johnston (2005), the five letters stand for:

P = Patient or population

I = Intervention or interest area

C = Comparison intervention or current practice

O = Outcome(s) desired

T = Time to achieve outcome (optional)

A clear discussion of this format is found in a March 2010 *AJN* article titled "Asking the Clinical Question: A Key Step in Evidence-Based Practice" (Stillwell, Fineout-Overholt, Melnyk, & Williamson, 2010). The following example was used: "In adult patients undergoing surgery, how does guided imagery compared with music therapy affect analgesia use within the first 24 hours post-op?" The population (P) was "adult patients undergoing surgery." The intervention of interest (I) was "guided imagery." The comparison intervention (C) was "music therapy." The outcome (O) was "analgesia use." Finally, the time (T) was "the first 24 hours post-op."

EVIDENCE-BASED NURSING PRACTICE CENTERS

Evidence-based practice centers in nursing are appearing in increasing numbers. Three examples—the Academic Center for Evidence-Based Practice, Joanna Briggs Institute, and Cole Hirsch Institute for Best Nursing Practices—are discussed next:

Academic Center for Evidence-Based Practice

The Academic Center for Evidence-Based Practice (ACE) is based at the School of Nursing of the University of Texas Health Science Center at San Antonio. The ACE center was established in 2000. The purpose of this center is "to advance cutting edge, state-of-the-art evidence-based nursing practice, research, and education within an interprofessional context" (http://acestar.uthscsa.edu/). The goal is "to turn research into action, improving health care and outcomes through evidence-based practice (EBP), research, and education." The slogan of the center is ". . . to the best of our knowledge!"

The ACE center provides a setting for evidence-based practice activities, which include education and interdisciplinary research projects. These projects concentrate on two objectives: (a) basic and professional level workforce development for EBP, and (b) the study of the processes and outcomes within evidence-based quality improvement.

Joanna Briggs Institute

The Joanna Briggs Institute (JBI), established in 1996, is an international collaboration involving nursing, medical, and allied health researchers; clinicians; academics; and quality managers. More than 90 countries are involved with the Institute, with more than 56 centers and groups. Since May 2010, the Institute has been housed in the Faculty of Health Sciences at the University of Adelaide, South Australia (http://joannabriggs.edu.au). The institute was named after Joanna Briggs (1805–1880), the first Matron (Head Nurse) of the Royal Adelaide Hospital in Australia.

The JBI coordinates the efforts of a group of self-governing collaborative centers. Goals are to promote evidence-based health care and training, conduct systematic reviews, develop Best Practice Information Sheets, implement evidence-based practice, and conduct evaluation cycles and primary research arising out of the systematic reviews.

There are four collaborating nursing centers in the United States: (a) Evidence Based Practice Center of Oklahoma (University of Oklahoma in Oklahoma City, OK), (b) Indiana Center for Evidence-Based Nursing Practice (Purdue University Calumet in Hammond, IN), (c) New Jersey Center for Evidence Based Nursing (University of Medicine and Dentistry of New Jersey in Newark, NJ); and (d) Texas Christian University Center for Evidence Based Practice and Medicine (Texas Christian University in Fort Worth, TX).

Sarah Cole Hirsh Institute for Best Nursing Practices

The Hirsh Institute is based at the Case Western Reserve University Frances Payne Bolton School of Nursing in Cleveland, Ohio. The Institute provides consulting services on evidence-based practice across health care settings and offers Certificate Programs to educate nurses on the best practice based on evidence. Also, literature searches are carried out and synthesized on current research topics. For more information go to http://fpb.case.edu/Centers/Hirsh/about.shtm.

SOURCES OF EVIDENCE FOR PRACTICE

Nurses are interested in conducting systematic or integrative reviews of research, just as physicians are. Some journals that publish review articles are *Clinical Nurse Specialist*, *Journal of Advanced Nursing*, *Journal of Clinical Nursing*, *Journal of Nursing Scholarship*, and *Pediatric, Oncology Nursing*.

According to Whittemore (2005), well-done reviews "present the state of the science, resolve conflicting reports of evidence, and have direct applicability to practice and policy" (p. 56). Windle (2010) asserted that nurses do not have the time to constantly review individual studies published in the literature. By reading systematic reviews, answers to clinical questions may be obtained in a timelier manner.

Meta-analysis is another method used by nurses to combine the results of several studies. Recall from Chapter 15 that a meta-analysis combines the statistical results of studies that have been conducted on the same topic. The purpose is to discover consistencies and inconsistencies in the results of these studies.

The following example presents an integrative review of studies that examined health care providers' attitudes regarding family presence during resuscitation of adults. The ensuing example summarizes the results of a meta-analysis on the predictors of anger in adolescents.

Integrative Review

An integrative review was conducted to determine health care providers' attitudes regarding family presence (FP) during resuscitation of adults (Howlett, Alexander, and Tsuchiya, 2010). Thirteen full-text articles met criteria for inclusion in the study. Factors that influenced attitudes toward FP included perceived burden on staff, perceived effects on family, lack of medical knowledge of family, and existence of a hospital policy on FP. Wide variation in support for FP was found among various health care professionals, with nurses generally being more favorable.

Meta-analysis

A meta-analytic study was conducted to determine predictors of anger in adolescents (Mahon, Yarcheski, Yarcheski, & Hanks, 2010). The literature review consisted of 288 published studies and 87 unpublished doctoral dissertation studies completed between 1980 and 2007. Eighty-eight of these studies met the inclusion criteria. Twelve prominent predictors of anger were identified. Five of these (trait anger, anxiety, depression, stress, and exposure to violence) had moderate to substantial effect sizes. Four predictors (victim of violence, hostility, self-esteem, and social support) had low to moderate effect sizes. The other three predictors (age, race/ethnicity, and gender) demonstrated only trivial effect sizes.

Controversy surrounds the sources of evidence for practice, especially for nursing practice. It appears that there is more agreement among physicians than among nurses. Many physicians agree with the levels of evidence originally presented by Archie Cochrane. He placed meta-analysis of randomized clinical trials at the top of the evidence hierarchy.

In nursing, Stetler et al. (1998) have suggested a hierarchy of levels of evidence for use in practice that is similar to that proposed by Cochrane. The first level is meta-analysis studies that provide evidence from multiple studies. Single experimental studies are the second level of evidence. The third level of evidence is quasi-experimental studies, such as cohort studies and time-series studies. Nonexperimental studies, such as comparative and correlational studies, constitute the fourth level of evidence. Program evaluation research and quality improvement projects provide the fifth level of evidence. Finally, opinions of authorities or experts is the sixth level of evidence. Within each of these levels, grades are assigned from A to D for the quality of the study.

One of the problems with this evidence hierarchy for nursing is that nurses have conducted few RCTs. Therefore, we often fail to reach the first or second level of evidence in our study findings. Another area of concern is that nurses deal with the psychological, social, cultural, and spiritual aspects of their patients/clients. Often these issues do not lend themselves to RCTs.

The Iowa Model of Evidence-Based Practice to Promote Quality Care (Titler et al., 2001) recognizes that other sources of evidence may be necessary for nursing practice. One step of the model shows that if there is not sufficient research data, practice may need to be based on case reports, expert opinion, scientific principles, and theory.

The multidisciplinary evidence-based practice model developed at the University of Colorado Hospital is discussed by Oman, Duran, and Fink (2008). This model places valid and current research at the core, along with nine other sources of evidence. These nine sources, depicted in the model as spokes coming out of the research core, are: pathophysiology; cost effectiveness analysis; benchmarking data; clinical expertise; patient preference; infection control data; international, national, and local standards; quality improvement and risk data; and retrospective or concurrent chart review.

Barr and Thomas (2005) have argued that many nursing clinical practices lack research evidence to support these practices. For example, they have called for the continued practice of aspiration prior to intramuscular (IM) injections because of the variation in individuals' anatomy and the dangers of inadvertent intravenous (IV) administration of IM drugs. Safety factors are thought to outweigh the drawbacks of this practice.

Many nurses are calling for the use of qualitative research study results as a source of evidence for practice (Callery, 2005; Chamberlain, 2009; Volante, 2008; Whittemore, 2005). Chamberlain (2009) asserted that some phenomena about human beings are not suitable for quantitative study.

CONSIDERATIONS FOR THE FUTURE

A fairly new concept in the area of evidence-based practice is care bundles. **Care bundles** group together several evidence-based practices. The belief behind care bundles is that when several practices or interventions are used in combination, or as a cluster, they have a greater effect on outcomes than if just one intervention was used. The idea, according to Fulbrook and Mooney (2003), is that the "whole is greater than the sum of its parts."

Harris (2010) described a urinary care bundle that was implemented at Our Lady of Lourdes Memorial Hospital in Binghamton, New York. The care bundled consisted of five main elements: (a) dependent and incontinent patients are toileted every 2 hours, (b) only justified catheters are inserted, and are removed as soon as they are no longer justified, (c) catheters are inserted properly using aseptic technique, (d) specimens are collected properly, and (e) catheters are properly cared for and maintained, based on recommended CDC guidelines.

A central-line care bundle used at Rady Children's Hospital in San Diego, California was described by Hatler, Hebden, Kaler, and Zack (2010). It includes the following components: (a) hand hygiene, (b) maximal barrier precautions during insertion, (c) chlorhexidine skin antisepsis, (d) optimal catheter-site selection with femoral-vein avoidance in adults, and (e) daily review of line necessity, with prompt removal of unnecessary lines.

Care Bundles to Reduce In-Hospital Mortality

Robb et al. (2010) evaluated the impact of eight care bundles implemented in several areas of 56 hospitals in the United Kingdom. Mortality rates were compared to the preceding year (from 2007 to 2006) for the 13 diagnoses targeted by the care bundles, for 43 nontargeted diagnoses, and for the hospitals' overall mortality rate. The researchers concluded that implementing care bundles reduces death rates in targeted clinical areas as well as the overall mortality rate.

Nursing practice today and in the future should be based on evidence. This is easy to say but difficult to ensure. Nurses may be reluctant to make practice changes, just as are other health care professionals. Change is stressful and the implementation of change sometimes takes time. Nurses will have to be convinced that evidence-based practice is in the best interests of their patients/clients and themselves. Also, we need to find ways to disseminate and implement research findings faster so that a patient does not have to wait for years to receive evidence-based care for a health care problem.

Use of Current Best Evidence

Ganz et al. (2009) studied nurses' oral-care practices related to the current best evidence for these practices. Nurses rated oral care a high priority, but many did not report implementing the latest evidence into their current practice. The level of research utilization was not related to personal or professional characteristics. Therefore, the researchers called for all ICU nurses to be educated and encouraged to implement evidence-based practices.

A body of evidence now exists on the routine use of episiotomies during childbirth. The evidence indicates that this practice is not in the best interests of women. Investigators for the Agency for Healthcare Research and Quality published results from a large systematic review of the literature on episiotomies (Hartmann et al., 2005). Data revealed that the episiotomy did not prevent fecal and urinary incontinence or relax the pelvic floor. The researchers therefore called for the practice to be abandoned. How long do you think it will take before episiotomies are discontinued, as a routine practice by obstetrical health care providers? Probably quite some time!

Another controversial issue is breast-self-examination (BSE). Studies have demonstrated that breast cancer mortality is not reduced by women's performance of BSE (see section on *Cochrane Reviews*). Are you going to be the nurse who tells a woman that there are no benefits to BSE? Not me!

SUMMARY

Evidence-based practice is a fairly new concept in health care. The movement began in medicine with the work of Archie Cochrane, a medical researcher and epidemiologist. In 1972 he published a book that pointed out the lack of solid evidence on the effects of health care. He suggested we should use our limited health care resources to provide the most effective health care.

Sackett et al. (1996) defined evidence-based medicine as "the conscientious, explicit, and judicious use of current best evidence in making decisions about the care of individual patients" (p. 71).

The Cochrane Collaboration is an international nonprofit organization that supports evidence-based practice. Cochrane Centers are located throughout the world. This organization conducts systematic reviews. A **systematic review** is a rigorous scientific approach that combines results from a group of original research studies and looks at the studies as a whole. *The Cochrane Library* is the medium used to publish the work of the Cochrane Collaboration.

The Agency for Healthcare Research and Quality (AHRQ) is a branch of the U.S. Department of Health and Human Services. There are 14 Evidence-Based Practice Centers (EPCs) in the United States and Canada. These centers develop evidence reports and technology assessments.

The U.S. Preventative Services Task Force (USPSTF) is sponsored by the AHRQ. It is the leading independent panel of private-sector experts in the area of primary care and preventative services. This task force reviews evidence provided by the 14 EPCs and then makes recommendations for or against preventative services.

The National Guideline Clearinghouse (NGC) is a public resource for evidence-based clinical practice guidelines. It is sponsored by the AHRQ. The NGC has published guidelines on such topics as pressure ulcer management and pain management.

Evidence-based nursing practice (EBNP) is broader in scope than research utilization. EBNP begins with a clinical problem for which there is no immediately apparent solution. Nurses then seek to find information about the best solution for this specific problem.

There is an increasing number of evidence-based practice centers in nursing. Three of these centers are: the Academic Center for Evidence-Based Nursing, located at the University of Texas Health Science Center at San Antonio; Joanna Briggs Institute, in Australia; and Sarah Cole Hirsh Institute for Best Nursing Practices Based on Evidence, based at the Case Western Reserve University Frances Payne Bolton School of Nursing in Cleveland, Ohio.

There is a great debate about the sources of evidence for making practice decisions. In the medical profession, meta-analysis of RCTs appears frequently at the top of the evidence hierarchy. Many nurses also give credence to this type of research, but are also calling for other sources of evidence, especially evidence from qualitative research studies.

A new concept in the area of evidence-based practice is care bundles. **Care bundles** group together several evidence-based practices. The belief behind care bundles is that when several practices or interventions are used in combination, or as a cluster, they will have a greater effect on outcomes than if just one intervention was used.

Nursing practice today and in the future should be based on evidence. However, nurses and other health care providers are resistant to change. Even when evidence clearly suggests a change in practice, sometimes change occurs slowly.

NURSING RESEARCH ON THE WEB

For additional online resources, research activities, and exercises, go to **www.mynursingkit. com.** Select Chapter 18 from the drop-down menu.

GET INVOLVED ACTIVITIES

1. Divide into groups and ask each group to pick a clinical topic of interest to the group. Search *The Cochrane Library* systematic reviews and see if any reviews have already been conducted on the topic.
2. Based on the *Cochrane Reviews* obtained in Activity 1, decide which reviews demonstrate the strongest evidence for implementation of the recommendations in practice.
3. Identify several barriers to the implementation of evidence-based nursing practice in a particular health care setting.
4. Divide into nine groups. Using the evidence-based practice model developed at the University of Colorado, each group will chose one of the types of evidence (other than research) and argue for the value of that source of evidence. For example, present your views on why preferences for care should be considered when making practice decisions.
5. Propose a nursing procedure for which you believe a care bundle is needed.
6. Using the PICOT format, develop a clinical question for an identified problem.

SELF-TEST

1. When was the concept of evidence-based practice first introduced?
   A. 1960s
   B. 1970s
   C. 1980s
   D. 1990s
2. What person or organization is generally credited with starting the movement toward evidence-based practice?
   A. Archie Cochrane
   B. Ed Sackett
   C. Cochrane Collaboration
   D. Agency for Healthcare Quality and Research

3. Which of the following countries *does not* have a Cochrane Center?
   A. Germany
   B. Italy
   C. Mexico
   D. Netherlands

4. Which level of evidence is most often placed at the top of the hierarchy of evidence for practice decisions?
   A. meta-analysis of multiple randomized clinical trials
   B. results from a single well-controlled experimental study
   C. a consensus of opinion from a group of experts on the topic
   D. case-control studies

5. Which of the following is *not* an example of an evidence-based nursing practice center?
   A. Joanna Briggs Institute
   B. Academic Center for Evidence-Based Nursing
   C. National Institute for Nursing Research
   D. Sarah Cole Hirsh Institute for Best Nursing Practices

6. When the U.S. Preventative Services Task Force assigns a "C" recommendation to a preventive service, it means
   A. the preventative service is being recommended, with reservations.
   B. a recommendation is made against providing the service.
   C. a recommendation is being made against routinely providing the service.

D. evidence is insufficient for making a recommendation for or against the service.

7. Care bundles have been used
   A. frequently in many areas of nursing and medicine.
   B. most often in critical care units.
   C. only in pilot studies.
   D. in emergency rooms.

8. Which of the following agencies is a source for clinical guidelines?
   A. National Guideline Clearinghouse
   B. National Institute of Nursing Research
   C. U. S. Guidelines Service
   D. Physicians' and Nurses' Guidelines Center

9. Which of the following nurses chaired the committee that developed practice guidelines for pressure ulcers?
   A. Florence Downs
   B. Nancy Bergstrom
   C. Tim Porter-O'Grady
   D. Bernadette Melnyk

10. Some nurses are calling for more emphasis to be placed on what type of evidence on which to base practice decisions?
    A. results from qualitative research studies
    B. expert opinions
    C. cost-containment data
    D. nurses' preferences for type of care they provide

REFERENCES

Barr, D. M., & Thomas, C. M. (2005, August 15). IM administration. *Advance for Nurses–Texas/Louisiana Metro Area*, 30.

Brewer, C. S., Kovner, C. T., Greene, W., & Cheng, Y. (2009). Predictors of RN's intent to work and work decisions 1 year later in a U.S. national sample. *International Journal of Nursing Studies, 46*, 940–956.

Callery, P. (2005). Needles and haystacks. *Paediatric Nursing, 17*(7), 14.

Chamberlain, B. (2009). Phenomenology: A qualitative method. *Clinical Nurse Specialist, 23*, 52–53.

Fawcett, J., & Garity, J. (2008). *Evaluating research for evidence-based nursing practice*. Philadelphia: F. A. Davis.

Fineout-Overholt, E., & Johnston, L. (2005). Teaching EBP: Asking searchable, answerable clinical questions. *Worldviews on Evidence-Based Nursing, 2*, 157–160.

Fulbrook, P., & Mooney, S. (2003). Care bundles in critical care: A practical approach to evidence-based practice. *British Association of Critical Care Nurses, Nursing in Critical Care, 8*, 249–255.

Ganz, F. D., Fink, N. F., Raanan, O., Asher, M., Bruttin, M., Nun, M. B., & Benbinishty, J. (2009). ICU nurses' oral-care practices and the current best evidence. *Journal of Nursing Scholarship, 41*, 132–138.

Harris, T. A. (2010). Changing practice to reduce the use of urinary catheters. *Nursing 2010, 40*, 18–20.

Hartmann, K., Viswanathan, M., Palmieri, R., Gartlehner, G, Thorp, J., & Lohr, K. N. (2005). Outcomes of routine episiotomy: A systematic review. *Journal of the American Medical Association, 293*, 2141–2148.

Hatler, C., Hebden, J., Kaler, W., & Zack, J. (2010). Walk the walk to reduce catheter-related bloodstream infections. *American Nurse Today, 5*, 26–30.

Hegyvary, S. T. (2006). A call for papers on evidence-based problems [Editorial]. *Journal of Nursing Scholarship, 38,* 1.

Howlett, M. S. L., Alexander, G. A., & Tsuchiya, B. (2010). Health care providers' attitudes regarding family presence during resuscitation of adults: An integrated review of the literature. *Clinical Nurse Specialist, 24,* 161–174.

Mahon, N. E., Yarcheski, A., Yarcheski, T. J., & Hanks, M. M. (2010). A meta-analytic study of predictors of anger in adolescents. *Nursing Research, 59,* 178–184.

Oman, K. S., Duran, C., & Fink, R. (2008). Evidence-based policy and procedures: An algorithm for success. *Journal of Nursing Administration, 38,* 47–51.

Robb, E., Jarman, B., Suntharalingam, G., Higgens, C., Tennant, R., Elcock, K. (2010). Using care bundles to reduce in-hospital mortality: Quantitative survey. *British Medical Journal, 340,* 861–863.

Sackett, D. L., Rosenberg, W. M., Gray, J. A., Haynes, R. B., & Richardson, W. S. (1996). Evidence based medicine: What it is and what it isn't. *British Medical Journal, 312,* 71–72.

Stetler, C. B., Brunnell, M., Guiliano, K. K., Morse, D., Prince, L., & Newell-Stokes, V. (1998). Evidence-based practice and the role of nursing leadership. *Journal of Nursing Administration, 28,* 45–53.

Stillwell, S. B., Fineout-Overholt, E., Melnyk, B. M., & Williamson, K. M. (2010). Asking the clinical question: A key step in evidence-based practice. *AJN, 110,* 58–61.

Titler, M. G., Kleiber, C., Steelman, V., Rakel, B., Budreau, G., Everett, L. Q., ... Goode. C. (2001). The Iowa Model of Evidence-Based Practice to Promote Quality Care. *Critical Care Nursing Clinics of North America, 13,* 497–509.

Titler, M. G., & Moore, J. (2010). Evidence-based practice [Editorial]. *Nursing Research, 59,* S2–S6.

Volante, M. (2008). Qualitative research. *Nurse Researcher, 16* (1), 4–6.

Whittemore, R. (2005). Combining evidence in nursing research: Methods and implications. *Nursing Research, 54,* 56–62.

Windle, P. E. (2010). The systematic review process: An overview. *Journal of PeriAnesthesia Nursing, 25,* 40–42.

CHAPTER 19

Nursing Research and Health Care Economics

—Michael L. Nieswiadomy and Rose M. Nieswiadomy

OUTLINE

Health Care Economics and Nursing
Nursing Research Cost-Effectiveness Studies
Need for More Research Studies
    on Nursing Care

Summary
Nursing Research on the Web
Get Involved Activities
Self-Test

OBJECTIVES

On completion of this chapter, you will be prepared to:
1. Discuss economic terms that have an impact on nursing
2. Articulate some of the reasons that nurses need to be familiar with economics
3. Determine the cost-effectiveness of nursing care based on the results of selected nursing research studies
4. Recognize the need for more cost-effectiveness studies on nursing care
5. Develop an idea for a nursing care cost-effectiveness study

NEW TERMS DEFINED IN THIS CHAPTER

derived demand, pg 291
diminishing marginal returns, pg 291
marginal benefit, pg 291
marginal expense, pg 291
marginal product, pg 291

marginal revenue, pg 291
monopsony, pg 291
pecuniary terms, pg 291
production function, pg 291

The nursing profession has been in existence throughout history. Today, it is a very admired profession. Since 1999, nurses have been included in the Gallup Poll that measures the general public's trust of various professionals in the United States. Nurses have been chosen as the most trusted professionals every year, except for 2001, when firefighters were selected.

Nurses have an obligation to live up to the trust that has been placed in us. We must continually demonstrate our knowledge and abilities in the health care arena. As members of the largest group of health care professionals, we should have a great deal of influence on health care.

With prospective payment systems determining the amount of reimbursements that hospitals receive, nursing care services are being closely examined. It is not difficult to determine that hospitals could cut costs by curtailing nursing services. However, if nursing care can be demonstrated to be cost effective, hospitals will look to other sources for trimming their budgets.

HEALTH CARE ECONOMICS AND NURSING

Nursing is an admirable profession, but it is also a business. In order for nurses to demonstrate their value, they must attempt to quantify this value in pecuniary terms. **Pecuniary terms** indicates that monetary values must be determined. Of course, only a portion of the services that professional nurses provide can be quantified in pecuniary terms (Dall et al., 2009). Nonetheless, we must begin this valuation process by estimating the monetary value of nursing care services. Nurses must become more aware of health care economics as the health care industry becomes more and more cost conscious. This section provides some of the insight needed to understand health care economics as it relates to nurses.

In order to understand economic issues affecting nursing, we must first understand the market forces that affect nurses. As in any market, two primary forces affect the number of nurses hired and the wage rate paid: the demand and supply for nursing skills. Let's start with a discussion of the demand for nurses by first examining a firm's demand for labor. A firm produces a good or service (e.g., treating patients), using what economists call a **production function**, which indicates the output that can be produced with a given set of inputs. In economic terms, we say that firms have a **derived demand** for labor because the demand for labor is *derived* from the demand for the product (or service) that the firm produces and sells. For example, a hospital hires nurses because their customers (i.e., patients) want to purchase medical care. A hospital, as a business entity, wants to maximize profits. (*Note*: This discussion also applies to a nonprofit hospital. It must compare its revenue to its costs.)

To determine the *profit maximizing* number of nurses (and other staff) to hire, a hospital must compare the marginal expense with the marginal benefit of hiring a nurse. The **marginal expense** of a worker is the additional cost of hiring one more worker. Usually, the marginal expense of hiring an additional worker is the market determined wage rate. The exception occurs when a **monopsony**, a large buyer of an input, such as the only hospital in town, sets the wage for nurses. For a discussion of this issue, see Feldstein (2004). The **marginal benefit** (also known as the marginal revenue product) of a worker is the product of two components: (a) the **marginal product** of labor—the additional output produced by an additional worker, and (b) the **marginal revenue**—the additional revenue generated by selling an additional unit of output.

The law of **diminishing marginal returns** says that as more of a variable input (like labor) is hired (and the amount of capital is fixed), the marginal product of a worker declines. Primarily due to this diminishing marginal product, the demand for labor curve is downward sloping. Once the hospital has determined the marginal benefit, it must compare this marginal benefit to the marginal expense of hiring another nurse. The hospital should hire additional nurses as long as the marginal benefit is greater than the wage rate (i.e., the marginal expense). The optimal number of nurses to hire occurs when the marginal benefit of the last nurse hired equals the marginal expense. The hospital must also decide how much of other inputs (e.g., computers, CT scanners) to use. The steps to determine the optimal combination of all inputs is somewhat complex and is not discussed here. Essentially, the marginal benefits must be compared to the marginal expenses.

A hospital (or other medical facility) has many similarities, along with some significant differences, with other firms. A hospital provides health care services and, thus, has a derived demand for many inputs such as doctors, nurses, equipment, and office staff. In this way a hospital is similar to many companies. However, a hospital administrator's task is very complex because it is much more difficult to measure the output of a hospital. Consequently, it is very difficult to measure the value (i.e., the marginal benefit) of a nurse. For example, it is easy for a paper mill to see how many feet of paper have been produced. But it is much more difficult to measure the output of a nurse's job because the output is ultimately measured in terms of the patient's health, something inherently difficult to measure. Herein lies the crux of the problem for the nursing profession: How do nurses demonstrate the value of their services? Although nurses pride themselves on being compassionate caregivers, they must recognize that they are ultimately an input used in providing health care, and, thus, there is a derived demand for their services. Nurses must be able to demonstrate the value of services for which they are paid or risk losing hospital nursing positions.

Recently, health care economists and nursing experts have begun to grapple with the issue of "costing out" nursing care. Part of the problem with determining the value of nursing care is that hospitals have not billed separately for nursing services. The cost of nursing services is bundled within a total hospital bill.

In the current system, hospitals can make more profit, in the short run, if they increase the workload of nurses. However, this strategy is likely to lead to long-term losses if the quality of care is significantly reduced. The hospitals will lose future customers as their reputations are tarnished. Even worse, hospitals may expose themselves to legal liabilities for harm caused to their patients. Thus, hospitals need to carefully examine the value of nursing care. And nurses need to play a pivotal role in this valuation process.

The Dall et al. (2009) study provides an excellent example of how to quantify the economic value (i.e., cost savings) of professional nursing. This study provides many interesting ideas for developing a cost-effectiveness study for nursing. The researchers examined the relationship between registered nurse staffing levels and nursing-sensitive patient outcomes (NSOs) in acute care hospitals. They synthesized findings from the literature and from hospital discharge data. These researchers examined patient risk for urinary tract infections, hospital-acquired pneumonia, pressure ulcer, upper gastrointestinal bleeding, sepsis, shock/cardiac failure, pulmonary failure, central nervous system complications, deep vein thrombosis, postoperative infection, adverse drug events, and patient falls. They also looked at in-hospital mortality (failure to rescue).

Estimates of the total cost were made by summing three categories of economic costs associated with NSOs: (a) medical costs, (b) patients' lost income due to increased length of stay, and (c) family lost income due to mortality of a member.

For the first cost category, they assumed that each inpatient day that is avoided generates cost savings of approximately $1,522 per patient day (the 2005 national average cost per inpatient day in community hospitals.) This is a very real savings to a hospital, especially as the federal government and private insurers increasingly refuse to pay for nosocomial complications.

For the second cost category, they assumed that each additional day of stay causes a person to lose income. The researchers used U.S. Bureau of Labor Statistics data on average earnings and labor force participation rates by age and gender to estimate the lost productive value to society of patients being delayed in returning to the workforce. A speedier return to the workforce results in a cost saving to the patient.

For the third cost category, they assumed that families of the deceased lose the lifetime stream of the deceased's income. They used standard economic assumptions on the growth in a worker's earnings and discounted these earnings to present value (the value in today's dollars of future losses). They multiplied the reduction in the probability of death (due to an increase in nurse staffing levels) times the lifetime earnings to obtain the expected cost savings.

The second and third cost categories are costs to the patient (and thus to society), but not necessarily to the hospital. However, as mentioned above, hospitals may bear the liability in lawsuits, which make these expected expenses very real costs. Thus, hospitals need to be keenly aware of these costs.

Dall et al.'s study results indicated that as nursing staffing levels increase, patient risk of nosocomial complications and hospital length of stay decrease. After combining the three above-mentioned cost saving categories, they estimated that adding 133,000 FTE (full-time equivalent) RNs to the acute care hospital workforce in the United States would save 5,900 lives per year. When medical savings and increased productivity were considered, the economic value of each additional RN was $57,700. They noted that this is only a partial estimate of the value of an additional nurse. Furthermore, their estimates consider only the marginal value. Because of diminishing marginal returns, the average value of a nurse is higher than the marginal value. Thus the average value of a nurse is higher than $57,700.

NURSING RESEARCH COST-EFFECTIVENESS STUDIES

As mentioned in Chapter 1, studies can be found in the literature that demonstrate the cost-effectiveness of nursing care. However, these studies are small in number. The results of some of these studies are presented here in chronological order. The areas studied include: care of early birth-weight infants, the cost-effectiveness of a nurse-practitioner-managed health care unit, a nurse case management program for patients experiencing syncope, and a collaborative nurse practitioner (NP) care management model on pharmaceutical usage, with a focus on antibiotics.

Brooten et al.'s (1986) study clearly demonstrates the cost-effectiveness of nursing care. This study examined early hospital discharge and home follow-up care of very-low-birth-weight infants. The researchers found that follow-up care by a nurse specialist is safe and cost-effective. This type of care potentially reduces hospital care costs, decreases iatrogenic illnesses and hospital-acquired infections, and enhances parent-infant interactions.

Ferguson (1996) analyzed the cost-effectiveness of a nurse practitioner–managed health care unit (HCU) that was implemented in a meat packing/rendering plant in the northern United States. During the first 5 years (1988–1992), a net savings of more than $1.3 million was realized in the cost of workers' compensation alone.

The cost savings of telephone nursing (TN) was reported by Greenberg (2000). Her study took place in a pediatric outpatient clinic setting in the southwest United States. Results of 90 calls (25% of the calls for 1 month) were examined. The dollar savings for 1 month was estimated to be $2,360. This figure was determined by subtracting the dollars ($2,216) spent on actual outcomes from the dollars ($4,576) that would have been spent based on outcomes without TN.

The cost-effectiveness of providing home nursing visits after newborn discharge was studied by Paul, Phillips, Widome, and Hollenbeak (2004). Nurse visits to newborns were made 1 to 2 days after their hospital discharge to determine if these visits would reduce the incidence of rehospitalization for jaundice and dehydration. These visits were found to reduce rehospitalization within the first 10 days of life from 2.8% of 2,641 newborns who were not seen by a nurse to only 0.6% of the 326 infants who received a home visit by a nurse. The home visits were significantly less costly than visits to the emergency department.

Bourdeaux et al. (2005) studied the use of a nurse case management program with patients experiencing syncope. The program was implemented at a large urban teaching hospital. The experimental (case management) group had 359 patients, and the control (no case management) group had 331 patients. Length of stay was reduced by 0.15 days over the 12 months of the case management program for diagnosis-related group (DRG) 141 (syncope and collapse with comorbidities). The decrease in direct cost was $376 per patient. Length of stay was decreased by 0.28 days for DRG 142 (syncope and collapse without comorbidities), with a cost savings of $292 per patient.

The staff of one Pennsylvania hospital created an admission nurse role (Hlipala, Meyer, Wallace, & Zaremba, 2005). This nurse initiates and completes the health history and assessment and promotes consumer satisfaction. A time study revealed that 30 to 60 minutes less staff nurse time was needed for new admissions. The annual cost savings, based on the salary of staff nurses, was between $100,000 and $201,296. Also, $64,000 a year was saved in overtime pay. Overtime pay related to admissions was found to be 93% less than prior to implementation of the admission nurse role.

Perinatal outcomes were evaluated based on a nurse-driven quality improvement program (Jallo, Bray, Padden, & Levin, 2009). Preterm birth, which is birth before 37 weeks gestation, is an acute and complex problem. A nursing team, composed of a perinatal clinical nurse specialist and several experienced obstetrical nurses, joined a large managed care organization (MCO) to develop and implement a program, Partners in Pregnancy (PnP), for pregnant women enrolled in the MCO. Four quarters of data from the pre-PnP program were compared to four quarters of data after the program was implemented. Neonatal Intensive Care Unit (NICU) length of stay (LOS) and cost data were compared. The LOS preprogram was 13.8 days, whereas the postprogram LOS was 11.6 days. The NICU payment per admission was reduced from $14,482 to $11,310.

A study was conducted to evaluate the economic impact of a collaborative nurse practitioner (NP) care management model on pharmaceutical usage, with a focus on antibiotics (Chen, McNeese-Smith, Cowan, Upenieks, & Afifi, 2009). The researchers used pharmaceutical claims data of 1,200 subjects who participated in the Multidisciplinary, Physician, and Nurse Practitioner Study from 2000 to 2004. The NP-led intervention group was associated with a significant reduction in overall drug cost, drug days, antibiotic cost, and antibiotic days per hospitalization episode. The researchers presented the advantages of "dedicating NPs in acute care settings to achieve quality care and contain inpatient drug costs" (p. 166).

NEED FOR MORE RESEARCH STUDIES ON NURSING CARE

Research is the means of demonstrating the value of nurses in the health care arena. Numerous sources call for more research on the economic value of nurses.

Chen et al. (2009) have called for future research that validates specific roles and functions of advanced nurse practitioners (ANPs) in regard to specific quality outcomes and cost-effectiveness measures. Bednarski (2009) reported that the American Association of Nephrology Nurses supports an evidence-based approach for delineating the value of nursing and wrote that is critical to connect nursing care with the outcomes of this care. Rausch and Bjorklund (2010) have called for more research in the use of bachelor's-prepared psychiatric nurses in the role of psychiatric liaison nurse in medical patient-care settings. Other experts call for research on how nursing intensity, academic preparation, licensure, certification, and other variables affect care cost and quality.

Peter Buerhaus, a member of the editorial board of *Nursing Economics$*, interviewed John Welton, PhD, RN, who is well known for his interest in the economic value of nursing. Welton argues, "We need to establish a price for nursing care and measure the clinical as well as economic contribution of nurses to patient care on an individual basis similar to physician care" (Buerhaus, 2010, p. 50). In economic terms, he says that we need to measure the marginal benefit of nursing care.

It is evident that more research is needed on the economic value of nursing. After reading this chapter on nursing research and health care economics, it is hoped that you will be more interested in the economic impact of nursing and be willing to participate in research to evaluate the importance of nursing in the health care arena.

SUMMARY

Nursing is an admired profession. However, it is necessary that nurses demonstrate their contributions to health care in monetary terms.

This chapter defines some economic terms that nurses need to understand. **Pecuniary terms** indicates that monetary values must be determined. A **production function** indicates the output that can be produced with a given set of inputs. A **derived demand** means that the demand for labor is derived from the demand for the product (or service) that a firm produces and sells. The **marginal expense** of a worker is the additional cost of hiring one more worker. The term **monopsony** is used to indicate a large buyer of an input, such as the only hospital in town, which is then able to set the wages for nurses. The **marginal benefit** of a worker has two components: (a) the **marginal product** of labor—the additional output produced by an additional worker, and (b) the **marginal revenue**—the additional revenue generated by selling an additional unit of output. The law of **diminishing marginal returns** means that as more of a variable input (like labor) is hired, and the amount of capital is fixed, the marginal product of a worker declines.

Findings from many nursing research studies have demonstrated the cost-effectiveness of nursing care. Brooten et al.'s (1986) study on very-low-birth-weight infants is a classic study that has been cited many times in the health care literature.

Many nursing and health care experts are calling for more research that will help determine the economic value of nursing care.

NURSING RESEARCH ON THE WEB

For additional online resources, research activities, and exercises, go to **www.mynursingkit. com.** Select Chapter 19 from the drop-down menu.

GET INVOLVED ACTIVITIES

1. Discuss the benefits to nurses of understanding economic terms that are relative to nursing practice.
2. Search the literature for a recent cost-effective nursing research study.
3. Divide into two debate teams. Argue the advantages and disadvantages of nursing care being "costed out" on a patient's hospital bill.

SELF-TEST

Circle the letter before the *best* answer:

1. The Gallup Poll has revealed that
   A. nursing is the most highly rated profession in the United States.
   B. nursing is the second most highly rated profession in the United States.
   C. the rating of the nursing profession has increased in recent years.
   D. the rating of the nursing profession has decreased slightly in recent years.

2. The demand for nursing is
   A. a derived demand.
   B. impossible to determine.
   C. not affected by demographic forces.
   D. not affected by technological advances.

3. Published studies involving the cost-effectiveness of nursing care
   A. are numerous in the literature.
   B. generally reveal that nursing care is cost-effective.
   C. have decreased in number in recent years.
   D. demonstrate mixed results on the cost-effectiveness of nursing care.

Write T (True) or F (False) beside the following statements:

____ 4. The economic value of nursing care is easier to determine than that of the services provided by many other occupations.

____ 5. Nurses do not need to be very interested in the monetary worth of the care they provide.

____ 6. A profit-maximizing firm should hire additional workers as long as the marginal benefit of an additional worker is greater than the marginal expense of the additional worker.

____ 7. One of the factors of nursing cost-effectiveness examined in the Dall et al. (2009) study was hospital-acquired pneumonia.

REFERENCES

Bednarski, D. (2009). The value of nursing. *Nephrology Nursing, 36,* 115–117.

Bourdeaux, L., Matthews, L., Richards, N. L., SanAgustin, G., Thomas, P., & Veltigian, S. (2005). Comparative study of case management program for patients with syncope. *Journal of Nursing Care Quality, 20,* 140–144.

Brooten, D., Kumar, S., Brown, L. P., Butts, P., Finkler, S. A., Bakewell-Sachs, S., ... Delivoria-Papadopoulos, M. (1986). A randomized clinical trial of early hospital discharge and home follow-up of very-low-birth-weight infants. *New England Journal of Medicine, 315,* 934–939.

Buerhaus, P. (2010). Health care payment reform: Implications for nurses. *Nursing Economics$, 26,* 49–54.

Chen, C., McNeese-Smith, D., Cowan, M., Upenieks, V., & Afifi, A. (2009). Evaluation of a nurse practitioner-led care management model in reducing inpatient drug utilization and cost. *Nursing Economics$, 27,* 160–169.

Dall, T. M., Chen, Y. J., Seifert, R. F., Maddox, P. J., & Hogan, P. F. (2009). The economic value of professional nursing. *Medical Care, 47,* 97–104.

Feldstein, Paul J. (2004). *Health care economics* (6th ed.). Albany, NY: Delmar.

Ferguson, L. A. (1996). Enhancing health care to underserved populations. *AAOHN Journal, 44,* 332–335.

Greenberg, M. E. (2000). Telephone nursing: Evidence of client and organizational benefits. *Nursing Economics$, 18,* 117–123.

Hlipala, S. I., Meyer, K. A., Wallace, T. O., & Zaremba, J. A. (2005). Profile of an admission nurse. *Nursing Management, 36,* 44–47.

Jallo, N., Bray, K., Padden, M., & Levin, D. (2009). A nurse-driven quality improvement program to improve perinatal outcomes. *Journal of Perinatal and Neonatal Nursing, 23,* 241–250.

Paul, I. M., Phillips, T. A., Widome, M. D., & Hollenbeak, C. S. (2004). Cost-effectiveness of postnatal home nursing visits for prevention of hospital care for jaundice and dehydration. *Pediatrics, 114,* 1015–1022.

Rausch, D. L., & Bjorklund, P. (2010). Decreasing the costs of constant observation. *The Journal of Nursing Administration, 40,* 75–81.

Critique of Research Reports

OUTLINE

OBJECTIVES

On completion of this chapter, you will be prepared to:
1. Discuss the guidelines for critiquing a quantitative research report
2. Discuss the guidelines for critiquing a qualitative research report
3. Critique selected quantitative research reports
4. Critique selected qualitative research reports
5. Determine both strengths and weaknesses of quantitative research reports
6. Determine both strengths and weaknesses of qualitative research reports

As all nurses and nursing students know, their practice should be based on evidence. Evidence-based practice (EBP) is probably one of the most prevalent terms found in the nursing literature in this first part of the 21st century. In Chapter 18, you learned more about EBP. You learned that research evidence is the most critical component of EBP. To use research evidence, one must be able to evaluate this evidence. Hence, nurses need critiquing skills. Stockhausen and Conrick (2003) have contended that learning how to critique research articles is one of the fundamental skills of scholarship in any discipline. Rempher and Silkman (2007) wrote that critiquing also shows your "commitment to evidence-informed practice and empowers you to create a practice culture based on the best available evidence" (p. 26).

As a reader of this book, you may take some consolation in knowing that you are not the only one who is *not* an expert in critiquing research articles. However, if you have made it all the way through to this page in the book, you have gained some knowledge that will help you critique published research articles.

You may believe that the only research articles that are published contain reports of "good" research. Unfortunately, this is not always true. Although the review process used by most nursing journals helps ensure the publication of valid research, some published studies contain serious flaws.

All studies have strong and weak points. The word *critique* is often equated with the word *criticism*. This is unfortunate because the purpose of a research critique is to assess the strengths as well as the weaknesses of a study. In the past, when my students have been given a critique assignment, I asked them to list the strengths of the study, as well as the weaknesses. Sometimes, it seems they enjoy pointing out the weaknesses rather than the strengths. They may then ask, "How did this study get published?" It is well to remember that the author of the published report had the courage and motivation to become involved in nursing research, whereas many other nurses have not. This is not to say that critiquers should be lenient in their evaluation of published research. It is important, however, that nursing research be conducted, and severe criticism of their work may dim the enthusiasm of some nurse researchers. This is especially true for those who are just beginning to become involved in nursing research. Keep in mind that it is much easier to evaluate the research of others than to conduct research yourself!

Frequently, there are no right or wrong answers when evaluating research reports. Even experts may disagree about certain aspects of a particular study. In evaluating research, reviewers should be as objective as possible and present a sound rationale for their judgments.

Duffy (2005) published an article in *Clinical Nurse Specialist* on critical appraisal resources that can be found on the Web. She suggested going to the search engine *Google* and typing "critical research appraisal and checklists." You will obtain thousands of "hits" and find checklists for critiquing various types of studies such as randomized control trials.

Critiquing research articles is particularly helpful to the beginning researcher because the critiquing process aids in the development of research skills. As the reader assesses the parts of a published study, ideas come to mind for the development of future research projects or for improvements in studies that have already been conducted or those that are in progress.

The research critique involves a thorough examination of all the parts of the study. Generally, the best way to conduct a critique is to read the entire study and make an initial evaluation of the report. Then, each part of the study should be subjected to an in-depth evaluation.

This chapter summarizes the material presented in other chapters on topics related to critiquing quantitative and qualitative study reports. The steps in critiquing qualitative studies are not as clear-cut and easily summarized as those of a quantitative study. Therefore, you may want to review other sources for critiquing certain aspects of qualitative study reports.

Some guidelines for evaluating research reports follow. These guidelines are certainly not an exhaustive list. Many other guidelines could be used and questions posed when reading research. As ideas come to mind while you are critiquing research reports, jot them down. In this way, you will be able to develop your own research critique assessment tool to use in the future.

CRIQITUING QUANTITATIVE RESEARCH REPORTS

Many nursing research textbooks contain information pertaining to the critique of quantitative studies. A number of published articles also contain guidelines for critiquing quantitative research reports (Dale, 2005; Rasmussen, O'Conner, Shinkle, & Thomas, 2000; Rempher & Silkman, 2007; Russell, 2005; Stockhausen & Conrick, 2003; Tanner, 2003).

When critiquing a quantitative study report, you generally begin with the abstract, placed either at the top of the article or along the left margin on the first page. The body of the article begins with an introductory section, which has no heading. A research article that discusses a quantitative study generally has four headings (there are variations): (a) "Literature Review," "Relevant Literature," or "Background," following the introduction; (b) "Methods"; (c) "Results"; and (d) "Discussion." Some articles contain additional headings for "Theoretical Framework" and "Conclusions." Even though the research article may contain only four or five headings, these sections should include all parts of the research study. For example, the "Methods" section generally contains information about the study design, setting, population, sample, data collection methods, and data collection instruments.

Probably the most important part of a research article to focus on, after a cursory review of the entire article, is where the design is discussed. As mentioned, information on the design is usually found in the "Methods" section. After you determine how the researcher actually carried out the study, you can go back and see if the other parts of the study are congruent. For example, if the design is described as a pretest-posttest design, two groups should be mentioned in the problem or purpose statement, the hypothesis, and when the population and sample are discussed.

Researcher Qualifications

The first question to ask about quantitative research studies concerns the individuals who conducted the research and their qualifications regarding that particular study. Non-nurses conducted many nursing studies in past years. As nurses have become more qualified to conduct research, they are now conducting the majority of these studies.

A brief biographical sketch will assist the reader in evaluating the qualifications of the author(s). If this type of information is not provided, the academic credentials after the name, such as MSN or PhD, informs the reader of the educational background of the researcher. Generally, the researcher's current affiliation with a university or health care institution is listed. If the research has been funded by a reputable organization, such as the American Nurses Foundation, the reader of the report should have more confidence in the study results and conclusions.

Title

Clarity and conciseness are the major considerations in evaluating the title of a research article or report. The focus of the research should be apparent in the study title. It should contain the population and major variable(s). According to the *Publication Manual of the American Psychological Association* (2010, p. 23), the title should be no more than 12 words, whereas the Contributor Guidelines for the journal *Nurse Researcher* call for the title to be no more than 8 words. Extraneous words like "A Study of . . . ," "The Relationship Between . . . ," or "The Effects of . . . ," should be avoided. Nouns serve as the keywords in the title.

Abstract

Research reports, particularly those published in journals, frequently contain an abstract or summary of the study. Because the abstract may be the only section of the article that is read, the researcher should present the essential components of the study in the abstract. Abstracts typically are 100 to 200 words in length and contain the purpose, hypothesis(es) or research question(s), methods, description of subjects, and major findings.

Introduction

Although a research report is not meant to be a literary work of art, there is no reason to write the report in a dull and uninteresting fashion. The introduction should catch the interest of the reader and set the stage for the presentation of the research report. The best way to accomplish this is through a brief exploration of the study area. Background information on the problem and the significance of this problem to nursing needs to be addressed. The study purpose may be included in this section.

Purpose

The author should leave no doubt in the reader's mind about the purpose of the study. The reason(s) for undertaking the study should have been clearly formulated before the research was begun, and the researcher should convey this information to the reader in the form of the study purpose. The broad purpose of the study may be made more specific in the form of objectives or goals. The purpose statement is usually found in the abstract and, again, at the end of the introductory section.

Problem Statement, Purpose Statement, Research Question

The problem of the study should be clearly identified. Generally, there is a discussion, early in the research report, of the broad problem area of the study. In the abstract and at the end of the introductory section of the report, you will generally find a more specific statement of the problem. This may be in the form of a declarative problem statement, a purpose statement, or a research question. As mentioned in Chapter 3 and Chapter 5, this author prefers the research question as the best way to demonstrate what will be studied. Questions demand answers more than declarative statements. The problem statement, purpose statement, or research question should contain the population and major variable(s) and indicate that data may be gathered empirically (through the senses). The feasibility and significance of the study should be apparent. Sometimes, it may appear that a researcher has made the study focus too broad and tried to examine too many variables in one study. Although the problem, purpose, and research question are separate entities, many research reports identify only one of these aspects of the research process. In many published reports, the purpose of the study may be identified more clearly than the specific statement of the problem or research question.

Review of the Literature

The literature review should flow logically. Generally, classic sources are presented, and current sources are discussed. Additionally, primary sources should be cited. If most of the references are from journals, you should have more confidence that primary sources were accessed. Key sources should be critically compared and appraised, rather than simply alluded to. Paraphrasing is preferred rather than the use of many direct quotations. A comprehensive literature review presents theory and research that both support and oppose the expected study results. Finally, the review should conclude with a sentence or two that indicates how the present study will contribute to the existing body of knowledge in that subject area.

Theoretical/Conceptual Framework

In searching for the study framework in a research report, the reader may find a clearly identified section for the framework, or this information may be found in the introductory section or literature review section of the research article or report. If a framework is identified, is this the most appropriate framework for the study? Is the framework based on a nursing theory or a theory from another discipline? With the great emphasis on theoretically based nursing research, nurse researchers are becoming aware of the need for a framework, but may not choose the most appropriate framework for the study. Support or lack of support for the framework, based on the findings, should be discussed at the end of the report.

Assumptions

All studies are based on assumptions. These assumptions may be of the universal type, such as "all human beings need to feel loved." Assumptions also come from theory and previous research. Finally, the researcher may make some commonsense assumptions that are necessary to proceed with the research. Such an assumption might be, "The respondents will answer the questions honestly." The reader should search for the researcher's explicit assumptions. Explicit assumptions are those asserted by the researcher and clearly identifiable by the reader. The reader should also try to identify assumptions that the researcher appears to have made, but never stated specifically. These implicit assumptions are those made by the researcher, but not clearly identified in the research report. For example, if the study sought to determine if giving a back rub at bedtime would decrease patients' requests for sleeping medications, the researcher has made at least three either explicitly stated or unstated implicit assumptions: (a) adequate sleep is necessary for patients, (b) sleeping medications are not the most healthful type of sleep enhancer, and (c) one of the roles of nurses is to try to assist patients in obtaining adequate sleep.

Limitations

The reader should not have to search out the limitations of a study. Frequently, the first mention is found in the discussion section. The author will, after the fact, comment on the inappropriateness of the instrument or small sample size. These limitations should be openly and honestly stated in the early part of a research report. The researcher should clearly identify those aspects of the research situation over which no control has been exercised. In experimental studies, internal and external threats to validity should be listed. As is the case with the assumptions of a study, many research reports do not contain a separate section on the study limitations. Because the researcher frequently acknowledges some of the study limitations in the discussion section, study limitations may be easier to identify than the assumptions on which the study was based. Additionally, readers frequently may be able to identify additional limitations of a study other than those acknowledged by the researcher.

Hypothesis(es)

Hypotheses should be clearly and concisely stated in a declarative sentence and in the present tense. Hypotheses should be based on theory or research findings. Directional research hypotheses, rather than null or nondirectional hypotheses, are the preferred type. The exception is those situations where there is no available research or theory that predicts the relationship between the variables being examined. The hypothesis should contain the population and the variables and reflect the problem statement, purpose, or research question. They should be empirically testable and contain only one prediction. To be testable, it must be possible to gather empirical or objective data on the variables of interest. Single predictions are necessary in a hypothesis to avoid the "partial support" crisis that occurs when two predictions are made and only one is supported. An error sometimes detected in published hypotheses is the multiple predictions they contain.

Definition of Terms

A separate section on definition of terms may not be included in a journal article because of space constraints. Definitions of key terms in a research report are necessary, however, to make explicit what is being studied. Replication of a study is aided by clear definitions of terms. The key terms generally reflect the theoretical or conceptual framework for the study; therefore, some of the definitions of the terms may be derived from the section on the discussion of the study framework. Operational definitions are also necessary. These definitions indicate the observable, measurable phenomena associated with the study variables. Frequently, operational definitions are indicated in the discussion of the research instruments that were used to gather data.

Research Design

The research design should be clearly identified and adequately described. In experimental studies, the research consumer is concerned with the experimental treatment. Is the treatment adequately described and appropriate for the particular study? Is the method of assigning subjects to groups discussed? Means to control threats to internal and external validity should be included in the section on research design. In nonexperimental quantitative studies, the means of selecting study participants should be discussed. Any extraneous variables that have been controlled, such as age and educational background of the respondents, should be identified.

Setting

The setting for the research project needs to be described. Many agencies do not want to be identified in research reports. The description of the setting is usually general. This description might be "a small private psychiatric institution in the southeastern United States." The reader must then determine if the setting seems appropriate for the particular study.

Population and Sample

Generally, the study sample is easily identified when reading a research article. The target population and the accessible population may not be so easy to identify. The author has the responsibility to mention the broad group of interest (target population) as well as that available group (accessible population) from which the sample was selected.

The section on the sample should identify and describe the specific probability or nonprobability sampling method that was used. This section should also describe the demographic characteristics of the sample and the sample size, and list the percentage of the population represented by the sample. Acknowledgment must be made of any dropout of subjects that occurred during the study and any other potential sampling biases that may have been recognized by the researcher. Finally, the section should discuss the methods taken to protect subjects' rights. Little information is generally provided about ethical issues because of space limitations in published articles. However, anonymity or confidentiality should be mentioned, and the permissions obtained to conduct the study noted.

Collection of Data

Five general questions to ask in evaluating the data-collection section are "who?, when?, where?, what?, and how?" "Who will collect the data?" "When will the data be collected?" "Where will the data be collected?" "What data will be collected?" and "How will the data be collected?" Use the acronym WWWWH. The specific data-collection method(s) will dictate additional questions that need to be asked. For example, if questionnaires were used, the research report should provide enough information for the reader to determine whether a questionnaire was the most appropriate method to collect data. If interviews were used, the interviewer training process should be explained. Observation research requires that the reader be told how observations were made, who made the observations, and how data were recorded. If physiological instruments were used, the means of assessing the accuracy of these instruments needs to be addressed.

Data-Collection Instruments

All of the data-collection instruments used in a study should be clearly identified and described. Scoring procedures and the range of possible scores on the instrument should also be included, where appropriate.

The characteristics of each instrument should be discussed. If an instrument has been used in previous research, the results of this use should be presented in the discussion of the instrument. The most important characteristics of an instrument concern its reliability and validity. The reader must determine whether the appropriate types of reliability and validity have been reported and the evidence of the reliability and validity is adequate for use of the instrument in the present study. Pilot study results should be included for any newly developed or revised instrument.

Analysis of Data

Many research consumers cringe when approaching the data analysis section of a research report because they are fearful of the statistics discussed in this section. A beginning knowledge of statistics is sufficient, however, to evaluate the majority of the published research findings. Descriptive statistics on the characteristics of the study sample should be presented first. Next, the subjects' scores on the various instruments need to be reported. Finally, inferential statistics should be presented if the study tested a hypothesis or hypotheses. The author should state whether each of the study hypotheses was supported or not supported. The results of the statistical test, the degrees of freedom, and the probability value should be given. These findings should be clearly presented in both the text and the tables.

Discussion of Findings

In the Discussion of Findings section of a research report, the author interprets the study results. This material may be more subjective than the information in the Findings section. The author should compare the present study findings with those of other studies discussed in the literature review. No new literature sources should be introduced that were not referred to in the review of literature. Study findings should be discussed in light of the theoretical or conceptual framework that was tested. The author must make it clear that the findings either supported or failed to support the study framework.

Both statistical and clinical significance should be discussed. These two types of significance are not always congruent. Findings that are statistically significant may have little or no clinical significance. On the other hand, results that were determined to be statistically nonsignificant could, in fact, have clinical significance. The researcher should also discuss the study limitations and how these limitations are thought to have affected the study results.

Conclusions

Conclusions answer the "so what?" question that might be posed to a researcher at the end of a study. Through the conclusions, the researcher demonstrates the meaning and worth of the research. The study conclusions attempt to make generalizations based on the study findings. Conclusions are often difficult to write, and many authors merely restate the findings or go to the other extreme and overgeneralize.

Conclusions are written tentatively, which means they are not written in stone. Words such as "seems" or "appears" are frequently found at the beginning of a stated conclusion. The findings are *bound* to the data; the conclusions are *based* on the data. For example, a finding might be "Postoperative hysterectomy patients who received a backrub at bedtime went to sleep 10.5 minutes faster than postoperative hysterectomy patients who did not receive a backrub." A conclusion related to this finding might be, "It appears that a backrub is an effective means of promoting sleep in postoperative hysterectomy patients." Can you tell, from this conclusion, that the researcher is attempting to generalize beyond the sample that was used in the study?

Implications

Implications need to be explicitly identified by the researcher for nursing practice, nursing education, or nursing research. The implications section of a research report contains the "shoulds" that result from the research findings. For example, nurse educators *should* include material in nursing curriculums on the topic of the study or nurse researchers *should* conduct more research in the area of interest. When the study findings are not statistically or clinically significant, the implications of the study may be that no changes are recommended as the result of the present study.

Recommendations

Although recommendations may be made for nursing practice and nursing education, recommendations found in a research report generally concern future research that is needed. A suggestion can be made that the study be replicated. Another suggestion may concern further development of the instrument or use of a larger sample size. Recommendations should take into consideration the limitations of the present study. The recommendations should consider the findings of previous studies. Nursing can ill afford to conduct impractical or irrelevant research or to reinvent the wheel, as it were.

Other Considerations

Although the most important areas to evaluate in a research report are the specific components of the research study, other areas also need to be evaluated. Correct grammar, sentence structure, and punctuation are essential. The research consumer may have difficulty concentrating on the merits of the research report if structural errors are found. The author's writing style and use of words, especially limiting the use of complex and technical words, are also important to the reader.

The accuracy and completeness of the reference list is also important. It is very discouraging to the reader to discover a source of interest in the literature review section and then be unable to find this source listed in the reference section. Also, it is not uncommon to find sources in the reference section that were never referred to in the research report. You may also find incomplete references or ones with essential elements missing. The last question to ask is, "After reading this research report, would I refer it to a colleague?"

CRITIQUING QUALITATIVE RESEARCH REPORTS

As previously mentioned, the critique of a qualitative study report is more difficult, at times, than the critique of a quantitative study. Your educational preparation likely did not include information about all of the types of qualitative designs and methodologies.

Members of disciplines, such as sociology and anthropology, often prefer a certain type of design. For example, sociologists may prefer a grounded theory design, whereas anthropologists may choose an ethnographic design. As a whole, nurses do not seem to be attached to any particular design, and many of us have not obtained knowledge about some of the available designs that can be used in qualitative research studies. If you choose to become a qualitative researcher or wish to critique qualitative studies, in depth, you may want to seek a mentor. If you are enrolled in a nursing educational program, you will probably have no difficulty in locating a qualitative researcher at your institution. The number of qualitative nurse researchers continues to increase. Qualitative nurse researchers are, generally, very happy to provide support to a nurse who is novice qualitative researcher or who is interested in qualitative research.

Some of the headings in a qualitative research article are similar to those of a quantitative study, such as the sections on Background or Literature Review, Methods, and Findings or Results. Some qualitative reports also contain a Data Collection, Conclusions, or Implications section. There is less similarity in headings in a qualitative research report than in a quantitative research report.

For guidance in critiquing qualitative research, numerous books and articles are available. Cheryl Tatano Beck published an informative article on critiquing qualitative research in the October 2009 issue of *AORN*.

Researcher Qualifications

It may be difficult to critique the expertise of researchers who conduct qualitative studies. Unless you have access to their educational preparation in qualitative research and are familiar with the qualitative research studies they have conducted, you will have no way of determining their qualifications to conduct a particular study. You will probably be able to determine the degrees they have completed and their present place of employment. Some articles contain an e-mail address for the author(s). If so, you may be able to contact them to obtain more information. Also, if the author is affiliated with an educational institution, you may be able to obtain pertinent information about the faculty member on the institution's Web site.

Title

The title of a qualitative study should indicate the phenomenon to be studied and the type of individuals who will be participants. Sometimes the title of a research study report provides a broad hint as to the type of study being discussed. This is true in both quantitative and qualitative reports. If the title indicates that open-heart surgery patients receiving a particular intervention are being compared to open-heart surgery patients receiving another intervention or the routine treatment, you will have no difficulty determining that you are reading about an experimental study. Another article's title may indicate that the report describes the feelings or emotions of certain people. For example, the title might be "The Lived Experience of Earthquake Survivors." Would you know immediately that you were about to read a qualitative research study report? Read through the table of contents of several issues of research journals, such as *Nursing Research*, and see how many titles clearly indicate quantitative or qualitative research reports.

Abstract

The abstract for a qualitative research report is located in the same place as in a quantitative report—at the top of the article or down the left side of the first page. Abstracts usually contain from 100 to 200 words. The abstract should summarize the main areas of the study, such as the purpose, design, type of participants, sample size, and any major themes uncovered in the data. The abstract is a very important part of a research report because, as mentioned in the section on critiquing quantitative study reports, this section may be the only one that is actually read.

Introduction

This section contains background material about the study and probably contains literature references about the topic. The problem statement, purpose statement, and/or research questions may be found in this introductory section. The main objective in critiquing the introductory section is to determine whether the important components are present and seem appropriate for the study and the material promotes the reader's interest in the report.

Problem of the Study

If the qualitative study report is presented appropriately, you should be able to locate the description of the problem of interest. Try to determine whether the study problem is clear or ambiguous. Does the problem seem significant to nursing? If you are familiar with the research design, does the problem seem to match the research tradition of that particular design? The study problem generally appears in the report's introductory section.

Purpose

The purpose of a research study should always be clear to the reader. The purpose statement is usually presented in a single sentence, and might read something like, "to explore the experience of living in a tent city for 6 months following a 7.0 earthquake that struck the homes of people in Haiti." The purpose may appear in the abstract and also at the end of the introductory section.

Research Question

A qualitative research report may present a broad research question, such as "What were the experiences of survivors of a 7.0 earthquake in Haiti?" The data collection section of the study may also list specific research questions, such as "What were your feelings as you tried to go to sleep in the tent city where you lived for 6 months?" and "What were your concerns about family members when you were separated from them for so long?" Are the research questions appropriate for the problem that was studied? Are they sufficient to gather the information needed for a comprehensive report of the phenomenon under study?

Research Design

This section may be difficult to critique unless you are familiar with all of the various qualitative research designs. The specific design is always mentioned in a research report, usually for the first time in the abstract. Once the design is identified, you may want to go to reference sources (even Wikipedia provides a simple explanation of designs) to gain an understanding of the specific design. This textbook provides some basic information about a number of the more common qualitative research designs (see Chapter 10). Again, you may want to seek the assistance of a mentor.

Review of the Literature

As you know, quantitative research studies always begin with a review of the literature. However, in order to critique this section of a qualitative research report, you need to be familiar with the study design. As mentioned in Chapter 4, some designs call for an early review of the literature, whereas others call for the review toward the completion of the study. Were classical and current references cited? Were primary sources cited? Does the literature review provide an adequate summary of the existing body of knowledge on the phenomenon of interest?

Selection of Sample

A purposive sample (see Chapter 11) is usually chosen for a qualitative study. Sometimes a convenience sample may be selected. In a qualitative study, the sample is of utmost importance. In a quantitative study, the population from which the sample is chosen is more important than the sample. The sample size in a qualitative study is usually small. Does the researcher discuss how the decision was made as to the number of participants to include in the study? For example, was the concept of "saturation" discussed (see Chapter 4)? How were the rights of participants protected? The researcher usually interacts directly with study participants in a qualitative study, and their identities are known. The report should indicate to the reader that the study was subject to external review. The researcher must also demonstrate that risks were minimized. However, as mentioned, because of space limitations, research articles usually contain little information about the protection of subjects' rights.

Collection of Data

The researcher must gain access to the study participants and determine where the data will be collected. Were the data collected in the participants' homes or at some neutral location? Did one researcher collect the data? If more than one researcher collected the data, were they properly trained? Data collection usually involves interviews. Were an adequate number of direct quotes collected to capture the true essence of what the participants were trying to say? These interviews must be recorded in some manner. Were these procedures described in sufficient detail? Were the transcripts of the interviews reviewed for accuracy? What were the qualifications of those individuals who reviewed the transcripts? Was agreement reached on the meaning of the participants' responses?

Analysis of Data

You may have a difficult time with this section of a qualitative research report. There are many ways to analyze data from a qualitative study. Analysis of data involves an examination of words rather than numbers. Coding is the basic data analysis scheme of qualitative researchers. All qualitative studies involve content analysis procedures. Content analysis varies according to the type of study design. Direct quotes are frequently used. In fact, if you scan a research article and see a number of direct quotes, you will probably conclude that you are examining a qualitative research report. Many qualitative researchers hand-analyze their data, whereas others use computer software in their data analysis. Some of these programs were mentioned in Chapter 4. Again, you may need assistance in critiquing this section of a qualitative research report.

Interpretation of Data

The interpretation of the data, once again, depends on the research design and research tradition used by the researcher. In the section where the researcher interprets the findings, you may see names like Merleau-Ponty, who focused on people's perceptions of their experiences through their bodily senses (tasting, touching, and hearing). Or you might read about Husserl, a leader of the German phenomenological movement. The researcher may have interpreted the data based on Merleau-Ponty's or Husserl's philosophical beliefs. Qualitative researchers interpret their findings based on the specific type of design used in the study, the ideas of experts in that area of design, and their own qualitative research beliefs. Finally, the research consumer should ask whether the researcher compared the findings to previous study results concerning the phenomenon of interest.

Recommendations

Every researcher makes recommendations based on their study results. Whether they have conducted a quantitative or a qualitative study, researchers generally call for more research on the topic of interest. Most research studies raise further questions that need to be answered. Recommendations are found at the end of each research report.

Other Considerations

The most important areas to evaluate in a qualitative research report are the actual components of the study. However, other areas also need to be evaluated. As in a quantitative report, correct grammar, sentence structure, and punctuation are essential. Was the report organized and easily understood? Was the writing style appealing? Were too many complex words or technical terms used? Would you recommend this research report to a colleague?

SUMMARY

Most research studies have both strong and weak points. A critical evaluation of all the sections of a research report is essential in determining the usefulness of the research results. Although many additional questions may be raised when examining research reports, this chapter presented some useful guidelines to the beginning researcher as he or she appraises published research reports of quantitative and qualitative studies.

REFERENCES

American Psychological Association. (2010). *Publication Manual of the American Psychological Association* (6th ed.). Washington, DC: Author.

Beck, C. T. (2009). Critiquing qualitative research. *AORN, 90,* 543–554.

Dale, J. C. (2005). Critiquing research for use in practice. *Journal of Pediatric Health Care, 19,* 183–186.

Duffy, M. E. (2005). Resources for critically appraising quantitative research evidence for nursing practice. *Clinical Nurse Specialist, 19,* 233–235.

Rasmussen, L., O'Conner, M., Shinkle, S., & Thomas, M. K. (2000). The basic research review checklist. *Journal of Continuing Education in Nursing, 31,* 13–17.

Rempher, K. J., & Silkman, C. (2007, January). How to appraise quantitative research articles. *American Nurse Today,* 26–28.

Russell, C. L. (2005). Evaluating quantitative research reports. *Nephrology Nursing Journal, 32,* 61–64.

Stockhausen, L., & Conrick, M. (2003). Making sense of research: A guide for critiquing a paper. *Contemporary Nurse, 14,* 38–48.

Tanner, J. (2003). Reading and critiquing research. *British Journal of Perioperative Nursing, 13,* 162.

Answers to Self-Tests

Chapter 1
1. C
2. A
3. C
4. A
5. B
6. A
7. A
8. A, B, C, D
9. C
10. A

Chapter 2
1. D
2. B
3. C
4. B
5. B
6. A
7. C
8. F
9. F

10. T
11. F
12. F

Chapter 3
1. D
2. B
3. A
4. D
5. A
6. C
7. A
8. B
9. D
10. B

Chapter 4
1. F
2. F
3. T
4. T
5. F

6. F
7. F
8. B
9. B
10. A

Chapter 5
1. D
2. D
3. A
4. A
5. D
6. B
7. D
8. A
9. B
10. C

Chapter 6
1. B
2. C
3. C

4. A
5. A
6. D
7. C
8. B
9. B
10. B

Chapter 7
1. B
2. A
3. D
4. C
5. E
6. C
7. A
8. A
9. C
10. C
11. B

Chapter 8

Identification of independent and dependent variables.

	Independent Variable(s)	Dependent Variable(s)
1.	gender of patients	requests for pain medications
2.	number of prenatal classes	fear concerning labor and delivery
3.	marital status	body image
4.	anxiety	requests for pain medication
5.	high school grade level	marijuana usage
6.	retirement	self-image
7.	length of employment	a. job turnover rate
		b. job dissatisfaction levels

Evaluation of hypotheses.
8. One level of the independent variable is missing. To what group is the baccalaureate-prepared nurse group being compared?
9. Did you notice the question mark at the end of the sentence? This statement is not a hypothesis.
10. The population is not identified.
11. Watch those value words like *better.* This is not a testable hypothesis.
12. This one looks good.

Chapter 9
1. E
2. A
3. D
4. B
5. C
6. C
7. D
8. B
9. A
10. C

Chapter 10
1. B
2. D
3. A
4. B
5. D
6. B
7. B
8. A
9. C
10. E

Chapter 11
1. F
2. F
3. T
4. T
5. convenience sampling
6. cluster sampling
7. systematic sampling
8. quota sampling
9. simple random sampling
10. snowball sampling

Chapter 12
1. stability reliability
2. face validity
3. construct validity
4. predictive validity
5. equivalence reliability
6. F
7. T
8. T
9. T
10. F

Chapter 13
1. Answers are not mutually exclusive. The categories overlap. A person who is 20, 25, or 30 years old might check two of the categories.
2. Answers are not exhaustive. There is no category for someone who has less than a grade school education. Also, the category "college graduate" does not include anyone who has a master's or doctoral degree.
3. B
4. C
5. B
6. D
7. A
8. C
9. B
10. E

Chapter 14
1. A
2. B
3. C
4. D
5. B
6. D
7. B
8. D
9. C
10. D

Chapter 15
1. C
2. A
3. A
4. D
5. A
6. C
7. C
8. B
9. B
10. B
11. A

Chapter 16
1. A
2. B
3. A
4. B
5. B
6. F
7. F
8. F
9. T
10. F
11. F
12. T

Chapter 17
1. B
2. D
3. B
4. A
5. B
6. F
7. T
8. F
9. F
10. F

Chapter 18
1. B
2. A
3. C
4. A
5. C
6. C
7. B
8. A
9. B
10. A

Chapter 19
1. A
2. A
3. B
4. F
5. F
6. T
7. T

Appendix A
Consent Form

Consent to Act as a Subject for Research and Investigation

I. I hereby authorize _____ to perform the following investigation:
The study will involve my 4-year-old child participating in an experiment. The investigation will consist of a physical examination of the eyes, ears, throat, elbow, and knee reflexes. Blood pressure and temperature will also be checked. The physical examination will require about 15 minutes. The child will receive a play session before the physical examination, or not, depending on the group to which he (she) is randomly assigned. If the child does not receive the play session before the physical examination, he (she) may receive the same play session after the physical examination. The physical examination and the play sessions will be conducted by registered nurses. The examining nurse will be experienced in the examination of children. The play sessions will be conducted by the researcher, who is experienced in working with children and with play techniques. Another registered nurse will observe the child during the physical examination.

II. The procedure or investigation listed in Paragraph I has been explained to me by _____.

III. I understand that the procedures or investigations described in Paragraph I involve the following possible risks or discomforts:
1. Confidential information from the study results might be accidentally released.
2. The child may feel anxious about the physical examination procedure.

IV. I understand that my child's rights and welfare will be protected as follows:
1. Safeguards against the accidental release of data will include the use of a code number, and only the investigator will know the name and the code number of each child. No names or code numbers will be used in the final research report. Only group statistics will be reported. There will be no way a reader of the final report can identify any of the participants. Any information pertaining to the identity of the participants will be destroyed when the study is completed.
2. The child will not be pressured into participating in the physical examination procedure. If the child does not want to participate in the activity, the child will not be examined.
3. The participation or nonparticipation of the child in the study will not influence care received at the day-care center. The child's participation in the study is strictly voluntary. The child may be withdrawn from the study at any time, without any penalty.
4. The participants who do not receive the play session before the physical examination will be given the opportunity for the play session in small groups after their physical examinations are done. The registered nurse conducting the play periods with the physical examination equipment is experienced in working with children and various play techniques.

V. I understand that the procedures and investigations described in Paragraph I have the following potential benefits to myself and others:
1. By participation in this study, the child will become more familiar with possible frightening equipment that is routinely used during physical examinations.
2. Because the child is more familiar with the equipment used, the child may be less anxious and more cooperative during the examination.

3. The results of physical examinations are more accurate if the child is not resistive during the procedures.

4. The child may have increased self-esteem because the child is better able to control behavior during the examination.

5. Participation in this study will help produce new knowledge that will assist child-care workers in dealing with young children.

VI. I understand that no medical service or compensation will be provided to the subjects by the university as a result of injury from participation in research.

VII. An offer has been made to answer all of my questions regarding the study. If alternative procedures are more advantageous to me, they have been explained. I understand that I may terminate my child's participation in the study at any time. The subject is a minor (age _____).

Signatures (One Required)

_____   _____
Father   Date

_____   _____
Mother   Date

_____   _____
Guardian   Date

Appendix B
Critiquing Exercise

Retrieve the following article:

Henneman, E. A., Roche, J. P., Fisher, D. L., Cunningham, H., Reilly, C. A., Nathanson, B. H., & Henneman, P. L. (2010). Error identification and recovery by student nurses using human patient simulation: Opportunity to improve patient safety. *Applied Nursing Research, 23*, 11–21.

Based on the information learned while reading this book, critique the article and answer the following questions:

1. **Title**—Is the title clear?

   Does it contain the population and the variables?

   Is the length appropriate?

   Are there any extraneous or unnecessary words?

2. **Researcher Qualifications**—Are you able to determine the researchers' educational and research qualifications to conduct the study?

   Three of the seven researchers do not have "RN" after their names. What disciplines do you think these three individuals represent, and what roles did they have in the study?

   Do you think one of these three individuals might have expertise in statistics?

   Was any funding obtained for this study?

   Conduct a computer search and see what information you can obtain about the researchers.

3. **Abstract**—Is the length appropriate?

   What elements of the study are contained in the abstract (Purpose? Hypotheses or Research Questions? Methods? Identification of participants? Major findings?) Does the abstract gain your attention and make you want to read the article?

4. **Introduction**—Does the Introduction section present pertinent information about the study problem?

   Is the significance of the research clearly identified?

   What components of the study are contained in this section of the report?

   Is appropriate background information presented?

5. **Purpose**—Is the purpose of the study made clear?

   Is the population identified?

   Are the major study variables included?

   The second page has a section titled "Specific Aims." How are these "aims" different from the study purpose?

6. **Review of the Literature**—Notice the section labeled "Review of the Literature and Significance." Is this the only location of literature sources?

   Are the literature sources pertinent to the study?

   Are direct quotes or paraphrases used?

   Are you able to determine if primary sources have been cited?

   What are the most recent and oldest references cited?

   The article was published in 2010; would you expect some references from 2008 and 2009 (notice the date of acceptance for publication)?

7. **Theoretical/Conceptual Framework**—This article contains a clearly labeled theoretical framework section.

   Is the framework from nursing or another discipline?

   Does the framework seem appropriate for the study?

   Can you clearly determine which part of the framework was tested in this study?

8. **Assumptions**—Can you identify at least three assumptions made by the researchers (beliefs or assertions that were not documented from literature sources). There are at least six.

9. **Limitations**—What are some of the study limitations identified by the researchers?

   Did you identify additional limitations of the study?

   Is it appropriate to discuss threats to internal and external validity in this type of study?

   What do you think is the greatest weakness of this study?

10. **Hypothesis(es)**—No hypotheses were stated in this article.

    Did the researchers have any basis (from the framework or the literature) for predicting study outcomes in the form of hypotheses?

    Although no hypotheses were stated, how many hypotheses were actually tested, based on data found in Table 1?

11. **Definition of Terms**—Determine what variables needed to be defined, and then search for the definitions provided by the researchers.

    Are both conceptual and operational definitions provided for the main study variables?

    Do the definitions provide observable, measurable criteria?

    Would you be able to replicate the study based on the definitions provided?

12. **Research Design**—The design section clearly lists the study as a "retrospective study design."

    What makes this design "retrospective"?

    Do you believe the design could be classified as any other type?

    How were students assigned to the two simulation groups?

    Was random assignment used?

13. **Setting**—The setting was identified as "a school of nursing at a large, research-intensive university in the northeastern United States." Is this description vague enough to prevent the identification of the setting?

    Do you think the study might have been conducted at the university where four of the nurse researchers were employed?

14. **Population and Sample**—Are the target populations and accessible populations identified?

    Is the sample clearly identified?

    What type of sampling method was used to select the sample?

    Does the sample size seem adequate?

    Was power analysis used to determine sample size?

    Was permission to conduct the study obtained from the appropriate authorities? Were students' rights protected?

15. **Data Collection**—Can you find information to answer the following five questions about data collection in this study:

    Who collected the data (researchers or research assistants)?

    When were the data collected (time period—how long)?

Where were the data collected (location of data collection)?
What data were collected (data to determine errors committed)?
How were the data collected (data collection method)?

16. **Data-Collection Instruments**—What type of instrument was used to collect data?

    Was the instrument appropriate to gather the data for the study?
    How were reliability and validity of the instrument assessed?

17. **Analysis of Data**—Are the statistical findings presented clearly?

    What type of statistics were used to present the data?
    Were demographic statistics presented on the sample?
    What statistic was used to present the number of errors made by students?
    Were you able to determine the total number of errors that it was possible for each student to commit?
    Why was the chi-square statistic used as an inferential statistical test? (*Hint*: What was the level of measurement of the data on the number of errors committed?)
    Based on Table 1, how many findings were significant?

18. **Discussion of Findings**—Were additional literature sources cited in this section?

    Were the findings discussed in regard to other studies in the literature?
    Were the findings related back to the theoretical framework?

19. **Conclusions**—A "Conclusions" section was included in the article. Were you able **to pick out** a conclusion or conclusions in this section that was/were based on th**e study fin**dings?

    Formulate a conclusion that is based on a comparison of error rates for the two simulation exercises.

20. **Implications**—What implications are pointed out by the researchers?

    Identify other possible implications of this study.
    Do you think this study has broad implications for many areas of nursing, such as nursing education, nursing practice, or nursing administration?

21. **Recommendations**—What recommendations were made by the researchers? Were recommendations found in one location in the article?

    Were study limitations considered in the recommendations made by the researchers?
    Do you think it would be feasible to use eye-tracking devices, as recommended by the researchers, to determine errors made by students?
    Are there other recommendations that you think could have been made by the researchers?

22. **Other Considerations**—

    What was the "lag time" for publication of this article?
    Was the article easy to read and understand?
    Was the use of technical terms limited?
    Were the tables and figures appropriate?
    Did you discover any typographical errors? (*Hint*: See page 13.)
    Were the references cited in the article also listed on the reference page?
    Were references cited complete and in APA format?
    Are there additional comments that you would like to make concerning this article?
    Would you recommend this article to a colleague?

Glossary

abstracts (research abstracts). Brief summaries of research studies; generally contain the purpose, methods, and major findings of the study.

accessible population. The group of people or objects that is available to the researcher for a particular study.

alpha (α). See level of significance.

alternate forms reliability. Results are compared using two forms or versions of the same instrument.

alternative hypothesis. See research hypothesis.

ambiguous questions. Questions containing words that may be interpreted in more than one way.

analysis of covariance (ANCOVA). A statistical test that allows the researcher to control statistically for some variable(s) that may have an influence on the dependent variable.

analysis of variance (ANOVA). A statistical test used to compare the difference between the means of two or more groups or sets of values.

anonymity. The identity of research subjects is unknown, even to the study investigator.

applied research. Research that is conducted to find a solution to an immediate practice problem.

assent. Agreement to participate in research by someone, especially a child older than 7 years, who is not capable cognitively of giving informed consent.

assumptions. Beliefs that are held to be true but have not necessarily been proven; assumptions may be explicit or implicit.

attitude scales. Self-report data collection instruments that ask respondents to report their attitudes or feelings on a continuum.

attribute variables. See demographic variables.

attrition. Study participant withdraws from a study.

bar graph. A figure used to represent a frequency distribution of nominal or ordinal data.

basic research. Research that is conducted to generate knowledge rather than to solve immediate problems.

beneficence. Research participants should be protected from harm.

beta (β). See type II error.

bimodal distribution. A frequency distribution that contains two identical high-frequency values.

bivariate study. A research study in which the relationship between two variables is examined.

blind review. Manuscript reviewers are not made aware of the author's identity before the manuscript is evaluated.

bracketing. A process in which qualitative researchers put aside their own feelings or beliefs about a phenomenon that is being studied to keep from biasing their observations.

call for abstract. A request for a summary of a study that the researcher wishes to present at a research conference.

canonical correlation. Examines the correlation between two or more independent variables and two or more dependent variables.

case studies. Research studies that involve an in-depth examination of a single person or a group of people. A case study might also examine an institution.

cause-and-effect relationship. One thing or event makes some other thing or event happen.

cells. Boxes in a table that are formed by the intersection of rows and columns.

central limit theorem. The phenomenon in which sample values tend to be normally distributed around the population value.

chi-square test (χ^2). A nonparametric statistical test used to compare sets of data that are in the form of frequencies or percentages (nominal level data).

class interval. A group of scores in a frequency distribution.

clinical nursing research. Nursing research studies involving clients or that have the potential for affecting clients.

clinical trials. Research studies conducted to evaluate new treatments, new drugs, and new or improved medical equipment.

closed-ended questions. Questions that require respondents to choose from given alternatives.

cluster random sampling. A random sampling process that involves two or more stages. The population is first listed by clusters or categories (e.g., hospitals) and then the sample elements (e.g., hospital administrators) are randomly selected from these clusters.

coefficient alpha. See Cronbach's alpha.

coefficient of determination (r^2, R^2). A statistic obtained by squaring a correlation coefficient and is interpreted as the percentage of variance shared by two variables.

cohort study. A special type of longitudinal study in which subjects are studied who have been born during one particular period or who have similar backgrounds.

collectively exhaustive categories. Categories are provided for every possible answer.

columns. Vertical entries in a table.

comparative studies. Studies in which intact groups are compared on some dependent variable. The researcher is not able to manipulate the independent variable, which is frequently some inherent characteristic of the subjects, such as age or educational level.

comparison group. A group of subjects in an experimental study that does not receive any experimental treatment or receives an alternate treatment such as the "normal" or routine treatment.

complex hypothesis. A hypothesis that concerns a relationship where two or more independent variables, two or more dependent variables, or both are being examined.

computer-assisted literature searches. The use of a computer to obtain bibliographic references that have been stored in a database.

computerized database. A compilation of information that can be retrieved by computer.

concept. A word picture or mental idea of a phenomenon.

conceptual definition. A dictionary or theoretical definition of an abstract idea that is being studied by the researcher.

conceptual framework. A background or foundation for a study; a less well-developed structure than a theoretical framework; concepts are related in a logical manner by the researcher.

conceptual model. Symbolic presentation of concepts and the relationships between these concepts.

concurrent validity. A type of criterion validity in which a determination is made of the instrument's ability to obtain a measurement of subjects' behavior that is comparable to some other criterion used to indicate that behavior.

confidence interval. A range of values that, with a specified degree of probability, is thought to contain the population value.

confidentiality. The identity of the research subjects is known only to the study investigator(s).

confounding variable. See extraneous variable.

constant comparison. Data gathered in a qualitative study are constantly or continually compared to data that have already been gathered.

construct. A highly abstract phenomenon that cannot be directly observed but must be inferred by certain concrete or less abstract indicators of the phenomenon.

construct validity. The ability of an instrument to measure the construct that it is intended to measure.

content analysis. A data collection method that examines communication messages that are usually in written form.

content validity. The degree to which an instrument covers the scope and range of information that is sought.

contingency questions. Questions that are relevant for some respondents and not for others.

contingency table. A table that visually displays the relationship between sets of nominal data.

control group. A group of subjects in an experimental study that does not receive the experimental treatment (see comparison group).

convenience sampling (accidental sampling). A nonprobability sampling procedure that involves the selection of the most readily available people or objects for a study.

correlation. The extent to which values of one variable (X) are related to the values of a second variable (Y). Correlations may be either positive or negative.

correlational studies. Research studies that examine the strength of relationships between variables.

correlation coefficient. A statistic that presents the magnitude and direction of a relationship between two variables. Correlation coefficients range from -1.00 (perfect negative relationship) to $+1.00$ (perfect positive relationship).

criterion validity. The extent to which an instrument corresponds or correlates with some criterion measure of the information that is being sought; the ability of an instrument to determine subjects' responses at present or predict subjects' responses in the future.

critical region (region of rejection). An area in a theoretical sampling distribution that contains the critical values, which are values considered to be statistically significant.

critical value. A scientific cutoff point that denotes the value in a theoretical distribution at which all obtained values from a sample that are equal to or beyond that point are said to be statistically significant.

critique (research critique).   Assesses the strengths and weaknesses of a study.

Cronbach's alpha.   Provides an estimate of the reliability of a written instrument when considering all possible ways to divide the items on the instrument into two halves.

cross-sectional study.   A research study that collects data on subjects at one point in time.

data.   The pieces of information or facts collected during a research study.

database.   See computerized database.

debriefing.   A meeting with research participants at the conclusion of a study that ensures their understanding of the reasons and the justification for the procedures used in the study.

deductive reasoning.   A reasoning process that proceeds from the general to the specific, from theory to empirical data.

degrees of freedom (df).   A concept in inferential statistics that concerns the number of values that are free to vary.

Delphi technique.   A data-collection method that uses several rounds of questions to seek a consensus on a particular topic from a group of experts on the topic.

demographic questions.   Questions that gather data on characteristics of the subjects (see demographic variables).

demographic variables.   Subject characteristics such as age, educational levels, and marital status.

dependent *t* test.   A form of the *t* test that is used when one set of scores or values is associated or dependent on another set of scores or values.

dependent variable.   The "effect"; a response or behavior that is influenced by the independent variable; sometimes called the criterion variable.

derived demand.   The demand for labor is *derived* from the demand for the product (or service) that the firm produces and sells.

descriptive statistics.   That group of statistics that organizes and summarizes numerical data obtained from populations and samples.

descriptive studies.   Research studies in which phenomena are described or the relationship between variables is examined; no attempt is made to determine cause-and-effect relationships.

design.   See research design.

diminishing marginal returns.   As more of a variable input (like labor) is hired, and the amount of

capital is fixed, the marginal product of a worker declines.

directional research hypothesis.   A type of hypothesis in which a prediction is made of the type of relationship that exists between variables.

disproportional stratified sampling.   Random selection of members from population strata where the number of members chosen for each stratum is not in proportion to the size of the stratum in the total population.

double-barreled questions.   Questions that ask two questions in one.

double-blind experiment.   An experiment in which neither the researcher nor the research participants know which participants are in the experimental and control groups.

dropout.   Study participant withdraws from a study.

effect size.   How useful a treatment or intervention was in several studies as indicated by the difference between data from control groups and experimental groups.

e-journal.   A journal that can be accessed online.

element.   A single member of a population.

empirical data.   Objective data gathered through the sense organs.

empirical generalization.   A summary statement about the occurrence of phenomena that is based on empirical data from a number of different research studies.

equivalence reliability.   The degree to which two forms of an instrument obtain the same results or two or more observers obtain the same results when using a single instrument to measure a variable.

ethnographic studies.   Research studies that involve the collection and analysis of data about cultural groups.

event sampling.   Observations made throughout the entire course of an event or behavior.

evidence-based nursing practice (EBNP).   Nursing practice that is based on the best available evidence, particularly research findings.

experimental design.   See quasi-experimental, preexperimental, and true experimental designs.

experimenter effect.   A threat to the external validity of a research study that occurs when the researcher's behavior influences the subjects' behavior in a way that is not intended by the researcher.

explanatory studies.   Research studies that search for causal explanations; usually experimental.

exploratory studies. Research studies that are conducted when little is known about the phenomenon being studied.

ex post facto studies. Studies in which the variation in the independent variable has already occurred in the past, and the researcher, "after the fact," is trying to determine if the variation that has occurred in the independent variable has any influence on the dependent variable being measured in the present.

external criticism (external appraisal, external examination). A type of examination of historical data that is concerned with the authenticity or genuineness of the data. External criticism might be used to determine if a letter was actually written by the person whose signature appeared on the letter.

external validity threats. The degree to which study results can be generalized to other people and other research settings.

extraneous variable. A type of variable that is not the variable of interest to a researcher but that may influence the results of a study. Other terms for extraneous variable are intervening variable and confounding variable.

e-zine. A magazine that can be accessed online.

face validity. A subjective determination that an instrument is adequate for obtaining the desired information; on the surface or the face of the instrument it appears to be an adequate means of obtaining the desired data.

factor analysis. A type of validity used to identify clusters of related items on an instrument or scale.

field studies. Research studies that are conducted in the field or in a real-life setting.

filler questions. Questions used to distract respondents from the purpose of other questions that are being asked.

focus group. A small group of individuals who meet together and are asked questions, by a moderator, about a certain topic or topics.

framework. See conceptual framework and theoretical framework.

frequency distribution. A listing of all scores or numerical values from a set of data and the number of times each score or value appears; scores may be listed from highest to lowest or lowest to highest.

frequency polygon. A graph that uses dots connected with straight lines to represent the frequency distribution of interval or ratio data. A dot is placed above the midpoint of each class interval.

galley proofs. Sheets of paper that show how an article or book will appear in typeset form.

generalization. See empirical generalization.

grand theories. Theories that are concerned with a broad range of phenomena in the environment or in the experiences of humans.

grounded theory studies. Research studies in which data are collected and analyzed, and then a theory is developed that is grounded in the data.

Hawthorne effect. A threat to the external validity of a research study that occurs when study participants respond in a certain manner because they are aware that they are involved in a research study.

histogram. A graph used to represent the frequency distribution of variables measured at the interval or ratio level.

historical studies. Research studies that are concerned with the identification, location, evaluation, and synthesis of data from the past.

history threat. A threat to the internal validity of an experimental research study; some event in addition to the experimental treatment occurs between the pretreatment and posttreatment measurement of the dependent variable, and this event influences the dependent variable.

hypothesis. A statement of the predicted relationship between two or more variables.

impact factor. A number used to evaluate the influence of a particular journal.

independent *t* test. A form of the *t* test that is used when there is no association between the two sets of scores or values being compared.

independent variable. The "cause" or the variable thought to influence the dependent variable; in experimental research it is the variable manipulated by the researcher.

indexes. Compilations of reference materials that provide information on books and periodicals.

inductive reasoning. A reasoning process that proceeds from the specific to the general, from empirical data to theory.

inferential statistics. That group of statistics concerned with the characteristics of populations and uses sample data to make an inference about a population.

informed consent. A subject voluntarily agrees to participate in a research study in which he or she has full understanding of the study before the study begins.

institutional review board (IRB). Every agency or institution that receives federal money for research must have an IRB to review research proposals.

instrument. A data-collection tool.

instrumentation change.   A threat to the internal validity of an experimental research study that involves changes from the pretest measurements to the posttest measurements as a result of inaccuracy of the instrument or the judges' ratings rather than as a result of the experimental treatment.

integrative review.   See systematic review.

interaction effect.   The result of two variables acting in conjunction with each other.

internal consistency reliability (scale homogeneity). The extent to which all items of an instrument measure the same variable.

internal criticism.   A type of examination of historical data that is concerned with the accuracy of the data. Internal criticism might be used to determine if a document contained an accurate recording of events as they actually happened.

internal validity threats.   The degree to which changes in the dependent variable (effect) can be attributed to the independent or experimental variable (cause) rather than to the effects of extraneous variables.

interobserver reliability.   See interrater reliability.

interquartile range.   Contains the middle half of the values in a frequency distribution.

interrater reliability (interobserver reliability). The degree to which two or more independent judges are in agreement about ratings or observations of events or behaviors.

interval level of measurement (interval data).   Data can be categorized, ranked, and the distance between the ranks can be specified; pulse rates and temperature readings are examples of interval data.

intervening variable.   See extraneous variable.

interview.   A method of data collection in which the interviewer obtains responses from a subject in a face-to-face encounter or through a telephone call.

interview schedule.   An instrument containing a set of questions, directions for asking these questions, and space to record the respondents' answers.

judgmental sample.   See purposive sample.

key informant.   A person who is knowledgeable about the culture that is being studied in ethnographic research.

known-groups procedure.   A research technique in which a research instrument is administered to two groups of people whose responses are expected to differ on the variable of interest.

laboratory studies.   Research studies in which subjects are studied in a special environment that has been created by the researcher.

level of measurement.   Indicates the precision with which data can be gathered and the mathematical operations that can be used with the data; the four levels of measurement are nominal, ordinal, interval, and ratio.

level of significance (probability level).   The probability of rejecting a null hypothesis when it is true; symbolized by lowercase Greek letter alpha (α); also symbolized by p.

Likert scale.   An attitude scale named after its developer, Rensis Likert. These scales usually contain five or seven responses for each item, ranging from "strongly agree" to "strongly disagree."

limitations.   Weaknesses in a study; uncontrolled variables.

longitudinal study.   Subjects are followed during a period in the future; data are collected at two or more different time periods.

manipulation.   The independent or experimental variable is controlled by the researcher to determine its effect on the dependent variable.

marginal benefit.   Also known as the marginal revenue product of a worker; has two components: (a) the **marginal product** of labor—the additional output produced by an additional worker, and (b) the **marginal revenue**—the additional revenue generated by selling an additional unit of output.

marginal expense.   The additional cost of hiring one more worker.

marginal product.   The additional output produced by an additional worker.

marginal revenue.   The additional revenue generated by selling an additional unit of output.

maturation.   A threat to the internal validity of an experimental research study that occurs when changes that take place within study subjects as a result of the passage of time (growing older, taller) affect the study results.

mean (M).   A measure of central tendency; the average of a set of values that is found by adding all values and dividing by the total number of values. The population symbol is μ, and the sample symbol is $\bar{x}$.

measurement.   A process in scientific research that uses rules to assign numbers to objects.

measures of central tendency.   Statistics that describe the average, typical, or most common value for a group of data.

measures of relationship.   Statistics that present the correlation between variables.

measures of variability.   Statistics that describe how spread out values are in a distribution of values (e.g., range, standard deviation).

measures to condense data. Statistics that are used to condense and summarize data.

median (Md, Mdn). A measure of central tendency; the middle score or value in a group of data.

meta-analysis. A technique that combines the results of several similar studies on a topic and statistically analyzes the results as if only one study had been conducted.

metasynthesis. A technique used in summarizing reports of two or more qualitative studies that cover the same topic.

methodological studies. Research studies that are concerned with the development, testing, and evaluation of research instruments and methods.

middle-range theories. Theories that have a narrow focus; concerned with only a small area of the environment or of human experiences.

mixed methods research. The combination of quantitative and qualitative methods in one study.

modal class. The category with the greatest frequency of observations; used with nominal and ordinal data.

mode (Mo). A measure of central tendency; the category or value that occurs most often in a set of data.

model. A symbolic representation of some phenomenon or phenomena.

monopsony. A large buyer of an input, such as the only hospital in town, that can therefore set wages.

mortality threat. A threat to the internal validity of an experimental research study that occurs when either the subject dropout rate is different, or characteristics are different, between those who drop out of the experimental group and those who drop out of the comparison group.

multimodal. A frequency distribution in which more than two values have the same high frequency.

multiple regression. A statistical procedure used to determine the influence of more than one independent variable on the dependent variable.

multivariate analysis of variance (MANOVA). A statistical test that examines the difference between the mean scores of two or more groups on two or more dependent variables that are measured at the same time.

multivariate study. A research study in which more than two variables are examined.

mutually exclusive categories. Categories are uniquely distinct; no overlap occurs between categories.

negatively skewed. A frequency distribution in which the tail of the distribution points to the left.

negative relationship (inverse relationship). A relationship between two variables in which there is a tendency for the values of one variable to increase as the values of the other variable decrease.

network sampling. See snowball sampling.

nominal level of measurement (nominal level of data). The lowest level of measurement; data are "named" or categorized, such as race and marital status.

nondirectional research hypothesis. A type of research hypothesis in which a prediction is made that a relationship exists between variables, but the type of relationship is not specified.

nonequivalent control group design. A type of quasi-experimental design; similar to the pretest-posttest control group experimental design, except that there is no random assignment of subjects to groups.

nonexperimental research. Research in which the researcher does not manipulate or control the independent variable.

nonparametric tests (distribution-free statistics). Types of inferential statistics that are not concerned with population parameters, and requirements for their use are less stringent; can be used with nominal and ordinal data and small sample sizes.

nonparticipant observer (covert). Research observer does not identify herself or himself to the subjects who are being observed.

nonparticipant observer (overt). Research observer openly identifies that she or he is conducting research and provides subjects with information about the type of data that will be collected.

nonprobability sampling. A sampling process in which a sample is selected from elements or members of a population through nonrandom methods; includes convenience, quota, and purposive.

nonrefereed journal. A journal that uses editorial staff members or consultants to review manuscripts.

nonsignificant results. Study results do not allow rejection of the null hypothesis.

nonsymmetrical distribution (skewed distribution). Frequency distribution in which the distribution has an off-center peak. If the tail of the distribution points to the right, the distribution is said to be positively skewed; if the tail of the distribution points to the left, the distribution is said to be negatively skewed.

normal curve.   A bell-shaped curve that graphically depicts a normally distributed frequency distribution (see normal distribution).

normal distribution.   A symmetrical bell-shaped theoretical distribution; has one central peak or set of values in the middle of the distribution.

null hypothesis (H_0).   A statistical hypothesis that predicts there is no relationship between variables; the hypothesis that is subjected to statistical analysis.

nursing research.   A systematic, objective process of analyzing phenomena of importance to nursing.

observation research.   A data-collection method in which data are collected through visual observations.

one-group pretest-posttest design.   A type of pre-experimental design; compares one group of subjects before and after an experimental treatment.

one-shot case study.   A type of pre-experimental design; a single group of subjects is observed after a treatment to determine the effects of the treatment. No pretest measurement is made.

one-tailed test of significance.   A test of statistical significance in which the critical values (statistically significant values) are sought in only one tail of the theoretical sampling distribution (either the right or the left tail).

open-ended questions.   Questions that allow respondents to answer in their own words.

operational definition.   The definition of a variable that identifies how the variable will be observed or measured.

ordinal level of measurement (ordinal data).   Data can be categorized and placed in order; small, medium, and large is an example of a set of ordinal data.

outcomes research.   Research that examines the outcomes or results of patient care interventions.

parallel forms reliability.   See alternate forms reliability.

parameter.   A numerical characteristic of a population (e.g., the average educational level of people living in the United States).

parametric statistical tests.   Types of inferential statistics that are concerned with population parameters. When parametric tests are used, assumptions are made that (a) the level of measurement of the data is interval or ratio, (b) data are taken from populations that are normally distributed on the variable being measured, and (c) data are taken from populations that have equal variances on the variable being measured.

participant observation.   Involves the direct observation and recording of information in a study and requires that the researcher become a part of the setting in which the person, group, or culture is being observed.

participant observer (covert).   Research observer interacts with the subjects and observes their behavior without their knowledge.

participant observer (overt).   Research observer interacts with subjects openly and with the full awareness of those people who are observed.

pecuniary terms.   Expressed in monetary values.

peer review.   The review of a research manuscript by professional colleagues who have content or methodological expertise concerning the material presented in the manuscript.

percentage (%).   A statistic that represents the proportion of a subgroup to a total group, expressed as a percentage ranging from 0% to 100%.

percentile.   A data point below which lies a certain percentage of the values in a frequency distribution.

personality inventories.   Self-report measures used to assess the differences in personality traits, needs, or values of people.

phenomenological studies.   Research studies that examine human experiences through the descriptions of the meanings of these experiences provided by the people involved.

pilot study.   A small-scale trial run of an actual research study.

population.   A complete set of persons or objects that possess some common characteristic of interest to the researcher.

positively skewed.   A frequency distribution in which the tail of the distribution points to the right.

positive relationship (direct relationship).   A relationship between two variables in which the variables tend to vary together; as the values of one variable increase or decrease, the values of the other variable increase or decrease.

posttest.   Data are collected after the researcher has administered the experimental treatment.

posttest-only control group design.   True experimental design in which subjects in the experimental and comparison groups are given a posttest after the experimental group receives the study treatment.

power analysis.   A procedure that is used to determine the sample size needed to prevent a type II error.

power of a statistical test.   The ability of a statistical test to reject a null hypothesis when it is false (and should be rejected).

predictive validity. A type of criterion validity of an instrument in which a determination is made of the instrument's ability to predict behavior of subjects in the future.

pre-existing data. Existing information that has not been collected for research purposes.

pre-experimental design. A type of experimental design in which the researcher has little control over the research situation; includes the one-shot case study and the one-group pretest-posttest design.

pretest. Data are collected before the researcher has administered the experimental treatment; data obtained in the pretest may also be called baseline data.

pretest-posttest control group design. True experimental design in which subjects in the experimental and comparison groups are given a pretest before and a posttest after the administration of the study treatment to the experimental group.

primary source. In the research literature, an account of a research study that has been written by the original researcher(s); in historical studies, firsthand information or direct evidence of an event.

principal investigator. The lead researcher; the person who has the primary responsibility for the study.

probability level (*p*). See level of significance.

probability sampling. The use of a random sampling procedure to select a sample from elements or members of a population; includes simple, stratified, cluster, and systematic random sampling techniques.

probes. Prompting questions that encourage the respondent to elaborate on the topic being discussed.

production function. Output that can be produced with a given set of input.

projective technique. Self-report measure in which a subject is asked to respond to stimuli that are designed to be ambiguous or to have no definite meaning. The responses reflect the internal feelings of the subject that are projected on the external stimuli.

proportional stratified sampling. Random selection of members from population strata where the number of members chosen from each stratum is in proportion to the size of the stratum in the total population.

propositional statement. A statement or assertion of the relationship between concepts.

prospective studies. Studies in which the independent variable or presumed cause is identified at the present time and then subjects are followed for some time in the future to observe the dependent variable or effect.

purposive sampling (judgmental sampling). A nonprobability sampling procedure in which the researcher uses personal judgment to select subjects considered to be representative of the population.

***p* value.** See level of significance.

Q sort (Q methodology). A data-collection method in which subjects are asked to sort statements into categories according to their attitudes toward, or rating of, the statements.

qualitative research. Research that is concerned with the subjective meaning of an experience to an individual.

quantitative research. Research that is concerned with objectivity, tight controls over the research situation, and the ability to generalize findings.

quasi-experimental design. A type of experimental design in which there is either no comparison group or no random assignment of subjects to groups; includes the nonequivalent control group design and time-series design.

query letter. A letter of inquiry sent to a journal to determine the editor's interest in publishing a manuscript. The letter usually contains an outline of the manuscript and important information about the content of the manuscript.

questionnaire. A paper-and-pencil self-report instrument used to gather data from subjects.

quota sampling. A nonprobability sampling procedure in which the researcher selects the sample to reflect certain characteristics of the population.

***r*.** The symbol for a correlation coefficient.

random assignment. A procedure used in an experimental study to ensure that each study subject has an equal chance of being placed into any one of the study groups.

random sampling. See probability sampling.

range. A measure of variability; the distance between the highest and lowest value in a group of values or scores.

ratio level of measurement (ratio data). Data can be categorized, ranked, the distance between ranks specified, and a "true" or natural zero point identified; the amount of money in a checking account or number of requests for pain medication are examples of ratio data.

reactive effects of the pretest. A threat to the external validity of a research study that occurs when subjects are sensitized to the experimental treatment by the pretest.

refereed journal. A journal that uses experts in a given field to review manuscripts.

region of rejection. See critical region.

reliability.   The consistency and dependability of a research instrument to measure a variable; types of reliability are stability, equivalence, and internal consistency.

replication study.   A research study that repeats or duplicates an earlier research study, with all of the essential elements of the original study held intact. A different sample or setting may be used.

research design.   The overall plan for gathering data in a research study.

research hypothesis (H_1).   An alternative hypothesis to the statistical null hypothesis; predicts the researcher's actual expectations about the outcome of a study; also called scientific, substantive, and theoretical.

research instruments (research tools).   Devices used to collect data in research studies.

research problem.   An area where knowledge is needed to advance the practice of nursing.

research question.   The specific question that the researcher expects to be answered in a study.

research report.   A written or oral summary of a research study.

research utilization.   The implementation of research findings into practice.

respondent.   A person in a study who provides answers or responses to the researcher.

retrospective studies.   Studies in which the dependent variable is identified in the present (e.g., a disease condition) and an attempt is made to determine the independent variable (e.g., cause of the disease) that occurred in the past.

Rosenthal effect.   The influence of interviewers on respondents' answers.

rows.   Horizontal entries in a table.

sample.   A subset of the population that is selected to represent the population.

sampling bias.   (a) The difference between sample data and population data that can be attributed to a faulty selection process; (b) a threat to the external validity of a research study that occurs when subjects are not randomly selected from the population.

sampling distribution.   A theoretical frequency distribution that is based on an infinite number of samples. Sampling distributions are based on mathematical formulas and logic.

sampling error.   Random fluctuations in data that occur when a sample is selected to represent a population.

sampling frame.   A listing of all the elements of the population from which a sample is to be chosen.

saturation.   The researcher hears a repetition of themes or ideas as additional participants are interviewed in a qualitative study.

scatter plot (scatter diagram, scattergram).   A graphic presentation of the relationship between two variables. The graph contains variables plotted on an X axis and a Y axis. Pairs of scores are plotted by the placement of dots to indicate where each pair of Xs and Ys intersect.

secondary source.   In the research literature, an account of a research study that has been written by someone other than the study investigators; in historical studies, secondhand information or data provided by someone who did not observe the event.

selection bias.   A threat to the internal validity of an experimental research study that occurs when study results are attributed to the experimental treatment when, in fact, the results may be related to pretreatment differences between the subjects in the experimental and comparison groups.

semantic differential.   Attitude scale that asks subjects to indicate their position or attitude about some concept along a continuum between two adjectives or phrases that are presented in relation to the concept being measured.

semiquartile range.   Determined by dividing the interquartile range in half (see interquartile range).

semistructured interviews.   Interviewers ask a certain number of specific questions, but additional questions or probes are used at the discretion of the interviewer.

simple hypothesis.   A hypothesis that predicts the relationship between one independent and one dependent variable.

simple random sampling.   A method of random sampling in which each element of the population has an equal and independent chance of being chosen for the sample.

simulation studies.   Laboratory studies in which subjects are presented with a description of a case study or situation intended to represent a real-life situation.

skewed.   A frequency distribution that is nonsymmetrical.

snowball sampling.   A sampling method that involves the assistance of study subjects to help obtain other potential subjects.

Solomon four-group design.   True experimental design that minimizes threats to internal and external validity.

stability reliability.   The consistency of a research instrument over time; test-retest procedures and repeated observations are methods to test the stability of an instrument.

standard deviation (SD; s).   A measure of variability; the statistic that indicates the average deviation or variation of all the values in a set of data from the mean value of that data.

standard error of the mean ($s_{\bar{x}}$).   The standard deviation of the sampling distribution of the mean.

statistic.   A numerical characteristic of a sample (e.g., the average educational level of a random sample of people living in the United States).

stratified random sampling.   A random sampling process in which a sample is selected after the population has been divided into subgroups or strata according to some variable of importance to the research study.

structured interviews.   Interviewers ask the same questions in the same manner of all respondents.

structured observations.   The researcher determines the behaviors to be observed before data collection. Usually some kind of checklist is used to record behaviors.

study limitations.   Weaknesses in a study that are not controlled by the researcher (e.g., educational level and age of participants).

subject dropout.   See attrition.

survey studies.   Research studies in which self-report data are collected from a sample to determine the characteristics of a population.

symmetrical distributions.   Frequency distributions in which both halves of the distribution are the same.

systematic random sampling.   A random sampling process in which every kth (e.g., every fifth) element or member of the population is selected for the sample.

systematic review.   A rigorous scientific approach that combines results from a group of research studies and looks at the studies as a whole; also called an integrative review, can summarize many studies at once, while focusing on a single area of interest.

table of random numbers.   A list of numbers that have been generated in such a manner that there is no order or sequencing of the numbers. Each number is equally likely to follow any other number.

target population.   The entire group of people or objects to which the researcher wishes to generalize the findings of a study.

telephone interviews.   Data are collected from subjects through the use of phone calls rather than in face-to-face encounters.

testing.   A threat to the internal validity of a research study that occurs when a pretest is administered to subjects; the effects of taking a pretest on responses on the posttest.

test-retest reliability.   See stability reliability.

theoretical framework.   A study framework based on propositional statements from a theory.

theoretical statement.   See propositional statement.

theory.   A set of related statements that describes or explains phenomena systematically.

time sampling.   Observations of events or behaviors that are made during certain specified time periods.

time-series design.   Quasi-experimental design in which the researcher periodically observes subjects and administers an experimental treatment between two of the observations.

triangulation.   The use of two or more different sampling strategies, data collectors, data collection procedures, or theories in one study.

true experimental design.   An experimental design in which the researcher (a) manipulates the experimental variable, (b) includes at least one experimental and one comparison group in the study, and (c) randomly assigns subjects to either the experimental or the comparison group; includes the pretest-posttest control group design, posttest-only control group design, and Solomon four-group design.

t test (t).   A parametric statistical test that examines the difference between the means of two groups of values. Types of t tests are the independent t test (independent samples t test) and the dependent t test (paired t test).

two-tailed test of significance.   A test of statistical significance in which critical values (statistically significant values) are sought in both tails of the sampling distribution; used when the researcher has not predicted the direction of the relationship between variables.

type I error. (α).   A decision is made to reject the null hypothesis when it is actually true; a decision is made that a relationship exists between variables when it does not.

type II error (β).   A decision is made not to reject the null hypothesis when it is false and should be rejected; a decision is made that no relationship exists between variables when, in fact, a relationship does exist.

unimodal.   A frequency distribution that contains one value that occurs more frequently than any other.

univariate study.   A research study in which only one variable is examined.

unstructured interviews.   The interviewer is given a great deal of freedom to direct the course of the interview; the interviewer's main goal is to encourage the respondent to talk freely about the topic being explored.

unstructured observations.   The researcher describes behaviors as they are viewed, with no preconceived ideas of what will be seen.

validity (of instruments).   The ability of an instrument to measure the variable that it is intended to measure. See also internal validity and external validity of experimental studies.

variable.   A characteristic or attribute of a person or object that differs among the persons or objects being studied (e.g., age, blood type).

variance (SD^2; s^2).   A measure of variability; the standard deviation squared.

visual analogue scale.   Subjects are presented with a straight line anchored on each end with words or phrases that represent the extremes of some phenomenon, such as pain. Subjects are asked to make a mark on the line at the point that corresponds to their experience of the phenomenon. Either a horizontal or vertical line may be used.

volunteers.   Subjects who have asked to participate in a study.

***z* score.**   A standard score that indicates how many standard deviations that a particular value is from the mean of the set of values.

Index

Italicized letters after page numbers indicate boxes (*b*), study examples (*e*), figures (*f*), and tables (*t*). Page numbers in bold indicate Glossary entries.